COMMUNICATION ACROSS CULTURES

EDITED BY
ELIZABETH CHRISTOPHER

palgrave
macmillan

First published 2012 by
PALGRAVE MACMILLAN

Palgrave Macmillan in the UK is an imprint of Macmillan Publishers Limited,
registered in England, company number 785998, of Houndmills, Basingstoke,
Hampshire RG21 6XS.

Palgrave Macmillan in the US is a division of St Martin's Press LLC,
175 Fifth Avenue, New York, NY 10010.

Palgrave Macmillan is the global academic imprint of the above companies
and has companies and representatives throughout the world.

Palgrave® and Macmillan® are registered trademarks in the United States,
the United Kingdom, Europe and other countries.

ISBN 978–0–230–27567–6

10 9 8 7 6 5 4 3 2 1
21 20 19 18 17 16 15 14 13 12

Printed in China

This book is dedicated to Anne Dunn, Helen Fulton, Cathy Stone and Dominic Stone, with love and gratitude for their never-ending support.

Contents

List of Tables

List of Figures

Preface

In 1982 I was awarded a fellowship to the East-West Center in Hawai'i. The EWC is a non-profit research institute, established by US Congress with funding from the federal government and additional support from individuals, agencies, foundations, corporations and governments in the region. Its mission is to promote better relations and understanding between the people and nations of the United States and Asia-Pacific.

My task was to conduct research on cultural differences in learning styles, and I was fortunate enough to work closely with academics and graduate students from literally dozens of countries. In some ways those years were the happiest and most rewarding of my life. I became immersed in a pool of international scholars of such calibre – and of such diverse experience and expertise – that I soaked up cross-cultural knowledge and understanding like a sponge. For the first time I learned to confront my own ethnocentricity and have been trying ever since to overcome my previously unassailable assumptions about gender, age, status, nationality, race, colour and creed.

Now, thirty years later and thanks to the editors of Palgrave Macmillan, I have been privileged again to work (albeit this time virtually) with a group of over thirty international scholars from all over the world and to put together some findings from their research and experience. To echo the words of the French Renaissance writer Michel de Montaigne, I have gathered a posy of other men's flowers, and nothing but the thread that binds them is my own. The men and women who between them have written this collection of essays have shared their knowledge and experience with such generosity that the book is full of unique insights; yet each individual perspective combines with the others to create an international overview.

Textbooks on cross-cultural communication are mostly secondary sources, and however competently the material is presented it cannot be written with the passion and commitment that result from truly original thinking and make for inspirational reading. I do not know of any relevant book that contains such nuances of thought, experience and expertise as in this edition.

The essays are set against the writers' backgrounds of Alaska, Asia, Australia, Brazil, Canada, Denmark, East Africa, France, Iceland, India, Nigeria, Sweden, the UK and the USA. Moreover they write from very different academic and vocational backgrounds – including communication; cross-cultural entrepreneurship; cultural psychology; diversity management; emotional intelligence; European–American relations; gender research; global leadership; the healthcare IT market; indigenous cultures; individual empowerment; innovation and technology management; intercultural sensitivity training; international business strategy; media studies; missionary theory and practice; social psychology; sociology; strategic alliances; teaching English to speakers of other languages; training, research and consultancy services; and world languages, literacy and culture.

The book is divided into four parts, each representing one dimension of communication across cultures. Part One sets the scene for the whole book: in three chapters it introduces the 'different voices' of cross-cultural communication. Chapter 1 begins by identifying the attribute all leaders seem to share – they are all good communicators. Yet their styles differ widely across cultures and sub-cultures, including those of gender, age, status, nationality, race and creed. Leadership diversity, as an aspect of communication across cultures, is discussed in contexts of the military, of mass media, of social change, in organisational settings; and as mythology.

Dharm Bhawuk's frame of reference is the US military, and he brings his extensive experience of cross-cultural training to discussion of diversity leadership. His co-authors are Keith Sakuda and Dan Landis. Anne Dunn cites role models in the media as ethical leaders, while Thomas Tufte writes on the need for ordinary citizens to become leaders in strategies for change. Diana Wong and Eric Kessler explore the motivations of global leaders through study of cultural mythologies.

Chapter 2 is entitled 'Like and Unlike: Different Communication Styles' and offers theoretical, practical and political views. Bhawuk discusses communication across cultures as a two-way process in which practice and theory interact. His essentially egalitarian view is balanced by the intriguing political thesis of Eunju Chen, that all cross-cultural communication in management contexts essentially consists of a struggle for power, in which people are empowered or disempowered by their gender, colour, status or ethnicity.

Chapter 3 takes us from 'noise to silence' in discussion of verbal and non-verbal communication. This last chapter in Part One deals with interpretation of meaning between languages and within a language. There is discussion of forms of non-verbal communication such as kinesics, proxemics, paralanguage, object language and use of time. As for spoken language, Sture Allén argues the need for simultaneous translation in international forums so members can speak in their native languages to counter the domination of English and encourage the preservation of less common languages.

But all languages rely to a greater or lesser extent on context for interpretation of meaning: thus Peter Buzzi and Claudia Megele see interpersonal communication as a form of drama, 'a game of masks' in which people as actors in all societies wear costumes and assume masks to create a context, like a form of theatre, by which to convey the importance of their social roles. They draw on Erving Goffman's 1959 work, *Presentation of Self in Everyday Life* (Doubleday) in which he stated that when people enter the presence of others, they commonly seek to acquire information about them or to bring into play information already possessed.

And so on to Part Two and the second dimension of communication across cultures: the work-related and problem-solving settings in which it takes place. In Chapter 4, on the micro-environment of gender factors and minority roles in workplaces, Gilles Asselin writes on achievement and affiliation as motivators for task-oriented or relationship-oriented behaviour. His essay contains helpful advice for employers and employees, and is illustrated with anecdotes and examples. Janet Haynes writes on the role of working women, based on her own experiences as an African-American woman. Sine Nørholm Just and Robyn Remke report on diversity management and describe three main policies: 'discrimination-and-fairness'; 'access-and-legitimacy'; and 'integration-and-learning'.

Chapter 5 continues the workplace theme by studying culture shock and adjustment to foreign postings. Hannah Mugambi's exotic setting is that of Northern Nigeria. Against a historical backdrop of British colonial domination she sets the scene for modern cultural conflict between expatriate members of western firms and native Nigerian companies. She focuses on differences between the thought-patterns and behaviour of members of mono-chronic and poly-chronic cultures, as defined by E.T. Hall; and suggests that more mutually positive attitudes are likely to develop in horizontally structured corporations.

Then, following a summary of Oberg's stages of adaptation by foreigners to host cultures, comes the delightful study by Bhawuk and Kathryn Anbe on the cultural changes newcomers need to embrace in Hawai'i if they are to work happily there. And Peter Petocz and Anna Reid survey international students' ideas on cross-cultural sensitivity. To add to the mix there is a case study of dysfunctional management.

Chapter 6 continues to develop the dimension of communication settings for working across cultures – by examining differences between traditional western and Asian teaching methods, learning and problem-solving styles. Suman Mishra, who grew up in West Bengal and has travelled extensively in India and the US, suggests how western teachers and trainers may learn from Asian teaching traditions; and Asians from western teaching methods, particularly in the sciences, technology and engineering, and business management. Adriana Medina-López-Portillo, Laura Rutter Strickling, Joan Kang Shin and Illysa Izenberg identify different ways in which people process information, and how these are connected to culture. The case study that follows is of robots that learn, and the chapter ends with a simulation game to raise players' awareness to learning style differences.

Part Three enters the third – global – dimension of communication across cultures. The first dimension, of 'different voices' in leadership, led upwards to the second dimension of international management contexts in which these different voices are heard. The chapters in Part Three take off from there to 'go global' into cross-border negotiations, alliances and networks.

The first contribution in Chapter 7 is by Philip Harris, with an account of China–Africa alliances. This raises larger issues of why corporations and governments form alliances, who benefits most from them and in what ways. He refers to Chinese expatriate management as highly ethnocentric, thus opening the topic of staffing policies for international alliances. After that there is another example, an account of Amazon's recent investment in Scotland. Meena Chavan writes about mergers and acquisitions as outcomes of corporate strategy. She distinguishes between vertical and horizontal integration and provides mini-case studies. She lists major reasons for failure of mergers and acquisitions, and her commentary supports the idea that negotiations in general run through five major stages. Neglect at any one stage is likely to lead to failure of the entire project. After this there are examples of alliances over a wide range, with the objective of identifying common characteristics of the communication tactics these respective allies employ in their very different settings.

Chapter 8 follows with a study of global networks, business and social. It illuminates the previous chapter by shedding light on reasons – some of them cultural – why three quarters of all joint ventures fail. Elizabeth Christopher begins by exploring the nature of service relationship networks. The discussion that follows is of Free Trade Agreements as international networks. A case of electronic networks studies the enormous worldwide popularity - and the exploitation – of online social forums such as Facebook, LinkedIn and Twitter. Ron Goodenow writes a personal memoir of decades of experience in electronic networking and asks a number of pertinent questions about the future of collaborative technologies across cultures.

Part Four moves up again, into a fourth dimension, beyond the planet and into cyberspace. From the first dimension of communication styles, through the second dimension of contexts and the third of alliances and networks, Part Four deals with electronic mass media.

Chapter 9 focuses on social change through ever-increasing digital media communication, including 'email etiquette' in business transactions. Thomas Tufte writes on 'glocal' development in the digital era, in which ordinary citizens are leaders, yet have to battle a climate of fear in cyberspace created by agencies with hidden agendas. Anne Jerslev reports on the relationship between viewers and 'live' television shows as reflected in internet debate forums. This raises further questions on how interpretation of messages is affected by the medium through which they are transmitted – following the pioneer work of Marshall McLuhan in recognising that 'the medium is the message'; meaning that the form of a medium embeds itself in the message. Thorbjörn Broddason and Kjartan Ólafsson argue that the introduction of digital media has already had a lasting impact on society and will continue to do so through new ways in which people – particularly young people – use them to interact with others. Mention of 'cyber rebels' leads to discussion of cultural factors in international conflicts as 'wars of words'.

Finally, we come to Chapter 10. Perhaps the most important aspect of communication across cultures has been left till last, as we move from rebellion and conflict to ethics and social responsibility in a digital age. This chapter continues from Chapter 9 the argument that social change involves social responsibility. It opens with a survey report on corporate initiatives by Asian firms – unfortunately generally conservative in the tradition that 'the business of business is business' and social responsibility is not central to competitive capitalism. Mention is made of Ebert and Griffiths' identification of four socially responsible levels of corporate behaviour, and there is an account of corporate irresponsibility over the recent Hungarian toxic mud disaster. And since religion is at the root of so much sectarian violence, Josh Brahinsky's contribution is very welcome, on the ethics of Christian missionary work. Reference is made also in the chapter to Berger and Huntingdon's claim that Evangelical Protestantism has become a globalising force representing a 'global culture' (along with the global cultures of business and non-government organisations and popular culture). Diana Wong stresses the importance of indigenous knowledge (too long ignored or dismissed as superstition) in western technological conservations plans. The discussion that follows offers a more cynical view of international managers' appropriation of indigenous knowledge.

As with all the chapters in the book, Chapter 10 ends with a conclusion, list of key points, experiential exercises to link practice to theory, internet resources and recommended reading (see the Introduction below for further details).

No single work can hope to paint a full picture of communication across cultures, no matter how many and how varied the artists. Nevertheless, thanks to its contributors, the coverage of topics in this textbook is impressive. It extends from leadership and motivation across cultures to verbal and non-verbal language differences in communication styles and in learning and teaching methods: from a micro-view of diversity in workplace communication to the macro-orientation of international negotiations and alliances: from personal culture shock to cross-cultural networks; and from mass media communication to international social responsibility.

It has been my responsibility and my privilege to link them together.

Elizabeth Christopher

Acknowledgements

Editor's acknowledgements

Many thanks to Palgrave Macmillan's international editorial staff and proof readers for their help and support. Grateful thanks also to all contributing authors for their unfailing generosity.

Publishers' acknowledgements

Every effort has been made to trace all copyright holders, but if any have been inadvertently overlooked, the publishers will be pleased to make the necessary arrangements at the first opportunity.

Notes on Contributors

Sture Allén was a Member of the Board of the Nobel Foundation 1986–99. He is Emeritus Professor at Göteborg University and recipient, among other literary prizes, of the Academy's Prize for Language Preservation. He was Permanent Secretary of the Swedish Academy from 1986 to 1999, and from 1991 he became successively pro-vice-chancellor of Göteborg University for five years and vice-chancellor for one year.

In 1974 he joined the Swedish Language Council, producing a number of articles on language preservation. He started the publication of a series of Swedish classics and cultural events at the Academy open to the public; and introduced data processing in the secretariat and the library. In 1986 he initiated *Svenska Akademiens grammatik* ('The Swedish Academy Grammar') in four volumes (completed in 1999) and was behind a large project that resulted in the *Svenska Akademiens ordbok* ('The Swedish Academy Dictionary'), continuously in preparation, available on the internet (http://g3.spraakdata.gu.se/saob/).

Sture was vice-chairman of the Swedish Language Council for twenty years and since 1984 chairman of the Swedish Society for Belles-Lettres. He has valuable contact surfaces with other fields as a member of, among others, The Royal Swedish Academy of Letters, History and Antiquities, The Royal Swedish Academy of Engineering Sciences, the Norwegian and Finnish academies of science and Academia Europaea; and as an honorary member of the Swedish Literary Society in Finland.

In 1999 a monumental selection of his essays over four decades was published, the 730-page *Modersmålet i fäderneslandet* ('Our mother-tongue in the land of our fathers').

Kathryn Anbe, with a doctorate from the University of Hawai'i, is a research scholar whose interests include multiculturalism, cultural psychology, positive psychology and indigenous cultures.

She has presented many papers at international conferences and was an organiser of the 6th Biennial Conference of the International Academy for Intercultural Research in Honolulu, Hawaii in August 2009.

Gilles Asselin is Founder and President of SoCoCo Intercultural, a training and consulting firm specialising in European–American relations. As a coach, consultant, facilitator and trainer, he works extensively with international teams as well as executives, managers and expatriate families to help them succeed across cultures or within a new environment.

Born and raised in France, Gilles became a French Certified Public Accountant in 1988 and spent more than seven years conducting and managing financial audit assignments, two of which took him to French-speaking Africa for three years – the French Peace Corps in Cameroon (Southwest province) and a World Bank project in the Congo (Brazzaville).

He first travelled to the United States as a graduate student and received a master's degree in business administration and a Masters of Science degree in industrial and organisation psychology from the University of Wisconsin-Oshkosh in 1994. He has completed additional studies in intercultural relations, including a research project on the meaning and importance of work among French and American employees, as well as a study about challenges and adaptation strategies of European expatriates in the US.

His interests lie in the human element: communicating, relating to one another, and sharing on a human level beyond cultures. This entails developing patterns for hosting meaningful conversations, enlivening places of exchange in organisations, and creating wherever possible 'communication havens' in a global world driven by speed, immediacy of information, increasing virtual relations and a constant search for greater efficiency.

Dharm P.S. Bhawuk is Professor of Management and Industrial Relations, University of Hawai'i at Manoa, He has held a number of positions as Visiting Fellow and Visiting Professor at various institutions, and is a former President of the International Training Institute, Kathmandu, Nepal. He has received many honours and awards and has published prolifically including books, book chapters and special issues of journals.

Dharm's creative work includes his creation with colleagues, including Richard Brislin, of the Multimedia Individualism and Collectivism Assimilator (1999), a one-hour CD-ROM cross-cultural training programme; and *Culture Means Thinking Differently About Business*, a 30-minute training video. He developed the Intercultural Sensitivity Inventory, a 46-item scale, published in the *International Journal of Intercultural Relations* (Bhawuk & Brislin, 1992); and also the Individualism and Collectivism Attitude 32-item Scale to synthesise similar scales developed by Triandis and colleagues in the 1980s. This was published in *Cross-Cultural Research* (Singelis, Triandis, Bhawuk & Gelfand, 1995).

His working papers include 'Integrating theory and practice: A framework for the study of diversity management'; 'Approaches to worker participation: An international comparison'; and 'Toward a theory of disconfirmed expectations: A synthesis of social expectancy theory, action theory, and learning theories in cross-cultural training'.

He has organised international conferences, including World Peace through Intercultural Understanding for the Academy of Intercultural Research (IAIR) Biennial Conference, Honolulu, in 2009; and the Fourth Asian Regional Conference of the International Association for Cross-cultural Psychology, in Nepal in 1992. Among his many conference presentations, his paper 'From social engineering to community transformation' (Bhawuk, Mrazek & Munusamy, 2009, presented at the Academy of Management Conference in Chicago, received the Rupert Chilsom Best Theory to Practice Paper Award from the Organization Development and Change Division of the Academy of Management, 2009.

Joshua Brahinsky is with the History of Consciousness Department at the University of California, Santa Cruz. His doctoral dissertation was based on participant observation and archival research at Bethany University, a Bible school within the largest Pentecostal denomination, the Assemblies of God.

His research on Pentecostal pedagogies details the shifting debates and practices of youthful missionaries in training. He finds them to be among the most effective organisers of the twentieth century; and that Pentecostal missionaries studying missiology – missions theory and practice – have inherited a rich lineage of both experiential and theoretical knowledge of the means to inspire commitment to change.

His findings also explore gendered generational shifts in culture, theology and politics that are refashioning the Christian Right; as well as more general dynamics between secular modernity and embodied religious devotion.

Josh's latest publication is 'Body logics: Cultivating a modern sensorium' in *Cultural Anthropology* (2011).

Thorbjörn Broddason is Professor of Sociology at the University of Iceland. He has been instrumental in the establishment of Sociology, Media and Communication Studies and Journalism and Mass Communication at the University of Iceland.

His research includes the long-term project 'Children and Television in Iceland', which originated in 1968 and continues to this day with repeated questionnaire surveys among random samples of 10- to 15-year-olds at six-year intervals. Some questions have remained stable, allowing for comparison between several generations of Icelandic youths, while other aspects of the questionnaire have evolved over the years in order to keep pace with the constantly changing media landscape. His other research has been aimed at the Icelandic media structure and a theoretical investigation of media professionalism.

Peter Buzzi is an author, researcher, mentor, consultant and lecturer with various research and publication interests in social psychology, psychotherapy, management and behavioural economics.

Peter's research interests include: the study of contemporary identity; interpersonal as well as other forms of communication; psychological and social capital as well as social change; social networking, liminality and hyper-reality; the study of violence, happiness and depression; management and governance; and social and economic policy/regeneration.

He is the Managing Director of 'A Sense Of Self', an organisation that offers services, programmes and training dedicated to mental health and empowering individuals to transform their lives and overcome challenges.

Meena Chavan was awarded a PhD from the University of Western Sydney and she is also a Bcom and an Mcom. She is a Senior Lecturer in Organisational and Management Studies in the Department of Marketing and Management within the Faculty of Business and Economics at Macquarie University, Sydney.

Prior to joining Macquarie University Meena held academic positions at UNSW and the University of Western Sydney from 1995 to 2008. She has held visiting academic roles at Purdue University, the University of Dubai and the Singapore National University.

Her research focuses on international business strategy, cross-cultural management and entrepreneurship. She has been published in academic journals such as the *Journal of Management Development*, the *International Journal of Entrepreneurship and Innovation*, the *Journal of Equal Opportunities* and the *Journal of Industry and Higher Education*.

She received the best paper award at the 48th ICSB conference in Belfast for her 2003 'Diversity – good for business' and was awarded the 2006 Emerald Literati award for excellence for her 2005 paper 'An appraisal of environment management systems: A competitive advantage for small business in the face of global competition' in *Management of Environment Quality: An International Journal*, 16, 5: 444–63.

Her teaching interests focus on international business and cross-cultural management, strategic management and entrepreneurship. She is an exponent of the experiential method of teaching.

Eunju C. Chen is a faculty member in the MA TESOL (Teaching English to Speakers of Other Languages) Program at the University of Maryland in Baltimore County and is the Coordinator of On-Line/Off-Campus Programs. She teaches courses that prepare in-service teachers as well as teacher candidates how to effectively work with English Language Learners (ELLs).

She received her MA in TESOL from the University of Maryland in Baltimore County and her PhD dissertation is within the Language, Literacy and Culture Program at that University. Her research focuses on intercultural communication and socio-cultural theories.

CSR Asia

CSR Asia is the leading provider of training, research and consultancy services on sustainable business practices in Asia.

Through offices in Beijing, Hong Kong, Kuala Lumpur, Shenzhen and Singapore, and partnerships in Vietnam, Thailand and Bangladesh, CSR Asia builds capacity and promotes awareness of corporate social responsibility to advance sustainable development across the region.

Anne Dunn is an Associate Professor in the Department of Media and Communications and formerly Pro-Dean Academic of the Faculty of Arts and Social Sciences, at the University of Sydney.

Prior to taking up a full-time academic career, Anne worked across the print, television and radio media. Altogether, Anne spent some 13 years with ABC Radio and Television, in management, in policy and in broadcasting, including as a presenter, journalist and producer.

She has also worked for the BBC in documentaries as well as in Australian commercial television as a journalist/researcher; for SBS Television as a reporter; and as a freelance director, reporter and writer in both the television and print media.

Her research interests include audience construction in the intersections between policy and practice in broadcast news production; impacts on radio journalists of digital convergence in the media; digital convergence; audiences; and public broadcasting.

Her publications include: co-authoring *Media, Markets and Morals*, with E. Spence, A. Alexander and A. Quinn (Wiley-Blackwell, 2011); co-authoring *Narrative and Media*, with H. Fulton, R. Huismann and J. Murphett (Cambridge University Press, 2005); and the chapter 'What have you done for us lately? Public service broadcasting and its audiences', in Michael Bromley (ed.), *No News is Bad News* (Longman, 2004)

Ron Goodenow has held academic and research appointments at several American and British universities, has edited or co-edited four books, and has published over 100 book chapters, articles and reviews in his chosen fields of history, comparative studies and information technology services in education and healthcare.

Ron is an independent writer, researcher and photographer, specialising in the healthcare IT market, and Senior Consultant to Avnet HealthPath Practice, Phoenix, Arizona.

Philip R. Harris is a Management/Space Psychologist, as well as a prolific author and futurist. He is president of Harris International, Ltd in La Jolla, California, a global management consultancy, and Visiting Professor in the California School of International Management. He is also a GS15 Federal Consultant.

Philip has edited three journals, published over 250 articles, and authored or edited more than forty books. In 2005, Human Resource Development Press published his *Managing the Knowledge Culture*, and previously his three-volume *New Work Culture Series*. In 2007, the seventh edition of his classic, *Managing Cultural Differences*, was released by Elsevier Science and adopted as a text in over 200 universities and colleges worldwide. It is the progenitor of some 12 supplementary titles in the *MCD Series*. He has completed his contribution (Unit 2) to the eighth edition, published in 2011. Also he co-authored the fourth edition of *Multicultural Law Enforcement* (Prentice Hall, 2011).

As a space psychologist Philip wrote *Living and Working in Space*, as well as a science-based novel, *Launch Out* (Univelt). With the assistance of Dave Schrunk, Philip has just completed a sequel to *Launch Out*. This work of fiction, *Lunar Pioneers*, examines living and working on the Moon in 2050. *Lunar Pioneers* is his fiftieth book.

For the past ten years he has been a member of the editorial advisory board for the *European Business Review* in England.

Janet Haynes is recognised as an educator, world-class facilitator, inspirational speaker and organisational consultant.

After receiving a BA in Organizational Administration and the Doctor of Education degree (EdD) in educational leadership from Fielding Graduate University, Janet rose to national prominence with action research studies of organisations, gender, leadership and management.

Illysa Izenberg is an adult educator specialising in management, leadership, and communication. She teaches Engineering undergraduate students at Johns Hopkins University and Science and Technology masters candidates at the University of Maryland, Baltimore County (UMBC). Illysa also creates and facilitates educational programmes for corporations, not-for-profits organisations and government agencies. She holds an MBA from Harvard Business School and a Certificate in Blended Teaching from Sloan-C.

Anne Jerslev is Professor, Film and Media Studies Section, Department of Media, Cognition, and Communication at the University of Copenhagen.

She has published a number of books, most recently *Det er bare film. Om unges videofællesskaber og vold på film* [It's only a movie. Young people's video communities and violence on film] (Gyldendal, 2000) and *Vi ses på tv. Medier og intimitet* [See you on TV. Media and intimacy] (Gyldendal, 2004). She has edited several anthologies in Danish and English, most recently *Performative Realism* with Rune Gade (Museum Tusculanum Press, 2005), and she has contributed to journals and anthologies with articles on youth and media, film-analytical subjects, film genres such as melodrama and film noir, reality television and documentary.

She has participated in a number of Danish and Nordic research projects funded by the National Research Council for the Humanities. She has also held a number of administrative posts including membership of the Humanistic Educational Council (1997–2001), head of department (2002–5) and chair of the Association of Danish Media Researchers (2001–4).

She was director of the research project 'High-tension Aesthetics. Ethics and Aesthetics in Contemporary Media' (2005–8).

Sine Nørholm Just is an Associate Professor at the Department of Business and Politics, Copenhagen Business School (CBS). She is also the programme director of a BA in Intercultural Marketing Communication. She holds a PhD in communication from CBS and an MA in rhetoric from the University of Copenhagen. Her research interests include intercultural communication generally and diversity management more specifically. She has studied processes of transnational and intercultural public debate as these unfold in the context of the European Union. Most recently she has taken up the study of rhetorical processes of market formation.

Eric H. Kessler is an expert in the field of management of innovation and technology. He is senior Professor of Management at Pace University in New York City and founding/current Director of their Business Honors Program, which prepares students with the knowledge and skills for successful careers in global business leadership.

He is a Fellow and Past President of the Eastern Academy of Management, the Northeastern United States Association of Business Management Scholars, where he designed and launched the EAM White Paper series to better apply management theory to business practice.

He has served on numerous editorial and advisory boards and as the guest editor for several of professional management journals, as well as with the United States National Security Education Program and the Pentagon's Joint Civilian Orientation Conference.

He has published or presented over 100 scholarly papers in academic outlets and conferences, won numerous research and teaching awards, and produced several critically acclaimed books, including: *The Handbook of Organizational and Managerial Wisdom* (Sage, 2008), *Cultural Mythology and Global Leadership* (Edward Elgar, 2009), and *Applying Management Theory to Practice: Real-World Lessons for Walking the Talk* (Palgrave Macmillan, 2010). Recently he was selected as the general editor for the Encyclopaedia of Management Theory.

He is a member of Phi Beta Kappa and has been inducted into national and international honour societies in business, economics, forensics and psychology. He instructs courses at the doctoral, masters and bachelors levels, and has worked as an executive educator, policy analyst and business consultant for public and private organisations. He has led numerous international field studies, and his professional travels have taken him across six continents.

Dan Landis is an Affiliate Professor of Psychology, University of Hawai'i at Manoa. Previously he was Professor of Psychology, Director of the Center for Applied Research and Evaluation and a former Dean of the Liberal Arts College at the University of Mississippi.

He is author and co-author of over 120 books, chapters and articles in refereed publications, and the founding and continuing editor of the *International Journal of Intercultural Relations*; he is also the founding president of the International Academy for Intercultural Research. He is a Fellow of the American Psychological Association, the Society for the Psychological Study of Social Issues, and the American Psychological Society. He is the co-editor/author of the *Handbook of Intercultural Training* (Pergamon Press, third edition, 2004).

In 1987, with Mickey Dansby, he developed the Military Equal Opportunity Climate Survey (MEOCS), which is now in wide use throughout the US Department of Defense and has been adapted for use in civilian organisations, universities and foreign institutions. During 1994–6 he was appointed the first Shirley J. Bach Visiting Professor at the Defense Equal Opportunity Management Institute, when he conducted further studies of equal opportunity climate in the US Armed Forces as well as investigating racial disparities in the administration of military justice.

He has consulted for, and received grants from, many government agencies (both federal and state) and private corporations as well as members of the legal profession. His grants and contracts with government agencies (over $3,000,000 total) have been for projects such as race relations and workforce diversity.

Adriana Medina-López-Portillo is Assistant Professor of Intercultural Communication in the Department of Modern Languages, Linguistics and Intercultural Communication at the University of Maryland, Baltimore County (UMBC).

She is the founder and president of the Society of Intercultural Education, Training, and Research (SIETAR) Baltimore; and an accomplished intercultural trainer, having designed and led workshops for numerous higher education, not-for-profit, governmental and corporate clients in the USA and abroad.

Among her favourite appointments were those of Training Officer for The Scholar Ship, a transnational academic programme housed on a passenger ship; and a member of the team of trainers who offered the first-year student pre-departure and onsite orientations for King Abdullah University of Science and Technology (KAUST).

Her research focuses on study abroad, teaching intercultural communication, intercultural competencies and emotional intelligence. Her latest publication, 'Interculturality vs. intercultural competencies in Latin America', can be found in The SAGE Handbook of Intercultural Competence.

Claudia Megele is an author, researcher, practitioner and lecturer. She is the Service Director of 'A Sense Of Self', an organisation that offers services, programmes and training at no or nominal cost, dedicated to empowering individuals to transform their lives and overcome challenges.

She is Vice Chair of Tower Hamlets Police and Community Safety Board (London); and a member of the editorial board of the *Race/Ethnicity Journal*, published by Kirwan Institute for the Study of Race and Ethnicity; of the Office of Minority Affairs at Ohio State University; of Indiana University Press; and of the advisory board of the *Journal of Sociological Imagination*. Her studies include sociology, psychology and social work; and her doctorate is in psychotherapy. Her diverse research interests include interpersonal communication, social networking, the study of violence, reflective practice and hyper-reality, management and governance, and social and economic policy/regeneration.

Suman Mishra is in the Department of Mass Communications, Southern Illinois University, Edwardsville, Illinois.

Growing up in West Bengal, Suman travelled much of India and the United States for her studies, earning a masters degree in advertising at Michigan State and a PhD in Mass Communication at Temple University in Philadelphia. She has also worked as a marketing communication consultant for several pharmaceutical companies in India.

She is an interdisciplinary scholar with a background in both science and art. She is currently teaching Media Law and Transnational Media and Research Methods, which gives her the opportunity to use her experience and multicultural background to help break down an often-criticised student apathy by impressing upon her students the importance of global issues.

Hannah M. Mugambi is Assistant Professor, School of Arts and Science, American University of Nigeria, Yola, Adamawa State, Nigeria.

Her research interests are in language literacy and culture. Her most recent publication is 'Nakuru women's culture-dependent responses to HIV prevention'. Other works are on the role of indigenous languages in Africa. She teaches Business Communication and Writing Skills and has launched a Basic English Literacy programme in Northern Nigeria.

She is also involved in community service, including HIV/AIDS prevention in Nigeria and Kenya.

Kjartan Ólafsson is a researcher at the RHA, The Research Centre of the University of Akureyri, Iceland and Assistant Professor at the University of Akureyri, Faculty of Law and Social Sciences.

He has been involved in various research projects related to youth and/or media. Among these are the long-term research project 'Children and Television in Iceland', the international WHO project 'Health Behaviour in School aged Children', the European School survey Project on Alcohol and other Drugs (ESPAD) and the Icelandic School Survey project.

He has acted as a principal researcher on various research projects at the RHA, including one of the largest social science research projects in Iceland on 'Monitoring the Social and Economic Impacts of Construction Projects in East Iceland'.

Peter Petocz is Associate Professor of Statistics in the Department of Statistics at Macquarie University, Sydney.

He has research interests in applied statistics, particularly in the area of health statistics, and also in pedagogy for statistics and other disciplines. He is the author of over 200 papers in academic journals, book chapters and conference proceedings. He has translated his pedagogic research into practical terms by developing a range of materials that can be used to enhance student learning – including eight videos and five textbooks in various aspects of mathematics, statistics and music.

Peter originally is from Budapest, Hungary, and he grew up in a refugee family with Hungarian as his first language before immigrating to Australia as a teenager.

Anna Reid is Professor of Music and Associate Dean Learning and Teaching at the Sydney Conservatorium of Music, University of Sydney.

She is a member of DOCTORALNET, an international group of researchers and HDR candidates who research higher, adult and work-based education.

Her research has spanned several disciplines and focuses on aspects of students' professional formation that will enhance their understanding of working within professional contexts; and the manner in which curriculum can be designed to focus on those elements.

Her current research projects focus on the professional formation of students and student engagement with their studies; peer learning in the music studio and in ensemble situations; curriculum implications of internationalisation; creativity, ethics, cross-cultural sensitivity and sustainability for professional formation; and leadership, mentoring and quality in HDR supervision.

She has become a skilled exponent of the qualitative research approach called phenomenography; and has published over 100 papers in academic journals. Also she has contributed chapters to books and conference proceedings. She has edited, together with Mary Hellstén, the recent book *Researching International Pedagogies* (Springer, 2008), which brings together research about approaches to helping diverse groups of tertiary students in the process of their learning.

Robyn Remke is Associate Professor in the Department of Intercultural Communication and Management at the Copenhagen Business School.

Motivated by questions of social and organisational injustice and discrimination, her research uses a critical/feminist lens to explore the gendered nature of organisations and organising. Her research focuses on the ways in which organisational members embody organisational practices such as leadership, diversity management programmes and parental leave policies through communication.

In addition, Robyn studies alternative forms of workplace organisational structures and gendered identity in the workplace. She has published journal articles in *Communication Studies* and *Communication Monographs*, and has co-authored a number of book chapters.

She is also President of the Organization for the Study of Communication, Language & Gender.

Keith H. Sakuda is an Assistant Professor of Management at the University of Hawai'i, West Oahu. He holds a PhD in International Management and a Japan-focused MBA from the University of Hawai'i at Manoa. His research interests include intercultural relations, cultural variation in task interdependence, and diversity. He has presented his research at conferences such as the Academy of Management, Western Academy of Management, and International Academy of Intercultural Research.

Joan Kang Shin is the Director of Teachers of English to Students of Other Languages (TESOL), Professional Training Programs at the English Language Center at the University of Maryland, Baltimore County (UMBC).

She is an administrator of the US Department of State's E-Teacher Scholarship Program, a fully online teacher training programme for English as a Foreign Language (EFL) teachers around the world. Also she is Project Director of the US Department of Education (USDOE)-funded Secondary Teacher Education and Professional Training for English Language Learners Program (STEP T for ELLs) in the Education Department at UMBC. This five-year programme provides online and face-to-face professional development to secondary math, science and social studies teachers in Maryland to instruct English-language learners.

In addition, she is an English Language Specialist for the Office of English Language Programs (OELP) in the US Department of State and has conducted EFL teacher training programmes with teachers in Russia, Libya, Egypt, Morocco, Saudi Arabia, Thailand, Laos, Cambodia, Vietnam, El Salvador, Guatemala and Peru.

Laura Rutter Strickling's doctorate is from the University of Maryland, Baltimore County (UMBC). She studies changes in educators' discourse after having participated in language variation professional development.

She holds two BA degrees, one in Art from Brigham Young University and one in Spanish from Augusta State University; and a MA in Intercultural Communication. She is National Board-Certified in World Languages, is a qualified administrator for the Intercultural Development Inventory and on the advisory board of SIETAR-Baltimore. She taught high-school Spanish for nine years when she developed an internship-tutoring programme for Latino elementary students and a Spanish immersion programme in Spain. Laura is currently a Spanish instructor at UMBC.

Thomas Tufte has been a Professor in Communication at the Department of Communication Studies of Roskilde University, Denmark, since 2004. He has an MA in cultural sociology (1989) and PhD in communication from the University of Copenhagen (1995).

From 2009 and until 2013 he will be principal investigator of the collaborative research programme Media, Empowerment and Democracy in East Africa (MEDIeA). He is also the co-director of Ørecomm, an international network originating at Malmö University (MAH) and Roskilde University (RUC) for research in the field of communication for development and social change. He has lectured at universities, and worked with communication consultancy, in more than 25 countries. He has written/edited ten books and numerous peer-reviewed articles. In 2003, he served as the UNESCO Chair of Communication at the Universidad Autónoma de Barcelona, Spain. For many years, his media and communication research concentrated on Latin America. His current research focuses primarily on Southern and Eastern Africa.

He serves on the council of the International Association for Media and Communication Research (IAMCR). He also serves on the advisory and/or editorial boards of a series of international journals in culture and communication, including *Communication, Culture and Critique* (ICA Journal), *Journal of Health Communication, Revista de Estudios Contemporáneos de la Comunicación y la Cultura*

(Universidad de Colima, México), *Intercom* (Brazil) and *Revista ALAIC* (edited by the Latin America Association on Information and Communication).

Diana J. Wong-MingJi is Associate Professor of Management, Eastern Michigan University.

Dr Wong's areas of research interests include strategic alliances, merger and acquisition integration, learning and technological innovations, and international management of global strategies. She chaired the planning committee for developing and implementing the International Cultural Competence Institute for faculty and staff at Eastern Michigan University; and in addition to committee work at different levels of the university she consults with executive managers who focus on strategic change for leading organisations.

Her professional involvement includes the Academy of Management, Academy of International Business, Strategic Management Society, North American Case Research Association, Eastern Academy of Management, Southern Academy of Management, and the Caribbean Studies Association. She reviews for various conferences and publications such as *Human Relations, Groups and Organization Management*, the *Journal of Business Research*, and the *Journal of Organization and Change Management*.

She teaches graduate and undergraduate strategic management, organisation development and change, entrepreneurship, and teams and teamwork. She also has experience teaching leadership, international management, research methods and data collection, and organisational behaviour to undergraduate, graduates and executive graduate students.

About the editor

Elizabeth Christopher is an academic and consultant in the field of cross-cultural studies. She spent many years working in the private sector before returning to a university environment. She taught at the University of New South Wales until 1983 and was awarded a PhD from the former School of Organisational Behaviour (now the Australian Graduate School of Management).

Through the 1980s and 1990s she was a visiting professor at various US universities and a visiting fellow at the East-West Center (EWC), Honolulu, Hawai'i. She is a part-time faculty member of the Honolulu-based Japan-American Institute of Management Science (JAIMS); and senior associate of a leadership training consultancy in Hawai'i, Christopher, Smith and Associates (www.csaworks.com). She is also Honorary Associate of Macquarie University, Sydney, Australia. Her publications since 2000 are:

August 2012: Elizabeth Christopher, *International management: Explorations across cultures* (Kogan Page, London)

2011: Helen Deresky and Elizabeth Christopher, *International Management: Managing across Borders and Cultures*, second edition (Pearson Education)

2010: Elizabeth Christopher 'The management of uncertainty and culture shock by graduate overseas students in Australia', *The International Journal of Arts and Sciences*, 3, 11: 35–53. ©InternationalJournal.org

2008: Helen Deresky and Elizabeth Christopher, *International Management: Managing across Borders and Cultures*, first edition (Pearson Education)

2007: Elizabeth Christopher (ed.), *Managing Cultural Diversity in International Business*, second edition (Pearson Education)

2007: Elizabeth Christopher, 'Give them a fish...', pp. 3–6; 'Human capacity building', pp. 41–2; and 'Political risk in international business: Keeping a low profile', pp. 139–41, in John J. Wild et al., *International Business: The Challenges of Globalization* (Pearson Education)

2006: Elizabeth Christopher, 'Political risk in international business: Trying to keep it down'; 'Political risk in international business: Keeping a low profile'; and 'Human capacity building': three international business case studies in John J. Wild et al., *International Business* (Pearson Education)

2005: Elizabeth Christopher, 'Little vineyard may grow a lot bigger overseas', in Prem Ramburuth and Catherine Welch (eds), *Casebook in International Business: Australian and Asia-Pacific Perspectives* (Pearson Prentice Hall)

2005: Elizabeth Christopher, 'Cultural convergence: A reality or merely wishful thinking?', *Journal of Asia Entrepreneurship and Sustainability* (peer-reviewed online edition, volume 1, issue II, October 2005, special edition): http://www.asiaentrepreneurshipjournal. com/sydneyconference.html

2004: Elizabeth Christopher, 'High- and low-context cultures: Communication problems for Thai and Norwegian graduate students at Macquarie University', in Anne Dunn (ed.), *Proceedings of the 2004 ANZCA Conference* (Faculty of Arts, Sydney University, online: http://conferences.arts.usyd.edu.au/viewabstract.php?id=23&cf=3)

2003: Elizabeth Christopher, *Cross-cultural Leadership and Management* (McGraw Hill Australia)

2002: Elizabeth Christopher: 'Are you being served? The relationship between service providers and clients in international contexts', in Mosad Zineldin (ed.), *Co-operation and Competition: 'Co-opetition'; the organization of the future* (Proceedings of the 2nd International Conference on Co-operation and Competition, C&C: Studenlitteratur, Lund, Sweden)

2001: Larry E. Smith and Elizabeth Christopher: 'Why can't they understand me when I speak English so clearly?, in Edwin Thumboo (ed.), *The Three Circles of English* (Unipress, Centre for the Arts, National University of Singapore, 2001)

2000: Christopher, Elizabeth: 'Some problems in using English as an intercultural means of communication', *Newsletter* No. 36, February 2000 (Intercultural Communications Institute, Kanda University of International Studies, Japan)

Introduction

This collection of writings by experts from a wide range of national and social cultures is on the general theme of communication across cultures. It examines ways of promoting mutual understanding in contemporary cross-cultural and international settings of human diversity. Specific objectives are to learn more about:

- Leading and motivating across cultures
- Cultural reasons for different communication styles
- Verbal and non-verbal communication
- Managing workforce diversity
- Culture shock and adjustment
- Learning and teaching across cultures
- International negotiations and alliances
- Organisational networks
- Mass media communication
- Corporate ethics and social responsibility.

The book is designed primarily to be set as required reading for a semester-long (half-yearly) teaching unit on cross-cultural communication within undergraduate and graduate university courses on international management. Each chapter offers a number of perspectives on the general topic, and in total they include sufficient theoretical and practical material to cover 10 weekly 3-hour periods of lectures and tutorials. All chapters follow the same format:

- Part number and name
- Chapter number and name
- Objectives of the chapter
- Outline of chapter
- Essay(s) followed by discussion points and questions
- Case studies and discussion points
- Conclusion and list of key points
- Experiential exercises
- Internet resources and recommended further reading.

For the purpose of the book, culture is defined in its widest sense as: cultivated behaviour, or the sum of individuals' social learning and experience through symbols deliberately perpetuated in a society through its institutions, accepted generally without question and passed along by communication and imitation from one generation to the next; a collective programming of the mind that distinguishes the members of one group or category of people from another. Thus culture is communication and communication is culture.

Each topic is presented as the content of a 3-hour teaching session, including an Instructors' Manual of lecture notes as PowerPoint presentations, discussion points and class activities. Reference notes and a list of recommended reading are included with each chapter, and the book has its own website. Classroom sessions are backed up on a website.

After studying this book, readers should be able to do the following:

- Identify culture-based reasons for different communication styles
- Recognise cultural differences in languages, verbal and non-verbal
- Assess critically the information provided over the internet
- Acquire new skills in the management of workplace diversity
- Become more functional in foreign environments
- Learn tactics for negotiating business and professional alliances across cultures
- Develop skills in creating and maintaining international networks
- Discuss similarities and differences in ethical concepts worldwide, including corporate social responsibility and protection of the environment
- Use appropriate learning and teaching methods depending on cultural context
- Adapt leadership style appropriately to situational context.

The book is distinctive and original in that there are very few, if any, publications that cover as many different perspectives on communicating across cultures or that constitute such a comprehensive teaching medium. Its organisation should satisfy the needs of all readers who seek an overview of interpersonal and impersonal communication in contexts of cultural diversity.

Its educational features are that each contribution is written by an expert in the given field and is academically sound (that is, each includes references and is comparable in format to any article in a refereed academic journal). The content is international and includes many cases and other interactive exercises to involve teachers and students in the process of their own learning, rather than passively reading the chapters. No one writer can be expert in all aspects of a topic, hence this wide range of interesting and current issues gathered together after 'picking the brains' of qualified colleagues. As a result the book has the same kind of individuality that the director stamps on a film to which many talents have contributed.

The overall style of the book is designed to convey immediacy, interest and humour. It is intended primarily for those who study in the field of international management, including non-native English speakers. Even the most complex ideas are described as simply as possible without being simplistic; emphasis is on discussion rather than lecture; and on finding practical applications of theoretical principles.

PART ONE

The First Dimension of Communication across Cultures: Different Voices

CHAPTER 1

Leading and Motivating across Cultures

Elizabeth Christopher; Dharm P.S. Bhawuk; Dan Landis;
Keith H. Sakuda; Diana J. Wong-MingJi;
Eric H. Kessler; Anne Dunn

Objective of the chapter

To examine a range of perspectives on leadership as introduction to a study of communication across cultures.

Chapter contents

- Outline of chapter
- Dharm P.S. Bhawuk; Dan Landis; Keith H. Sakuda: Leadership in military retention
- Discussion
- Case study: The Tailhook scandal
- Diana J. Wong-MingJi and Eric H. Kessler: Motivations of global leaders from cultural mythologies
- Discussion
- Anne Dunn: Role models in the media as ethical motivators
- Discussion
- Case study: The trading scandal of Salomon Brothers
- Questions
- Conclusion
- Key points
- Experiential exercise
- Further recommended reading
- References

Outline of chapter

Leadership styles vary, but possibly the single characteristic shared by all leaders, regardless of culture, background and situation, is that they are effective communicators in writing and through the spoken word. Therefore the opening chapter in this study of communication across cultures deals with the behaviour of leaders in a number of different contexts.

The first contribution is by Bhawuk, Landis and Sakuda. Their context is organisational, and the topic is leadership in policies and practices for employment retention programmes. Their argument is that if organisational leaders cannot instil a sense of commitment in their followers they will lose them, to the high cost of the organisation on a number of levels.

The writers' case study is the US military, and recommendations emerge from it for various ways in which effective communication by senior managers can improve retention rates in organisations characterised by diversity.

The report that accompanies Bhawuk et al.'s essay is an example of the disastrous effects of poor leadership communication, as is the trading scandal of Salomon Brothers, described later in the chapter.

Writing of leaders as heroes, Wong and Kessler explain how cultural mythologies shape global leaders' behaviour. They focus on traditional myths from four different regions to illustrate culture-based interpretations of 'heroic' leaders' behaviour.

This theme of role models is followed by Dunn. Her setting is the media industry, and she offers a number of examples of ethical leadership.

These essays are punctuated by discussions, questions and cases; and the chapter ends with a conclusion and summary of key points; experiential exercises, and reading resources.

LEADERSHIP IN MILITARY RETENTION	Dharm P.S. Bhawuk; Dan Landis; Keith H. Sakuda

Retention woes plague the modern US military. In 2005 the media pounced on then Secretary Rumsfeld's concession that operations in the Middle East and elsewhere have overcommitted US forces (Englehardt, 2006). This prompted talk-show pundits to suggest that ongoing operations in Iraq and Afghanistan might have compromised military readiness to respond to emerging threats.

A stop-loss policy (Powers, 2004) was instituted as a reactionary attempt to curb the loss of skilled soldiers. It consisted partly of compulsory extension of service members' active duty beyond their initial end of term of service. However, the policy drew tremendous criticism, protests, legal challenges and even a motion picture by Paramount Pictures (*Stop-Loss*, a 2008 US drama film directed by Kimberly Peirce). Although later rescinded, the policy provoked a backlash of negative sentiment that may affect the military for many years.

Effective retention policies must acknowledge the different motivations that affect personal decisions to remain in the military. An effective, though costly, approach has been to align service people's needs and motives with appropriate rewards. The aim was to increase commitment by increasing dependency on, and perceived benefit from, the military. This 'normative commitment' approach (inducing individual commitment through a sense of obligation) (Meyer et al., 2002) can be successful, but it risks turning retention into a mercenary-like bidding process. A more effective and less costly approach is to instil 'affective commitment' through emotional attachment to, and identification with, the organisation (ibid.).

Acculturation theory (see, e.g., Berry, 1990) suggests that retention policies will be more effective if recruits are socialised into the military from the beginning. The term 'acculturation' is used deliberately since the military has its own unique roles, norms and values, which are the hallmark of a culture (Trianidis, 1994). From a cultural perspective, the decision to join the military can be compared to the decision to emigrate to another country.

Intercultural training always risks invoking strong negative emotions. One key reason is ethnocentrism – evaluating the behaviour of people from other cultures through one's own cultural references. Organisational environments often create situations where people from different cultures are forced to interact. This often results in misunderstandings; conflicts may emerge and group dynamics may deteriorate. Reframing intercultural encounters from judgement-of-difference to perception-of-similarity is an essential component of intercultural training (Bhawuk et al., 2006). Factors like common organisational goals, common friends, consideration for others' languages and social interactions can lead to perception of similarity and improve interpersonal interactions.

Organisational leaders can also contribute to the process by creating equality between members of different ethnic groups and providing opportunities for them to interact in professional and social settings. From the military's perspective, individuals' intercultural experience is often the decision point for retention and re-enlistment.

The contact hypothesis of Gordon Allport (Allport, 1954) has formed the basis for much of the training to reduce prejudice against minority group members. Allport proposed that prejudice:

> ... may be reduced by equal status contact between majority and minority groups in the pursuit of common goals. The effect is greatly enhanced if this contact is sanctioned by institutional supports ... and provided it is of a sort that leads to the perception of common interests and common humanity between members of the two groups.

Many of Allport's conditions are clearly applicable to the military. Directives and policies have clearly demonstrated institutional support for equal treatment, but it is less clear if equal status contact actually occurs within the military's vast hierarchical structure. Enlisted people are likely to have a high school degree and come from middle class or lower middle class strata of society, whereas officers are likely to have a college degree and come from the middle class. This class structure in the military can be a source of cultural conflict (Cortright, 1975). Also, many of the enlisted African-American, Hispanic or other minority group members are likely to come from the inner cities, and may bring with them into the military what Triandis (1976) describes as an 'eco-system distrust'.

Military leaders may believe that basic training completely assimilates enlisted people into the military. However, such a belief would clash with Brewer's theory (Brewer, 1991) that human beings strive to retain their individual distinctiveness. This suggests the need for training programmes in conceptual understanding of acculturation issues, and behavioural training to help people integrate with military society. However, the institution itself may be resistant to admissions of discrimination and individuals who draw attention to its failings may be victimised for doing so.

Protection should be given to these 'whistleblowers', who often find themselves under character attack. For example, the naval officer who brought the Tailhook scandal to public awareness was effectively forced to resign from the military, and an admiral who appears to have been implicated later committed suicide.

In the military people spend most of their time in group activities, and they do not have a choice to pick who they work with. Therefore in social hours they prefer to spend time with people with similar race, gender or sexual preference. Historically the military has allowed this, but from an intercultural perspective it is a symptom of separation. A cognitive approach to acculturation training would emphasise the benefits of integration beyond work hours. Opportunities might be created for people to interact those different from themselves, learn their worldviews and develop cross-cultural networks (Bennett, 1986).

Military training should be evaluated as a holistic package with the ultimate aim of creating readiness to serve in a truly international and intercultural institution (Bhawuk, 1990). For example, the current emphasis on physical training in boot camp and other training programmes should include some elements of psycho-social training (Sam and Berry, 2006). If people harbour fear, suspicion and resentment of the military or their fellow soldiers, their readiness will be limited.

The military frowns on fraternisation between officers and soldiers, but this policy results in some disadvantages for integration of the military community. Officers sometimes are penalised if found fraternising with subordinates; but socialisation serves a critical function in the transmission of tacit knowledge and social information. Exposing enlisted soldiers to officers of the same ethnic group may help diffuse perceptions of 'glass ceilings' or covert discrimination. Socialisation also provides informal opportunities for the officers to mentor enlisted soldiers, which may include views on military life from a culturally similar perspective. Thus, properly managed, socialisation may contribute to the psychological readiness of the soldiers.

Discussion

Acculturation researchers have spent more than half a century learning how to prepare people for intercultural experiences. Few organisations in the world need to socialise such a large and diverse number of 'outsiders' into a strong and distinctive culture as does the military. Therefore study of diversity leadership in the military provides useful suggestions for managers in general.

New recruits – to whatever organisation – will experience different cognitive, affective and behavioural responses to their new environment depending on their cultural backgrounds. Failure to cater to these differences is likely to lead to many new employees' failure to become socialised into the values and beliefs of the organisation. It is highly likely that those who do not fully accept the culture of their workplace will soon to seek employment elsewhere. As in the military, the loss of trained and experienced people means a loss of valuable human resources to the employing institution. Effective retention policies must recognise the different motivations that affect personal decisions to remain with the firm.

Leadership strategies for retention include a 'normative commitment' approach by which employees are motivated by a sense of obligation – a feeling that the company is treating them so well that they owe loyalty in return – and motivation by 'affective commitment' through emotional attachment to, and identification with, the organisation. However, acculturation theory suggests that retention policies will be more effective if recruits are socialised into it from the beginning. That is, if they are taught the unique roles, norms and values which are the hallmark of every organisational culture.

This is not as easy as it sounds. Workplaces today are diverse environments in which people from different cultures are forced to interact. This often results in misunderstandings, even conflict, and poor group dynamics. Perceptions of similarities is an essential part of intercultural training; and organisational leaders can contribute to the process by creating equality between members of different ethnic groups and providing opportunities for them to interact in professional and social settings. Positive intercultural experiences are often a major reason for employees' decision to stay with the firm – or, in the military, to re-enlist.

Case study: The Tailhook scandal

Paula A. Coughlin, a decorated former Navy pilot and lieutenant, who blew the whistle on the debauchery at the US Navy's 1991 Tailhook Association convention of naval aviators in Las Vegas, settled her lawsuit in May 1995 with the group that sponsored the affair, and in May 1997 a federal appeals court upheld the multimillion-dollar damage award she won against Hilton Hotels for a breakdown in security at the convention.

1n 1991 Lieutenant Coughlin was grabbed and groped in a gauntlet of drunken aviators as she walked down a hotel corridor at the convention, organised by a private group of active-duty and retired naval aviators. After she went public with her accusations the Navy found she was one of more than 80 women who had been sexually molested, assaulted or harassed. Her testimony and the subsequent Pentagon investigations rocked the highest levels of the Navy and caused the service to rewrite its protocols for relations between the genders. Despite the Navy's findings, it was never able to successfully prosecute anyone, and many of the women say stubborn institutional barriers and chauvinistic mores remain.

Reports of widespread misbehaviour at the convention were at first played down by Navy brass with the standard explanation 'boys will be boys'. Paula Coughlin went to her military superiors, asking that the guilty men should be held accountable, but was accused of breaking rank and turning on fellow officers. She was made a pariah and an object of ridicule. One colleague wondered openly whether 'this woman is complaining of being groped, or not being groped'.

In 1994 Paula Coughlin resigned from the Navy. No reason was given, but CBS News and NBC News reported that she was quitting because of continued harassment over the Tailhook scandal. NBC and CBS both obtained copies of her letter of resignation, and each reported that Ms Coughlin cited the Tailhook case as her reason for leaving. NBC quoted her letter as saying, 'The physical attack on me by the naval aviators at the 1991 Tailhook convention and the covert attacks on me that followed have stripped me of my ability to serve.'

The scandal led to a Congressional shake-up, fuelled by women members of both houses. Both the highly respected Vice Chief of Naval Operations, Stanley R. Arthur, and a hero of the Gulf War, Comdr Robert E. Stumpf, found their careers suddenly blocked; and it was suggested that the post-Tailhook enquiry may have contributed to the suicide in 1996 of Admiral Jeremy M. Boorda, the Chief of Naval Operations.

Bhawuk and his colleagues propose various ways in which managers can help new recruits achieve solidarity within a highly diverse workforce; but note that the policies and practices of the employing institution may in effect promote discrimination, hence the importance of encouraging and protecting 'whistleblowers' – individuals who speak out on behalf of the majority to reveal injustices – instead of allowing them to be victimised.

They mention the Tailhook scandal as an example of such victimisation. The account is also an implicit argument for self-regulation by leaders of all organisations. Corporate leaders are not usually in favour of government interference in the way their run their institutions, therefore it is their responsibility to keep it to a minimum by modelling and promoting the highest ethical standards of behaviour.

Sources

Fernandez, S. 2011. 'Empowering public sector employees to improve performance: Does it work?', *The American Review of Public Administration*, 1 January 2011, 41: 23–47.

Goodman, W. 1996. 'Tailhook scandal's long shadows', *New York Times*, 15 October; http://www.nytimes.com/1996/10/15/arts/tailhook-scandal-s-long-shadows.html?ref=jeremymboorda 'INSIDE' published 20 May 1996 [accessed 3 April 2012].

Labaton, S. 1994. 'Women in the navy; A settlement is reached in the Tailhook scandal', *New York Times*, 11 September; http://www.nytimes.com/1994/09/11/weekinreview/sept-4-10-women-in-the-navy-a-settlement-is-reached-in-the-tailhook-scandal.html?src=pm [accessed 3 April 2012].

Kaifeng Yang and Anthony Kassekert. 'Linking management reform with employee job satisfaction: Evidence from federal agencies'. *Journal of Public Administration Research and Theory*, 1 April 2010, 20, pp. 413–36.

Meyer, J.P. and Allen, N.J. 1991. 'A three-component conceptualization of organizational commitment: Some methodological considerations'. *Human Resource Management Review*, 1, pp. 61–98.

O'Connor, J. 1995. 'How the Tailhook party turned into a scandal', *New York Times*, 22 May; http://www.nytimes.com/1995/05/22/arts/television-review-how-the-tailhook-party-turned-into-a-scandal.html?src=pm [accessed 3 April 2012].

Park, S.M. and Rainey, H.G. 2007. 'Antecedents, mediators, and consequences of affective, normative, and continuance commitment: Empirical tests of commitment effects in Federal Agencies'. *Review of Public Personnel Administration*, September, 27 (3), pp. 197–226.

Schmitt, E. 1992. 'Congressional roundup: 1,126 officers are promoted', *New York Times*, 2 July; http://www.nytimes.com/1992/07/02/us/congressional-roundup-1126-officers-are-promoted.html?src=pm [accessed 3 April 2012].

'Tailhook case: Whistle-blower quits navy', *New York Times*, 11 February 1994; http://www.nytimes.com/1994/02/11/us/tailhook-case-whistle-blower-quits-navy.html?src=pm [accessed 3 April 2012].

'Verdict against hotel upheld in Tailhook case', *New York* Times, 5 May 1997; http://www.nytimes.com/1997/05/05/us/verdict-against-hotel-upheld-in-tailhook-case.html [accessed 3 April 2012].

Discussion

1. High employee turnover is a problem that all managers want to avoid. Retention policies will be more effective if employees are acculturated into the organisation from the beginning.

2. However, most workforces today are diverse – diversity being defined as any significant difference that distinguishes one individual from another (e.g., race and gender are only two of many diversity factors).

3. People from different cultures are forced to interact, which often results in misunderstandings and conflicts. Nevertheless most people tend to prefer working in homogeneous groups and tend to avoid and resist change. Therefore workplace diversity management should develop an environment that works for all employees.

4. No single solution will create lasting change. Successful diversity comes through action at all levels of an organization

5. Nevertheless top leadership commitment is essential to strategic planning for diversity linked to performance and subject accountability.

6. Finally, there need to be systemic efforts to inform and educate management and staff about diversity's benefits to the organisation as a whole.

Questions

1. Do you have personal experience of an organisation that incorporates diversity management with recruitment and hiring? If you are in your final year of university studies maybe you have been approached by representatives of various firms to discuss a possible career with their company; or perhaps you have attended promotional public lectures on campus by some of these people? If so, what impression did you gain of their commitment to human diversity in employment policies?

2. Have you ever experienced discrimination in employment (or in any other aspect of your life) on the grounds of your gender, nationality, race, religion, marital status, sexual preference, or any other? If so, would you be willing to discuss it in class?

3. If you were an employer, how would you attract qualified and diverse applicants in order to develop a rich mix of talents within your firm?

MOTIVATIONS OF GLOBAL LEADERS FROM CULTURAL MYTHOLOGIES   Diana J. Wong-MingJi and Eric H. Kessler

Introduction

A study of key mythological figures provides insights not only to values underlying the motivation of global leaders but also to understanding different cultures.

The term mythology is composed of '*mythos*' meaning 'word' and '*logos*' meaning 'the science or study of' (Levin, 1959). Mythology has also come to mean not just the study of myths but also of a particular group of people, such as the ancient Greeks.

Joseph Campbell (1988: 163) considers myth to indicate what is universally permanent in human nature; because all societies create myths over the course of history that spans at least 70,000 years. Popper (1963) discusses how criticisms of myth gave rise to science. Malinowski (1948) considers myth as explanation for structural patterns of moral behaviour. Cassirer (1946) views myth as a language of metaphors and symbols; and Barthes (1973) sees it as a type of speech in a semiological system. Freud (1999) developed theoretical explanations about his patients' insecurities by extracting from Greek mythology and identifying the Oedipus complex. Jung (1912) also conceived of myth as a 'collective unconscious'.

Kostera (2008) and Gabriel (2004) write of the significance of myths in contemporary organisations. Kostera constructed a trilogy from three major themes – the heroes and heroines of organisational myths; mythical features of organisational epics and sagas; and mythmaking inspirations for organisational realities. Gabriel's essays demonstrate how the retelling and reinterpretations of ancient myths in today's organisations shed light on the psycho-social dynamics of how organisations work and what drives the motivation of organisational members.

Gabriel defines myths as sacred stories with sweeping grandeur, emotional intensity and complex narratives. Myths are often unique, unusual and unlikely stories. Heroes, villains and impossible conquests occur in myths, repeated in many forms such as plays, movies, books, poems, songs, etc. Myths are often associated with recurring themes across different cultures, which include creation of the world, universal truths and values, birth and return of the hero, trials and quests (Bierlein, 1994; Bowles, 1989).

The stream of research on values driving the attitudes, motivations and behaviours of global managers and leaders continues with an ever-growing list of cultural variables for comparison (see, e.g., England, 1975; Hofstede, 1980, 1983, 1993, 2001; Hofstede and McCrae, 2004; Javidan et al., 2006; Morrison, 2001; Schwartz, 1992; Trompenaars, 1993; Trompenaars and Hampden-Turner, 1998; Trompenaars and Woolliams, 1999). However the limitation of all theoretical description is that it neglects to demonstrate how these values are expressed in interpersonal interactions and cultural differences in interpretation. Cultural mythologies can build bridges across boundaries where cross-cultural relationships and interactions matter the most. This is a critical role because it can enable global leaders to understand underlying meaning for motivations within a particular context of time and space.

Heroic figures in different cultural mythologies often face insurmountable challenges, and the feats they engage in can defy human belief. Global leaders entering into new lands might well identify with such challenges. The plot lines of a culture's mythology provide templates for what behaviour and action are considered appropriate in cross-cultural communication.

Cultural mythologies are readily available today beyond oral tradition in print, drama, film, comic books and various art expressions: and regardless of the channel mythologies create a common cultural platform for both locals and strangers to share experience. The telling of myths down through generations provides a source of connections in the present by collectively drawing upon the past to navigate the future. This holds major significance for intergenerational dynamics because one of the key responsibilities of managers in multinational organisations is to develop successors from different cultures. The telling of sacred stories from the respective cultures of team members can create a platform of interpretations, inspirations and aspirations. Though myths cannot be taken as literal truth, they communicate essential truths that capture the imagination to challenge each one to grow beyond their existing limits.

In sum, understanding the relationship between cultural mythologies and cross-cultural communication can help to shape and motivate global leaders. Cultural mythology offers a complementary, reciprocal and extended relationship to the current body of knowledge in cross-cultural communication. Where generalised variables leave off, cultural mythology can be specific to the understanding of cultural differences on interpersonal levels. As a result, global leaders and managers can become more fully equipped to learn about each others' motivation in crossing the chaotic divides of cultural boundaries.

Cultural mythologies are multidimensional in nature. They hold meaning across vast expanses of time and yet their meanings evolve in real time at the moment of as myths are communicated. In this manner, cultures and myths evolve together in an interdependent fashion. Campbell (1949, 1959, 1976) defined three key functions of myth:

1. As an experience for placing people's position in relation to the universe; to enable them to make sense of their purpose by answering the question, 'why are we here?'. Jung (1912) argued that all human beings need to believe in some kind of mythology.
2. To integrate the accumulation of knowledge and set of ideas existing at the time of the telling of the myth. Myth socialises members into a culture; to relate and support the values, attitudes and behaviours of the society's insiders;
3. As a template to help people move towards self-realisation.

Kirk (1970) also suggested three major functions of myths: as entertaining narratives and stories that go beyond storytelling; as operative, iterative and validating repetitions, central to rituals and ceremonies where significant cultural value and meaning are conveyed. They confirm, maintain, authorise and institutionalise existing cultural relationships, order and systems. Finally they function as speculative explanations of how problems and dilemmas might be resolved.

Myths establish standards of conduct by creating, maintaining and legitimising actions and outcomes; they manage political interests and value systems of the status quo; construct cause–effect relationships; create and explain organisational phenomena; rationalise and enable stability in complex and turbulent environments. Myths from four geographically disparate regions of the world provide brief illustrations of the above, and of deep motivating forces that shape the mental, behavioural and emotional orientations of global leaders.

Ireland

The Mythological Cycle, also known as the Golden Age, accounts for the collection of myths about the origins of Ireland and extends back to a hazy ancient time of gods. The Book of Invasions describes a succession of five mythical battles and occupations of various gods. The foundational myth of Ireland is the Tuatha De Danann, the tribe of the Goddess Danu. When the Celts arrived and took over Ireland, the Thuatha retreated underground and became known as the 'little people' or leprechauns and fairies (Ellis, 2002; Yeats, 2003).

The Ulster Cycle is the second set of myths, which is also known as the Heroic Age, with the most prominent epic being The Cattle Raid of Cooley (*Tain Bo Cuailnge*). The myth is a series of conflicts and battles with an array of characters between two northern Irish territories. Most notable, Cuchulainn, the son of Lug and the defender of Ulster, was chosen as the Irish champion after defeating the water giant Uath to face off against an invasion by the Goddess-Queen Medb of Connacht. Fears of death in battle were mitigated by a belief in reincarnation after the soul entered into paradise for a respite before re-entering into the human world.

The Fenian Cycle encompasses myths set around 300 BC. They focus on adventures of Finn mac Cool, a great hero, and his followers, the Fian or Fianna. He was a warrior, hunter and a prophet who fought against Ireland's enemies with such power that he was often identified with Lugh, the ancient Celtic god. His battles included defeating Aillen mac Midgna, an Otherworld fire-breathing musician. Much of the Fenian Cycle centres on professional warriors with myths told in verse form about hunting, fighting and having adventures in the supernatural spirit world. At the same time, warriors were expected to be proficient in poetry.

The Kings Cycle is a collection of Celtic myths that extended beyond the current borders of Ireland into Wales and Britain. The *Mabinogion* dated back to the twelfth century about four branches of families – the Pwyll, Branwen, Manawydan and Math. Some of the myths echoed the ones from the Tuatha De Danaan. From the eleven tales, the legendary myths of King Arthur took shape, with battles for independence against the Anglo-Saxons and resemblances of Christian influence in the quest for the Holy Grail.

In sum, overarching themes in Irish mythology are combat between individual god-like heroes and other supernatural beings, a mix of victories and losses that are not necessarily aligned with good or evil, and knowledge and wisdom intimately rooted in spirits of the natural world. Descriptors of the Celts include a clannish fraternity and brotherhood with loud boisterous behaviour, including much feasting and drinking that are often associated with preparations for battle. In addition, Celts were also free-spirited, poetic, romantic, artistic and deeply religious in their relationship with ancient spiritual connections with gods from the natural world.

Relating the rich collection of Celtic mythologies from Ireland to the motivation of global leadership suggests a human propensity for combative competition between individuals and groups who battle on behalf of the larger community while appealing to supernatural forces for aid. The purpose of battle may not always be clear or understood as a worthwhile cause and may be sparked by mishaps and misunderstandings. For example, the great epic of the Cattle Raid of Cooley began with an argument between Queen Maeve of Connacht and her husband, Ailill, about who had the finer possessions. The argument escalated into a full-scale war against the neighbouring kingdom of Ulster, which ended with the loss of many lives and a battle between two bulls, with both dying, as well as the death of Queen Maeve herself. Out of the story arose Ireland's greatest Celtic hero, Cuchulainn, who led a short, glorious life.

As Herzberg defined motivator factors (1993), the Celtic mythologies often illustrate how individual autonomy and responsibility drive one towards achievement and winning in battles. Various Celtic myths also reveal motivation based on needs related strongly to affiliation for connections among clan members and comrades in battle while the need for achievement and power also strongly resonates.

These characteristics also relate to Hofstede's (1993) results for Ireland on the different cultural dimensions, which indicate close-to-moderate positions on all of them with only slight tendencies towards any end of any continuum.

Even on the masculinity–femininity dimension, Ireland is positioned slightly towards the feminine, which is consistent with the number of goddess-heroines that possess significant powers in their battles and rule over kingdoms. At the same time, male and female roles are somewhat more blurred, as illustrated in the myth of the knight Sir Ector who was given the child Arthur to nurture as an ordinary child when his father King Uther Pendragon handed the baby into Merlin's care and protection.

Both expectancy theory (Vroom and Yetton, 1973; Vroom and Jago, 1988) and reinforcement theories (Skinner, 1953) of motivation apply to many of the Celtic myths. Expectancy of winning is often high when a god-hero possesses athletic prowess, vast intellect and knowledge, and supernatural powers. The instrumentality to achieving outcome is high when the outcomes are protection of the clan and glory of heroism. Valence of how much the god-heroes value the outcomes varies because sometimes the need to step into battle is a result of one's station and duty, such as being a prince, versus voluntary individual choice. In addition, Celtic god-heroes often rise with multiple sources of positive reinforcement because the most negative one, being the fear of death, is substantially mitigated by the spiritual perspective of reincarnation and a soul resting place in paradise until being reborn.

Overall, the implications for global leaders with a heritage of Celtic mythologies include a willingness to engage in combative competition that is heralded with a pre-celebratory launch. All three dimensions of intellectual, physical prowess and spiritual forces will be brought forth. The loss of a battle may not necessarily mean the end of a war even with the demise of a leader. Thus, encounters with Irish leaders require a strong fortitude for both combativeness and camaraderie with strong social bonding on multiple levels.

Nigeria

African mythologies have many complex stories that were passed on by word of mouth from one generation to the next. Recent colonial historical events created arbitrary political lines that are often drawn through the same cultural society while at the same creating composites of multiple cultures under a single statehood. Thus, the cultural mythologies of countries such as Nigeria need to account for the complex cultural composite of mythologies in its geopolitical founding.

Evidence of the earliest human existence comes from Africa and with the development of societies in Nigeria going back as far as 9000 BC. Today, it is the eighth most populated country in the world, with the largest black population of any nation. Three major groups of people, known as the Yoruba, Igbo and Hausa, make up most of Nigeria. This means that Nigerian cultural mythologies form somewhat of a kaleidoscope in which a rich array of myths prevail over many aspects of life. Continuity faced disruption and reinterpretations, first by Islam and then Christianity, which attempted to replace ancient ideas and languages with the conquerors' version of god, truth and civilisation (Davis, 2005).

The Yoruba have a pantheon of over 1,700 divinities that are also referred to as orishas. The supreme god of the heaven and sky known as Olodumare or Olorun created seven princes. The first six took the best gifts and left the youngest with a chicken, the iron bars, and an ambiguous unknown substance wrapped in a cloth. The prince, Oranmiyan, threw the substance on the water and the chicken jumped to scatter it far and wide to create the land. Ile-Ife is identified by the Yoruba as the special place where the Earth was created.

Then Oranmiyan transformed the iron bars into weapons. An important role of the king is to rule with the skilful combat and might of the strongest warrior to protect his people from invaders. As a result, Oranmiyan became king of the Yoruba and established the greatness of his tribe. He allowed his older brothers to rule a small portion of the land but required all their descendants to be subjects of his descendants forever. In a different version of this myth, Olorun only had two sons but still only one went forth to create the world while the other got drunk and fell asleep.

In the face of might and strength, an important character that appears in many African myths is the trickster. A variety of myths tell of how a small, weaker character employs cunning and trickery to defeat a much stronger opponent. The trickster requires an effective combination of intelligence, quick thinking and gall with little regard for the outcomes. Different myths have the trickster as Eshu, a god who brings chaos. More often than not, the trickster is an animal such as a rabbit, but Anansi the spider is a famous animal trickster.

Similar to various African mythologies, Nigerian myths portray gods that exist everywhere with little hierarchy or regard for an after-life. The focus is on the present and issues confronting daily life.

The rich collection of Nigerian mythologies provides insight to the underlying motivations of global leaders from Nigeria. First, there is the valuing of leaders who provide protection through both might and intelligence. The strongest and bravest has responsibility to protect those who are weaker and less able to fend for themselves until such time when another stronger and more able body can defeat the leader. Second, a leader must take care of familial responsibilities but the rule is very much autocratic and top-down, which requires respect from those below. Last, intelligence and cunning wit are capable of overcoming brute force.

Thus Nigerian mythology shapes its leaders with a distinct collection of myths, which also function to hold certain values, beliefs and attitudes with degree of consistency. The complexity of the sacred stories reflects a highly interwoven set of attitudes as they form layers of influences on actions and communication styles. By engaging in the increasing importance of the global marketplace, myths equip Nigerian leaders with particular lenses for interpreting different cross-cultural interactions while also having a vehicle to interpret new ideas.

China

Chinese mythology encompasses a vast collection of myths extending as far back as 3000 BC within a broad cosmological context. Chinese cosmology considers '... that all parts of the entire cosmos belong to one organic whole and that they all interact as participants in one spontaneously self-generating life process' (Mote, 1989: 15). The notion of interdependence exists in a Chinese cosmological order where a change in one part impacts other parts of a system. This is related to the contemporary idea of a collectivist orientation in the Chinese culture as described by Hofstede (2001, 1983).

The collectivist orientation in Chinese leadership characteristics, traits, values, cultural orientations and behavioural practices encompasses strong filial responsibility as a prominent family value, *guanxi*, in developing community and business network relationships, trust and face. These leadership qualities are interrelated to each other and integrated within the relationships of a Chinese leader. Various Chinese mythologies illustrate the complexities of the interwoven dynamics of Chinese leadership qualities.

Some of the famous Chinese mythologies about leadership are the Yellow Emperor (*Huang Di*), Qin Shi, Queen Mother of the West (*Xi Wang Mu*), Kuan Yin, the Monkey King's Journey to the West, Five Virtuous Emperors, the Three Sovereigns or Three August Ones, Eight Immortals and Four Supreme Bodhisattvas. Many of the Chinese myths have an ensemble of leaders who act in concert with each other to support, motivate and collaborate in confronting challenges to the benefit of the greater collective. Chinese myths of individual leaders are often ones of transformational leadership, such as the Queen Mother of the West who serves peaches of immortality to transform mortals to immortals. The motivation driving the transformational Chinese leaders vary as illustrated by two notable emperors who hold venerable position positions in the Chinese psyche and culture.

The Yellow Emperor is considered to be the benevolent 'Ancestor of the Chinese' and 'Originator of the Chinese civilisation', who was born of a stormy divine birth and established the foundation of the Chinese culture. He introduced the art of war, rules of government, agriculture, animal husbandry, traditional Chinese medicine and acupuncture, an ideogram-writing system, mathematical system, astronomy and the calendar, a 12-tone musical scale, musical instruments, and inventions such as building architectural structures, wheel and cart, weaving and clothing, and boats.

Two important volumes of writings are attributed to him: *The Yellow Emperor's Canon of Medicine* formed the foundation of traditional Chinese medicine for over 24 centuries and the *Handbooks of Sex* (2697–2598 BC) outline ideas of love. The Yellow Emperor's hundred years of rule ended with ascension to heaven in a chariot filled with an entourage; hence, he and subsequent Chinese rulers are referred to as the 'Son of Heaven'. Many of the essential foundations of the Chinese cultures are attributed to the benevolence, compassion and creative intelligence of the rule of the Yellow Emperor. The leadership motivation of the Yellow Emperor can be related to Aristotle's four cardinal virtues – prudence, justice, fortitude and temperance, which are in substantial contrast to Maslow's hierarchy or Herzberg's two-factor theory of motivation (see laynetworks.com). His transformational leadership style is intertwined with the exercise of legitimate and expert power (French and Raven, 1959).

Qin Shi Huang Di (260–210 BC), also known as the First Emperor, is famous for creating the Qin dynasty, the first one of many dynasties until 1912. He unified China through an extensive infrastructure of roads, canals and the Great Wall with standard cart-sizes for his transportation system. He also standardised the currency, writing system, legal codes and bureaucracy to unify the Chinese. To prepare for the after-life, Qin Shi's burial included the thousands of life-size terracotta warriors near Xian, which was discovered only recently in 1974. The absoluteness of the Emperor's power also entailed significant dominance over human life where many lives were lost and buried in building the Great Wall; and where over 300 concubines without children were buried alive with the Emperor and the secrecy of the burial location ensured by executing all who knew of the site.

The myth of Qin Shi illustrates a complex interaction of leadership motivation with a need for achievement and power as defined by McClelland et al. (1953) in an authoritarian type of leadership. Qin Shi also systematically built an empire by exercising different types of power including legitimate, coercive and expert (French and Raven, 1959). An important cultural dimension shaping Chinese leadership from the myths is the large power distance (Hofstede, 2001) between those in positions of authority and their followers.

Understanding the motivation of Chinese leaders through the mythology of the culture requires going beyond many of the motivational theories in western management. While a few of the motivational theories can be related, the heavy focus on individualist theories – such as Maslow's hierarchy of needs, Alderfer's ERG theory, job characteristic model, expectancy theory, reinforcement theory and equity theory (see laynetworks.com) – needs to account for interpretations of the cultural orientations of Chinese leadership. The multi-stream natural and nurtured bases of motivation (Dyck and Neubert, 2010) provide an important direction by accounting for motivation to live a virtuous life, create harmony with embracing the diversity of individuals, have a life worth living, and make an enduring contribution to others.

The USA

American superhero mythology developed through a relatively brief but rich history of frontier exploration, cultural conglomeration, industrial and techno-logical development, and geopolitical engagement. It tends to revolve around valiant figures of many shapes and sizes displaying a rugged individualism and engaged spirit such as: heroic engineer Casey Jones, brave woodsman Davy Crockett, gruff leader Ethan Allen, mighty steel-driver John Henry, benevolent naturalist Johnny Appleseed, imposing woodsman Paul Bunyan, cowboy hero Pecos Bill, sharp-shooting Annie Oakley and witty Brer Rabbit (see american-folklore.net).

With advances in media American myths have also been played out on the big screen through characters such as the idealistic Atticus Finch, resourceful Indiana Jones, clever Rick Blain, macho John Wayne, indomitable Rocky Balboa, noble George Bailey and courageous Ellen Ripley. With the popularity of athletics sports pages and bubble-gum cards have been filled with the mythical exploits of Babe Ruth, Jim Thorpe, Johnny Unitas, Michael Jordan and Muhammad Ali. With expansion of business and industry they have taken shape in the corner office with iconic figures such as Walton, Disney, Ford, Sloan, Rockefeller, Watson, Hewlett, Turner, Welch, Gates and Jobs. But perhaps the most colourful and revealing manifestation of this mythology is in its comic book superheroes.

Superheroes connote distinct values, ideas, methods of play, genres of experi-ences and diverse cognitive structures to their audiences that manifest themselves into leadership styles. They are is a sense mechanisms for socialisation which serve as role models for conveying core values and modes of behaviour (Bandura, 1977) as well as larger-than-life figures with enduring legacies and lessons (Hunt, 1999; Patterson, 2007)).

Although the 'hero journey' is a somewhat universal mythology the American superhero is a rather particular manifestation of the lone individualist calling up uncommon powers to overcome evil and rescue the powerless (Faludi, 2007; Lawrence and Jewett, 2002; Shamir, 2006). This is consistent with studies (e.g., Hofstede, 1980) characterising the American culture as highly individualistic, assertive and performance oriented. Moreover, although hero idolisation is not *per se* American, what is unique is the degree to which their values impact the social fabric (Kamm, 2001) as well as their level of penetration in the American consumer and mass-media market (Postrel, 2006).

Some prototypical American superheroes are offered for illustration. First, the caped crusader Batman, a master scientist and criminologist, leverages state-of-the-art technology to fight evil but also struggles with his own inner daemons. Batman harkens us to consider the intersection of leadership and innovation, personal introspection and the need for strategic flexibility and adaptive decision-making under uncertainty.

A second example is Spiderman, a transformed teen who possesses spider-like attributes of climbing, leaping, web-slinging and a special sense-of-danger. Spiderman prompts us to examine issues of identity and ego, public image, the role of intuition and the burden as well as social dimension of leadership embodied in the lesson that 'with great power comes great responsibility'.

Thirdly, Superman might be seen as the most universal and formidable American superhero. He is an immigrant who fights to protect his adopted land and boasts of amazing strength, the power of flight, impenetrable skin and X-ray vision. However, he must constantly be wary of 'strategic kryptonites' and over-confidence. All in all, the prototypical American superhero leader can be seen to illustrate the value of creatively developing and exploiting unique competitive advantages, becoming self-reliant yet compassionate, proactively managing reputation and image, self-reflecting on identity and purpose, acting strong and brave, leveraging cutting-edge resources, and ultimately fighting for noble personal and societal goals.

Enhancing this generic profile, a critical aspect of American mythology (much like its central characters) is that it is not so much a static caricature but more resembling of an unfolding cinema. The images morph to fit their task domain and social context. They develop to reflect their time and era underlining the analogy between superheroes and America itself. For example, with shifting trends, issues and affinities the superhero genre also changes. This is evidenced in the transition from simpler conceptions of Batman and Captain America to more reflective and complex modern characterisations.

The mythology also seeks to reconcile the schism between heroic and a more 'post-heroic' leadership that emphasises collaboration (Dutton, 1996; Taylor and Greve, 2006) and team orientation (e.g., Fantastic Four, X-Men, Justice League). Moving forward, perhaps the greatest communication dynamic in making sense of and applying this evolving mythological saga is such – the ability to be both heroic and post-heroic to navigate the intricacies of an increasingly interconnected and interdependent world of interlaced stakeholders facing monumental challenges.

Discussion

Cultural mythologies offer three major insights for global leaders in international management. First, they enable a first step towards cultural understanding and appreciation. Hence, a global leader can build cultural competence to forge constructive organisational relationships in the chaotic and complex dynamics of international business.

Second, cultural mythologies provide a way of accessing insights into the contextual meanings of ideas in action over time. When collectivism in Chinese and Irish mythologies is compared, the interpretation of collectivism takes on very different meaning. In the Chinese culture, collectivism refers to filial responsibilities and *guanxi* relationships. In the Irish culture, collectivism refers to one's clan members that may or may not be related by blood but certainly in tightly woven historical community of brotherhood and sisterhood-like relationships against outsiders.

Thus the underlying motivations that drive collectivism or other cultural tendencies are embedded in a cultural context. In turn, the cultural context of an idea or concept evolves over time with shared historical and collective experiences to construct a culture's collective interpretations and meanings. Hence motivating factors evolve within a cultural context that can be extrapolated from the big stories that matter, the cultural mythologies.

Last, while cultural mythologies rarely hold literal facts, they are the vehicles for cultural truths and beliefs that enable the multiple functions of myths as discussed above. Facts rarely entertain and capture the imagination. But myths have the power to do so and support both the stability and transformation of a culture at the same time. The US cultural mythology of Superman from the 1930s shifted from a lone superhero who fights crime and evildoers to being part of a team with the Justice League of America and others. By 1996, Superman does marry his long-time love, Lois Lane, and settles into living through various martial issues as well as becoming a vegetarian in 2000.

As an evolving mythology reflective of the US culture, the lone superhero reflects the Great Man and leadership traits theories of management with values of idealism, compassion and justice. In keeping with the times, the same character encompasses additional issues. Thus, cultural myths act as adaptive and regenerative mechanisms to develop cultural identities across time.

Motivation theories from management researchers enable global managers to understand what drives people towards different behaviour and performance in organisations. But most of the research has cultural roots in a western management culture, primarily the US and among undergraduate students who provided the data. In an era of increasing globalisation, different voices are necessary for international management. The different voices from cultural mythologies go much deeper into the underlying cultural roots where integration of values, beliefs and historical context formulate motivations and subsequent, interpretations, meanings and behaviour. Global leaders need to listen to cultural mythologies not only to participate more effectively in cross-cultural negotiation but also to find role-models of leadership from their own cultural heritages.

ROLE MODELS IN THE MEDIA AS ETHICAL MOTIVATORS	Anne Dunn

This contribution draws on material written by Anne Dunn and was originally published in Spence, E., Alexander, A., Quinn, A. and Dunn, A. (2011), *Media, Markets and Morals* (London and New York: Wiley Blackwell). It is reproduced with the permission of the author.

The bane of a free economy is external compliance through regulation. Since media organisations are run as businesses, ethical role models would potentially enhance the moral standing – and hence effectiveness – of self-regulation; thus rendering external regulation less necessary.

Media practitioners should aim to act in ways that are morally excellent. However, what is meant by moral excellence? How can morally excellent media practice be encouraged? The central argument here is that *role models* are important in the education of media practitioners.

One definition of journalism is of 'contributing to public discourse by providing factual, reliable, timely and meaningful information' (Hayes, Singer and Ceppos, 2007: 265). In other words, it is an activity in the service of the public, to enable discussion and participation in public affairs.

Moral excellence is thus both a function of individual character and of the profession itself: but all ethical decisions have to be made within contextual frameworks. Context can make conflicting demands on judgement as to the right behaviour. A majority of media professionals are employed in organisations that are also businesses. Individual practitioners may come under pressure from employers to cut ethical corners in the pursuit of profit. In such situations, a strong hold on the virtues of professional practice is essential, and this is learnt through right upbringing and education, and through experience. Major news organisations may enjoy a reputation for credible, trustworthy information, and this is likely both to benefit journalists who work for that organisation and to identify individual employees who undermine that reputation through unethical behaviour. From an ethical point of view, however, an individual must exercise personal moral responsibility to attain moral excellence, and cannot derive it from an organisation (Hayes, Singer and Ceppos, 2007: 270).

The education of media practitioners today takes place much more often in universities than it did twenty or thirty years ago. James Carey (1980) has made a forceful argument in favour of educating journalists in the humanities and social sciences. Lee Bollinger, the President of Columbia University, home of the Pulitzer Prize for journalism, enumerated (2003) the 'basic capacities' that a journalism school should instil in its students. These included familiarity with the history of their field and its great figures, and 'the moral and ethical standards that should guide professional behaviour'. In so saying, the Columbia University president was acknowledging the importance both of education in ethical behaviour and of role models.

We learn what is considered right and what wrong in interaction with others (parents, friends, teachers, colleagues). All of them are in some respects role models, not all necessarily good ones. There are, after all, unethical practitioners – quacks and crooks – in every profession. When it comes to selecting good role models, some may be inclined to think people in media professions such as journalism or public relations or advertising would find this hard to do. Moreover, it may not be easy to find any role model who is wholly and unequivocally virtuous; human beings are more complicated than this. It can be instructive, however, to give consideration to whether or not a particular practitioner might be called a good role model for the profession. Let us consider some examples from journalism.

Edward R. Murrow (1908–65)

This legendary American journalist was a pioneer of television news broadcasting, having established his reputation for truthful and courageous reporting in a series of radio broadcasts for CBS during the Second World War.

Murrow was also a powerful mentor not only to journalists but also to the camera operators and producers who worked with him. He recruited a team of journalists who became known in the industry as 'Murrow's Boys' (few women were working as broadcast correspondents in the 1930s and 1940s).

During his regular broadcasts for CBS from London during the Blitz, Morrow developed a signature sign-off that would become the title of a 2005 movie: 'Good night, and good luck'. Early in the 1950s Murrow and his producer Fred Friendly took to television a current affairs format they had introduced on radio as *Hear it Now*, calling it, reasonably enough, *See it Now*. This was very early in the life of television as a mass medium, and Murrow introduced his new series with the words 'This is an old team, trying to learn a new trade.' Murrow was already a role model for broadcast journalists, celebrated for his honesty and integrity, virtues of character that he was to demonstrate in his new medium.

It was a time to challenge the ethics of any citizen, never mind any journalist. The United States and its allies were in the grip of the Cold War, with the Soviet Union and all forms of Communism perceived as a direct threat to democracy and to the principle of freedom. At the height of the Cold War, in 1953 and 1954, Senator Joseph McCarthy used his position as chairman of the Senate Permanent Subcommittee on Investigations to launch an anti-Communist crusade, subpoenaing witnesses on short notice and often being the only Senator to attend closed-door hearings. Transcripts of hearings, released in 2003, showed that McCarthy manipulated hearings by calling only witnesses he could intimidate and avoiding those likely to stand up to him.

The coining of the term 'McCarthyism' to describe this genre of punitive anti-Communist fervour, a prominent characteristic of the era, demonstrates the pervasiveness of the senator's influence on American society. The special edition of *See it Now* that Murrow broadcast on 9 March 1954, called 'A Report on Senator Joseph McCarthy', is credited with beginning a backlash against McCarthy that would end his reign of terror. Murrow showed both courage and practical judgement in the way he and his team carefully researched and delivered their report, specifically targeting McCarthy in spite of the general public level of fear, of McCarthy's threats to subpoena him and an implied threat to the career of Murrow's brother, a general in the US Air Force (Wersba, n.d.).

Murrow is often quoted as having had doubts about using the power of television to attack an individual; but he reached an ethical decision that the greater public good lay in revealing McCarthy's manipulative behaviour. The network, CBS, would not permit Murrow and Friendly, his producer, to use CBS money to advertise the programme, nor use the network logo in the ads, so the journalist and his producer paid for newspaper advertisements themselves. After the broadcast, tens of thousands of letters, telegrams and phone calls poured into CBS, running 15 to 1 in Murrow's favour. In December of that year, the US Senate voted to censure Joseph McCarthy, making him one of the few senators ever to be so disciplined; he died in hospital three years later.

Edward R. Murrow is still considered one of journalism's greatest role models. In the movie *The Insider*, a television producer who succumbs to advertiser pressure to tone down a piece of investigative journalism exposing unethical behaviour in the tobacco industry is accused of 'betraying the legacy of Edward R. Murrow'. What makes Murrow an excellent role model is that his actions exemplify the cardinal virtues and are evidence of his practical wisdom. In Murrow we see that combination of justification, motivation and internal compliance, which is how personal, individual ethical conduct comes about.

Chris Masters

This Australian television reporter was responsible for a programme broadcast in 1987 called 'The Moonlight State' that rocked the country. It instigated a Royal Commission (known as the Fitzgerald Inquiry) into police corruption in the Australian state of Queensland, which in turn produced a large number of convictions of corrupt police, including of a former Queensland Police Commissioner, Sir Terence Lewis. Masters has written (1992) that what he discovered about the extent and nature of police corruption severely tested his fundamental belief 'that people are basically good'.

Although the final television programme, aired as part of the investigative documentary series *Four Corners*, by the national public service broadcaster, the Australian Broadcasting Corporation, can certainly be held to have improved the nation's moral condition, Masters and the ABC were to face more than a decade of legal action, as a result of Australia's defamation laws. As a result, despite still believing that what he did was worthwhile, Masters has expressed concern that the price of 'the death by a thousand courts' was too high to encourage young journalists to follow his example (Masters, 2001).

There are examples aplenty of Masters' courage. He recounts how nearly he came to being set up on a trumped-up charge that would nevertheless have ruined his reputation. There is also an illustration of how Masters' own courage gave courage to others, in the seven key witnesses who eventually agreed to be filmed for the programme, all of whom put themselves at real risk to do so. Masters acknowledges that the risks of the investigation 'were not just mine to take' (1992: 68) and recounts a moment when he inadvertently put another witness in danger. He argues that 'there are times when you can't help but take chances in order to get a little closer to the truth' (ibid.). Here we have the challenge of right judgement, of knowing the difference between risk that is 'sensible, professional' and risk that is not.

Veronica Guerin

The case of this Irish journalist, murdered by drug dealers in 1996, illustrates the complexity of role models. Her name became internationally known after Australian actress Cate Blanchett played the title role in the 2003 movie, *Veronica Guerin*.

Guerin had been a renowned and fearless crime reporter for the Irish *Sunday Independent* newspaper. Over the two years prior to her death she had been investigating drugs gangs in Dublin. Two drug dealers were found guilty of her murder. Her reports had seriously hampered the illegal operations of the drugs gangs, and the judge who sentenced her killers said her death had not been in vain, because of the many young people her work had spared 'from the scourge of drugs' (Laville, 1999). Guerin would confront those whom she was investigating, going to their homes alone to interview them; on one occasion, in 1995, she was attacked and beaten by a man said to be the boss of the Dublin drugs gang that murdered her a year later.

In the 2003 film, Guerin as played by Cate Blanchett, is clearly meant to be seen as heroic; indeed, the director of the film alluded to Guerin as a real-life hero. At the time of Guerin's death, her editor described her in heroic terms: 'She insisted on the freedom to do her job and, armed only with her pen, she set about doing that' (Muir, 1996). But Guerin was also a wife and mother; her son was six years old when she died. Some argued that for her to continue her investigative work after such violence and threat was not courageous, but 'recklessness' (Taylor, 2003).

Here we appear to have an example of a journalist determined to inform the public, to reveal the truth about what was happening in society. Her death was met with widespread shock and a response that connected it with the moral role of journalism. The Irish Prime Minister called it 'an attack on democracy', and a joint statement of prominent newspaper editors in Ireland and England spoke of her murder as 'a fundamental attack on the free press'. Their statement concluded 'Journalists will not be intimidated.' And Guerin did make a difference. After her death, the Irish government launched its biggest-ever criminal investigation, eventually changing the law to give it the power to seize assets bought with the proceeds of crime, and to prevent criminals benefiting financially from their crimes.

In Veronica Guerin, we have a case study of the complexity of acting virtuously in the Aristotelian sense described at the beginning of the chapter, and of the importance of contextual factors.

Anna Politkovskaya

This Russian journalist was an outspoken critic of the war in Chechnya. She was found dead in her apartment building in Moscow in October 2006; she had been shot.

Chechnya is a Muslim republic trying to break away from Moscow; Russia has waged two wars against it since the mid-1990s. Politkovskaya's reporting on Chechnya began in 1999, at the start of the second of these wars. She concentrated her attention on the impact of the fighting on the civilian population, on the brutal behaviour of both the Russian and the Chechen forces. She was one of the few people to enter the Moscow theatre where Chechen militants took hundreds hostage, in 2002.

Politkovskaya documented killings, torture and beatings of civilians. She was not afraid to name those she accused, such as Russian police officer Sergei Lapin. He was detained, but the case was dismissed; and Politkovskaya had made another enemy. Foreign journalists based in Moscow, and other Russian journalists were united in the view that Politkovskaya was 'in a class of her own' and 'the first name that came to mind' as an example of honest journalism in Russia (Parfitt, 2006).

Despite repeated threats to her life, Politkovskaya would not be silenced, nor did she think of herself as a hero, saying 'I'm just trying to do my job, to let people know what's happening in our country' (Parfitt, 2006). She thus, like Guerin, drew attention to the aim or goal of journalism, as her own moral compass. Her stand was the more remarkable because so few journalists in Russia, working largely for state-owned or controlled publications, were prepared to report on events in Chechnya.

International news agencies were grateful for the information only she was brave enough to make public. Politkovskaya received international awards for her writing, but also the criticism that her journalism was biased against Russia and President Vladimir Putin. Her defenders countered that she was as willing to expose Chechen rebel tactics as to criticise the Russian forces.

After her death, Politkovskaya was mourned by thousands of ordinary Russians, who held vigils in Moscow and St Petersburg. There seemed little doubt in the minds of the people there as to who had killed her. A giant photograph of her in Pushkin Square, Moscow had written across it: 'The Kremlin has killed freedom of speech'; on another photo, of Mr Putin, were the words: 'You are responsible for everything' (Blomfield, 2006).

Discussion

'Moral excellence' in professional behaviour is closely connected to excellent professional practice. Individuals must take ultimate responsibility for ethical decision-making, no matter how ethically excellent (or corrupt) an organisation might be. Individuals develop moral frameworks over time and through socialisation, including education. Moral education for professionals must surely go beyond technical training. It needs to encompass knowledge and appreciation of the history of the profession and its conceptual frameworks; and of those whose contribution is widely acknowledged as epitomising its goals and principles. This is where role models can provide a valuable starting point for reflection. The cases of Veronica Guerin and Anna Politkovskaya demonstrate that even the apparently heroic pursuit of truth and its disclosure in the face of threats and intimidation may not always be simply as virtuous as they seem.

Acknowledging the superior power of a global, public ethical framework, media professionals have a primary role to disseminate information – which itself has an inherent normative structure – and this role determines their professional ethical framework, or role morality. Good role models, then, demonstrate both the virtues that characterise the role morality of their profession and an understanding, demonstrated in actions and beliefs, of what is universally right and good.

In the media professions, this role morality lies in characters who automatically and consistently demonstrate, in the exercise of their profession, honesty and accuracy, sincerity, fairness and courage. These in turn exemplify the universal ethical principles of truthfulness and justice. It would be unrealistic to expect all media professionals to display all of these virtues all of the time; but those who consistently act according to even one of the key principles are likely to provide a better role model than those who cannot or will not do so.

Case Study: The trading scandal of Salomon Brothers

The Tailhook scandal, described above, illustrates how unethical organisational cultures develop under bad leadership; and the *Journal of Business Ethics* is a good source for more examples of good and bad leadership models. For instance, Ronald Sims and Johannes Brinkman (2009) describe and discuss unethical behaviour in organisations as a result of interaction between disputable leadership and ethical climate. They analyse the bond trading scandal at Salomon Brothers to demonstrate the development of an unethical organisational culture under the leadership of John Gutfreund (Lewis, 2011, 1990; Mayer, 1993). They argue that leaders shape and reinforce an ethical or unethical organisational climate by what they pay attention to, how they react to crises, how they behave, how they allocate rewards and how they hire and fire individuals.

John Gutfreund, ex-chairman and chief executive officer of Salomon Brothers, Wall Street's largest investment banking house, joined the firm as a municipal bond trader in 1953. When William R. Salomon, the firm's managing partner, retired in 1978, Gutfreund replaced him, treating subordinates with contempt while embarking on enormous corporate spending enterprises, which in the words of Martin Mayer 'made the excesses of the most free-spending Roman emperors pale by comparison'.

Those surrounding Gutfreund could not check (and often imitated) his high-handedness. He became a symbol of the excess that defined the 1980s business culture in the US; in 1985, *Business Week* gave him the nickname 'King of Wall Street'. In 1985, its peak year, the company brought in $760 million in pretax profits, more than the entire securities industry earned in 1978. Riding the crest, John Gutfreund planned to take Salomon out of its long-time offices at One New York Plaza, in lower Manhattan, and erect what was to have been the city's most glittery new office tower as its headquarters, uptown, on Columbus Circle. The project was abandoned after the 22 May 1991 auction of US treasury bonds brought to a crisis a calamity that had been building for years.

Federal law prohibits any one buyer from bidding for more than 35 per cent of the treasury bonds available at an auction. However, it permits brokerage houses to bid for clients who order bonds and these bids do not count against the firm's 35 per cent limit. Salomon, long an outspoken critic of the limitation, regularly entered bids in clients' names, unbeknown to them. After the 22 May auction Salomon walked away with $10.6 billion of the $11.3 billion available in US treasuries. After the government launched an investigation it emerged that Paul Mozer, a rogue trader with Salomon Brothers, had submitted bids in excess of Treasury rules. When this was discovered Gutfreund did not immediately suspend Mozer, to the disapproval of Warren Buffett who had just acquired a stock position in Salomon Brothers for Berkshire Hathaway.

In August, 1991, John Gutfreund resigned after accusations of involvement of Salomon's senior management in the bidding violations and a public announcement by the Treasury that as chairman and chief executive officer he should bear ultimate responsibility for supervision of the wrongdoer. Gutfreund paid a fine, and undertook not to serve in future as chairman or chief executive officer of a securities firm without the prior approval of the SEC. Paul Mozer later went to prison.

Sources

Ellis, C.D. and Vertin, J.R. 2001. *Wall Street People: True Stories of Today's Masters and Moguls*, vol. 2. New York: Wiley.

Mayer, M. 1993. *Nightmare on Wall Street: Salomon Brothers and the Corruption of the Marketplace*. New York: Simon & Schuster.

Parfitt, P. 2006. 'Assassin's bullet kills fiery critic of Putin'. *The Observer*, Sunday, 8 October. http://www.guardian.co.uk/world/2006/oct/08/media.pressandpublishing

Sterngold, J. 1988. 'Too far, too fast; Salomon Brothers' John Gutfreund', *New York Times*, 10 January. http://www.nytimes.com/1988/01/10/magazine/too-far-too-fast-salomon-brothers-john-gutfreund.html.

Questions

Have you studied cases of corrupt, negligent or irresponsible corporate leadership? If so, share them with the class. Alternatively, in small groups, carry out small research projects to find these examples, and pool the results.

Conclusion

Virtually a prerequisite for leadership is possession of a communication style that is effective in its given context. Thus – as in the military – all leadership should be to motivate followers towards individual commitment to the cause or the institution through emotional attachment and identification; poor leadership, by contrast, has the opposite effect. Commitment is not just for followers. Leaders in cross-cultural environments need the courage and vision to change any organisational structure and processes that hinder the creation of workforce diversity. These qualities go with moral and ethical standards: leaders need to be heroes, as illustrated by cultural mythologies, and all industries and sectors of society provide modern examples of men and women as role models.

Key points

1. Diversity management should develop an environment in which treatment and opportunities are the same for all members.

2. Implementing diversity in the workplace is difficult because people prefer working in homogeneous groups; and they tend to avoid and resist change.

3. Successful leadership of diversity is more a matter of communicating conviction than changing habits of compliance. This requires top leadership commitment; inclusion in strategic plans; linking diversity to performance; quantitative and qualitative measurement of diversity programmes; linking performance assessment and compensation to the progress of diversity initiatives; succession planning; diversity in recruitment and diversity training.

4. Leaders of organisations characterised by diversity will find their task easier if acculturation training is provided for new recruits at the start of their employment. In particular, retention rates will be higher if recruits gain a sense of commitment to the organisation from the beginning.

5. Leaders are likely to gain followers' commitment through appeals to three basic mind sets: normative, affective and continuance. Normative commitment occurs when employees remain with the organisation from feelings of obligation. Affective commitment occurs when employees strongly identify with the goals of the organisation and want to remain part of it. Continuance commitment occurs from a perception of the disadvantages of losing the benefits of organisational membership.

6. Many lessons in the management of diversity can be learned from ecosystem models. Mono-cropping destroys biological diversity, and so does mono-managing destroy diversity within organisations. A single focus, for example on recruitment, will not create lasting change. This will occur only through commitment from the most senior managers and appropriate adjustments to organisational strategy, communication, structure and processes.

7. Emergent and potential leaders need role models of leadership behaviour. These can be found in all industries and walks of life; and in cultural mythologies: but like all models, some are better than others. Unethical organisational cultures develop under bad leadership.

Looking ahead

Chapter 2 continues the theme of diversity by identifying culture-based reasons for different communication styles. The discussion is broadened to include not only leaders but people in general. The term 'culture' is used in its widest sense, to indicate differences in values, beliefs and behaviour of members in collectives such as age, gender, colour, race and creed, family, class and status as well as of neighbourhoods, countries and regions. Examples are offered from such diverse sources as housing, advertising, politics and robot technology to illustrate how different cultural contexts, power hierarchies and group compositions affect the ways in which people interact.

Experiential exercise

MAIN (Motivating, Authoritarian, Inclusive, Normalising) leadership style quiz: instructions

In each pair of statements please circle the one you feel applies more to you (or you may find it easier make your choice by rejecting the statement you feel does not apply to you!). Make your choice as spontaneously as possible – there are no wrong answers. If you find it difficult to choose one of any pair of statements, leave it, move on to the next and come back to it later. Some pairs seem oddly matched, but don't let that worry you. When you have finished, write the number of each choice on the score sheet

1. I like action.
2. I try to deal with problems logically and systematically.

3. I believe that 'two heads are better than one' and that teams are more effective than individuals.

4. I enjoy innovation and the excitement of new ideas.

----

5. I am more interested in the future than the past.

6. I enjoy working with people.

----

7. I like meetings to be well organised.

8. I am good at meeting deadlines.

----

9. I get impatient quickly with delays and postponements.

10. New ideas should be tested before being put into practice.

----

11. I enjoy working with other people.

12. I am always looking for new possibilities.

----

13. I need freedom to set my own goals.

14. When I start something I like to finish it.

----

15. I try to understand other people's emotions.

16. I am aware I challenge/confront people.

----

17. I need feedback on my performance from people whose opinion I value.

18. I like step-by-step problem-solving.

----

19. I think I am good at 'reading' people.

20. I like creative problem-solving.

----

21. I like to extend and enlarge ideas.

22. I am sensitive to others' needs.

----

23. Planning is the key to success.

24. I become impatient with lengthy discussions and deliberations.

----

25. I stay calm under pressure.

26. I value learning from experience.

----

27. I listen to people.
28. People say I'm a quick thinker.

----

29. Cooperation is important to me.
30. I use logical methods to test a variety of possibilities.

----

31. I like to handle several projects at once.
32. I always question myself.

----

33. I learn by doing.
34. My heart rules my head.

----

35. I can predict how otherswill react.
36. I can't be bothered with details.

----

37. Analysis should precede action.
38. I am able to judge the 'climate' of a group.

----

39. Often I start things and don't finish them.
40. I am decisive.

----

41. I seek challenging tasks.
42. I rely on facts and figures.

----

43. I can express my feelings openly.
44. I like to design new projects.

----

45. I enjoy reading.
46. I am a good facilitator.

----

47. I like to deal with one issue at a time.
48. I like to achieve.

----

49. I enjoy learning about other people.
50. I like variety.

----

51. Facts speak for themselves.
52. I use my imagination.

----

53. I get impatient with long, slow assignments.
54. My mind never stops working.

---

55. Important decisions should be made with caution.
56. People need each other to get work done.

---

57. I make decisions without too much thought.
58. Emotions create problems.

---

59. I want people to like me.
60. I can put two and two together.

---

61. I try out my new ideas on people.
62. I believe in a systematic, scientific approach to problems.

---

63. I like to get things done.
64. Good relationships are essential.

---

65. I am impulsive.
66. I accept differences in people.

---

67. Communicating with people is an end in itself.
68. I need intellectual stimulation.

---

69. I like to organise.
70. I usually jump from one task to another.

---

71. Talking and working with people are creative acts.
72. Self-growth and personal development are key themes for me.

---

73. I enjoy playing with ideas.
74. I don't like wasting time.

---

75. I enjoy doing things I'm good at.
76. I learn by interacting with others.

---

77. I find abstractions interesting and enjoyable.
78. I am patient with details.

---

79. I like statements to be short and to the point.

80. I feel confident in myself.

Score sheet: what is your MAIN leadership style?

Draw a circle round the number for each of your choices on one of the four scales below. For example: if your choices were 1, 4, 5, 7, 10, 11, 13, 16, and so on, then you would circle those numbers in Styles 1, 4, 4, 2, 2, 3, 1, 4 respectively; and so on.

M: Motivator style 1 (WHY?):

4   5   12   16   20   21   28   32   36   39   44
45   52   54   60   61   68   72   73   77

A: Authoritarian leadership style 2 (WHAT?)

1   8   9   13   17   24   26   31   33   40   41
48   50   53   57   63   65   70   74   79

I: Involver style 3 (WHO?)

3   6   11   15   19   22   27   29   35   38   43
46   49   56   59   64   67   71   76   80

N: Normaliser style 4 (HOW?)

2   7   10   14   18   23   25   30   34   37   42
47   51   55   58   62   66   69   75   78

Now add up the total number of CIRCLES (not the numbers inside the circles). The maximum is 20 per style and the total for the four styles should be 40.

In which style or styles do you have relatively high scores?

The answers should tell you how you prefer to negotiate with others and what kind of leader or negotiator other people perceive you to be.

Style 1: Motivating – WHY? and WHY NOT?

People with a strong 'Why?' style are visionaries and dreamers. They can be difficult to negotiate with because they tend to resist obvious answers, to pursue ideas, concepts, theories and innovations. Charismatic leaders fall into this category.

Style 2: Authoritarian – WHAT?

These are leaders who want ACTION. They want to get things done; to achieve something; to do something. They may seek power and influence over others to achieve their goals.

Style 3: Involving – WHO?

For these leaders, PEOPLE are all-important. They will negotiate through communication; relationships; teamwork.

Style 4: Normalising – HOW?

People with this style are PLANNERS. They need to manage by PROCESS. They devise strategies, they organise; they get the facts. They seek order and balance and distrust change.

Negotiating with people of different communication styles

Communicating with a MOTIVATIONAL leader (Style 1: 'WHY?')

- Allow enough time for discussion.
- Do not get impatient when the person goes off at a tangent.
- In your opening, try to relate the discussion to a broader framework; be conceptual.
- Stress the unique qualities of the idea or topic at hand.
- Emphasise the value, or the impact of the idea in the future.
- If writing, try to stress from the beginning the key concepts that underlie your proposal or recommendation. Start off with an overview before beginning to fill in the details.

Communicating with an AUTHORITARIAN leader (Style 2: 'WHAT?')

- Focus on the results first; state the conclusion right at the outset.
- State your best recommendation; do not offer many alternatives.
- Be as brief as possible; emphasise the practicality of your ideas; Use visual aids.

Communicating with an INVOLVING leader (Style 3: 'WHO?')

- Allow for small talk, do not start the discussion straight away.
- Stress the relationships between your proposal and the people concerned.
- Show how the idea has worked well in the past.
- Indicate support from well-respected people.
- Use an informal writing style.

Communicating with a NORMALISING leader (Style 4: 'HOW?')

- Be precise, state the facts.
- Organise your presentation in logical order:
  - Background;
  - Present situation;
  - Outcome.
- Break down your recommendations.
- Include options; consider alternatives with pros and cons.
- Do not rush a process-oriented person.
- Outline your proposal: 1 – 2 – 3.

Table 1.1 Personality type behaviour in leadership

| | Motivation | Authority | Involvement | Normalisation |
	M	A	I	N
Scores:				
First impressions	Verbal, confident, enthusiastic, attractive	Direct, important, forceful, commanding	Warmth, friendliness, openness	Calmness, reserve
Basic motivation	To influence others	To have power	Cooperation	Order
'Hard' leadership strategies	Own vision; radical transformation, control of task	Uses rules, laws as power tools; rapid frequent structural changes, command and control	Capable of authority; prefers input from a range of sources; agreement by consensus	Uses rules for order, accuracy, detail; sound research and impersonal decisions
'Soft' leadership strategies	Personal charisma as motivator rather than rules and rationality; willing to delegate and negotiate; empowers group members	Limited delegation of authority; often unwilling to listen to others' views or criticism. Cultural change through structural change; takes (sometimes unacceptably high) risks	Builds harmonious teams; flexible over rules, encourages continuous improvement and individual responsibility. Finds difficulty in handling real conflict; takes problems personally	Resists change; delegates; works for continuous improvement and individual empowerment but switches to 'hard' strategy when in doubt; prefers structural changes based on careful planning
Examples	Winston Churchill Mahatma Gandhi Abraham Lincoln Nelson Mandela Mustapha Kemal (Attaturk)	Fidel Castro Julius Caesar Catherine the Great John Foster Dulles	Eleanor of Aquitaine Willy Brandt Joseph Chamberlain Luis Drago	Buddha Confucius Socrates The Prophet Jesus

Table 1.2 What do we talk about when we negotiate? How do we do it?

Style	Talk about?	
1 'WHY?'	Concepts	New ways
	Innovation	New methods
	Creativity	Improving
	Opportunities	Problems
	Possibilities	Potential
	Grand designs	Alternatives
	Issues	What's new
	Interdependence	
2 'WHAT?'	Results	Feedback
	Objectives	Experience
	Performance	Challenges
	Productivity	Achievements
	Efficiency	Change
	Moving ahead	Decisions
	Responsibility	Action
3 'WHO?'	People	Sensitivity
	Needs	Awareness
	Motivations	Cooperation
	Teamwork	Beliefs
	Communication	Values
	Feelings	Expectations
	Team spirit	Relationships
	Understanding	Self-development
4 'HOW?'	Facts	Trying out, testing
	Procedures	Analysis
	Planning	Observations
	Organising	Proof
	Controlling	Details
	Testing	Time frames

Further recommended reading

Books

Allport, Gordon W. 1954. *The Nature of Prejudice*. Reading, MA: Addison-Wesley.

Bauman, Z. 2010. *Living on Borrowed Time*. Cambridge: Polity.

Brislin, R. W. (ed.) 1990. *Applied Cross-Cultural Psychology*. Newbury Park, CA: Sage.

Castells, M. 2009. *Communication Power*. Oxford: Oxford University Press.

Dyck, B. and Neubert, M.J. 2010. *Management: Current Practices and New Directions*. New York: Houghton Mifflin Harcourt.

Featherstone, M., Lash, S. and Robertson, R. 1995. *Global Modernities*. Newbury Park, CA: Sage.

Furedi, F. 2002. *Culture of Fear. Risk-Taking and the Morality of Low Expectation*. London: Continuum.

Herzberg, F., Mausner, B. and Snyderman, B. B. 1993. *The Motivation to Work*. Piscataway, NJ: Transaction Publishers.

Hofstede, G. 2001. *Culture's Consequences: Comparing Values, Behaviors, Institutions, and Organizations across Nations*, 2nd edn. Thousand Oaks, CA: Sage.

Jung, C.G. 1912. *Psychology of the Unconscious*, English translation by Beatrice M. Hinkle, 1916. London: Kegan Paul Trench & Trubner.

Kahane, A. 2010. *Power and Love: A Theory and Practice of Social Change.* San Francisco: Berrett-Koehler.

Lewis, M. 1990. *Liar's Poker.* New York: W.W. Norton.

—— 2011. *The Big Short: Inside the Doomsday Machine.* New York: W.W. Norton.

McClelland, D., Atkinson, J., Clark, R. and Lowell, E. 1953. *The Achievement Motive.* New York: Appleton-Century-Crofts.

McGrew, A. and Poku, N. K. (eds) 2007. *Globalization, Development and Human Security.* Cambridge: Polity.

Masters, C. 1992. *Inside Story.* Sydney: Angus & Robertson.

Mor Barak, M. 2005. *Managing Diversity: Toward a Globally Inclusive Workplace.* Thousand Oaks, CA: Sage.

Sam, David. L. and Berry, John W. (eds) 2006. *The Cambridge Handbook of Acculturation Psychology.* Cambridge: Cambridge University Press.

Silverstone, R. 2007. *Media and Morality: On the Rise of the Mediapolis.* Cambridge: Polity.

Skinner, B.F. 1953. *Science and Human Behavior.* New York: Macmillan.

Triandis, H.C. 1994. *Culture and Social Behavior.* New York: McGraw-Hill.

Trompenaars, F. 1993. *Riding the Waves of Culture.* London: Economist Books.

Vroom, V. H. and Jago, A. G. 1988. *The New Leadership: Managing Participation in Organizations.* New York: Prentice-Hall.

Journals

Association Management
Business and Society Review
Carleton Journalism Review
Creativity and Innovation Management
Harvard Business Review
HR Magazine
International Journal of Intercultural Relations
Journal of the Academy of International Business
Journal of European Industrial Training
Journal of Library Administration
Journal of Management in Engineering
Journal of Mass Media Ethics
Journal of Vocational Behavior
Personality and Social Psychology Bulletin
Review of Public Personnel Administration
Sloan Management Review
Training and Development Journal
Wall Street Journal

References

Allport, Gordon W. 1954. *The Nature of Prejudice.* Reading, MA: Addison-Wesley.

Americanfolklore: http://www.americanfolklore.net [accessed 15 February 2011].

Aronson, D. 2002. 'Managing the diversity revolution: Best practices for 21st century business'. *Civil Rights Journal*, 6, pp. 46–66.

Bandura, A. 1977. *Social Learning Theory.* Englewood Cliffs, NJ: Prentice Hall.

Barthes, R. 1973. *Mythologies*, translated by A. Lavers. London: Granada. [Originally published 1957.]

Bassett-Jones, N. 2005. 'The paradox of diversity management, creativity and innovation'. *Creativity and Innovation Management*, 14, pp. 169–75.

Bennett, M.J. 1986. 'A developmental approach to training for intercultural sensitivity'. *International Journal of Intercultural Relations*, 10, pp. 179–85.

Berry, J.W. 1990. 'Psychology of acculturation: Understanding individuals moving between cultures'. In R.W. Brislin (ed.), *Applied Cross-Cultural Psychology*. Newbury Park, CA: Sage.

Bhawuk, D.P.S. 1990. 'Cross-cultural orientation programs'. In R.W. Brislin (ed.), *Applied Cross-Cultural Psychology*. Newbury Park, CA: Sage.

Bhawuk, Dharm P.S., Landis, Dan and Lo, Kevin D. 2006. 'Intercultural training'. In D. L. Sam. and J. W. Berry (eds), *The Cambridge Handbook of Acculturation Psychology*. Cambridge: Cambridge University Press, pp. 504–24.

Bierlein, J.F. 1994. *Parallel Myths*. New York: Random House.

Blomfield, A. 2006. 'Is this the killer of Russian journalist?', *The Telegraph*, 10 October. http://www.telegraph.co.uk/news/main.jhtml?xml=/news/2006/10/09/wrussia09.xml [accessed 18 February 2008].

Bollinger, L. 2003. 'President Bollinger's statement on the future of journalism education', *Columbia News*, 17 April. http://www.columbia.edu/cu/news/03/04/lcb_j_task_force.html [accessed 17 February 2008].

Bowles, M.L. 1989. 'Myth, meaning and work organization'. *Organization Studies*, 10 (3), pp. 405–21.

Brewer, M.B. 1991. 'The social self: On being the same and different at the same time'. *Personality and Social Psychology Bulletin*, 17, pp. 475–85.

Campbell, J. 1949. *Hero with a Thousand Faces*. Princeton, NJ: Bollingen Foundation & Pantheon Books.

—— 1959. 'The historical development of mythology'. *Daedalus*, 88 (2), pp. 232–54.

—— 1976. *Primitive Mythology*. Harmondsworth: Penguin.

Campbell, J. with Moyers, B. 1988. 'The power of myth'. In B. S. Flowers (ed.), *The Power of Myth*. New York: Doubleday.

Carey, J. 1980. 'The university tradition in journalism education'. *Carleton Journalism Review*, 2 (6), pp. 3–7.

Cassirer, E. 1946. *Language and Myth*, translated by S. Langer. New York: Dover.

Chozick, A. 2005. 'Beyond the numbers: One expert says the real challenge for employers isn't in hiring: it's in making the most of a varied workforce'. Interview with R. Roosevelt Thomas, Jr', Leadership, a Special Report, *Wall Street Journal* (Eastern Edition), 14 November, p. R4.

Coats, R., Goodwin, J. and Bangs, P. 2000. 'Seeking the best path: Assessing a library's diversity climate'. *Library Administration & Management*, 14, pp. 148–54.

Cortright, D. 1975. *Soldiers in Revolt: The American military today*. New York: Anchor/Doubleday.

Cox, T. Jr 2001. *Creating the Multicultural Organization: A Strategy for Capturing the Power of Diversity*. San Francisco: Jossey-Bass.

Davis, K.C. 2005. *Don't Know Much about Mythology: Everything You Need to Know about the Greatest Stories in History But Never Learned*. New York: HarperCollins.

Digh, P. 1998. 'Coming to terms with diversity'. *HR Magazine*, 43 (12), p. 117. http://www.shrm.org/hrmagazine/articles/1198digh.asp [accessed 13 February 2007].

Dutton, G. 1996. 'Leadership in a post-heroic age'. *Management Review*, 85 (10), p. 7.

Dyck, B. and Neubert, M.J. 2010. *Management: Current Practices and New Directions*. Boston, MA: Houghton Mifflin Harcourt.

Ellis, P.B. 2002. *Celtic Myths and Legends*. Philadelphia, PA: Running Press.

England, G.W. 1975. *The Manager and His Values: An International Perspective*. Cambridge, MA: Ballinger.

Englehardt, T. 2006. 'The delusions of global hegemony: Tom Englehardt interviews Andrew Bacevich'. http://antiwar.com/englehardt/?articleid=9027, 24 May.

Faludi, S. 2007. 'Post 9/11, a more macho America'. *US News and World Report*, 22 October, p. 30.

Freud, S. 1999. *The Standard Edition of the Complete Psychological Works of Sigmund Freud*, translated from the German under the general editorship of James Strachey, in collaboration with Anna Freud, assisted by Alix Strachey and Alan Tyson, 24 vols. New York: Vintage.

French, J. R. P. and Raven, B. 1959. 'The basis of social power'. In D. Cartwright and A. Zander (eds), *Studies in Social Power*. Ann Arbor, MI: University of Michigan, Institute for Social Research, pp. 150–67.

Gabriel, Y. (ed.) 2004. *Myths, Stories, and Organizations: Premodern Narratives for Our Times*. Oxford: Oxford University Press.

Galagan, P.A. 1993. 'Navigating the differences'. *Training and Development*, April: 29–33.

Government Accountability Office (GAO) 2005. 'Diversity management: Expert-identified leading practices and agency examples'. GAO-05-90 (Washington, DC: GAO Online report, available at http://gao.gov/new.items/d0590.pdf).

Hayes, A., Singer, J. and Ceppos, J. 2007. 'Shifting roles, enduring values: The credible journalist in a digital age'. *Journal of Mass Media Ethics*, 22 (4), pp. 262–79.

Herzberg, F., Mausner, B. and Snyderman, B. B. 1993. *The Motivation to Work*. Piscataway, NJ: Transaction Publishers.

Hofstede, G. 1980. *Culture's Consequences: International Differences in Work-Related Values*. Beverley Hills, CA: Sage.

—— 1983. 'The cultural relativity of organizational practices and theories'. *Journal of International Business Studies*, 14, pp. 75–89.

—— 1993. 'Cultural constraints in management theories'. *Academy of Management Executive*, 7 (1), pp. 81–94.

—— 2001. *Culture's Consequences: Comparing Values, Behaviors, Institutions, And Organizations Across Nations*, 2nd edn. Thousand Oaks, CA: Sage.

Hofstede, G.H. and McCrae, R.R. 2004. 'Personality and culture revisited: Linking traits and dimensions of culture'. *Cross Cultural Research*, 38, pp. 52–88.

Hunt, A.R. 1999. 'The century's larger-than-life leaders'. *Wall Street Journal*, 30 December, p. A-13:3.

Javidan, M., Dorfman, P.W., Sully de Luque, M. and House, R.J. .2006. 'In the eye of the beholder: Cross cultural lessons from Project GLOBE'. *Academy of Management Perspective*, 20 (1), pp. 67–90.

Johnson, J.P. III 2003. 'Creating a diverse workforce'. http://www.shrm.org/hrresources/whitepapers_published/CMS_005379.asp#P_0 [accessed 13 February 2007].

Jones, D. 1999. 'The definition of diversity: Two views. A more inclusive definition'. *Journal of Library Administration*, 27, pp. 5–15.

Jones, R.T. 1989. 'How do you manage a diverse workforce?'. *Training and Development Journal*, 43, pp. 13–21.

Jung, C.G. 1912. *Psychology of the Unconscious*, translated by Beatrice M. Hinkle, 1916. London: Kegan Paul, Trench & Trubner.

Kamm, R.H. 2001. 'The Superman syndrome'. *Journal for Quality and Participation*, 24 (2), pp. 38–40.

Kirk, G.S. 1970. *Myth: Its Meaning and Functions in Ancient and Other Cultures*. Berkeley, CA: University of California Press.

Kossek, E.E. and Lobel, S.A. (eds) 1996. *Managing Diversity: Human Resources Strategies for Transforming the Workplace*. Cambridge, MA: Blackwell.

Kostera, M. (ed.) (2008) *Mythical Inspirations for Organizational Realities* (New York: Palgrave Macmillan).

Lauring, J. and Ross, C. 2004. 'Research notes: Cultural diversity and organizational efficiency'. *New Zealand Journal of Employment Relations*, 29, pp. 89–103.

Laville, S. 1999. 'Veronica Guerin: Praise for reporter as second man gets life'. *Electronic Telegraph*, 30 July. http://www.telegraph.co.uk/html/Content.jhtml?=/archive/1999/0730/nveron30.html [accessed11 January 2008].

Lawrence, J.S. and Jewett, R. 2002. *The Myth of the American Superhero*. Grand Rapids, MI: Eerdmans.

Laynetworks: http://www.laynetworks.com/Theories-of-Motivation.html [accessed 15 February 2011].

Levin, H. 1959. 'Some meanings of myth'. *Daedalus*, 88 (2), pp. 223–31.

Lewis, M. 1990. *Liar's Poker*. New York: W.W. Norton.

—— 2011. *The Big Short: Inside the Doomsday Machine*. New York: W.W. Norton.

McLelland, D., Atkinson, J., Clark, R. and Lowell, E. 1953. *The Achievement Motive*. New York: Appleton-Century-Crofts).

McMahon, A.M. 2006. 'Responses to diversity: Approaches and initiatives'. http://www.shrm.org/hrresources/whitepapers_published/CMS_017028.asp [accessed 13 February 2007).

Makower, J. 1995. 'Managing diversity in the workplace', *Business and Society Review*, 92, pp. 48–54.

Malinowsky, B. 1948. 'Myth in primitive psychology'. In his *Magic, Science and Religion, and Other Essays*. Boston, MA: Beacon Press.

Masters, C. 1992. *Inside Story*. Sydney: Angus & Robertson.

—— 2001. 'Interview for the 40th year of Four Corners'. http://www.abc.net.au/4corners/4c40/interviews/masters.html [accessed 2 August 2008].

Mayer, M. 1993. *Nightmare on Wall Street: Salomon Brothers and the Corruption of the Marketplace*. New York: Simon & Schuster.

Meyer, J. P., Stanley, D. J., Herscovitch, L. and Topolyntsky, L. 2002. 'Affective, continuance, and normative commitment to the organization: A meta-analysis of antecedents, correlates, and consequences'. *Journal of Vocational Behavior*, 61 (1), August, pp. 20–52.

Moore, S. 1999. 'Understanding and managing diversity among groups at work: Key issues for organizational training and development'. *Journal of European Industrial Training*, 23, pp. 208–17.

Mor Barak, M. 2005. *Managing Diversity: Toward a Globally Inclusive Workplace*. Thousand Oaks, CA: Sage.

Morrison, A. 2001. 'Integrity and global leadership'. *Journal of Business Ethics*, 31 (1), pp. 65–76.

Mote, F.W. 1989. *Intellectual Foundations of China*, 2nd edn. New York: McGraw-Hill.

Muir, H. 1996. 'Journalist who exposed underworld is shot dead'. *Electronic Telegraph*, 27 June. http://telegraph.co.uk/html/Content.jhtml?=archive/1996/06/27/whack27.html [accessed 11 January 2008].

Patterson, J. 2007. 'A time for heroes'. *Guardian*, 17 February, p. 10.

Pitts, D.W. 2006. 'Modeling the impact of diversity management'. *Review of Public Personnel Administration*, 26, pp. 245–68.

Popper, K. 1963. *Conjectures and Refutations: The Growth of Scientific Knowledge*. London: Routledge & Kegan Paul.

Postrel, V. 2006. 'Superhero worship', *Atlantic Monthly*, 298 (3), pp. 140–4.

Powers, R. 2004. 'Military STOP LOSS: Is it a "back-door draft"?' *About.com Guide*; http://usmilitary.aboutcom/od/deploymentsconflicts/a/stoploss.htm, 17 December.

Sam, David L. and Berry, John W. (eds), *The Cambridge Handbook of Acculturation Psychology*. Cambridge: Cambridge University Press.

Schwartz, S.H. 1992. 'Universals in content and structure of values: Theoretical advances and empirical tests in 20 countries'. In M. P. Zanna (ed.), *Advances in Experimental Social Psychology*. San Diego, CA: Academic Press, pp. 1–65.

Shamir, B. 2006. 'Review of *In Their Time: The Greatest Business Leaders of the Twentieth Century*'. *Academy of Management Review*, 31 (3), pp. 760–3.

Simmons-Welburn, J. 1999. 'Diversity dialogue groups: A model for enhancing workplace diversity'. *Journal of Library Administration*, 27. pp. 111–21.

Sims, R. and Brinkman, J. 2009. 'Leaders as moral role models: The case of John Gutfreund at Salomon Brothers'. *Journal of Business Ethics*, 35 (4), pp. 327–39.

Skinner, B.F. 1953. *Science and Human Behavior*. New York: Macmillan.

Soutar, S. 2004. 'Beyond the rainbow'. *Association Management*, 56, pp. 26–33.

Taylor, A. and Greve, H.R. 2006. 'Superman or The Fantastic Four: Knowledge combination and experience in innovative teams'. *Academy of Management Review*, 39 (4), pp. 723–40.

Taylor, C. 2003. 'Veronica Guerin', *Salon.com*, 17 October. http://www.dir.salon.com/story/ent/movies/review/2003/10/07/veronica/ [accessed 10 January 2008].

Thomas, R.R. Jr 1990. 'From affirmative action to affirming diversity'. *Harvard Business Review*, 68, pp. 107–17.

—— .1992. *Beyond Race and Gender: Unleashing the Power of Your Local Workforce by Managing Diversity.* New York: AMACOM.

Triandis, H.C. 1976. *Variations in Black and White Perceptions of the Social Environment.* Evanston, IL: University of Illinois Press.

—— 1994. *Culture and Social Behavior.* New York: McGraw-Hill.

Trompenaars, F. 1993. *Riding the Waves of Culture.* London: Economist Books.

Trompenaars, F. and Hampden-Turner, C. 1998. *Understanding Cultural Diversity in Business.* London: Irwin.

Trompenaars, F. and Woolliams, P. 1999. 'Trans-cultural competence'. *People Management*, 5 (8).

Vroom, Victor H. and Jago, Arthur G. 1988. *The New Leadership: Managing Participation in Organizations.* Englewood Cliffs, NJ: Prentice Hall.

Vroom, Victor H. and Yetton, Phillip W. 1973. *Leadership and Decision-Making.* Pittsburgh, PA: University of Pittsburgh Press.

Welburn, W.C. 1999. 'Multicultural curriculum in higher education'. *Journal of Library Administration*, 27, pp. 157–69.

Wersba, J. n.d. 'Edward R. Murrow and the time of his time'. *Eve's Magazine*; http://www.evesmag.com/murrowx.html [accessed 2 August 2008].

Yeats, W.B. 2003. *Irish Fairy and Folk Tales.* New York: Random House.

CHAPTER 2

Like and Unlike: Different Communication Styles

Elizabeth Christopher; Dharm P.S. Bhawuk; Eunju Chung Chen

Objective of the chapter

To identify culture-based reasons for different communication styles, including leadership styles; and to recognise the visual impact of communication media.

Chapter contents

Outline of chapter

Chapter 1 was about downward communication – from leaders to followers in contexts of human diversity. Chapter 2 includes two core essays that continue to explore the implications of diverse communication styles, upwards as well as downwards through the ranks. Though the respective writers take very different approaches, between them they provide an overview of the whole field of intercultural communication. Two of the most important differences between cultural values – reflected in all human interaction – are relative emphases on importance of the individual versus that of society; and on power imbalances in societies (Hofstede, 1991, 1980). These views are illustrated by news items and other examples.

Bhawuk applies theories of individualism and collectivism to communicative styles, based on research of scholars such as Hofstede, Hall and Triandis. Within this framework he discusses concepts of internal and external locus of control; digital and analogue sense of self; and monochronic and polychronic sense of time.

The concept of individualism versus collectivism is illustrated by a report from Paris on a specific example of culture-based communication: between people who live in city apartments and have to yield some individualism to the collective needs of apartment life. The report includes a cross-cultural project initiated by the Mayor of Paris to provide government-subsidised housing for poor people in wealthy areas of the city occupied by high-income dwellers. The intention is to break down, to some extent, the communication barriers of power imbalances between those who have, and those who have not.

This notion is pursued, though indirectly, by Chen. Her thesis is that all cross-cultural communication in social, political and management contexts consists essentially of struggles for power. She discusses ways in which people are empowered or disempowered because of gender, colour, race or ethnicity.

Since leadership is the exercise of power, the discussion that follows Chen's essay identifies different leadership styles and their respective effects on followers' behaviour. The theme of individualism versus collectivism is evident again here.

Then a report based on research by Trendwatch.com provides a different example of communicative power – that of consumers internationally to affect the commercial provision of goods and services. The report suggests that since consumers are becoming more individualistic through urbanisation and the Internet, resulting in a 'mature materialism' of increasing sophistication, marketers should take advantage of this trend by creating and maintaining a demand for unusual brands and products.

Then the importance of visual elements in written communication is illustrated by discussion of typefaces; and finally a possible future is envisaged in which robots learn either to become members of a collectivist culture whose values are to store, retrieve and share information; or of an individualistic culture in which they are taught to respond to particular human needs!

Essays are followed by discussion points and questions; key points are summarised, with experiential exercises to take them further. Internet resources are listed, together with reference notes and a list of recommended further reading.

DIVERSITY AND INTERCULTURAL COMMUNICATION: THE INFLUENCE OF INDIVIDUALISM AND COLLECTIVISM	Dharm P.S. Bhawuk

The field of cross-cultural communication is primarily a study of interpersonal psycho-dynamics (Pederson, 1994), but is broad enough to accommodate psychologists, sociologists, political scientists, anthropologists and communication researchers. Each discipline brings its own methods, perspectives and contexts (Kim et al., 1994), therefore the field must be multidisciplinary.

Studies of intercultural communication have evolved from being driven completely by passionate practitioners wanting to share their cross-cultural war stories (Gercik, 1992; Han and Park, 1995) to a somewhat theory-driven field of research (Gudykunst et al., 1996).

This evolution is quite natural in any applied field; however here the interaction between theory and practice is particularly significant. Theory can help improve practitioners' interactions in the field while practitioners' experience and insights can lead to the improvement of theory (Brislin et al., 1986).

Research is broadly focused on international aspects of intercultural communication but as there are very few countries that are extremely homogenous, the lessons learnt from the international domain are quite applicable to domestic settings, and vice versa; therefore there is much to be gained by analysing the conversation between broad social groups such as those of gender, class, caste and others in cross-cultural terms (Triandis, 1994). For example, development scholars have looked at the intercultural interaction between donors and receivers from the perspective of power (Bhawuk and Brislin, 2001), and the same perspective has proved useful in gender studies (Ragins and Sundstrom, 1989). Cultural differences can lead to the creation of ingroups and outgroups, which is exactly what caste and class differences lead to. Thus cross-cultural perspectives on class, gender and so forth are likely to be useful for both research and practice.

Triandis (1975) identified many factors that are effective in cross-cultural interactions but not specific to any culture. Some are general, such as his observation that people are ethnocentric in every culture; that attributions made by hosts are usually different from those of guests; that most sojourners need to see a positive aspect in every situation; that they need to find new recreational activities in the host culture to avoid overdependence on the expatriate community, and so forth. Others are more specific and require particular skills for effective behaviour in another culture. These skills include learning how to differentiate what is personal from what is national (for example, US Americans may have to bear individually the brunt of criticism for their country's national policies); taking the lead in starting a conversation with hosts to learn more about their culture;

learning to live with ambiguity and to suspend judgement, and learning how to transcend differences in attitudes and values. These are all essential skills for many cross-cultural situations; they can be called meta-skills. It can be argued that their acquisition makes extreme positions on the use of culture-specific versus culture general training irrelevant.

Individualism and collectivism (Hofstede, 2001) and intercultural communication

Triandis, Brislin and Hui (1988) have presented a summary of research on individualism and collectivism, and provided many helpful hints for individualists to interact with collectivists and vice versa. They suggest that other culture theories, like tightness versus looseness or internal versus external control of motivation, can be similarly summarised with advice on how to improve intercultural effectiveness. Examples of individualistic national cultures include those of the USA and Australia; while collectivist cultures include those of China, Japan and Turkey.

In the two decades and more since publication of the article by Triandis et al., the theory of individualism and collectivism has undergone much development (Triandis, Chen and Chan, 1998) and has been used extensively to study intercultural communication. No other culture theory has been developed sufficiently to help trainers improve effectiveness in intercultural communication. However, Bhawuk has presented new developments in a theoretical framework (Bhawuk and Brislin, 2001), and suggested how it might provide such training, thus extending the work of Triandis and colleagues.

Consistent with the literature, Triandis, Brislin and Hui (1998) visualised individualism and collectivism as a bipolar construct. For example, one of the key differences is argued to be how people prioritise their goals. In collectivist cultures 'individuals subordinate their goals to the goals of some collectives', whereas in individualist cultures 'individuals subordinate the goals of collectives to their personal goals' (ibid.: 271). Though these characteristics remain as important defining attributes, the field has evolved to consider independent and interdependent concepts of self (Markus and Kitayama, 1991) at the core of the definition (Bhawuk and Brislin, 2001). It is also generally accepted that individualism and collectivism are separate constructs each with its own latent factors (Hui and Triandis, 1986).

Based on this bipartite concept of individualism and collectivism it is possible to predict and explain in broad terms communicative and other human behaviour. For example, collectivists such as Japanese are likely to share work tools as common property without asking permission to use them: but individualistic US Americans are much more likely to expect others to ask their permission before using what they consider to be their own private property.

Another difference is that during communication, individualists use 'I' a lot, whereas collectivists use 'we' a lot. They may drop the pronoun 'I' altogether and allow the context to specify the subject (Kashima and Kashima, 1998, 2003). Moreover individualists cannot usually tolerate silence in communication; they fill it with spoken thoughts and ideas, whereas collectivists can almost invariably out-wait them and remain silent until others make a comment. Silence may even be construed as a sign of strength for some collectivists and talkativeness as a sign of weakness (Fernández et al., 2000). Further, for many collectivists communication is quite indirect, and body language is significantly more important than for individualists.

Many more general propositions can be made on the basis of the concepts of individualism and collectivism, for example by Triandis, Brislin and Hui (1988); but they all share a significant disadvantage: they ignore the innumerable differences in communication *within* individualistic and collectivist cultures. Thus these general constructs become a kind of catch-all and they have been criticised for being too broad (Schwartz, 1990).

A good example of collectivist values within an individualistic mainstream comes from Australia. The nation's white post-colonial citizens are identified in the literature as members of a strongly individualistic culture (e.g. in http://geert-hofstede.com/hofstede_australia.shtml). However, the concept of 'mateship' (e.g. http://www.cultureandrecreation.gov.au/articles/mateship) can be traced back to early colonial times when the harsh environment in which convicts and new settlers found themselves meant that men and women closely relied on each other for all sorts of help. Today in Australia, a 'mate' is more than just a friend; it is a term that implies a sense of shared experience, mutual respect and unconditional assistance.

To counter the criticism that the concepts of 'individualistic' and 'collectivist' cultures are too broad, Bhawuk and Brsilin present (2001) a theoretical framework that puts 'concept of self' in the centre of the frame, round which are grouped ways in which individuals interact with other people, groups and society at large. Bhawuk argues that the self-concept is basic to human behaviour.

Cross-cultural researchers have known for a long time that people view themselves differently in different cultures, and 'concept of self' has been the focus of anthropological as well as psychological and sociological research (Belay, 1996; Rosenberger, 1992). What is new is the suggestion that in some cultures (again taking Australia as an example) people see themselves as independent; while in others (for instance, that of China) as interdependent: a suggestions that fits with, and is an extension of, the concepts of individualism and collectivism (Markus and Kitayama, 1991; Triandis, 1995).

A sense of oneself as interdependent with others has less rigid boundaries than a self-concept of independence (Beattie, 1980). In collectivist cultures human nature is seen as part of everything else in nature and inseparable from it (Galtung, 1981). This holistic view is in sharp contrast to the Cartesian perspective taken by members of individualist cultures and derived from Rene Descartes' thesis (1641) that the mind and body are distinct and separate. The central point of what became known as Cartesian dualism (in honour of Descartes) is that people look on their worlds as direct reflections of themselves, their values, beliefs, experiences, conditions and development.

Therefore a sense of close relationship between self, others and nature leads people to develop an interdependent concept of self, whereas in individualist cultures the self is perceived as independent of nature, people and situations. Thus, compared to collectivists, individualists assume more control over nature and situations and feel more responsible for their own behaviour.

A similar argument exists for a difference between individuals' 'locus of control'. This concept was developed by Julian B. Rotter in 1954 and has become an important element in personality studies. 'Locus of control' refers to the extent to which individuals believe they can control events that affect them. Individuals with a high *internal locus of control* believe that events result primarily from their own behaviour and actions. Those with a high *external locus of control* believe that powerful others, fate or chance primarily determine events whereas those with a high *internal locus of control* are more likely to assume that their efforts will be successful in bringing about desired change.

Bhawuk (2001) devised yet another theory: that the concept of self can be viewed as *digital* (for individualists, i.e., as single entities) or *analogue* (for collectivists, i.e., as parts of a whole). Individualists view themselves in a more definitive way – 'This is me, and that is not me.' For example, they are not likely to think of their parents, spouse, children, even the closest members of the nuclear family, as a part of themselves. There is no overlap between themselves and others. In other words, their view of themselves is digital. On the other hand, collectivists view people in their family (parents, spouse, children, siblings), as part of themselves. Similar closeness is felt for other relatives, and even friends. Thus it can be said they have an analogue self. Of course, the biological self is digital for both individualists and collectivists; it is the socially constructed self that is digital or analogue.

Instead of using the broad constructs of individualism and collectivism, using the concept of self makes better sense of the proposition that collectivists emphasise the group in communication, and to say 'we' more than do individualists who tend more to say 'I'. Individualists are likely to use 'I' more because they have a digital self, and they like to separate themselves from things and people around them. Collectivists, on the other hand, need to include their immediate family and friends in their self, and hence find it more comfortable to use the term 'we'.

It follows that people with an independent concept of self are likely to be more direct in their communication than people whose sense of self is interdependent, and therefore apt to be more sensitive to the idea of face-saving. For example, independent-self people are likely to communicate organisational schedules and deadlines more firmly, even with stipulation of punishment if the schedule is not followed; whereas interdependent-self people tend to engage in more tacit communication about resource-sharing, preferring face-to-face communication instead of the more impersonal channels that independent-self people seem more to adopt.

Bhawuk (2001) argues that people develop different types of affinity to groups, depending on how they see themselves. For example, those with an independent concept of self tend to develop ties with others primarily to satisfy their own needs and may not give a great deal of importance to the needs of others. On the other hand, those with an interdependent concept of self may develop ties with other people to satisfy not only their own needs but also those of the others included in their collective.

There are many other aspects of interaction with groups that deserve attention. For example, individualists tend to take advantage of groups, and may indulge in 'social loafing' more than collectivists (Earley, 1989, 1993). Social loafing ('the Ringelmann effect'), a phenomenon first identified in 1913 by Max Ringelmann (Kravitz and Martin, 1986), describes the tendency of individuals to make less effort when they are part of a group. Because all members of the group are pooling their resources to achieve a common goal, each member of the group may contribute less than they would do if they were individually responsible.

Collectivists are equally prone to social loafing when interacting with outgroup members in a group setting but make significantly large concessions to ingroup members whereas individualists tend not to differentiate between ingroup and outgroup members (Carnevale, 1995) and to allocate rewards based on the principle of equity. Collectivists use equality for ingroup members, and equity for outgroup members (Han and Park, 1995) (equality in this sense means 'we all deserve the same so we will all get the same' while equity means 'each of us gets what we deserve so some of us will get more than others').

Collectivists are likely be informal with ingroup members and formal with outgroup members, whereas individualists are likely to be informal (as in the US) or formal (British and German) in dealing both with ingroups or outgroups.

Edward T. Hall (1996) identified a major cultural difference in conceptualising time; and found that this is related to differences between individualistic and collectivist cultures. Individualists are likely to be what Hall calls monochronic in their use of time when interacting with other people whereas collectivists are likely to be polychronic when dealing with ingroups but monochronic with outgroups.

Hall writes that in monochronic cultures it is expected that people will do one thing at a time, concentrate on the job, take time commitments (deadlines, schedules) seriously, need a great deal of information, be committed to the job, stick religiously to plans, be concerned about not disturbing others; and follow rules of privacy and consideration. They will show great respect for private property, seldom borrow or lend, emphasise promptness and be accustomed to short-term relationships.

On the other hand, people in polychronic cultures are accustomed to doing many things at once; they are easily distracted and interrupted. They consider time commitments to be theoretically desirable objectives but not essential. They are highly aware of context and therefore already have a lot of the information needed to complete a task. They are committed to people and human relationships, therefore plans change plans often and easily; are more concerned with close relations (family, friends, close business associates) than with privacy; borrow and lend often and easily; base promptness on the relationship and show a strong tendency to build lifetime relationships.

In any case early socialisation leads people to interact with groups differently. For example, both collectivist and individualistic students have been found to be motivated to learn when they are rewarded for learning. However, collectivists such as Chinese, unlike individualists such as US Americans, showed motivation to learn even when only the teacher was rewarded (Haruki et al., 1984).

The researchers explained this phenomenon by suggesting that socialisation of children is different in the two cultures and that Chinese children are acculturated early in life to observe and respond to others' feelings. A Chinese mother may say 'I am happy' or 'I am sad' to provide positive or negative reinforcement rather than directly saying 'You are right' or 'You are wrong', which is usually the case in US families.

Another reason for making this distinction between motivations is collectivists' perception of a common fate with their family, kin, friends and co-workers (Hui and Triandis, 1986). For example, the divorce rate is high in individualistic societies because one or both partners are unwilling to compromise their careers, whereas collectivists (usually the women) often sacrifice career opportunities to take care of their family needs (ingroup goals), and derive satisfaction in doing so.

Individualists are likely to emphasise the value for the person in trying to inspire people towards organisational goals, whereas collectivists are likely to emphasise the value for the group. Telling people 'You should do this task because it is good for you' is likely to be a motivation strategy for individualists, whereas 'You should do it because it is good for the collective (e.g., family, unit, organization, etc.)' is likely to be inspirational for collectivists.

Shame is a likely tool for collectivists to discourage people from social loafing, whereas guilt is the likely tool for individualists.

Part of managing interdependencies is to develop goals that meet the needs of more than oneself. In taking care of the needs of one's ingroup members a social mechanism evolves in collectivist cultures that is driven by norms. It is much easier to resort to methods that have been tried in the past for interacting with people at large. Hence the difference between following personal beliefs and conforming to the norms of society becomes a salient difference between individualist and collectivist cultures.

One reason for collectivists' desire to conform results from their need to pay attention to what their extended family, friends, colleagues and neighbours have to say about what they do and how they do it. A sense of duty guides them towards social norms both in the workplace and interpersonal relationships. Individualists, on the other hand, are more concerned about their personal attitudes and values. They care much less than collectivists about what their family members have to say, let alone the extended family, friends or neighbours. Often, in individualist cultures there are fewer social and workplace assumptions about 'the right way to do things' than in collectivist cultures.

This does not mean that that individualist cultures develop no social norms for behaviour, including interpersonal communication, or that collectivist cultures do not permit individual deviations. However, granted there are exceptions, in general in individualistic cultures there are fewer norms, less severely imposed than in collectivist cultures where social behaviour is strictly monitored while 'deviance' is often hidden from public eyes. In collectivist cultures effective communications are likely to be those that follow social prescription; not only what but also *how* something is said is critical, whereas in individualist cultures effective communications are likely to be those that produce a desired outcome: *what* is said is critical, rather than how it is said. It follows that in collectivist cultures non-verbal behaviour is likely to be critical because it contextualises communication, whereas in individualist cultures non-verbal behaviour is less significant since context is less important.

In collectivist cultures phenomena described by Japanese as '*tatemae*' and '*honne*' (behaviour and opinions one displays in public versus true feelings and desires) are likely to exist because knowing and maintaining norms is important, whereas in individualistic cultures such difference is unnecessary because people are more driven by personal attitudes, values and beliefs.

When the self is viewed as independent, interpersonal relationships are developed to meet the need of the self to maximise the benefits to the self. Thus, social exchange is based on the principle of equal exchange, and people form new relationships to meet their changing needs based on cost benefit analysis. To this extent individualists are rational in their social exchange. On the other hand, those with an interdependent concept of self and relationships that are inherited are likely to view their relationships as long-term in nature and, therefore, unlikely to break a relationship even if it is not cost effective. Thus, collectivists value relationships for their own sake, and nurture them with unequal social exchanges over a long period of time.

Exchanges have a different character among collectivists and individualists (Triandis and Bhawuk, 1997). Collectivists usually play relationships by ear, and do not expect a clear plan about what is going to happen. On the other hand, individualists are more likely to spell things out categorically, much like 'if ... then' statements.

For example, in individualist cultures a commuter driver between home and office may offer to provide transport for a neighbour who works for the same firm; and in exchange the passenger pays for the petrol. In a collectivist culture such reciprocity is likely to take place less explicitly. The driver continues to pay all the costs of the journey, with nothing said about a contribution from the passenger: but the driver will receive a gift of equal or more in value or be invited occasionally to lunch or dinner.

The time perspective is longer. The need to return favours is not urgent; it can be after days, months or even years, and exchange will not necessarily be of equal value or even of the same kind. Love, status, information, money, goods or services are in this sense interchangeable (Foa and Foa, 1996). Individualists, on the other hand, are likely to exchange the same type of resource, love for love, money for money, lunch for lunch, and so forth. In these ways interpersonal communication is marked by exchange of resources for collectivists, but not for individualists.

Collectivists seem to be more empathic (Realo and Luik, 2002) in their social interactions and adaptation to behavioural settings. Individualists tend more to assume that people know what their preferences are, and will ask for what they need. Therefore, individualists often ask others about what they want, whereas collectivists try to find out what people like in advance and provide them that without asking.

Variations occur across cultures in what is exchanged, and also across rural and urban settings. For example, in rural settings exchanges are likely to involve goods (vegetables, fruits and other foods) and services (helping in field or yard, helping with children). Foster (1967) found that in a Mexican peasant village usually there was a series of exchanges between people whereby what was given never quite matched what was received. Kagitcibasi (1990) suggested that also there may be class difference in exchanges. She noted that in Turkey middle-class and affluent people, unlike the lower classes, make fewer financial social transactions (borrowing money or sharing financial resources) among extended family members; but they provide emotional support to each other through social gatherings.

Collectivists do not need to constantly communicate to maintain relationships, whereas individualists do. Stoppage of communication marks the end of a relationship, whereas collectivists can stop communication without breaking a relationship, and can actually pick up a relationship even after a gap of many years. Communication is peripheral to the relationship whereas for individualists it is central.

Triandis (in Singelis et al., 1995) also proposed that individualism and collectivism are of two types, vertical and horizontal, depending on whether people view themselves as 'same as' or 'different from' others. In vertical collectivism (VC) and individualism (VI), people view themselves as different; India and China provide examples of vertical collectivism, whereas the US and France exemplify vertical individualism. In horizontal collectivism (HC) and individualism (HI), people view themselves as the same as others; the Israeli kibbutz and Eskimo cultures provide examples of horizontal collectivism, whereas Sweden and Australia approach horizontal individualism (see Lee and Choi, 2005).

Table 2.1   The types of individualism and collectivism (after Singelis et al., 1995)

Vertical individualism	Horizontal individualism	Vertical collectivism	Horizontal collectivism
'People are different'; hierarchy is emphasised; 'I want to do my own thing and be the best'	'We are all the same'; equality is emphasised; 'doing one's own thing' without regard to standards of excellence	Submission to hierarchy defined by ingroups; willingness to sacrifice for ingroup	Democratic cooperation within ingroups
The USA	Sweden	India	Israeli kibbutz
France	Australia	China	Inuit (Eskimo)

Triandis and Bhawuk (1997) discuss how this culture theory helps to explain and predict workplace behaviour and other communication and organisational issues. Measurement of these four types of cultural syndromes can be found in the work of Triandis and colleagues (1998).

Disconfirmed expectation and communication

This is another theoretical concept that has not received much attention in the literature but can be used to sharpen intercultural communication skills, and provides the basis for further research in this field.

'Disconfirmed expectation' refers to situations where sojourners expect certain behaviour from host nationals, who in turn assume the foreigners will behave in a certain way – but their expectations are not met or confirmed; particularly in differences in work ethics, roles, learning styles, and use of time and space.

Communication can be improved if foreigners prepare themselves to avoid a hurried conclusion about the cause of their hosts' behaviour when it does not meet their expectations – and vice versa – since such conclusions can lead to negative stereotyping that may prejudice future interactions.

Jackson (1995) reports how Hughes-Weiner – building on Kolb's learning styles model (1984) – has created a learning-how-to-learn model for intercultural communication and training. Her basic idea is that starting from concrete experience, learners can move to reflective observation, abstract conceptualisation and active experimentation. If they stop at concrete experience, they remain ethnocentric. They fail to understand intercultural interactions and misattribute them to some kind of weakness in the people concerned (they are idiots!) or to their culture (what backward people!). This supports the notion that everybody is ethnocentric to some degree (Triandis, 1994) and fits with Bennett's intercultural development model (1986) in which people are clearly not interested in growth.

Through reflective observation it is possible to learn about cultural differences, and often some emic (specific) aspect of the culture involved. Reflective observers learn also about their own culture, especially if the other cultural practices are drastically different (mediated by cultural distance) and experience some personal intercultural growth.

However, to go beyond reflective observation into abstract conceptualisation (theory-building) it is possible to acquire theoretical insights to many experiences. This leads to culture-general understanding and is a clear advancement from the earlier stages of learning; moreover more understanding is gained of one's own culture. We know better why we do what we do. In this phase learning is supplemented by understanding. However, by stopping here, insight may not lead to behaviour that demonstrates understanding.

Active experimentation completes the cycle in that learners are now testing new theories and ideas. They are no longer social small-talk interculturalists but experimenters who try out new learning. Thus disconfirmed expectation can be used as an opportunity to develop intercultural communication skills.

Isomorphic attribution in intercultural communication

'Isomorphic' refers to the assumption that two things are the same because they look the same; and a major source of misunderstandings in human relationships is when people believe specific behaviour is always for similar reasons. For example, if employees are late for work their supervisors may assume they are lazy: but there may be other explanations such as the employee missing the bus. Making non-isomorphic attributions (Triandis, 1975) means that the same behaviour is seen as having possibly very different meanings.

Isomorphic attribution in this context refers to sojourners making approximately the same judgement about the cause of behaviour in the host country as they would for people in their home culture (Triandis, 1975): they impose their own cultural perspectives instead of trying to see the point of view of members of the host culture.

Collectivists tend to attribute events and situations to external causes; while individualists are more likely to attribute events to internal individual causes (Morris and Peng, 1994). As a result, individualists may make the 'fundamental attribution error' of over-stressing internal, relative to external, causes of behaviour more frequently than collectivists (Smith et al., 2006). For example, to the question 'Why did he fail?' individualists are more likely to answer: 'he does not have the ability', rather than 'his co-workers did not give him clear instructions'. The collectivists are more likely to see environmental factors as the cause of the behaviour. Success is attributed by collectivists to the help of others; but by individualists to their own ability. Failure is attributed to lack of effort by collectivists; to task difficulty or bad luck by individualists.

Collectivists do not use the Performance = Ability × Effort formulation that is common among individualists (Gannon and Newman, 2002). More often they use Performance = Ability + Effort. Since individualists see performance as a personal quality, then lack of performance must be due to individual lack of ability or laziness. Collectivists see performance as a group quality, therefore it is possible to succeed if one member of the group has ability and the others make the effort. Effort is a quality that can be changed by the individual, while ability is less changeable, thus it is much better to make effort attributions. Dweck and Leggett (1988) showed that people can be trained to make such attributions to improve their performance.

In conclusion, intercultural communication as a field has blossomed, and many theories are now available for experiment. In this study the theory of individualism and collectivism has been used to suggest how intercultural communication differences can be explained. These ideas are also useful in the classroom, especially with students who have some intercultural experience (Landis and Bhagat, 1996). They learn more to explain their own experience in terms of theoretical ideas. No doubt practitioners will explore other theoretical paradigms and test them in practice.

Table 2.2   A summary of typical traits of collectivism and individualism

Collectivism	Individualism
Emphasis on group; use of 'we'	Emphasis on self; use of 'I'
Success is with help from others; failure is from lack of effort	Success is by own ability; failure is from difficulty or bad luck
Interdependent ('analogue') concept of self	Independent ('digital') concept of self
Ties with other people to satisfy own and others' needs	Ties with other people to satisfy own needs
Motivation through value to group in achieving organisational goals	Motivation through value to individual in achieving organisational goals
High *external locus of control*; events are beyond individual control	High *internal locus of control*; more sense of responsibility for own behaviour; assumption that one's own efforts can effect desired change
Need to save face: indirect and tacit communication	Direct channels of communication
High awareness of context; no need to spell everything out	Low attention to context; need for much information

(continued)

Table 2.2   Continued

Collectivism	Individualism
Preference for face-to-face communication	Preference for impersonal forms of communication
Ability to tolerate silence as a form of strength	Intolerant of silence as a form of weakness
Body language is important	Relatively little reliance on body language
Social loafing only with outgroup members	General tendency to social loafing in groups
Equality for ingroup members, equity for outgroup members	Equity for all (not necessarily equality)
Informality with ingroup members; formality with outgroup members	Consistency in informal or formal behaviour
Polychronic; many things at once; easily distracted and interrupted	Monochronic; one thing at a time; concentrate on the job
Time commitments theoretically desirable but not essential	Schedules and deadlines very important
Plans change plans often and easily; promptness based on the relationship	Stick religiously to plans; punctual and punctilious
More concerned with close relations than with privacy	Concern not to disturb others, personal privacy very important
Borrow and lend often and easily	Strong sense of personal possessions; seldom borrow or lend; great respect for private property
Favours to be returned over time and in many forms	Favours to be returned soon and in kind
Strong tendency to build lifetime relationships; not essential to 'keep in touch' frequently	Short-term relationships; 'out of sight, out of mind'
Feelings of shame discourages collectivists from anti-social behaviour	Feelings of guilt restrain individualists from anti-social behaviour

Discussion questions

1. Bhawuk offers the suggestion that members of collectivist cultures are likely to share work tools as common property and use them as needed; whereas individualists are more likely to ask each other's permission to use tools or equipment. At work or study, if your desk is beside that of someone else, would you assume you could lean over and take their pen, scissors or stapler without asking? Discuss your answer!

2. Do you think, in general terms, that you have a stronger *internal* or *external* locus of control? For example, how often do you qualify your decisions by

saying something like 'other things permitting'? Compare your answers with those of your group members.

3. Again in general terms, do you think of yourself in *digital* or *analogue* terms, as defined by Bhawuk? For example, to what extent do you see your loved ones as part of you, or separate from you? How do other members of your group feel about this? Do your responses support or refute other aspects in yourselves of individualism (digital) or collectivism (analogue)?

4. In class, discuss these issues from the perspective of management of cultural diversity. For example, what might be the most effective method of allocating resources, respectively, in teams whose members are from collectivist and from individualistic cultures? What clues might help managers to decide whether their team members accept stronger internal or external loci of control?

Case study: the Parisian apartment code of conduct

The following account provides a good example of the influence of context on communication style. In April 2011 Hugh Schofield reported from Paris to BBC News on the possibility that the type of housing a city provides for its residents influences their behaviour towards a spirit of social mingling – or 'la mixite'.

He observed that people who are culturally accustomed, as in France, to living in flats learn to accommodate to high-density living and tend to be highly considerate of others. They know the rules of apartment life and not to break them. Parisians have always lived in flats. In the old days, the houses were divided so that the wealthier the tenants the higher they lived; and over the years, that proximity has led to codes of behaviour.

Apartments dwellers get to know their neighbours perhaps more intimately than they would prefer, so they keep their relationship to one of formal distance, respectful but not friendly. They learn not to express their independence too readily by playing music late or having parties, or running a bath at midnight. And they learn there are overarching institutions that decide things for them, such as whether to plant flowers in the communal garden or how much to pay the concierge. In short, they learn to surrender some of their individual liberty in return for a more social, communal life.

This seems to impact on the larger society. Linked to the habits of apartment living, French and other Europeans are more socially minded, both less free and less individualistic than, say, their British counterparts: though it is a moot point whether people live in flats because they are more communal-minded, or they are more communally minded because they live in flats.

In 2005 Adam Sage wrote in the *New Statesman* about a new type of resident who would be moving into the elegant seventh *arrondissement* in central Paris when a sports field opposite a four-star hotel in the rue de la Federation on the banks of the Seine was to be developed for housing to include 120 council flats. Sage noted that with the present residential mix in the area, of professionals, managing directors and people who own their own businesses, such a development would be the equivalent of putting new council houses in Chelsea or Mayfair.

The mayor of Paris, Bertrand Delanoë, did not want the city to look like London, with a very wealthy population in some areas and much poorer people in others. He believed it is the social balance that makes Paris what it is. Delanoë was elected in 2001 as Paris' first Socialist mayor in recent times. He instituted a series of popular cultural initiatives and pledged to create 5,000 council flats a year – not in the three poor *arrondissements* in the north and east of Paris that already contain 70 per cent of the city's municipal housing, but in the wealthy districts of the west and south. At least in theory this would bring unemployed Algerian immigrants into districts where a three-bedroomed flat sells for over €1m.

Many towns around Paris have been deserted by the middle classes, leaving behind largely immigrant populations. But Paris itself has maintained *la mixite sociale*. The city's rulers seem determined to keep it that way. However, significant changes are afoot. In France, more and more people are not living in apartments. In the Paris region hundreds of dormitory settlements are building up. Moreover once-typical rural villages are being transformed into commuter towns, not with tier upon tier of flats, but row upon row of bijou houses, each with its private strip of garden.

Maybe France is going the way of the 'little boxes on the hillside, little boxes all the same', as in the US politically satirical song about the development of suburbia and associated conformist middle-class attitudes. Maybe France too is suburbanising fast and heading into town on the Paris commuter rail system, the Reseau Express Regional or RER.

Sources

Reynolds, M. 'Little boxes'. http://ingeb.org/songs/littlebo.html.
Sage, A. 2005. 'Paris opts for *la mixite sociale*', *New Statesman*, 24 January. http://www.newstatesman.com/200501240009.
Schofield, H. 2011. 'The Parisian apartment code of conduct', BBC News, Paris, 23 April. http://news.bbc.co.uk/2/hi/programmes/from_our_own_correspondent/9463155.stm.
Stevens, A. and Monaghan, J. 2008. 'Bertrand Delanoë, Mayor of Paris', 20 March. http://www.citymayors.com/mayors/paris_mayor.html.

Class exercise

An interesting class exercise would be to divide students into two groups, of those who live (or have lived) in apartments and those who live (or have lived) in houses; then pair them off, one member of each pair to be a flat-dweller, the other a house-dweller. All pairs can discuss the statement: 'Living in an apartment permits less individuality than living in a house.'

GAPS IN INTERCULTURAL COMMUNICATION LITERATURE	Eunju Chung Chen

The following study is based on the author's original research at the University of Maryland in Baltimore, and is reproduced with her permission.

Chen argues that globalisation has made it possible, indeed probable, to experience intercultural encounters without ever leaving home. Students of international management in classrooms across the world have become increasingly diverse, especially in language and culture. They demand that their lecturers shall engage with, and operate within, this multicultural learning environment. She finds two problems in doing so: one is failure to find an adequate working definition of culture; and the other is lack of recognition of the importance of power relations in studies of intercultural encounters.

Chen bases her argument on Bourdieu's theory (1977) that all interactions in socio-political contexts (and these include managerial contexts) consist essentially of struggles for power. Failure to recognise this element in intercultural communication results in failure to understand its complexities; and in culture being too pragmatically defined.

Because of the difficulties in defining culture many theorists resort to generalities by discussing culture as of nationality, or even more broadly, of global regions (Jandt, 2007; Moodian, 2009; Neuliep, 2008; Schmidt et al., 2007). These general descriptions are helpful and necessary, and broad strokes make a good start in studying cultures other than one's own. Nevertheless investigation should include more critical appreciation of the dynamics of intercultural communication.

Study of the topic was based originally on the theoretical structures of psychology and communication, with emphasis on observable facts (Lockett et al., 2006). Consequently until very recently there has been no room to consider power dynamics in intercultural encounters because emphasis has been on *differences* rather than the *different positions* in the power hierarchy (Tomaselli, 1999).

Nevertheless definition of culture has to begin with defining boundaries, borders and distinctive features of identified cultural groups: and when cultural descriptions are given within socio-historical contexts, they necessarily describe the power hierarchies within which these groups exist. The global history of imperialism, colonialism and Western hegemony makes it crucial to consider issues of power when different groups encounter each other. These omissions outline significant theoretical gaps in intercultural communication literature.

According to Bourdieu, the field of power is a dynamic site of struggle where unequal distributions of economic and cultural capital create power hierarchies. Those who possess a greater share of economic and cultural capital wield greater power in dominant social classes. Those with no access to these resources remain powerless and dominated. Thus Bourdieu considers conflict to be the fundamental dynamic of all social life.

One of his key claims is that this struggle is carried out over symbolic capital as well as material resources. Swartz (1997: 136–7) comments:

> [T]wo major competing principles of social hierarchy ... shape the struggle for power... : the distribution of economic capital (wealth, income, and property) ... and the distribution of cultural capital (knowledge, culture, and educational credentials).... This fundamental opposition between cultural capital and economic capital delineates Bourdieu's field of power.

While this dynamism explains the processes of social interaction there is another factor. There can be shifts in hierarchies due to different and varying values of cultural capital. Different positions in power hierarchies are determined objectively by possession or absence of various forms of capital. These differences – in addition to cultural differences – impact intercultural encounters. However, values attributed to various forms of cultural capital (that make up those hierarchies) are highly subjective in nature. They are governed by the respective cultures' beliefs and assumptions under which 'the natural and social world appear as self-evident and undisputed' (Bourdieu, 1977: 164).

Bourdieu suggests there are three conceptions of social beliefs and values: *doxa*, *orthodoxy* and *heterodoxy*. *Doxa* is a constructed vision of 'reality' so naturalised that it appears to be the *only* vision of reality. Thus it is 'self-evident' and 'undisputed' in US culture that democracy is the best form of government and capitalism the best form of economy: but though these are seen as real and true they are actually relatively arbitrary and artificial constructions.

Orthodoxy is defence of *doxa*. Orthodox opinions enhance, and maintain the status quo, the existing state of affairs. Again referring to the *doxa* that democracy is the best form of government, an example of relevant *orthodox* opinion is a quotation from John Dryden: 'Democracy does not guarantee equality of conditions – it only guarantees equality of opportunity' (http://www.best-quotes-poems.com/democracy-quotes.html). And even though Alfred Emanuel Smith wrote cynically that 'It's not the voting that's democracy, it's the counting of the votes' (ibid.), he was still being orthodox. He wanted to draw attention to the corrupt practice of vote-tampering but he was not attacking democracy as such – indeed he was trying to protect it.

On the other hand, *heterodoxy* resists the *doxa*, struggling to overturn social structures that exist to create, enhance and maintain power of the few over the many (Bourdieu, 1977: 169). For example, 'Black Power' is both a political slogan and a phrase to describe political movements worldwide by people of Black African descent in defence against racial oppression and in support of separate social institutions and a self-sufficient economy (separatism). All disempowered members of society have an interest in pushing back the limits of orthodoxy and questioning the 'taken-for- granted'.

The conflict between orthodoxy and heterodoxy in intercultural encounters is played out with the currency of cultural capital – such as skin colour, religion, achievement, gender or even level of English proficiency. Ownership of these social currencies affects the dynamics of interpersonal communication. For example, in some contexts there is greater cultural capital (correlated to greater power) in being a man, in others in being a woman. Context is crucial in deciding the value of certain cultural capital, and therefore individuals' positions in the power hierarchy. Context is an essential component in all cultural descriptions, and to group cultures by nation and global region is to create gross simplifications.

A historical view helps to identify how the values of different forms of cultural capital have been established, circulated and reproduced. The global community is not made up of groups of people or nations who are different but equal (Ansell-Pearson et al., 1997; Said, 1978, 1994, 2001). The power hierarchies in which intercultural encounters take place are comprised of many layers: personal, professional, local, national, global, etc. A sense of history aids understanding why the West has more power than the East (at any rate up to the present time) and why lighter skin has more power than darker skin.

Values are further complicated by the fact that these assignments of cultural capital are dynamic. Twenty-five years ago, Japanese was the popular language for Westerners to learn. Today, learning Mandarin is in much greater demand, though English as an international language surpasses both.

At another level, in intercultural communication studies, heterodoxy has criticised the field from within, arguing that omission of power relations is a form of orthodoxy, supporting the current global and local power structures by acquiescence. Broader conceptions of culture would accept a heterodoxy that would allow for more productive discussion.

For example, until fairly recently the majority of lecturers in Western universities were white and from middle-class backgrounds. There was disconnection between these academics and their increasingly multicultural students, and several dimensions of power were typically at work in their classrooms: teacher/student, white/non-white, full English proficiency/limited English proficiency. These represented the values of cultural capital in a power hierarchy in which teachers had greater power than students, whiteness had greater power than non-whiteness, and so on. However, the structure of universities, their curricula, standards, social processes and economics of education have changed enormously with shifts in their national economies; and these have power implications.

The Australian national newspaper, *The Australian*, reported in October 2008 that the number of international students in higher education in Australia had increased 52 per cent from 2002 to 2007. The Australian Department of Education, Employment and Workplace Relations in December 2008 published a review of higher education in Australia. Some findings relevant to this research were that

> *Our educational institutions and, in particular, our universities have built Australia's third-largest export industry – in education services – in the last two decades. A quarter of our higher education students are from other countries and they make an enormous contribution to our economy, our relationships with the region and our demand for graduates.*
>
> (Christopher, 2010)

Today Australia is the third most popular study destination in the English-speaking world, with more than 200,000 international students in Australian institutions across all education sectors. In 2009 at Macquarie University in Sydney overseas postgraduate students were enrolled from mainland China, France, Germany, Hong Kong, India, Indonesia, South Korea, Malaysia, Netherlands, Russia, Taiwan, Thailand and Turkey. Not surprisingly, the Australian government sees the quality of overseas student experience to be of prime importance, part of a national strategy, because of the contribution to the national economy by higher education students from other countries and to Australia's relationships with the Australasian region with its increasing demand for graduates.

Thus the power has shifted from universities to their clients – not only in Australia but generally in Western institutes of higher education worldwide; and there are many dimensions of power that have been affected by this shift, not the least of which are skin colour and English fluency. A great deal of cultural capital was attributed in the past to white, native English speakers – a product of centuries of global history during which economic and cultural capital shaped the power hierarchies in which they operated.

Along with recognition that economic capital has changed hands, so to speak, came the belief that major cultural differences between overseas students and their host lecturers were the principal cause of academic success or failure; and that academics should cater to these differences. However, present thinking is that with more and more cultural convergence, more focus on teaching skills is needed rather than worrying too much about cultural differences in students. One recent study (Christopher, 2010) found that from China to Turkey, from Europe to Asia, overseas students in common appear to be individualistic, self-motivated, low in need to avoid uncertainty, comparatively low in power distance, with high expectations of themselves and their teachers. Therefore academics should employ the same teaching skills for overseas graduate students' learning as they would for comparable local students. In fact to do otherwise, such as focusing on cross-cultural differences rather than on pedagogy, would be to do them a disservice.

Conclusion

Bourdieu's contention, that unequal distributions of economic and cultural capital create power hierarchies, is useful for the study of international management. He argued that dominant social classes, possessing a greater share of economic and cultural capital, wield power over those with no access to these resources; and that this disparity creates conflict as a fundamental dynamic of all social life. Moreover this struggle is carried out over symbolic capital as well as material resources, such as being white and a native English speaker.

Starting from these premises it is relatively easy to see how these fields of conflict have shifted and levelled with the movement called globalisation or internationalisation. International managers, whether of business firms, government or non-government agencies, educational institutions and curricula, now come from, and have to cater to, a very wide range of social groups, more and more of which are both different and but equal.

Discussion questions

1. What experiences can you remember of 'intercultural encounters without ever leaving home'? (Hint: think of your neighbourhood, school, sport or religious associations, clubs, etc!)

2. Can you think of a practical example to support or refute the statement that conflict is 'the fundamental dynamic of all social life'? Before you answer, consider how you define 'conflict'. If your definition can include any tussle of

wills between people, however essentially friendly and loving, will this affect your answer?

3. Why do some of us own more cultural capital – and therefore can exercise greater power – than others? What kind of cultural capital are we talking about? What kind of power? Can you apply your answers to the management of cultural diversity?

Case study: All interactions in socio-political contexts essentially are struggles for power

In the UK in September 2010, as it became clear that second-preference votes had carried Ed Miliband to the Labour Party leadership, the loser, his older brother David, was the first to congratulate and embrace him. The sound of applause at the Labour Party conference was louder than the victory announcement. Later David issued a rallying call to the Labour conference, saying the party now had a 'great leader'.

He was generous in defeat since Ed's victory ended his hopes of ever becoming prime minister. He had given no sign that he was prepared for defeat as the votes were read out, seemingly confident in stark contrast to Ed's serious, almost sad appearance.

It had been an extraordinary decision by Ed to take on his own brother but he knew another chance might never come, and nobody wanted a repeat of the 'Granita' deal in 2003 under which the then Prime Minister Tony Blair agreed to make Gordon Brown a very powerful Chancellor of the Exchequer, with a remit covering not only the economy but also large areas of welfare and social policy. It involved agreement not only on Brown's control over policy but the nomination of key Brownian allies to strategic ministerial positions; and poisoned the party during the Blair–Brown years.

'Am I really not going to stand because my brother is standing?' Ed had asked. 'If he wasn't in the race, I would not have had any hesitation.'

All his life he had walked in shadow of his brother, first at school then at Oxford, where he chose not only the same course but the same college. Finally he joined David in the House of Commons and sat at the same table as him as a cabinet minister. On 26 September 2010, standing on the podium as the new leader of the Labour Party, Ed turned to his brother and said: 'David, I love you so much as a brother.' He later paid tribute to him for the 'gracefulness and generosity of spirit' he had shown in defeat, adding: 'He deserves all our support and he will be a vital part of our party.'

For his part, David refused to discuss his own future, insisting the day belonged to Ed. He said that 'obviously' he was genuinely delighted for his brother and that if he himself couldn't win, then Ed should lead the party. In any case 'It's a huge day for the Miliband family' and he added wryly that though it wasn't quite the day for the Miliband family he would have wanted – Miliband D. rather than Miliband E. – that's the way things go.

Sources

'David Miliband rallying call: Ed's a great leader'; BBC News, 27 September 2010; http://www.bbc.co.uk/news/uk-politics-11415568.

Doward, J. and Asthana, A. 2010. Sunday, 26 September, guardian.co.uk.
Keegan, W. 2003. 'Numbers and napkins: The Granita deal'. *The Observer*, Sunday, 28 September; http://www.guardian.co.uk/business/2003/sep/28/theobserver. observerbusiness12.

Discussion question

Why was this report chosen as an illustration of Chen's argument that essentially all interpersonal communication in socio-political contexts is about power? (Hint: what are the various levels of relationship between David and Ed? What is the context in which this case study is set?)

LEADERSHIP STYLES AS FORMS OF POWER   Elizabeth Christopher

Over 70 years ago Kurt Lewin and his colleagues (Lewin, Lippit and White, 1939) identified three different communication styles by which Western leaders attempt to control followers' behaviour: they called them autocratic, democratic and laissez-faire.

Autocratic leaders are extremely individualistic, highly motivated by need for personal power (a motivation identified by David McClelland (McClelland et al., 1953) and discussed in Chapter 1) and take decisions without consultation. This often causes a great deal of discontent but works well when there is no need for input by other people and when followers are content not to be included in the decision (Vroom and Yetton, 1973).

Democratic leaders involve others, though the final decision may or may not remain with them. The process usually is appreciated by the people concerned, especially if it comes as a welcome change from previous autocratic leaders, but it can be problematic when there is a wide range of opinions and no clear way to find a solution fair to everybody.

The laissez-faire style minimises leaders' involvement. It allows people to make their own decisions, although the formal leaders may still be responsible for the outcome (as, for example, in the case of the Salomon Brothers scandal discussed in Chapter 1). Laissez-faire works best when people are capable and motivated to make their own decisions, and where there is no requirement for a central coordination, for example, in sharing resources across a range of different people and groups.

Lewin's conclusion as a Western researcher was that the most effective leadership style is democratic; but in itself this was a culturally biased choice. It was not until the 1950s that the notion of 'situational leadership' was offered by management theorists from Ohio State University and the University of Michigan (Bass et al., 2003). They carried out a series of studies on whether leaders should be more task or relationship (people) oriented, concluding that leaders tend to have a dominant style they use in a wide variety of situations but that there is no one 'best' style. Behaviour should be adjusted appropriately for the situation, in awareness of three critical factors common to all:

- The organisational culture (linked to national culture) in which leaders operate;
- The relevant organisational structure, i.e., whether it favours or limits autocratic leadership (Yukl, 1994);
- The degree to which leaders are prepared to empower their followers (Stogdill and Bass, 1974).

Moreover the following factors always seem to be relevant (Fiedler, 1967; Hersey et al., 2007; House, 1971:
The nature of the task:

- Is the task well defined?
- Do all team members perceive the task in the same light as the team leader?
- Is the task relatively easy or difficult, long- or short-term?

The personality of the leader:

- Task-minded or relationship-minded?

The readiness of team members to follow the leader:

- What is the nature of the relationship between team members; and between team members and their leader? How homogeneous or heterogeneous is the team?

More recently there has been study of 'transactional' versus 'transformational' leadership styles (Luthans, 2005). Transactional leadership emphasises the status quo, and a 'by the book' approach in which leaders work within the rules, as in large bureaucratic organisations. On the other hand, the primary focus of transformational leadership is to make change happen, to initiate change. Competent leadership needs to adopt either style as circumstances dictate. For example, when everything is running smoothly there is need only for a firm hand on the tiller; but when a storm blows up, the skipper must order navigational changes to deal with the new situation.

Another study has been of 'soft' versus 'hard' leadership styles. 'Soft leadership' tends to create adaptive and flexible structures that promote particular kinds of organisational cultures, for example, semi-autonomous work teams, merchant banks, stockbroking firms, franchises, joint ventures, business partnerships, federations, networks and alliances. 'Soft' leadership seeks continuous improvement of quality and quantity of output by empowered workers.

On the other hand, 'hard' leadership favours authoritative command. This tends to create rational and rigid structures based on rules and precepts; but subject to radical change and transformation. Examples are military forces and police services.

Another way of looking at leadership is to identify four kinds of leader: visionary motivators and power-driven authoritarians both tend to adopt 'hard' management styles; while people-oriented, involving, leaders and problem-solving, stabilising, status quo leaders tend to use a 'softer' approach.

All research findings agree that everybody is capable to some extent of using a basic set of leadership skills, but most people are likely to feel more comfortable with one style than the others and to be a more effective leader in some situations than in others; and that culture influences leadership behaviour. Depending on the situation, one leadership style is more likely to be effective than another; thus leaders need to be able to switch from one style to another at need. For example, even if a leader's preferred style is to give orders, there may be times – such as when directing an international team of informed and competent specialists – when it is necessary to delegate decisions to the team.

Generally speaking, there seems to be a contrast between (a) task-oriented, (b) relationship-oriented and (c) problem-solving behaviour: (a) focuses on goal-setting and achieving; (b) on giving support, promoting interaction, listening and providing helpful feedback: (c) more often seeks relationships between things rather than people, for example, through research to find patterns of activity from which to draw generalisations in the field of study. Leaders who seem naturally to adopt this style tend to be observers rather than doers; they delegate action in order to leave themselves time to plan and ponder and solve problems.

Questions

How would you characterise your own preferred leadership style? Are you fairly flexible in adapting it to particular circumstances and followers?

Case study: Increasing individualism through globalisation

The following report on increasing individualism arising through globalisation is based on a posting by Trendwatching.com (http://www.trendwatching.com/trends/maturialism), one of the world's leading trend firms who scan the globe for emerging consumer trends: in this case a growing international trend towards individualism in consumerism and a demand for brands that are 'more daring, outspoken, even a bit more risqué'. The following was posted in September 2010:

> As the busiest time of the year is about to kick in for many of you, we thought we'd keep things light-hearted this month. Check out the rise in 'mature materialism': experienced, less-easily shocked, outspoken consumers who appreciate brands that are more daring, outspoken, even a bit more risqué.

Trendwatching.com cited three drivers behind the 'maturialism' trend: the anything-goes online culture, the slowly creeping spread of liberal culture, and the ongoing shift of how status is defined.

With the popularity of social media networks, millions of consumers can easily post their comments about brands, companies, bad customer service or defective products (Holzer, 2010). Some firms have been quick to adjust to these changes, appointing managers to monitor Twitter, Facebook and other social media networks (Shih, 2009).

Another example of consumer power was that when the iPhone 4 was first introduced, Apple users generally praised it. But the apparent antennae problems, and the company's stubborn refusal to acknowledge it, led to an anti-Apple backlash for a while (*Wall Street Journal*, 2010).

Also consumers expect transparency from companies, and are not afraid to voice their comments and criticisms. Trendwatching.com said:

> *The gap between the sanitized, litigious, politically correct corporate world and mature consumers wanting to experience something more daring and unscripted has never been bigger. Case in point: the increasing popularity of anything that's 'live' ... Live experiences can't be edited or controlled or censored, and thus offer the rare possibility of surprise, excitement and 'realness' that mature consumers enjoy.*

In particular, urban consumers have become more exposed to, and interested in, alternative goods, services and lifestyles, moving away from traditional social structures and looking eagerly for the next big status marker. Wealthy and urban consumers are looking for more innovative, creative and unconventional products, services and experiences.

To address the new demands of consumers, companies have to walk the fine line between being naughty and indecent. Cathy Garcia, writing in the *Korea Times* in September 2010, reported that South Korean companies were following examples of the materialism trend from other countries; and in New York the previous July, Calvin Klein Jeans (Indvik, 2010) posted a large QR code on two billboards for its new collection, with the words 'Get it Uncensored'. Smartphone users were able to capture the code, which linked them to a racy 40-second uncensored commercial featuring supermodel Lara Stone.

Air New Zealand's ad campaign highlighted its transparent prices by showing employees wearing nothing but body paint (nothing to hide, 2010). Levi's Jeans launched Curve ID (softpedia.com, 2010), a new line of jeans designed based on women's body shapes, not waist size. Levi's identified three universal body shapes for women: slight curve, demi-curve and bold curve, for the jeans.

Ice cream is being positioned in a different way for the mature crowd (how-to-branding.com, 2010). A UK brand came out with premium X-rated flavours, and Wine Cellar Sorbet introduced alcohol-infused sorbets.

Hagen Daz ice cream advertisements are now targeting adults rather than children. One showed a woman lying in bed with Hagen Daz Caramel Biscuit and Cream ice cream. US-based Ben & Jerry's renamed their Chubby Hubby flavour as Hubby Hubby in celebration of the legalisation of same-sex marriage in Vermont state in 2009. Burger King now targets a non-traditional market with a 24-hour Whopper Bar offering a specialised menu that allows patrons to customise their sandwiches and burgers; and beer is served.

The Disloyalty Card (nickwade.com, 2010) is another simple – but brilliant – example of unconventional advertising. Gwilym Davies of Prufrock Coffee is a world barista champion who in 2010 was running a small store on Shoreditch High Street, London. Keen to encourage a genuine interest in an emerging scene, he introduced his Disloyalty Card. If customers drink at eight other coffee stores they can claim a free coffee from him. The stores are mainly scattered across East London, and all are (just about) within walking distance of each other. They're listed on a business card, and for each one visitors receive a stamp as proof of purchase.

Thus for grown-up brands in tune with consumer values, materialism creates amazing opportunities for entrepreneurs. Mature consumers expect communications and innovations to be candid, to have personality and passion, and sometimes to push the boundaries.

Discussion questions

Apparently even developing economies such as that of South Korea are now jumping on to the 'maturialism' bandwagon in response to mass communication media. Geert Hofstede's website classifies the culture of South Korea as comparatively very low in individualism.

To what social or other factors do you attribute what seems to be an increase in this cultural dimension, not only in South Korea but across the globe?

How might your answers affect foreign investment in South Korea, including the management of foreign-owned local subsidiaries?

TRUE TO TYPE: WHAT MESSAGES DO TYPEFACES CONVEY?	Elizabeth Christopher

Commercial advertisers are very conscious of visual appeal as a communication technique, and this should be noted by all those who deliberately try to influence others through written language. One comparatively easy way to do so is by use of particular typefaces – as will be made plain in discussion of 'flaming emails' in Chapter 9. To give one example here of offensive use of typeface in email correspondence, Garfield (2010) tells the story of a woman, Vicki Walker, working as an accountant in a New Zealand health agency. She wanted to send an email but ignored the unwritten rule that CAPITAL LETTERS LOOK LIKE YOU HATE SOMEONE AND ARE SHOUTING.

She emailed this instruction: TO ENSURE YOUR STAFF CLAIM IS PROCESSED AND PAID, PLEASE DO FOLLOW THE BELOW CHECKLIST.

Garfield reports that Walker was sacked three months later, on the grounds that her email caused 'disharmony in the workplace'. This seems laughable but it caused a great deal of distress. Vicki had to remortgage her house and borrow money from her sister to fight her case. Nearly two years later she appealed successfully for unfair dismissal, and was awarded $17,000 (£10,000).

With the invention of 'desktop publishing', designers began setting type on their computers for the first time; and maybe for the first time became aware of the power of typeface to influence reader response. For example Harris (2000) wrote that authors should choose typefaces 'that have similar feelings'; and Garfield (2010) – who believes in general that typefaces should 'inform but not alarm' – cites the choice of Arquitectura and Centaur as typefaces for the male and female lines respectively in John Gray's bestselling book *Men are from Mars, Women are from Venus* (2003). Garfield argues that Arquitectura:

looks manly because it is tall, solid, slightly space-age, rooted and implacable. Centaur, despite its bullish name, looks like it has been written by hand, has thin and thick strokes, and is charming and elegant.

Garfield suggests this is an example of sexual stereotyping, suitable for Gray's book of 'pop-psychology'; and that it illustrates how typefaces can have gender.

Strizver (2001) writes of the importance of training one's eye to notice differences between typefaces by examining the anatomy of the characters that make up our alphabet. Harris notes that 'bargain-basement' fonts, such as those sold by the thousand for a few dollars, are poor copies of originals and badly digitalised. He points out that use of such inferior typefaces makes the text look bad and consequently downgrades the value of the content.

Margaret Calvert and Jock Kinneir were the designers of the type used for the signs on Britain's motorways and streets: 'one of the most ambitious and effective information design projects ever executed in Britain' (designmuseum,org). The Design Museum describes the project as 'Intellectually rigorous yet inclusive and engaging ... a role model for modern road signage all over the world.' The system consisted of carefully coordinated lettering, colours, shapes and symbols and was introduced in the late 1950s for all motorways and for all other roads in the mid-1960s. Calvert and Kinneir found that at speed drivers are better able to read place names and directions in a mixture of upper- and lower-case, rather than signs in all-capitals that had been favoured.

Neville Brody (fontshop.com) is perhaps the best-known graphic designer of his generation. He first was noticed for his record cover designs in the early 1980s and the innovative styling of *The Face* magazine (1981–6). He won much public acclaim for his ideas on incorporating and combining typefaces into design, later designing his own typefaces and opening the way for digital type design. In 1987 he founded The Studio in London, and his unusual computer-generated designs received a great deal of recognition, especially abroad. His work has been commissioned by such major organisations as Berlin's Haus der Kulturen der Welt, Greenpeace, Japanese companies Men's Bigi and Parco, the Dutch Postal Service, the German cable channel Premiere and Austria's ORF TV channel. Often referred to as a 'star typographer', Brody has designed a number of very well-known typefaces.

Erik Spiekermann's (2002) fonts display signs on the Berlin transit network, the Deutsche Bahn national railway and the headquarters of the Berlin Philharmonic. Eric Gill (1993) is remembered – among many other reasons – for his typefaces, notably Gill Sans, one of the twentieth century's earliest and classic sans serif fonts. Unfortunately for Gill's reputation Fiona McCarthy published a biography of Gill (1989) that described his sexual experimentation with incest and bestiality, with the result that even today some people won't use any of his beautiful types: a sad illustration of the power of perception to affect communication.

Discussion questions

What typeface do you prefer to use? Why? Might it be for any of the reasons suggested above: that some typefaces seem more 'masculine', some 'feminine'; some more aesthetic than others; easier to read; more modern....?

Do you agree with Marshall McLuhan that the appearance of a text is in itself a medium of communication; that the medium is the message?

Case study: Are robots individualists or collectivists?

Any discussion of communication media should include robotic engineering as a form of communication across cultures. Compiled from BBC News sources, the following report suggests that robots may develop either a collectivist or an individualist culture through different forms of communication!

Robots to get their own Internet; and will learn to read your mind to train themselves

Robots could soon have an equivalent of the Internet and Wikipedia. European scientists have embarked on a project to let robots share and store what they discover about the world. Called RoboEarth, it will be a place from which robots can upload data to master a task, and ask for help in carrying out new ones. Researchers behind it hope it will allow robots to come into service more quickly, armed with a growing library of knowledge about their human masters.

The idea behind RoboEarth is to develop methods that help robots encode, exchange and reuse knowledge, said RoboEarth researcher Dr Markus Waibel from the Swiss Federal Institute of Technology in Zurich. He commented that most researchers using robots typically develop individual ways for that machine to build up a body of data about the world. This makes it very difficult for roboticists to share knowledge or for the field to advance rapidly.

By contrast, RoboEarth hopes to show how the information that robots discover can be shared, as in a collective, so any other robot can find it and use it. RoboEarth will be a communication system and database with maps of places where robots work, descriptions of objects they encounter and instructions for how to complete distinct actions. According to Dr Waibel, the human equivalent would be Wikipedia, something that humans use to share knowledge, that everyone can edit, contribute knowledge to and access. Currently nothing like this exists for robots.

RoboEarth is likely to become a tool for the growing number of service and domestic robots that many expect to become a feature in homes in coming decades. Domestic settings might teach robots about the objects that fill the human world and their relationships to each other. For instance, RoboEarth could help robots understand how to set the table for a meal.

The EU-funded project has about 35 researchers working on it and hopes to demonstrate how the system might work by the end of its four-year duration. Early work has resulted in a way to download descriptions of tasks that are then executed by a robot. Improved maps of locations can also be uploaded.

On the other hand, Rajesh Rao takes a different approach to robots' learning. He believes that the best type of robotic helper is one who can read individual human minds. He believes in training them through the power of thought alone. His team at the Neural Systems Laboratory, University of Washington, hopes to take brain-computer interface (BCI) technology to the next level by attempting to teach robots new skills directly via brain signals.

Robotic surrogates that offer paralysed people freedom to explore their environment, manipulate objects or simply fetch things have been the holy grail of BCI research for a long time. Dr Rao's team began by programming a humanoid robot with simple behaviours, which users could then select with a wearable electroencephalogram (EEG) cap that picked up their brain activity. The brain generates what is known as a P300, or P3, signal involuntarily, each time it recognises an object. This signal is caused by millions of neurons firing together in a synchronised fashion. It has been used by many researchers worldwide to create BCI-based applications that allow users to spell a word, identify images, select buttons in a virtual environment and more recently, even play in an orchestra or send a Twitter message.

The team's initial goal was for users to send commands that a robot would process into a movement. However, this requires programming robots with predefined sets of very basic behaviours, a very limiting approach. The team reasoned that giving the robot the ability to learn would allow a greater range of movements and responses: and the way to do it was to tap into the human brain's 'hierarchical' system to control the body. The brain is organised into multiple levels of control including the spinal cord at the low level to the neocortex at the high level. The low-level circuits take care of behaviour such as walking while the higher level allows other behaviour – such as driving a car: this is first learnt but later becomes an almost autonomous lower-level behaviour, freeing the driver to recognise and wave to a friend on the street while driving.

To emulate this kind of behaviour – albeit in a more simplistic fashion – Dr Rao and his team are developing a hierarchical brain-computer interface for controlling the robot. A behaviour initially taught by the user is translated into a higher-level command. When invoked later, the details of the behaviour are handled by the robot.

A number of groups worldwide are attempting to create thought-controlled robots for various applications. Early last year Honda demonstrated how their robot Asimo could lift an arm or a leg through signals sent wirelessly from a system operated by a user with an EEG cap. Scientists at the University of Zaragoza in Spain are working on creating robotic wheelchairs that can be manipulated by thought.

Rao's latest robot prototype is 'Mitra' – meaning 'friend'. It's a two-foot tall humanoid that can walk, look for familiar objects and pick up or drop off objects. The team is building a BCI that can be used to train Mitra to walk to different locations within a room. Once a person puts on the EEG cap they can choose to either teach the robot a new skill or execute a known command through a menu. In the 'teaching' mode, machine learning algorithms are used to map the sensor readings the robot gets to appropriate commands. If the robot is successful in learning the new behaviour then the user can ask the system to store it as a new high-level command that will appear on the list of available choices the next time.

The resulting system is both adaptive and hierarchical – adaptive because it learns from the user and hierarchical because new commands can be composed as sequences of previously learnt commands. The major challenge is accuracy. While EEG can be used to teach the robot simple skills such as navigating to a new location, it may not be possible to teach robots complex skills that involve fine manipulation, such as opening a medicine bottle or tying shoelaces. It may be possible to attain a finer degree of control either by using an invasive BCI or by allowing users to select from videos of useful human actions that robots might be able to learn. A parallel effort in the same laboratory is working on imitation-based learning algorithms that would allow a robot to imitate complex actions such as kicking a ball or lifting objects by watching a human do the task.

Dr Rao believes that there are very interesting times ahead as researchers explore whether the human brain can truly exert direct control over non-biological robotic devices. In some ways, the mind has already overcome some limitations of the body by designing cars and airplanes that travel faster than pedestrians, mobile phones to communicate further than by immediate speech, books and the Internet to store more information than can fit into any one brain.

Being able to exert direct control on the physical environment instead of through hands and feet might represent the next step in this progression: but there may be ethical issues involved that would need to be adequately addressed.

Sources

Sandhana, L. (technology journalist) 2010. BBC News, 25 October, 'The robot that reads your mind to train itself'. http://www.bbc.co.uk/news/technology-11457127.
Ward, M. (technology correspondent) 2011. BBC News, 9 February, 'Robots to get their own internet'; http://www.bbc.co.uk/news/technology-12400647.

Conclusion

This chapter has offered two main suggestions. One: that an essential difference in social values – and therefore in the ways in which people interact – is between an individualistic and a collective view of society. Two: that these interactions are profoundly affected also by the power imbalances that exist in all societies by which people are empowered or disempowered for a huge number of reasons including their gender, colour, race or ethnicity, social status and so on.

Within the difference of individualism versus collectivism are concepts of internal and external locus of control; digital and analogue sense of self; and monochronic and polychronic sense of time. As for power, since leadership is the exercise of power, different leadership styles will have different effects on follow-ers' behaviour. This refers to downward command, from leaders to followers; but an example of upward control is that of members of society over corporate leaders in the provision of goods and services.

Since so much communication is in written form, the importance of visual elements has been discussed with examples of emotive elements in typefaces. A report on robotic communication ends the chapter.

Key points

1. Study of communication across cultures is multidisciplinary; international findings can be applied to domestic settings and vice versa, between members of different gender, class and caste and to differences in ownership of power; because cultural differences lead to creation of ingroups and outgroups,

2. Particular problems arise when individualists interact with collectivists. Examples of individualistic national cultures include those of the USA and Australia; while collectivist cultures include those of China, Japan and Turkey.

3. Self-concept is basic to human behaviour: in individualistic societies people tend to see themselves as independent; in collectivist societies, as interdependent. Individualists assume more control over nature and situations, and feel more responsible for their own behaviour under an internal locus of control; whereas more members of collectivist cultures possess a higher external locus of control and believe more firmly that external factors finally determine events. Concept of self can be viewed as digital (for individualists, i.e., as single entities) or analogue (for collectivists, i.e. as parts of a whole).

4. People with an independent concept of self are likely to be more monochronic in their use of time, but those whose sense of self is interdependent are likely to be polychronic with ingroups but monochronic with outgroups. Individualists are likely to be guided by personal beliefs and to be motivated by personal goals, and collectivists to conform to social norms and to be motivated by adding value to the group.

5. The degree of individualism varies within as well as between cultures and with context. For example, in political elections the struggle for individual power may set brother against brother. And in commercial transactions, thanks to the Internet and urbanisation, consumers are becoming more individualistic, sophisticated and demanding; and increasing materialism creates new opportunities for enterprising marketers.

6. Also social factors within a society, such as type of housing, will influence communication. People who live in apartments learn more collective behaviour than those in private dwellings.

7. Government policies on the location of subsidised housing for low-income residents will affect intra-cultural communication within the relevant population when poor people are housed in city areas formerly reserved for the financially elite.

8. In any case globalisation may be motivating apartment dwellers towards a more individualistic, conservative lifestyle of suburban house ownership.

9. These international social trends illustrate that all human interaction consists essentially of struggles for different positions in power hierarchies created by unequal distributions of economic and cultural capital. These hierarchies may be of class and status; or of political ideology or leadership. Cultural capital, which makes up the hierarchies, is defined by the respective cultures' beliefs and assumptions about what is natural and right.

10. Orthodox opinions enhance and maintain existing states of affairs. Heterodoxy struggles to overturn social structures that create and maintain power of the few over the many.

11. The conflict between orthodoxy and heterodoxy in intercultural encounters is played out with the currency of cultural capital – such as skin colour, religion, achievement, gender or even level of English proficiency. Ownership of these social currencies affects the dynamics of interpersonal communication. Thus context is an essential component of all power hierarchies.

12. Cultural capital is dynamic, and the global community increasingly is made up of people who are different but equal. International management studies take place nowadays in educational environments to which people bring their own unique contexts.

13. Advances in modern technologies affect interpersonal communication in unanticipated ways. For example, social networking over the Internet is essentially egalitarian and promotes the expression of individual ideas and opinions; but it can also be the driver of collective action, as in mass political protests.

14. Interpretation of meanings through social networking and other forms of written communication is affected by visual elements such as the appearance of the typeface.

15. The design of robotic communication may arm robots with a growing collective library of shared knowledge about their human masters that they can edit, contribute to and access; also they may learn new skills directly via an individual's brain signals.

Looking ahead

Chapter 3 follows the path blazed by the contributors to Chapters 1 and 2: from leadership communication in contexts of human diversity, through more general discussion of the influences of culture and context on human interactions and on to communication through language, verbal and non-verbal, written and spoken.

Experiential exercises

1. In groups of three (as cross-cultural as possible), choose one member to take notes while the other two talk to each other on any agreed topic for about 3 minutes. Meanwhile the writer notes how often each speaker uses the words 'I' and 'we'. After 3 minutes change roles so the writer has a chance to be speaker, and vice versa. Finally, tot up the scores and discuss the results in terms of individualist/collectivist societies.

2. Ask the group, 'How would you describe your culture?' Ask everybody to write down some words or phrases. Then compare them. Can members of any one culture find cultural attributes that describe them all? If there is some agreement are there also exceptions? Ask everybody to discuss why some characteristics have become popular stereotypes of particular cultures; and

whether it is possible to make any general statements about any one culture because of its diverse population.

Suggestions for further reading

Books

Brislin, R.W., Bochner, S. and Lonner, W. 1999. (eds) *Cross-cultural Perspectives on Learning.* Beverley Hills, CA: Sage.

Hall, E. T. 1985. *Hidden Differences: Studies in International Communication.* Hamburg: Grunder & Jahr.

Hofstede, G. 1980. *Culture's Consequences: International Differences In Work-Related Values.* Beverley Hills, CA: Sage.

—— 1991. *Cultures and Organizations: Software of the Mind.* New York: McGraw Hill.

Lewis, R. D. 1999. *When Cultures Collide: Managing Successfully across Cultures.* London: Nicholas Brealey.

Mead, R. B. 1990. *Cross-Cultural Management Communication.* Chichester, UK: Wiley.

Moran, R. T., Harris, P. R. and Moran, S. V. 2010. *Managing Cultural Differences: Global Leadership Strategies for Cross-Cultural Business Success.* New York: Routledge.

—— 1981. *Managing Cultural Synergy,* vol. 2. Gulf Publishing Company.

Schneider, S. and Barsoux, J.-L. 1997. *Management across Cultures.* New York: Prentice Hall.

Tayeb, M. H. 1988. *Organisations and National Culture: A Comparative Analysis.* London: Sage.

—— 2000. *The Management of International Enterprises: A Socio-Political View.* Basingstoke: Macmillan.

Triandis, H. C. 1999. 'Cross-cultural psychology', *Asian Journal of Social Psychology,* 2, pp. 127–143.

Trompenaars, F.and Hampden-Turner, C. 1997. *Riding the Waves of Culture: Understanding Cultural Diversity in Business.* London: Nicholas Brealey.

Journals

International Association for Applied Psychology
International Journal of Arts and Sciences
International Journal of Intercultural Relations
Journal of Cross-Cultural Psychology
Journal of Management Studies
Journal of Personality and Social Psychology
Psychological Bulletin
Social Science Information

References

Ansell-Pearson, K., Parry, B. and Squires, J. 1997. 'Introduction'. In K. Ansell-Pearson, B. Parry and J. Squires (eds), *Cultural Readings of Imperialism: Edward Said and the Gravity of History.* New York: St Martin's Press, pp. 8–27.

Bass, Bernard M., Avolio, Bruce J., Jung, Dong I. and Berso, Yair (2003) 'Predicting unit performance by assessing transformational and transactional leadership', *Journal of Applied Psychology,* 88: 207–18.

Beattie, J. 1980. 'Representations of the self in traditional Africa', *Africa,* 50 (3), pp. 313–20.

Belay, G. .1996. '(Re)construction and negotiation of cultural identities in the age of globalization', *Information and Behavior,* 5, pp. 319–46.

Bennett, M. J. 1986. 'A developmental approach to training for intercultural sensitivity'. *International Journal of Intercultural Relations,* 10 (2), pp. 179–96.

Bhawuk, D. and Brislin, R. 2001. 'Cross-cultural training: A review', article first published online, 25 December 2000; *International Association for Applied Psychology*, 2000.

Bourdieu, P. 1977. *Outline of a Theory of Practice*, translated by Richard Nice. Cambridge: Cambridge University Press. [Original work published in 1972.]

Brislin, R.W., Cushner, K., Cherrie, C. and Yong, M. 1986.. *Intercultural Interactions: A Practical Guide*. Beverley Hills, CA: Sage.

Brody, N.: http://www.fontshop.com/fonts/designer/neville_brody/.

Carnevale, P.J. 1995. 'Property, culture, and negotiation'. In R. Kramer and D. M. Messick (eds), *Negotiation as a Social Process*. Newbury Park, CA: Sage.

Christopher, E. 2010. 'The management of uncertainty and culture shock by graduate overseas students in Australia'. *International Journal of Arts and Sciences*, 3(11), pp. 35–53; Google Scholar: http://openaccesslibrary.org/images/XEW151_Elizabeth_Christopher.pdf.

Descartes, R. 1641. 'Meditations on first philosophy'. In *The Philosophical Writings of René Descartes*, translated by J. Cottingham, R. Stoothoff and D. Murdoch. Cambridge: Cambridge University Press, 1984, vol. 2, pp. 1–62.

Design Museum: http://designmuseum.org/design/jock-kinneir-margaret-calvert.

Dweck, C.S. and Leggett, E.L. 1988. 'A social-cognitive approach to motivation and personality'. *Psychological Review*, 95, pp. 256–73.

Earley, P.C. 1989. 'Social loafing and collectivism: A comparison of the United States and the People's Republic of China'. *Administrative Science Quarterly*, 34, pp. 565–81.

—— 1993. 'East meets West meets Mideast: Further explorations of collectivistic and individualistic work groups'. *Academy of Management Journal*, 36, pp. 271–88.

Fernández, I., Carrera, P., Sánchez, F., Paez, Darío and Candia, L. 2000. 'Differences between cultures in emotional verbal and non-verbal reactions'. *Psicothema*, 12, Supp., pp. 83–92; http://www.psicothema.com/pdf/401.pdf.

Fiedler, F. E. 1967. *A Theory of Leadership Effectiveness*. New York: McGraw-Hill.

Foa, U. G. and Foa, E. B. 1996. 'Perception in behavior in reciprocal roles: The ringex model'. *Psychological Monographs*, 80, p. 15 (American Psychological Association).

Foster, G.M. 1967. 'The dyadic contract: A model for the social structure of a Mexican peasant village'. In J.M Potter, M.N. Diaz and G.M. Foster (eds), *Peasant Society*. Boston: Little, Brown, pp. 213–29.

Galtung, J. 1981. 'Structure, culture, and intellectual style: An essay comparing Saxonic, Teutonic, Gallic, and Nipponic approaches'. *Social Science Information*, 20, pp. 817–56.

Gannon, M. J. and Newman, K. L. 2002. *The Blackwell Handbook of Cross-cultural Management*. Oxford: Wiley-Blackwell.

Garcia, Cathy Rose, A. 2010. 'More daring ads, brands for urban consumers'. *Korea Times*, 24 September; http://www.koreatimes.co.kr/www/news/biz/2010/09/123_73430.html.

Garfield, S. 2010. *Just My Type: A Book about Fonts*. London: Profile Books.

Gercik, P. 1992. *On Track with the Japanese: A Case-by-Case Approach to Building Successful Relationships*. New York: Kodansha International.

Gill, E. 1993. *Essay on Typography*. New York: David R. Godine.

Gray, J. 2003. *Men are from Mars, Women are from Venus*. New York: HarperCollins.

Gudykunst, W. B., Ting-Toomey, S. and Nishida, T. 1996. *Communication in Personal Relationships across Cultures*. Newbury Park, CA: Sage.

Hall, E. T. 1996. *The Dance of Life: The Other Dimension of Time*. New York: Doubleday.

Han, G. and Park, B. 1995. 'Children's choice in conflict: Application of the theory of individualism-collectivism'. *Journal of Cross-Cultural Psychology*, 26 (3), pp. 298–313.

Harris, W. 2000. http://www.will-harris.com/typepairs.htm.

Haruki, Y., Shigehisa, T., Nedate, K., Wajima, M. and Ogawa, R. 1984. 'Effects of alien-reinforcement and its combined type on learning behavior and efficacy in relation to personality', *International Journal of Psychology*, 19, pp. 527–45.

Hersey, P., Blanchard, K.H. and Johnson, D.E. 2007. *Management of Organizational Behavior: Leading Human Resources*. Englewood Cliffs, NJ: Prentice Hall.

Hofstede, G. 1980. *Culture's Consequences: International Differences in Work-Related Values*. Beverley Hills, CA: Sage.

—— 1991. *Cultures and Organizations: Software of the Mind*. New York: McGraw-Hill.

—— 2001. *Culture's Consequences: Comparing Values, Behaviors, Institutions, and Organizations across Nations*. Thousand Oaks, CA: Sage.

Holzer, S. 2010. *Facebook Marketing: Designing Your Next Marketing Campaign*. Harlow: Que Publishing.

House, R. J. 1971. 'A path-goal theory of leader effectiveness'. *Administrative Science Quarterly*, 16, pp. 321–39.

Hui, C. H. and Triandis, H. C. 1986. 'Individualism-collectivism: A study of cross-cultural researchers'. *Journal of Cross-Cultural Psychology*, 17 (2), pp. 225–48.

Indvik, L. 2010. 'Calvin Klein Jeans replaces racy billboards with QR Codes'. *Mashable Business*, 13 July; http://mashable.com/2010/07/13/calvin-klein-qr-code-billboard/.

Jackson, T. 1995. 'European management learning: A cross-cultural interpretation of Kolb's learning cycle'. *Journal of Management Development*, 14 (6), pp. 42–50.

Jandt, F.E. 2007. *An Introduction to Intercultural Communication: Identities in a Global Community*. Thousand Oaks, CA: Sage.

Kağitçibaşi, Ç. 1990. 'Family and socialization in cross-cultural perspective: A model of change'. In J. Berman (ed.), *Cross-Cultural Perspectives*. Lincoln, NB: University of Nebraska Press, pp. 135–200.

Kashima, E.S. and Kashima, Y. 1998. 'Culture and language: The case of cultural dimensions and personal pronoun use'. *Journal of Cross-Cultural Psychology*, 29, pp. 461–86.

Kashima, Y. and Kashima, E.S. 2003. 'Individualism, GNP, climate, and pronoun drop: Is individualism determined by affluence and climate, or does language use play a role? *Journal of Cross-Cultural Psychology*, 34, pp. 125–34.

Kim, U., Triandis, H.C., Kagitcibasi, C., Choi, S. and Yoon, G. (eds) 1994. *Individualism and Collectivism: Theory, method, and applications* (Newbury Park, CA: Sage).

Kolb, D.A. 1984. *Experiential Learning*. Englewood Cliffs, NJ: Prentice Hall.

Kravitz, D.A. and Martin, B. 1986. 'Ringelmann Rediscovered: The Original Article'. *Journal of Personality and Social Psychology*, 50, pp. 936–41.

Landis, D. and Bhagat, R. (eds) 1996. *Handbook of Intercultural Training*. Newbury Park, CA: Sage.

Lee, W.-N. and Choi, S.M. 2005. 'The role of horizontal and vertical individualism and collectivism in online consumers' response toward persuasive communication on the Web', *Journal of Computer-Mediated Communication*, 11 (1), article 1; http://jcmc.indiana.edu/vol11/issue1/wnlee.html.

Lewin, K., Lippit, R. and White, R.K. 1939. 'Patterns of aggressive behavior in experimentally created social climates'. *Journal of Social Psychology*, 10, pp. 271–301.

Lockett, A., Moon, J. and Visser, W. 2006. 'Corporate social responsibility in management research: Focus, nature, salience and sources of influence', first published online, 10 January 2006; DOI: 10.1111/j.1467-6486.2006.00585.x; *Journal of Management Studies*, 43 (1), pp. 115–36.

Luthans, F. 2005. *Organizational Behavior*. Boston, MA: McGraw-Hill Irwin.

MacCarthy, F. 1989. *Eric Gill*. London: Faber & Faber.

McClelland, D., Atkinson, J., Clark, R. and Lowell, E. 1953. *The Achievement Motive*. New York: Appleton-Century-Crofts.

Markus, H.R. and Kitayama, S. 1991. 'Culture and the self: Implications for cognition, emotion, and motivation'. *Psychological Review*, 98, pp. 224–53.

Moodian, M.A. (ed.) 2009. *Contemporary Leadership and Intercultural Competence: Exploring the Cross-Cultural Dynamics within Organizations*. Thousand Oaks, CA: Sage.

'More ways to differentiate'; http://www.how-to-branding.com/More-Ways-to-Differentiate.html [accessed December 2010].

Morris, M.W. and Peng, K. 1994. 'Culture and cause: American and Chinese attributions for social and physical events'. *Journal of Personality and Social Psychology*, 67, pp. 949–71.

Neuliep, J. 2008. *Intercultural Communication: A Contextual Approach*, 4th edn. Thousand Oaks, CA: Sage.

'Nothing to hide'; http://www.nothingtohide.co.nz/ [accessed December 2010].

Pederson, P. 1994. *A Handbook for Developing Multicultural Awareness*. Alexandria, VA: American Counseling Association.

Ragins, B.R. and Sundstrom, E. 1989. 'Gender and power in organizations: A longitudinal perspective'. *Psychological Bulletin*, 105 (1), pp. 51–88.

Realo, A. and Luik, M. 2002. 'On the relationship between collectivism and empathy in the context of personality traits', *TRAMES: Journal of the Humanities and Social Sciences*, 6 (3), pp. 218.

Rosenberger, N.R. (ed.) 1992. *Japanese Sense of Self*. Cambridge: Cambridge University Press.

Rotter, J.B. 1954. *Social Learning and Clinical Psychology*. Englewood Cliffs, NJ: Prentice Hall.

Said, E. 1978. *Orientalism*. New York: Random House: Introduction.

——— 1994. *Orientalism*. New York: Random House, Afterword.

——— 2001. 'Orientalism and after'. In G. Viswanathan (ed.), *Power, Politics, and Culture: Interviews with Edward W. Said*. New York: Pantheon Books, pp. 208–32.

Schmidt, W.V., Conaway, R.N., Easton, S.S. and Wardrope, W.J. 2007. *Communicating Globally: Intercultural Communication and International Business*. Thousand Oaks, CA: Sage.

Schwartz, S.H. 1990. 'Individualism-collectivism: Critique and proposed refinements'. *Journal of Cross-Cultural Psychology*, 21. pp. 139–57.

Shih, C. 2009. *The Facebook Era: Tapping Online Social Networks to Build Better Products, Reach New Audiences and Sell More Stuff*. Englewood Cliffs, NJ: Prentice Hall.

Singelis, T.M., Triandis, H.C., Bhawuk, D.P.S. and Gelfand, M. 1995. 'Horizontal and vertical dimensions of individualism and collectivism: A theoretical and measurement refinement', *Cross-Cultural Research*, 29, pp. 240–75.

Softpedia.com 2010. 'Levi's to launch Curve ID, the jeans that fit all body types', 30 August: http://news.softpedia.com/news/Levi-s-to-Launch-Curve-ID-the-Jeans-that-Fit-All-Body-Types-154264.shtml.

Smith, P.B., Bond, M.H. and Kağitçibaşi, Ç. 2006. *Understanding Social Psychology across Cultures: Living and Working in a Changing World*, 3rd rev. edn. London: Sage.

Spiekermann, E. 2002. *Stop Stealing Sheep & Find Out How Type Works*. Berkeley, CA: Adobe Press.

Stogdill, R. M. and Bass, B. M. 1974. *Handbook of Leadership: A Survey of Theory and Research*. New York: Free Press.

Strizver, I. 2001. *Type Rules!* Cotati, CA: North Light Books.

Swartz, D. 1997. *Culture & Power*. Chicago: University of Chicago Press.

Tomaselli, K.G. 1999. 'Misappropriating discourses: Intercultural communication theory in South Africa, 1980–1995'. *Communal/Plural*, 7 (2), pp. 137–58.

Trendwatching.com 2010. 'Maturialism: Time to loosen up a little', September; http://trendwatching.com/trends/maturialism/.

Triandis, H.C. 1975. 'Culture training, cognitive complexity, and interpersonal attitudes'. In R.W. Brislin, S. Bochner and W. Lonner (eds), *Cross-cultural Perspectives on Learning*. Beverley Hills, CA: Sage, pp. 39–77.

——— 1994. *Culture and Social Behavior*. New York: McGraw-Hill.

Triandis, H.C., Brislin, R.W. and Hui, C.H. 1988. 'Cross-cultural training across the individualism and collectivism divide'. *International Journal of Intercultural Relations*, 12, pp. 269–89.

Triandis, H.C., Chen, X.P. and Chan, D.K.-S. 1998. 'Scenarios for the measurement of collectivism and individualism', *Journal of Cross-Cultural Psychology*, 29, pp. 275–89.

Vroom, Victor H. and Yetton, Phillip W. 1973. *Leadership and Decision Making*. Pittsburgh, PA: University of Pittsburgh Press.

Wade, N.: http://www.nickwade.com/the-east-london-coffee-disloyalty-card-tour [accessed 20 November 2010].

Wall Street Journal 2010. 'Apple knew of iPhone issue; Engineers aware of antenna risks before release, but CEO Jobs liked design', Personal Technology, 16 July; http://online.wsj.com/article/SB10001424052748704682604575369311876558240.html.

Yukl, G. 1994. *Leadership in Organizations*. Englewood Cliffs, NJ: Prentice Hall.

CHAPTER 3

Noise and Silence: Verbal and Non-Verbal Communication

Elizabeth Christopher; Sture Allén; Peter Buzzi; Claudia Megele

Objectives of the chapter

To examine how meaning is communicated through language, verbal and non-verbal, written and spoken; and how international managers can improve their communication skills.

Chapter contents

- Outline of chapter
- Sture Allén: Language as cultural communication: Speaking European
- Discussion points, questions and exercises
- Classroom exercise
- Case study: Press releases
- Class exercises
- Peter Buzzi and Claudia Megele: *Honne* and *Tatemae*: A world dominated by a 'game of masks'
- Discussion points, questions, exercises
- Questions to discuss in class
- Elizabeth Christopher (2011): Verbal and non-verbal communication across cultures
- Discussion questions for classrooms
- Conclusion
- Key points
- Experiential exercise for the classroom
- Recommended reading
- References

Outline of chapter

This is the final chapter in Part One, on 'different voices' as the first dimension of communication across cultures, an overview of the whole concept.

Chapters 1 and 2 were concerned with general discussion of cultural factors in human interactions. Chapter 3 deals more specifically with language diversity and with subtleties of interpretation within a language: the difference between what is said, how, why and with what consequences.

The first contributor is Sture Allén who argues the need to respect all human languages as expressions of cultural diversity – a need that is becoming more and more important for international managers as they operate increasingly in multilingual environments. Allén commends simultaneous translation in international forums so that members can speak in their native languages. He suggests this will help to counter the domination of English as a global language and encourage the preservation of less common languages. His frame of reference is Europe, but his comments apply equally to all nations and regions.

The case study that follows it, 'Press Releases', illustrates another aspect of translation and interpretation: the importance of reading 'between the lines' for intended propaganda hidden in apparently value-free text.

Contributors Peter Buzzi and Claudia Megele then discuss the importance of context in interpretation of language; and interpersonal communication as forms of theatre in which people as individuals and in teams play social roles.

Finally, Elizabeth Christopher writes on verbal and non-verbal communication across cultures; she examines the causes of interference with interpretations of meanings, including psychological variables such as thought patterns, attributions, perceptions, stereotyping and attitudes. She refers to factors of social organisation that affect interaction: roles, verbal and non-verbal 'language' including kinesics, proxemics, paralanguage, object language and use of time.

Discussion points, questions and exercises run through the chapter, and it ends with a conclusion and summary of key points; experiential exercises; suggestions for further reading; and references.

LANGUAGE AS CULTURAL COMMUNICATION: SPEAKING EUROPEAN	Sture Allén

This article is based on an address at a seminar on openness and clear language in the EU Stockholm, given on 8 September 2009, and an interview in the journal *Nordeuropa* (1994 (2): 24–7) itled 'Sprachliche Demokratie – europaweit! Sture Allén zu den Perspektiven der nordischen Sprachen in einer erweiterten EU'.

An important and excellent example of one aspect of cultural communication was once given by George Bernard Shaw (see http://nobelprize.org/nobel_prizes/literature/laureates/1925). After being awarded the Nobel Prize for literature in 1925, he proposed that the money be used to establish a fund to encourage exchange and understanding in literature and art between Sweden and the British Isles.

The Nobel Prize in itself is an overall form of cultural communication. However, more direct issues concern us today, the main theme being openness and clear language, two forces interacting in the best interests of all concerned.

Openness is a prerequisite for democracy, and so is clear language. Human language is a fantastic resource, infinite in scope and potential. Every language has unique assets – semantic, stylistic and culture-historic. All offer enormous possibilities for communication but also make demands on the users. The process involves senders and receivers, media and messages. Notice that McLuhan's slogan 'the medium is the message' does not imply any fundamental identity between the channel and the content of a manifestation but rather the influence of the medium on the message (McLuhan, 1964).

Solid insights into one's own culture and sense of identity are considered keystones of openness and respect for linguistic and cultural diversity. Native speakers of any language should be able to distinguish between, and use, different kinds of texts and to formulate and express arguments in writing and speech in convincing and appropriate ways. A positive attitude to communication in one's native tongue means a focus on critical and constructive dialogue, ability to make aesthetic judgements and intention to achieve quality. This is not in any way to belittle the value of knowledge of foreign languages. Such knowledge can give insight into new contexts, expand cultural perspectives and expedite contacts in everyday life.

In this context it is relevant to refer to the UNESCO Declaration on Tolerance (signed 16 November 1995: see http://www.unesco.org/cpp/uk/declarations/tolerance.pdf). It includes the need for respect, recognition and appreciation of the richness and diversity of cultural heritage and forms of expression. The term *European languages* is taken to mean all the languages spoken in the geographical area called Europe, irrespective of what groups they belong to or whether they have status as majority languages. The vast majority of inhabitants in this part of the world use at least one of the twenty-three official languages of the EU: Bulgarian, Czech, Danish, Dutch, English, Estonian, Finnish, French, German, Greek, Hungarian, Irish, Italian, Latvian, Lithuanian, Maltese, Polish, Portuguese, Romanian, Slovak, Slovene, Spanish and Swedish. Of these, nineteen belong to the Indo-European language group, three are Finno-Ugric (Estonian, Finnish and Hungarian) and one is a Semitic language (Maltese).

Native speakers of these languages often share a long history and are or have been longstanding neighbours. Therefore between them their 500 million users in many respects share the same values and this helps to create mutual understanding. Thus, it can be said that when speaking one of the EU's official languages, speakers are talking *European*. Speaking European includes speaking your own native tongue and getting professional simultaneous interpretation to the native languages of the other participants in the meeting. In this way, everybody can take part in negotiation on an equal footing. This basically simple model could make the EU globally unique in the domain of cultural communication. It could also make a fundamental contribution to the battle against a monolingual international culture, a dystopian concept in that it would contribute to the destruction of human diversity.

Because of cultural, linguistic and historical differences, translations can never be exact copies that convey all and nothing but the qualities of the originals. Nevertheless translation goes a long way towards overcoming language barriers and the preservation of the linguistic basis of culture. It is also important to support teaching of native languages and to look critically at the role of English in the schools. Studies have shown that teaching in the medium of English, generally speaking, does not have the positive effect that many people believe it has.

Attention should also be drawn to the shortcomings of major computer applications in failing to respect languages other than English – both in the applications themselves and in the manuals that go with them. It would be a valuable task for government authorities to ensure that computers are for people and not the other way around. For example, there are millions of us who are looking forward to the day when our names will be spelt correctly in electronic communication.

Those who have English as their native language have a major advantage in all communication in their native tongue. This is a built-in injustice, an obvious example of inequality that truly disadvantages clear language in the complete meaning of the term. The EU should adopt a fair-play principle, by which everybody speaks their native tongue and professional interpretation is provided as a matter of course. Failure to do so on the grounds of cost would be to waste our greatest wealth, the cultural and linguistic diversity that makes the EU unique in today's world.

Discussion points, questions and exercises

1. Allén reminds his readers of the importance of open and clear language. There are many examples in organisational and political contexts of conflict arising from lack of such language. For instance, in July 2010 in the UK, Housing Minister Grant Shapps made what seemed to be a clear commitment to the British people but in fact was nothing of the kind: 'This government are committed to ensuring that all new homes post-2016 can be zero-carbon.' Four months later zero became 56 per cent (see George Monbiot's blog, 8 December 2010, http://www.guardian.co.uk/environment/georgemonbiot). Can you think of some corporate examples of disingenuous language? If not, conduct an online search.

2. Allén's next point is that every language is a unique medium and each makes its own demands on senders and receivers' choices of media through which to send their messages. He quotes McLuhan's slogan that 'the medium is the message; and suggests that speakers of any language should be acquire skills in expressing convincing arguments in writing and speech.

   Since managers are in constant communication with an infinite variety of recipients, it is self-evident that language skills and fluency are essential. One example is the ability to influence people's opinion of something or somebody by choosing a particular noun to describe them; such as:

   – Ellis is the senior executive (makes Ellis sound important);
   – Ellis is a senior executive (less important);
   – Ellis is a female executive (least important).

   Another example is in public relations in which the phrase 'spin doctor' is often used to describe experts as well as political or corporate representatives whose task is to put a 'positive spin' on events or situations. Thus 'spin' is a form of propaganda (Safire, 1996), the persuasive interpretation of events in favour of or against an organisation or public figure. A good example is from cigarette companies that sell products known to be harmful. To deter negative publicity they fund sporting and charitable events, donate money to social projects and in other ways try to 'spin' a bad image around into one of corporate social responsibility.

A good class exercise is for students to find their own examples of skilful use of language to serve particular communication needs!

3. Allén's third point is the need for respect, recognition and appreciation of all languages as diverse forms of expression; and for using translation and interpretation media in resistance to what he calls a 'monolingual international culture' that would 'help to ruin human diversity'.

Increasingly, national and state governments worldwide are taking pride in the language diversity of their populations. For example, while English is the dominant language in Australia, collectively Australians speak over 200 languages and about 16 per cent speak a language other than English within their families and communities, including Italian, Greek, Cantonese, Arabic, Mandarin and Vietnamese (Australian Bureau of Statistics, 2007). This linguistic diversity is argued to be an asset for Australia, to make the country more competitive in international trade as well as fostering international ties and cultural exchanges.

In the UK, linguists have challenged politicians over their attitude towards asylum seekers, arguing that demands for spoken English are parochial and dangerous (Plomin, 2001). During a conference organised by the British Council in Cardiff in September 2001, on less-used languages, criticism was made of Labour's Ann Cryer MP, who suggested asylum seekers should show evidence of their ability to speak English before being admitted to the country. Speakers claimed that instead of celebrating diversity within the country, foreign-language speakers are regarded as a problem and that comments such as those make by Ann Cryer could promote intolerance between different communities.

Another issue raised at the conference (whose theme was how languages spoken by a small percentage of the population contribute to society) was that the UK school system is as much to blame as politicians. For example, native English-speaking students can get examination credits for foreign language learning but non-native-speaking students, studying in English and fluent at home in perhaps two languages, get no credit for functional trilingualism.

Speakers applauded the speech by Robin Cook (2001), the then foreign secretary, in April of that year when he said that pluralism is not a burden to be reluctantly accepted but an immense asset that contributes to the cultural and economic vitality of the nation.

Classroom exercise

Think about this in relation to your own life experience. If you are a native English speaker, to what extent do you feel you should learn a foreign host country language if you were posted there as a manager? If you are not a native speaker, do you feel resentful that native speakers seem to make so little effort to learn your language? Discuss this with the class.

Case study: Press releases

Press releases are forms of news items, written in the third person to promote the importance of a person, event, service or product. They are sent by email, fax or mail; as part of a press kit or with a promotional letter. Usually the headline states the release's most exciting news in as few words as possible for maximum effect. The balance of the press release backs up whatever claims were made in the headline.

In the *Wall Street Journal* of 7 December 2010, journalist Dave Kansas (2010) reported on a press release issue by 3M, headlined '3M outlines strategy for accelerated growth in sales, profits and cash flow'. He translated the statement of: '... the company's ongoing commitment to investing in its core businesses ...' to mean: 'We're spending more than we should, but we've got to do it', arguing that this was what the phrase 'commitment to investing' usually means. He suggested there was more than a hint of desperation in the statement that:

> *'Our continuing strong performance clearly demonstrates that our growth strategy is working' and of defensiveness in the claim that '3M's innovation engine has been revitalized...'*

since use of the word 'revitalized' was probably a tactic to blame past failures on the former administration – though replaced five years previously.

He quoted another statement from the release, of

> *... the company's continuing commitment to growing its core businesses and expanding market share through increased investments in R&D, sales and marketing and new manufacturing capacity, particularly in fast growth developing economies. ... Developing markets currently represent one-third of 3M sales and will likely reach forty-five percent by 2015.*

Kansas translated this to mean: 'Again, we're spending more than we ought to, but we got to do it' and that 'boosting developing market sales from 33% to 45% over the next four years' was not only a timid resolve but also carefully hedged ('will likely reach'). Moreover he pointed out that readers should always pay careful attention when writers shift from fractions ('one-third') to numbers ('45%') because this can be misleading.

The release affirmed also

> *... the company's focus on complementary acquisitions of both technologies and businesses to pursue adjacent market opportunities and to build new platforms for future growth (citing) 3M's recent purchases of Cogent Inc. and Attenti Holdings S.A. in the security market space and Arizant Inc. in the healthcare market as examples of new high growth platforms for 3M.*

Kansas interpreted this to mean: 'We will not do any transformative deals, but will keep nibbling at the small fry.' And he suggested the statement that: 'Additional presenters at the conference will include (a list of company executives)' really meant that big investors were absent.

In the press release 3M also provided its 2011 sales and earnings outlook – hailed by Kansas as actual news, saved for the last paragraph and including hyperbole meant to point readers towards the 'adjusted' figures – which were the last numbers cited and the most attractive.

Kansas' final comment was that though the release was not a bad piece of sales presentation, it could not hide the fact that 3M was short of its stated growth goal, and perhaps this was why investors were unhappy with the press release and therefore were selling the stock.

Sources

Kansas, D. 2010. 'Translation time! 3M Press Release touts growth, stock falls', 7 December, *Wall Street Journal*; http://blogs.wsj.com/.
'Press release: Nevada to get $112,500 under $67m multistate settlement with B of A', *Wall Street Journal*; http://online.wsj.com/article/bt-co-20101207-710834.html.
PublicityInsider.com; http://www.publicityinsider.com/release.asp [accessed 9 December 2010]

Class exercises

Find some more examples of press releases and discuss what is actually written and how it might be translated as meaning something else. What do you understand by the phrase 'spin doctors'? Does this case illustrate that there is a special 'language' that spin doctors use?

HONNE AND *TATEMAE*: A WORLD DOMINATED BY A 'GAME OF MASKS'	Peter Buzzi and Claudia Megele

We utter sounds that are understood by others as words and language. To an English speaker who does not understand a word of German, Greek, Chinese or Japanese, any conversation in those languages will at best seem like a sequence of utterances that make no sense.

The purpose of communication is to convey a message, that is, to generate, co-create or share joint meanings. Hence sounds generated by people as their spoken language are part of a code or convention of utterances that comprises its words, phrases and expressions. Each word either refers to something actually and physically existing or to the idea of something. This suggests that language is a symbolic game where each word refers or points to a given, signified, meaning. For instance, the word 'bird', either refers to an actual bird or to the idea of a bird.

However, in everyday life the meaning of words is generated contextually and depending on their use. For instance, if someone with hostile intentions broke into the room you might use a chair to protect yourself or to fend off the attack. In this case, the chair may be called your 'shield'. Or, in a camping trip you may sit on a tree stump and may refer to the stump as your 'chair'.

J.L. Austin (1962) extended an analysis of contextual meaning to formulate what became known as speech act theory. He argued that statements and words do not only describe a situation or state a fact, but also perform a certain action by themselves. For instance, the sentence 'You have beautiful eyes' can be either true or false. However, Austin suggests that this utterance is more than a mere description and does things on its own. Depending on the context and its use, this sentence can have different functions such as praise, irony, flirtation or flattery, maybe as a preamble for asking a favour.

Therefore Austin makes a distinction between utterance-as-description and utterance-as-action – action such as naming a ship the Queen Elizabeth or saying 'yes, I do' in a wedding ceremony. These utterances are not true or false, are not just reporting or describing something but doing something.

Austin divides speech acts into three categories: what is said; what the speaker actually intended to say; and what happens as a consequence. For instance, the sentence 'You can't do that' is the actual utterance; the speaker's intention may be to stop you from doing something, and the consequence may be that you actually stop doing that thing – or continue to do it as an act of defiance, the consequence of interpreting the demand as interference.

Austin argues that speakers rely on the power of socially accepted conventions to lend force to their utterances. However, Strawson (1969) and Grice (1996) are two writers who critique Austin and suggest that speech is dependent on speakers' intention rather than convention. Nonetheless, Austin's speech act theory was a significant contribution to the study of language and meaning. He successfully relocated meaning in the use of words and context rather than in a fixed linguistic connection by which each word refers to a given meaning.

However, the main difficulty with Austin's speech act theory and its variations is that all these approaches are based on a speaker-centred model of meaning in communication, which discounts the role of listener and the nature of communication as dialogue. Geertz (1993) defines culture as 'webs of significance' spun between people through their actions and interactions. Through this dynamic, identities, actions, practices, communities, subjects and objects become cultural through more or less structured webs of significance, and this is the foundation of subjective understanding and cultural identity (Jansson, 2002).

Therefore meaning is not created in a void; it is structured and sustained by the socio-cultural influences and the environment within which it is generated. In fact, at times the same utterance can have opposite meanings in different cultures. For instance, the proverb 'a rolling stone gathers no moss' in English signifies that if one is sufficiently dynamic one does not become obsolete ('gather moss'). In this context 'moss' has a negative connotation, and the proverb is used to depict a positive characteristic (mobility). On the contrary, the same maxim in Japanese means that one cannot become mature if one changes place too often. Hence 'moss' in this context signifies maturity and has a positive connotation, while the proverb itself is used to depict a negative characteristic (that of excessive mobility).

Wittgenstein (1953) emphasises the importance of context and culture in determining meaning and states that 'the speaking of language is part of an activity or of a life-form' (1953: 10), and that meaning is deeply rooted in the value system in one's life or 'language game'.

Erving Goffman (1959) offers a new appreciation of the multifaceted nature of context. He presents an innovative approach to the understanding of social interaction, language and meaning as well as intra-cultural and inter-cultural communications. Goffman can be considered one of the greatest sociologists of the latter half of the twentieth century. Indeed, since his book *The Presentation of Self in Everyday Life* there has been no complete alternative to his analysis of interaction and his rich and meaningful metaphor of life as theatre. This is not to say that Goffman's work has gone without criticism, but his theory and analysis remain both influential and relevant in contemporary social contexts.

Goffman focuses on the micro-level interaction between individuals in society and offers an impressive analysis of how those interactions sociologically constitute the human experience. He elucidates how individuals and collectives work together to construct a common understanding and representation of 'reality'. Of particular significance is the analysis of dramaturgical elements and processes embedded in social interaction. This in turn raises the question of 'impression management' and how individuals and groups, through the use of scripted dialogues, gestures, props, costumes and so on, create a reality for their 'audience' with the aim of communicating a particular impression of the world to others.

For Goffmann 'self' is not a fixed entity 'owned' by social actors; it is rather dynamically and collaboratively (re)enacted, (re)constituted and (re)performed in social actions and interactions, and as such remains a fluid and ever-evolving phenomenon. He does not consider the individual as totally autonomous, rather as in relation to a social whole. In Goffman's theory, not individuals but 'teams' are responsible for cooperatively creating and constituting a particular impression of reality or a particular experience, much like the presentation of a theatre play.

An example of such role-playing is how sales agents must adopt the roles of competent, knowledgeable, honest and professional individuals in order to sell their products and services. Being perceived as professionals provides them with credibility; moreover their role may be repositioned and reframed, for example, from an sales agent selling insurance policies to a financial advising role in which – based on their specialised knowledge and skills – they offer expert advice to assist clients in solving their problems and achieving their financial objectives.

Another example is a job interview where the candidates aim to fit the 'role' for which they are being interviewed in order to create the impression of suitability for that role, and consequently be hired by the employer/organisation.

Goffman suggests that 'scripts' are vital to interpersonal communication. Many of the everyday 'routine' interactions (e.g., initial greetings, the usual niceties, and so on) are 'scripted'. For instance, asking an acquaintance or a colleague 'How are you?' usually solicits a response of 'Fine thank you, and yourself?' rather than a detailed and sincere answer about the other person's feelings, health or well-being. This is a routine so familiar that it is performed almost automatically. Such scripts offer people convenient solutions to social expectations and norms.

Organisations and business establishments often make use of formal scripts to communicate messages to their target audience. Such scripts can range from the initial greeting by the company's telephone operator to the cold-call telephone solicitations by various marketing agents. They convey a standardised message and communicate a given meaning with the hope of enacting and generating a desired effect and soliciting a desired response, usually in order to control the interaction, and hence the customers.

Individuals form first impressions based on people's appearance and what they wear. Therefore wardrobe is important in presenting the person's role and social status in the 'episode' of the life 'drama' being played at the time. For instance, a pinstripe suit usually projects a conservative and professional image.

Stage and sets constitute part of the context for interaction. If used effectively they can help convince the 'other' to adopt the version of reality that the 'team' would like to convey. For instance, a candlelit dinner, a company conference room, an executive office, a nursery playground – each offers a physical environment, a 'stage', designed to induce a desired effect and outcome. Manipulation of the scenery, the stage and set usually involves a conscious effort to replace the ordinary with the extraordinary and to generate a desired 'mood' or 'ambience'.

The stage is divided into front-stage and back-stage. Front-stage is what the audience sees, while back-stage provides the space for all the paraphernalia and support activities (as in the storage room of a retail shop). Also it offers a space for emotional maintenance of team members where they can take a break from their role and the performance (as in the staff room in a company suite of offices). Team members can also use the back-stage for discussions, information sharing, evaluating the performance, providing feedback, strategising, and so on.

Nishiyama (1971) has analysed the relation between the two values of *honne* and *tatemae* in Japanese culture. *Honne* may be defined as true feelings and intentions, which may be contrary to *giri* (social obligations); while *tatemae* literally means façade or 'front' and refers to behaviour and opinions displayed in public – to conform to the social expectations embedded in individuals' positions in given contexts.

From a dramaturgical perspective the concepts of *honne* and *tatemae* can be related to the back-stage and front-stage performances of social actors. As in theatre performances, in communication and social interactions the actors assume different roles and identities between back-stage (*honne*) and front-stage (*tatemae*). This raises important ethical questions in relation to image management, sincerity, authenticity, truth, deception and cynicism in social interactions.

An excellent example is the Japanese *kaigi* or face-to-face business meeting/ conference. Although on the surface, this may appear similar, say, to a US business meeting, there are significant differences, including differences in purpose and objectives. Whereas an American business meeting is to facilitate decision-making, the Japanese business meeting is aimed at formalising what has already been decided informally (a process referred to as *nemawashi*).

In Western business cultures it is acceptable to change one's mind about decisions made or conclusions reached, based on new information and emergent discussions. In Japanese business meetings such a change of mind is considered a serious breach of trust, since most agreements reached during informal consultation must be respected and adhered to in formal business meetings. Although *kiagi* may include the ritual of asking questions and providing answers, such questions are usually points that have already been discussed beforehand. The meeting participants will not appreciate surprise questions or strong objections during the actual meeting. This is contrary to American business meetings where open discussion and debate are welcomed, where the participants are encouraged to actively engage and to raise any relevant issues or points that may add value to the decision-making process and/or organisation.

Also Japanese participants in business meetings play different roles from their American counterparts. For instance, the American chairperson would take direct control over the conduct of the meeting and would encourage direct and spontaneous participation from all participants, with the aim of stirring a lively discussion to work out and reconcile differences. The Japanese counterpart would aim to mediate consensus among participants, and will leave the role of aggressive and/or direct control to a *buchoo* (department head), who will also coordinate the sequence of interventions and participants' presentations based on a predetermined order.

The dramaturgical aspects of business relations are particularly evident in the interaction between junior and senior participants in meetings and business communication. For instance, in *kiagi* junior participants must express their questions and opinions with humility and by underlining their lack of experience. Hence, in asking questions or expressing opinions a junior participant may begin with a sentence such as 'I may be asking this question due to my inexperience, and may be wrong, but …' or 'I may be wrong and beg your indulgence for my inexperience, but …'. Such tentative approaches to expressing one's opinion and to business discussion and decision-making (*ringi*) are part of the rituals of Japanese 'conflict-avoiding' culture, which values consensus and harmony.

This does not mean that Japanese do not ever exchange honest and frank opinions. However, this is done in the context of informal meetings and other 'non-official' opportunities. For instance, Japanese businesspersons often meet their counterparts in after-office gatherings to exchange opinions and discuss various matters; at times this is referred to as 'nomication', a contraction for *nomini* (drinking) and communication. Nomication provides a social space similar to back-stage for participants where they can express their opinions and feelings more freely.

Even in the nomication context members must know their positions with respect to other participants; however, expressing discontent and even complaining about one's superior during nomication highlight the dramaturgical aspects of this type of social performance in Japanese culture. For instance, during nomication, junior participants may complain about their superior's action or treatment, by pretending to be inebriated. The following morning, however, the 'drunk' participants must apologise for their behaviour to maintain *tatemae* by saying something like: 'I am sorry for becoming drunk last night. I can't remember what I said.' Although they may very well remember every detail of the conversation and, in their *honne*, have no remorse about their complaints or expressions the previous evening.

The cultural differences and challenges of intercultural communication are exacerbated by individual differences and the difficulties inherent in individual thinking and identity. These include individual perception, patterns of thinking and cognition, non-verbal communication and so on. Perception is the internal process by which we select, evaluate and organise the stimuli of the outside world. Individual perceptions are strongly influenced by culture. Culture conditions individual preferences, likes and dislikes and the way people see, hear, feel, experience and even taste and smell the world. Therefore, individuals' notion of beauty, concept of self and attitude towards and relationship with others depend on their culture and values. Perception is an important aspect of intercultural communication. People from dissimilar cultures usually assign different meanings to the same environmental stimulus (such as objects, events, ideas, signs, symbol, and so on), and therefore experience and perceive the world differently.

People usually think in schemas – sets of interrelated cognitions that allow them to quickly make sense of a person, situation, event or a place on the basis of limited information. In practice, certain cues activate schemas, which then fill in the missing details. Schemas are therefore preconceptions and general expectations based on our system of values, our identity and our experiences, and are learned through experience and socialisation. The more entrenched a schema the more difficult it is to modify it. We use schemas to select and process incoming information from the social environment. Hence schemas play an important functional and essential role in screening and interpreting environmental stimuli, and help us understand the complexity of social life.

There are generally considered to be four types of schemas (Fiske and Taylor, 1991; Taylor and Crocker, 1981): person schemas (opinions/expectations about a person); role schemas (expectations about a role, e.g., how politicians, policemen, nurses, etc. should behave); self schemas (view/expectations of self); and event schemas (expectations about an event).

Culture also influences individuals' thinking and cognitive patterns, which in turn influence the way they relate to and interact with one another. Therefore individual reasoning and problem-solving are culturally dependent and at times result in different ways of learning, understanding and doing things. Nisbett (2003) notes that Northeast Asians (e.g., Chinese, Japanese and Koreans) deploy a holistic thinking pattern while Western cultures prefer a cause-and-effect model, which approaches problem-solving with a systematic analysis of various factors and components from simple to more complex and with a focus on correlations and causality.

Considering that cognitive patterns are culturally based, they facilitate communication within similar cultures by sustaining similar ways of thinking and reasoning and by sharing common meanings. However, they can be a source of misunderstanding and difficulty in intercultural communication between dissimilar cultures. For instance, in international business negotiations between Japan and the US, the Japanese have a tendency to go back and reopen what their US counterparts consider closed issues since from their perspective the new discussions and information have a bearing on previous decisions and/or agreement. This can prove frustrating from a Western cultural perspective.

Another example is when Japanese are asked whether they agree with a given conclusion or the general discussion. They might respond: 'Yes, I don't agree with you,' which actually means 'Yes, you are right. I don't agree with you.'

Hence it is important to gain an appreciation of the divergent patterns of cognition based on cultural orientations, and to develop strategies for dealing with and reconciling such differences in intercultural communications.

Furthermore, individual differences in cognitive styles affect perceptions of reality. For instance, some individuals adopt an open-minded-approach to decision-making by seeking additional information and alternative opinions before arriving at a conclusion. Such individuals usually formulate their final opinion and/or decision only after having gathered what they consider sufficient information. On the contrary, individuals with a closed-minded cognitive style often formulate their opinion and/or decision, at least partially, before seeking further information. At times, such individuals seek others' opinions hoping only to receive a revalidation of their own opinions, decisions and/or conclusions.

Another example of divergent cognitive styles is that of associative thinkers versus abstract thinkers. Associative thinkers filter and codify data and environmental stimuli based on experience while abstract thinkers can readily imagine something new.

A critically important factor in intercultural communication is non-verbal behaviour, including various non-verbal cues, gestures, facial and/or bodily expressions, gaze, posture and movement, sense of touch, pause, silence, dress, and the use of space and time. Non-verbal communication is often closely interlinked to verbal communication and can at times convey more meaning, and therefore be more important and revealing than verbal communication.

Non-verbal behaviour and communication are rooted in culture and societal norms and are processed (produced/coded and interpreted/decoded) based on these. Given that the process can take place at conscious as well as subconscious level, at times non-verbal communication can be more powerful and influential in our actions and decisions than verbal communication. Furthermore, non-verbal communication can readily become a source of misunderstanding and even conflict. Non-verbal communication has significant variations across cultural boundaries. Greeting behaviour is an example of non-verbal behaviours with significant intercultural variations, ranging from Latin embrace (Mexican *abrazo*), to Indian *namaste*, to Japanese bow, and to various types of handshakes and so on.

On the stage of life and with the advent of new technologies, individuals have many alternatives for manipulating 'reality' and the impressions and images they project onto the world. However, a theatre actor playing Hamlet, after his performance knows that he is not a Danish prince. This raises the question: what are the consequences of continuous and consistent role-plays within a 'constructed reality' as part of the dramaturgy of 'everyday life'? What are its implications for actors and the audiences' psyches and identities? In an incessant act of performance the inescapable question is what are the confines of 'truth' and 'pretence'? Where does the 'play' end and 'life' begin? Or are they inextricably and unrecognisably merged and fused? Or yet, are they one and the same? What delineates the confines of sincerity and cynicism?

Goffman candidly claims that when adopting various roles actors have to take a position in relation to both their role and their values and identity – they must decide whether the impression of reality that they project is 'true'. He suggests that the actors can be taken in by their roles. Individuals' perception of their actual performance and the effects of their performance allow attribution of relative value to their roles. Actors who have no belief in their own performance and no concern for its consequences or its effects on audiences are labelled as 'deceitful' or 'cynical', while those actors who believe in their own performance are considered 'sincere'.

Given the individual differences in identity, values and culture, attitudes and thinking, every social interaction and/or communication can be considered as an act of translation, both intra- and inter-cultural. It takes place through the processes of signification and interpretation, verbal and non-verbal, from one person's system of signs, standards and values to those of another. We can therefore conclude that if culture is the circulatory system of society, then language is the blood that circulates within that system. As blood is the source of life and brings arteries and veins to life, language in its infinite colours, varieties and expressions, and communicated through varied media, brings culture alive and encapsulates human thought.

It is this process of translative articulation that is the supreme expression, and the very essence, of cultural praxis and the fertile ground for individual growth and identity. It is in this context and upon this dramaturgical stage dominated by the game of masks that everyday life drama unfolds. As the curtain calls of *honne* and *tatemae* are enacted and (re)performed in the limits of front- and back-stage, the diversity of cultures and languages confront us with the incessant need for shared meaning through 'translation'. Thus translation becomes an act of articulation in the diversity of a shrinking global village of disparate dependencies. In this context, language is the transformative elixir and the empowering agent that ushers particularities on to the stage of universality.

Discussion points, questions, exercises

The authors suggest that language is a kind of game in which players match words to given meanings – thus, for example, in the game of 'speaking English' they all understand that 'fire' refers to flames and burning – but context affects interpretation. For example, how would hearers interpret the phrase 'being fired' in the following contexts?

- A boss referring to an employee;
- A circus clown and a mock cannon;
- A potter about to complete work on a new clay artefact.

A second point made in the essay is that there is a difference in speech between what is said, what the speaker actually intends to say and what happens as a consequence. An example is that an office manager can't find a document and says to a very young, very new filing clerk: 'Why can't I find the report on the 2010 conference?' The manager may intend a simple query but the new recruit may well interpret it as an indirect criticism and feel humiliated in consequence. On the other hand, the manager may have intended a reproof, but the clerk may have interpreted it as a sign of the manager's incompetence and feel superior in consequence.

This illustrates why perception is such an important aspect of communication, particularly when intercultural in any sense.

Questions to discuss in class

1. What are 'schemas' and what purpose do they serve in interpersonal communication?
2. What examples are offered in the essay of ways in which culture influences individuals' thinking patterns and ways they relate to and interact with one another?
3. What is non-verbal behaviour and how does it affect verbal communication?
4. Consider your classroom as a stage and the people on it as players. What expectations do stage and costumes set up about the kind of drama that will be played out here?
5. How would you set the stage and costume yourself to enact the following social 'dramas'?

   – 'Interviewing candidates for a job looking after small children in a day-care centre';
   – 'Interviewing candidates for a job as a bank clerk';
   – 'The boss is coming to dinner';
   – 'Your job has been made redundant'.

VERBAL AND NON-VERBAL COMMUNICATION ACROSS CULTURES	Elizabeth Christopher (2011)

What is communication?

Communication is the exchange and flow of information and ideas, effective only if it is received as intended by senders. It involves thinking, encoding, channelling, sending, decoding and feedback. Information exists in the mind of the senders and is transmitted via some sort of common 'code', such as words in a particular language, culturally determined non-verbal behaviour and so on, via a selected 'channel' (face-to-face, telephone, Internet, etc.). Thus intended meanings are translated into symbols. Marshall McLuhan (1964) wrote that the medium is the message. The form of the message influences interpretation of its content, for example, handwritten messages send different signals from emails.

Receivers translate messages into concepts or information they can understand and feedback their response (Clark, 2005). At any stage, meaning can be distorted. Anything that interferes with accurate understanding is referred to in the literature as 'noise' (Jenkins, 1999). Ways to avoid or minimise noise include using different words and media, for instance, by following up an email with a letter rephrasing the same information with a request for comment; then to telephone the receiver to make sure all is well. Two-way communication is essential for mutual understanding; repeated efforts are needed to ensure it.

Causes of interference

The primary cause of interference with accurate sending and receiving of messages ('noise') is that senders and receivers all exist in their own unique and private worlds. These life spaces are each filled with experiences and ideas based on unique combinations of cultural background and individual personality. Thus they filter, or selectively censor, messages to fit with their own expectations, perceptions of reality, values and norms of behaviour.

Studies by Mintzberg (see http://www.henrymintzberg.com) demonstrate the importance of verbal communication: he found that most managers spend between 50 and 90 per cent of their time talking to people. Thus a major challenge for managers – as for anybody – is to find the appropriate behaviour, verbal and non-verbal, that will most effectively communicate their wants and needs in any given situation.

For example, a manager may say to a worker: 'I need you to work overtime tonight.' An Australian employee may interpret this either as 'Oh, good, I shall earn some extra money' or 'Not bloody likely!' A Norwegian employee may think 'Oh, no, I want to go home to my family.' A Thai employee may respond to the manager's need without thinking about extra money – but will expect the manager to see she gets home safely if she has to work late at night; and so on.

The more dissimilar the culture, the more the likelihood of misinterpretation: that is, noise. Communication, therefore, is a complex process of linking up or sharing perceptions.

It has been said before that one of the reasons English has become, by default, the international language is that it is so flexible. It can accommodate itself to almost any grammatical distortion, with possibly the one exception of reference to gender. It is simply not possible in English to say 'he' or 'him' when one means 'she' or 'her'. Turks, for example, when speaking English often muddle the two – to the complete, if momentary, confusion of their hearers – because there is no such distinction in Turkish. However Turks (and speakers of many other languages) cannot simply refer to 'my sister', for example, as in English, because there is a different word in Turkish for younger and older sisters.

Moreover, Triandis is one of a large number of writers to point out that in a great many other languages (European, Asian, Middle Eastern) there are several words for 'I' and 'you', depending on the relationship between the speakers (see http://www.psych.uiuc.edu/people/showprofile.php?id=564). The French verb *tutoyer* denotes the difference between the formal use of 'you' (*vous*) and the informal 'you' (*tu*). In Japanese there are different ways to address men and women, and so on. Thus it is perfectly possible to cause unintended offence (and therefore to create noise in communication) when native English speakers try to communicate in a foreign language that contains these subtleties.

The writer's mother was in France when the late John Kennedy visited that country as US President in the 1960s. She described how his wife – a fluent but non-native French speaker – referred to him in a TV interview as *ce type* (meaning 'this guy'). In US English this would be an informal but not offensive way to refer to one's husband even, and especially, if he were of high rank. However, some sixty years ago the phrase in French carried very informal connotations. Jackie Kennedy's use of it caused a storm of media reaction and she was accused of belittling her husband in public (Knudsen, 1963).

Samovar and Porter (1999) and Harris and Moran (1996), among others, have identified psychological variables likely to influence communication. These include thought patterns, attribution, perception, stereotyping and attitude. Other relevant factors include social organisation, roles, language (spoken or written), non-verbal communication (including kinesic behaviour, proxemics, paralanguage and object language) and time.

Attribution

Attribution happens when people look for explanations of others' apparently incomprehensible behaviour. Thus, in the words of Hall and Hall (1990), they may blame their lack of understanding on the other party's stupidity, deceit or craziness. Alternatively, they may attribute superior wisdom to them. People also may make attributions in accordance with an external locus of control, as described in Rotter's social learning theory (1954). This refers to the extent to which people believe they can control events that affect them. Individuals with a high internal locus of control believe that events result primarily from their own behaviour and actions. Those with a high external locus of control believe that powerful others, fate or chance primarily determine events – as religious people do when they attribute events to the will of God, or when they say, 'Events were beyond my control.'

Perceptions and stereotypes

People perceive reality from the perspective of their own world of values, and stereotyping is a common cause of misunderstanding in intercultural communication. Macrae et al. (1996) have written a comprehensive overview of contemporary research on stereotypes, which they describe as structured sets of beliefs about the characteristics of members of social categories, influencing how people attend to, encode, represent and retrieve information about others, and how they judge and respond to them.

Attitudes

It seems to be generally understood that people's attitudes underlie the way they behave and communicate and the ways in which they interpret messages from others. For example, the results of a study (Treviño et al., 2000) of attitudes towards media communication suggested that recipients' general attitudes towards different media are influenced most consistently by perceived medium richness, including the degree of interaction provided between people and technology. This may help to explain the worldwide popularity of interactive computer games.

Communication confusions and breakdowns

Confusions and breakdowns can occur through inability to speak the local language, poor translation, ignorance of idioms, lack of perception of the meaning of non-verbal language and symbols. Even between people who share a language, problems can arise from the subtleties and nuances inherent in local uses. More than just conveying objective information, language also conveys cultural and social understandings from one generation to the next. Anything that can be said in one language can be translated into another; but sometimes one word will need several in translation. This provides clues to cultural priorities.

The English word 'mate' carries different socio-cultural connotations from those of the French *copain*, for example, which denotes a man or boyfriend, whereas 'mate' – at least in Australia – includes the concept of an equal partner in an enterprise who is usually but not necessarily male. The French verb quoted above, *tutoyer*, cannot be translated into English except as 'to talk to you as a friend' – or some similar phrase – because the English language, like its native speakers, is pragmatic more than inter-relational.

There are many different single Arabic words to denote some kind of camel. They can all be translated into English but only by using more than one word – because camels are not part of English-speaking cultures. In English there is only one word for 'rice', though it can be qualified by adding more words, such as 'long grain'; but in rice cultures, such as that of Japan, there are many single words for different kinds of rice. In Icelandic there are many single words for 'snow'.

In US English the word for a cellular telephone is 'cellphone' (or just 'cell'); it describes the object in terms of its technology. In Australian English the word is 'mobile'; the object is described in terms of its flexibility. In French it is a 'portable', something that people carry like a briefcase. In German, 'handy' describes it in terms of function (the word is a corruption of the *Handfunktelefon* marketed by electronic firms such as Bosch and Hagenuk). Each description indicates, to a small extent, a particular cultural perspective.

In as much as language conveys culture, technology and priorities, it also serves to separate and perpetuate subcultures. In India, 14 official and many unofficial languages are used, and over 800 languages are spoken on the African continent.

Because of increasing workforce diversity around the world, international business managers deal with a medley of languages. For example, assembly-line workers at the Ford plant in Cologne, Germany, speak Turkish and Spanish as well as German. In Malaysia, Indonesia and Thailand many of the buyers and traders are Chinese. Not all Arabs speak Arabic in business transactions: in Tunisia and Lebanon, for example, French is the language of commerce. Therefore international managers need either a very good command of the local language or competent interpreters.

But even direct translation of specific words does not guarantee congruence of meaning, as with the word 'yes' said by Asians, which usually means only that they are listening attentively, not necessarily that they agree with you. Thus politeness or a desire to say only what the listener wants to hear may create noise. This applies even between native speakers, for example, between Britons and US Americans. Britons tend to be polite with strangers, to avoid confrontation, to say comparatively little and listen a lot. US Americans, though equally polite, tend to be direct and to talk rather than listen. Thus the British may think their US counterparts are too talkative while the Americans may find them too reserved.

Non-verbal communication

As the phrase implies, this is without words (although it is often accompanied by words). Even minor variations in body language, as well as speech rhythms, send messages to observers, to be interpreted favourably or unfavourably, depending on the total situation. Non-verbal behaviour includes seating arrangements, personal distance and sense of time.

For example, young Thai students at Western universities, if they want to remain after class to talk privately to their lecturers, will often squat down on their heels beside them if they are seated so their heads will be on a lower level than those of their teachers, as a mark of respect. They will talk earnestly and at length, even if students are queuing up behind them and the next class is waiting to enter the room. They will continue to talk as they follow the lecturer out of the room, down the corridor and even into the toilet if they are of the same gender.

In contrast, Northern Europeans quite happily will tower over their seated lecturers and tend to be more aware of time. They are likely to arrange a special appointment if their query is lengthy, rather than keeping other students waiting.

Another aspect of non-verbal communication is seen in different approaches to 'knowing'. European-based cultures traditionally have valued theoretical and verbal reasoning above learning from experience and intuition. On the other hand, Asian, Middle Eastern and African cultures have always recognised the importance of experience, of describing the world in symbolic imagery as well as by facts and figures. Music, drama, dance and rhythm are as valuable as more formal communication media.

Kinesics

Anthropologist Ray Birdwhistell (1952) used the term 'kinesic behaviour' to refer to communication through body movements: posture, gestures, facial expressions and eye contact. Marjorie Vargas (1986) wrote:

> *A man stands inside of a closed glass phone booth. You cannot hear a word he says, but you see his postures, gestures, and facial expressions. You see his kinesics.*

Although some actions may be universal, often their meaning is not. Because kinesic systems are culturally specific and learnt they cannot be generalised across cultures. Even displays of the basic emotions of happiness or misery, friendship or anger, shock or delight will vary. Many businesspeople and visitors in foreign countries react negatively to what they feel are inappropriate facial expressions. Foreigners are often disconcerted when Japanese laugh as a way to avoid showing negative emotions such as embarrassment or even grief. Another example is that in many Asian cultures it is considered rude to stare. The British share this feeling, but not the French. Such subtle differences in eye behaviour ('oculesics') can cause communication breakdown if they are not anticipated. Eye behaviour includes differences not only in eye contact but also in the use of eyes to convey other messages – as in flirting, for instance.

Gestures – or lack of them – also can be confusing to foreigners. For instance, Chinese sometimes hold up two crossed forefingers to signify something is wrong; but Westerners may interpret this as a religious gesture. Northern Europeans use few gestures of any kind and tend to talk quietly without much emphasis – unlike their neighbours on the Mediterranean. Non-native English speakers may find this impassivity a real barrier to understanding.

Proxemics

This concept deals with the influence of space on communication – personal space, and exterior and interior designs. For example, the British preference is for natural-looking parks and landscapes, but the French tradition is for formal landscaping rather than 'unspoiled nature' since the former expresses aesthetic values.

The British tradition is that interiors provide private space for each person (separate bedrooms, offices, etc.) and the more senior the employees, the larger and more private are the spaces allotted them. A reserved car space in the company car park is a definite 'perk' of office. This is not the case in most of Europe or Asia, where the custom is more to provide open office space, with people at all levels working and talking in close proximity.

Regarding personal space, South Americans, Southern and Eastern Europeans, Indonesians, Indians and Arabs are members of what Edward T. Hall (1959) calls 'high-contact cultures': that is, they prefer to stand close, touch a great deal and experience a 'close' sensory involvement. Conversely, following Hall's arguments, Australians, Canadians, Chinese and Northern Europeans belong to low-contact cultures and prefer much less sensory involvement, standing farther apart and touching far less. They have a more 'distant' style of body language.

Personal contact

There seems to be a link between degree of individualism (as defined by Hofstede (1991), for instance) and culturally acceptable levels of personal contact. In general, people from individualistic cultures tend to adopt more remote and distant behaviour with colleagues, whereas those from collectivist cultures are more likely to work in closer proximity. This is noticeable in subcultures also: for instance, young people tend to be like puppies in a basket, happy to huddle up to each other in confined spaces, but older people need more room.

Paralanguage

Paralanguage refers to how something is said rather than the content: rate of speech, tone and inflection of voice, laughing, whispering, shouting. Silence also is a powerful communicator. It may be a way of saying no, of indicating offence or simply waiting for more information. Most US Americans don't seem able to cope with more than 10 or 15 seconds of silence – whereas in general Asians can endure silence for much longer periods than can Westerners.

Object language

Object language refers to how people communicate through material artefacts, whether in architecture, office design and furniture, clothing, cars or cosmetics. Material culture communicates what people hold as important in the material world. An example from the emerging wealthy middle class of Chinese professionals and business people is their preference for goods with internationally famous brand names, as an indicator of personal wealth (*Journal of Asia Business Studies*, 2008).

Time

As for attitudes towards time as a form of communication, Bluedorn (2002) refers to a German preference for doing 'one thing at a time'; and the culturally based ways in which people regard and use time is a critical variable in the success or otherwise of cross-cultural communication. US Americans tend to be very punctual people ('time is money'), but in the state of Hawaii they are forgiven for being about 15 minutes late for appointments. Residents explain apologetically to their fellow nationals from other states, that 'Hawaii time' (i.e., running late) is acceptable in deference to the strong South Pacific local culture.

Edward T. Hall (1959, 1966, 1976, 1983) was one of the founders of intercultural communication study. He suggested that in what he called 'monochronic' cultures (such as those of Switzerland, Germany and the US) time is experienced in a linear way, with a past, a present and a future. Time is treated as something to be spent, saved, made up or wasted. This attitude is a learned part of Western culture and probably began with the invention of clocks. Thus monochronic members of individualistic cultures, such as Germany or the US, generally prefer to concentrate on one thing at a time ('Finish one thing before you start another!'), adhere to time commitments ('You mustn't keep people waiting!'), and to be accustomed to relatively short-term relationships ('I want a divorce!').

Though members of Western cultures almost intuitively seem to seek closure – i.e. to declare a task completed and to move on to the next – members of Asian cultures, equally apparently intuitively, seem to resist closure, preferring always to leave options open. A major problem for some Asian students in Western universities is to complete their dissertations – for example, for doctoral degrees. They find it almost impossible to accept that they have done enough research, that the report must be written and an imaginary line drawn under it with the words 'The End'.

Thus people in 'polychronic' cultures are more likely to tolerate many things occurring simultaneously; and they emphasise involvement with people over worrying about deadlines. Members of Latin cultures in general are likely to continue a conversation with a friend even if it means being a few minutes late for a business meeting. Punctuality carries nothing of the same moral weight as in Germany or the US.

Time and space

The relationship between time and space also affects communication. Polychronic people, for example, are likely to hold open meetings, moving around and conducting transactions with one party and then another rather than compartmentalising topics, as do monochronic people.

It is important to note gender differences. In every society men are socialised so differently from women it can be said they belong to different cultures. Men are brought up from birth to be monochronic and practical; women, polychronic and emotional. In the past these 'female' tendencies were regarded by men as faults in women, as evidence they 'let feelings interfere with judgement' and 'can never stick to one thing at a time'.

Awareness of context

Edward T. Hall first used the terms high- and low-context cultures to identify differences in communication style between members of different societies (see Beer, n.d.).

By 'high context' Hall meant the kind of communication that occurs in collectivist societies or groups. Many aspects of cultural behaviour are not made explicit because most members know what is expected of them, and they share assumptions about the need to show mutual respect and to maintain harmony in day-to-day interchanges. Families (if they are functional families) are examples of high-context groups.

'Low context' refers to communication in more individualistic societies where non-verbal communication is limited because less can be taken for granted without explanation. Feelings – such as the need to 'save face' – are not considered so relevant; factual information is more important. A legal courtroom is an example of a low-context environment.

People in high-context cultures expect others to understand unarticulated moods, subtle gestures and environmental clues that people from low-context cultures simply do not recognise. The writer witnessed in the UK an incident of total mutual misunderstanding from this cause. An Indian woman had flown to London from Calcutta to take part in a high-level international forum on famine relief. Her flight was delayed and she arrived only just in time for the first session. She was tired and tense, but when the English secretary asked if she would like a cup of tea she replied: 'Oh no, please don't trouble to make tea.'

In her culture this was a clear message that her refusal was from good manners and should not be taken literally. In fact she would have welcomed a hot drink, and she assumed the secretary would know this and would say something like: 'But you must have something, what can I get you?' After that it would be socially acceptable to ask for what she wanted. However, the secretary, being a member of a relatively low-context culture, took the refusal at face value, said nothing more about refreshment and escorted the poor thirsty delegate to her place at the forum.

High-context people tend to distrust low-context communication for being too verbally literal, too obvious, crass, redundant and undignified. On the other hand, low-context people sometimes perceive their high-context counterparts as secretive, even hypocritical and untrustworthy. In the anecdote above, when the English secretary was made aware of the Indian delegate's plight she snapped indignantly: 'Well, why on earth couldn't she say what she wanted? How was I supposed to guess?'

Even under the most auspicious circumstances, finding the balance between high- and low-context communication can be tricky. Too much information may lead people to feel they are being 'talked down to'; too little can make people feel left out.

The Athenian philosopher Plato said: '*Wise men talk because they have something to say fools, because they have to say something.*' The English poet and dramatist John Dryden wrote that '*far more numerous was the herd of such, Who think too little and who talk too much.*' But maybe the most entertaining comment on this topic came from the late actor John Wayne, famous for his roles as a taciturn cowboy in the days of the 'wild west' of what is now the USA: '*talk low, talk slow, and don't talk too much*'.

Information flow

Context also affects information flow. In high-context cultures, such as in Thailand, information spreads rapidly but informally because of constant close contact and implicit ties between people and organisations. One result is that rumours abound, often unfounded. Workers rely on their immediate supervisors as the link between themselves and senior management, and also rely on them to protect the group's interests.

In low-context organisational cultures (such as those of Germany and the US) information flows through formal, legitimised channels such as memos, newsletters and emails from head office. In countries such as Indonesia, Malaysia and Papua New Guinea (PNG) foreigners must rely on local informants to find out what is going on. Representatives of transnationals like IBM, who travel all the time, are constantly in touch with local IBM employees who are their mediators with the local environment.

Information speed

The speed of information systems is another key variable. US businesspeople expect to give and receive information quickly and clearly, moving through details and stages in a linear fashion to the conclusion. They use a wide range of media for fast messages: letters containing facts and plans, telephone calls and teleconferences, emails, faxes and face-to-face meetings. In contrast, French written communication tends to be formal and tentative with subsequent letters slowly building up to a new proposal. This echoes a need for formality in business relationships; and results in a slowing down of message transmission that often seems as unnecessary to US Americans as does US haste to the French.

Patterns of speed and flow

In all organisations there needs to be a systematic pattern for information flow (Bavelas, 1950), and there are a number of such patterns.

The chain pattern is hierarchical: formal information flow is from top to bottom, as in the military. In business firms, when organisational changes are made at top level the relevant information is emailed or otherwise passed from the top down to executives and then from executives to professional grades to ensure that the higher executives know first.

In the US F.W. Taylor (1911) believed that management could be formulated as an academic discipline, and that the best results would come from the partnership between a trained and qualified management and a cooperative and innovative workforce. Organisations should be arranged in a hierarchy with systems of abstract rules and impersonal relationships between staff. In Germany Max Weber (1846–1920) (see http://www.sociosite.net/topics/weber.php) argued for bureaucracies with a clearly defined hierarchy of positions within a firm system of supervision based on clear levels of authority. In France Henri Fayol's administrative principles of management (1916) included division of work under a centralised unity of command and direction (what he called a 'scalar chain') and the concept of line and staff. Two functions of management are to command and coordinate so that 'each official knows whom to report to with specified rights of control...'

In a wheel pattern, direction is passed from the hub of the wheel down each of the spokes to the individuals at the rim. There is no exchange of information between the spokes of the wheel. An example would be of a small firm in which the owner-manager directs each employer individually on their duties and each works on their own. Experiments at MIT in the 1950s (see http://www. iq.harvard.edu/blog/netgov/2007/04/bavelas_revisited_hubspoke_vs.html [accessed 23 April 2007] indicated that information tends to flow faster by this means than in decentralised networks in which, in the extreme, everyone can communicate with everyone else. The basic logic seems to be that in decentralised networks information floats around inefficiently.

The star pattern is common to most businesses. Groups or individuals are all related to one central source from which the transfer of information flows, but they are often independent of each other. The central source handles all messages whereas employees who occupy positions at the edges of the star send and receive fewer messages, and have little or no control over the flow of information. They can communicate with only one or two others and depend on others to relay any messages beyond their own range.

After experimenting with groups in chain, wheel and star configurations, Bavelas (1950: 10) suggested that in patterns with central positions such as the wheel and the star, organisations develop quickly around the people in these positions. Also organisations seem to be more stable, with fewer performance errors, than in communications patterns with lower degrees of centrality such as the circle. However, he found that employee morale in high-centrality organisations is relatively low. He speculated that in the long run this might lower the accuracy and speed of such networks.

Bavelas concluded from his laboratory experiments that the structure of communications within any organisation will have a significant influence on the accuracy of decisions, the speed with which they can be reached and the satisfaction of the people involved. In networks where responsibility for initiating and passing along messages is shared evenly among members, employee morale is higher in the long term.

An all-channel network involves information being freely distributed: 'it suggests democracy and sharing, the free and complete flow of information' (Clarke, 2003). It is an elaboration of Bavelas' circle (Borgatti, 1997) used by Guetzkow (Guetzkow and Simon, 1955), and can be compared to the free flow of communication in a group that encourages all of its members to become involved in its decisions. The all-channel network may also be compared to some of the informal communication networks.

The Internet

As for communication via the Internet, Whitney (2009) agrees that it is getting friendlier for a significant chunk of the world. A proposal in 2009 was that web addresses should include non-English characters, and now Internationalised Domain Names (IDNs) accept non-Latin characters in the entire address. This allows people who write in Chinese, Korean or Arabic to use their own languages to surf the web, and it jump-started Internet use in many regions across the globe. Not only cross-culturally but intra-culturally the Internet is proving to be more and more essential as a communication tool across a whole range of topics and uses, from the most personal to the most factual. Email has become a regular part of life.

In summary

Breakdowns in mutual understanding are to be expected – but not necessarily accepted – between people from different cultures and backgrounds. Cultural differences are reflected in communication and constitute 'noise' or interference with intended meanings. Negotiators across cultures need to be flexible, and to adjust their communication styles appropriately.

Discussion questions for classrooms

1. What is stereotyping? Can you give some examples?
2. How might people stereotype you?

3. How does a socio-type differ from a stereotype? (Hint: Think of socio-typing as creating cultural patterns or profiles; and stereotyping as attributing simplified and distorted aspects of those profiles to individuals.)

4. Can you think of an example of the relationship between language and culture, apart from those above? One example would be that in some cultures the language puts the verb, the action word, at the end of the sentence (e.g., Japanese, German). Thus you have to hear the whole sentence before you can guess at the meaning. But in English the verb is near the beginning, which makes it easier to act on assumption.

5. Does this hint towards a culture-based difference in emphasis between 'Look before you leap' (long-term orientation and need to avoid uncertainty as much as possible) and 'Strike while the iron is hot' (short term orientation and 'masculine' culture)?

6. Are there other examples of the link between culture and language?

7. Give some examples of cultural differences in the interpretation of body language. What is the role of such non-verbal communication in business relationships? (Hint: Who do you shake hands with? When? Why?)

8. Give an example of a difference between monochronic and polychronic use of time. (Here's a thought to get you started: did your parents teach you to 'finish one thing before you start another'? If so, do you think they emphasised this more to the boys than the girls?)

9. What would be an example of a difference between high and low awareness of context, respectively, in a conversation between two people? This is one suggestion:

High context:

A: (Plainly very anxious that the answer be 'yes'):
Do you think the chairman will ask me to speak at the meeting?
B: It is possible. The agenda is tight but to stretch it would be a compliment to you, and I see from your appearance and laptop that you are well prepared.

Low context:

A: (Plainly very anxious that the answer be 'yes'):
Do you think the chairman will ask me to speak at the meeting?
B: I shouldn't think so, it's a very tight agenda.

10. Can you suggest one way in which information systems vary from country to country, and why? (Hint: How do you communicate with your friends? How does your grandmother keep in touch with her friends? Is there a difference between these subcultures of age?) Think also of the senior members of any firm you have ever worked for, or the senior teachers in your school. It is quite likely you can identify differences in the way they use communication media – the telephone, emails, PowerPoint, laptops, letters, memos, etc.

Conclusion

This third and last chapter in Part One has dealt with language interpretation – not translation from one language to another but within a language. All languages should be respected and supported, and all languages to a greater or lesser extent rely on context for interpretation of meaning. Therefore people every-where, in all societies, use context in their favour as a form of theatre in which they wear costumes and masks to convey the importance of their social roles. This is an example of non-verbal communication – as are kinesics, proxemics, paralanguage, object language and use of time. Here as well as in verbal interac-tions people's thought patterns and attributions come into play, which further influences interpretation.

Key points

1. The focus of this chapter has been on the management of verbal and non-verbal languages as manipulative (or persuasive) communication media.

2. International managers operate increasingly in multilingual environments. All languages should be respected as expressions of cultural diversity.

3. Simultaneous interpretation of speeches and translation of written documents are important media for organisational communication across cultures to overcome the barrier of language difference and to weaken the hegemony of English as an international *lingua franca*.

4. However, verbal and non-verbal communication vary across cultures, and these variations may cause 'noise' or interference with understanding.

5. There are major differences between spoken and written language, between formal and informal language; and spontaneous, improvised language and language as a crafted tool for propaganda, that is, persuasion and manipula-tion of audiences for the benefit of the authors. Information is not knowl-edge. Interpretation is essential to identify and counter propaganda under the guise of information.

6. The context in which the language is used is a critical factor, as well as the actual language.

7. Shakespeare, in the play *As You Like It*, wrote:

> *All the world's a stage,*
> *And all the men and women merely players:*
> *They have their exits and their entrances;*
> *And one man in his time plays many parts ...*

Thus life may be seen as theatre in which people as individuals and in groups play social roles in various dramas and design settings and costumes in the presentation of self in everyday life. People talk, walk, dress and in general behave as actors playing their parts according to the setting of the social stage. Moreover 'back-stage' behaviour is different from 'front of stage'.

8. Not only printed words but their typefaces convey messages – of strength and masculinity, for example, or elegance and femininity. This is an example of 'the medium is the message', and suggests strategies for designs of organisational communication media such that their form will reinforce the content of the messages.

9. Individual characteristics also affect interpretation of meanings, such as thought patterns, attributions, perceptions, stereotyping and attitudes.

10. Time also is a factor in communication. Different attitudes towards time (culture-based) are recognisable in the difference between adages such as: 'Strike while the iron is hot' ('Act now!', a largely Western motivation); 'If Allah wills it' ('It will happen if it happens', an Islamic view); and '*Mañana*' ('Tomorrow will do', a Latin American view).

Looking ahead

The next section of the book, Part Two, contains two chapters along the second dimension of communication across cultures: that of context. Chapter 4 surveys the micro-environment of workplace diversity, conflict and collaboration; and Chapter 5 deals with sojourners' adjustment to the macro-environment of living and working in foreign cultures.

Experiential exercise for the classroom

The phrase 'impression management' refers to ways in which individuals and groups use scripted dialogues, gestures, props and costumes to create a reality for their 'audience', to make a desired impression, rather like the presentation of a theatre play. How would students 'play' the following social roles as a team? They should think about appearance of the various players, their verbal styles and non-verbal language:

- An important job interview;
- Negotiating a contract with a corporate client;
- A social post-merger get-to-know-you gathering.

How would the team 'set the stage' for the above, if they were in charge of organising them? What 'back-stage' arrangements might they make, in terms of Buzzi's and Megele's arguments?

Recommended reading

Austin, J.L. 1962. *How to Do Things with Words*. Cambridge, MA: Harvard University Press.

Birdwhistell, R. L. 1952. *Kinesics and Context: Essays on Body Motion Communication*. Philadelphia: University of Pennsylvania Press.

Deresky, H. and Christopher, E. 2011. *International Management; Managing Cultural Diversity*, 2nd edn. Frenchs Forest, NSW: Pearson Education Australia.

Fayol, H. 1916. *Functions and Principles of Management*, translated by Constance Storrs; http://www.bola.biz/competence/fayol.html.

Geertz, C. 1993. *The Interpretation of Cultures: Selected Essays.* London: Fontana Press.

Goffman, E. 1959. *The Presentation of Self in Everyday Life.* New York: Doubleday.

Hall, E. T. 1959. *The Silent Language.* New York: Doubleday.

Harris, P. R. and Moran, R. T. 1996. *Managing Cultural Differences.* Houston, TX: Gulf.

Higgins, E.T., Herman, C.P. and Zanna, M.P. 1978. *Social Cognition.* Hillsdale, NJ: L. Erlbaum Associates.

Hofstede, G. 1991. *Cultures and Organizations: Software of the Mind.* New York: McGraw-Hill.

McLuhan, M. 1964. *Understanding Media: The Extensions of Man.* New York: Mentor (reissued 1994, MIT Press, with an introduction by Lewis Lapham).

Macrae, N. C., Stangor, C. and Hewstone, M. 1996. *Stereotypes and Stereotyping.* New York: Guildford Press.

Mintzberg, H. 1989. *Mintzberg on Management: Inside Our Strange World of Organizations.* New York: Free Press.

Nisbett, R. 2003. *The Geography of Thought.* New York: Free Press.

Samovar, L. and Porter, R. E. 1999. *Intercultural Communication: A Reader.* London: Thomson Learning.

Taylor, F.W. 1911. *The Principles of Scientific Management.* New York: Harper & Row.

Weber, M. and Parsons, T. 2003. *The Protestant Ethic and the Spirit of Capitalism.* Chelmsford, MA: Courier Dover Publications.

References

Austin, J.L. 1962. *How to Do Things with Words* Cambridge, MA: Harvard University Press.

Australian Bureau of Statistics 2007. 'Main language other than English spoken at home/proficiency in spoken English'; www.abs.gov.au/AUSSTATS/abs@.nsf/0/5C5E4429075FC19FCA25737F001682F6?opendocument.

Bavelas, A. 1950. 'Communication patterns in task-oriented groups'. *Journal of the Acoustical Society of America*, 22, pp. 725–30.

Beer, J.E. n.d. 'High and low context'; http://www.culture-at-work.com/highlow.html.

Birdwhistell, R.L. 1952. *Kinesics and Context: Essays on Body Motion Communication.* Philadelphia: University of Pennsylvania Press.

Bluedorn, A.C. 2002. *The Human Organization of Time: Temporal Realities and Experience.* Stanford, CA: Stanford University Press.

Borgatti, S.P. 1997. 'Communication structure and its effects on task performance'; http://www.analytictech.com/networks/commstruc.htm.

Clark, D. 2005. 'Communication and leadership', 17 July; http://www.nwlink.com/~donclark/leader/leadcom.html.

Clarke, S. 2003. 'School leadership and complexity theory', *Journal of Educational Administration*, 41 (4), pp. 445–8.

Cook, R. 2001. 'Robin Cook's chicken tikka masala speech: Extracts from a speech by the foreign secretary to the Social Market Foundation in London', *Guardian*, 19 April; http://www.guardian.co.uk/world/2001/apr/19/race.britishidentity.

Deresky, H. and Christopher, E. 2011. *International Management: Managing Cultural Diversity*, 2nd edn. Frenchs Forest, NSW: Pearson Education Australia.

Fayol, H. 1916. *Functions and Principles of Management*, translated by Constance Storrs; http://www.bola.biz/competence/fayol.html.

Fiske, S. and Taylor, S. 1991. *Social Perception: Cognition.* New York: McGraw-Hill.

Geertz, C. 1993. *The Interpretation of Cultures: Selected Essays.* London: Fontana Press.

Goffman, E. 1959. *The Presentation of Self in Everyday Life.* New York: Doubleday.

Grice, H.P. 1996. 'Meaning'. In A.P. Martinich, (ed.), *The Philosophy of Language*, 3rd edn. New York: Oxford University Press, pp. 85–91.

Guetzkow, H. and Simon, H.A. 1955. 'The impact of certain communication nets upon organ-ization and performance in task-oriented groups'. *Management Science*, 1, pp. 233–50.

Hall, E.T. 1959. *The Silent Language*. New York: Doubleday.

——— 1966. *The Hidden Dimension*. New York: Doubleday.

——— 1976. *Beyond Culture*. New York: Doubleday.

——— 1983. *The Dance of Life: The Other Dimension of Time*. New York: Doubleday.

Hall, E.T. and Hall, M.R. 1990. *Understanding Cultural Differences: Germans, French and Americans*. Boston, MA: Intercultural Press.

Harris, P.R. and Moran, R.T. 1996. *Managing Cultural Differences*. Houston, TX: Gulf.

Hofstede, G. 1991. *Cultures and Organizations: Software of the Mind*. New York: McGraw-Hill.

Jansson, A. 2002. 'The mediatization of consumption: Toward an analytical framework of image culture'. *Journal of Consumer Culture*, 2 (1), pp. 5–31.

Jenkins, O.B. 1999. 'Worldview: Noise in communication'; http://strategyleader.org/worldview/worldvnoise.html.

Journal of Asia Business Studies 2008. 'Does consumer ethnocentrism affect purchase inten-tions of Chinese consumers? Mediating effect of brand sensitivity and moderating effect of product cues', 22 September, vol. 7, pp. 23–33.

Kansas, D. 2010. 'Translation time! 3M Press Release touts growth, stock falls', 7 December, *Wall Street Journal*; http://blogs.wsj.com/marketbeat/2010/12/07/translation-time-3m-press-release-touts-growth-stock-falls/.

Knudsen, R. 1963. 'President's trip to Europe' (Berlin: Executive Office of the President), 26 June.

McLuhan, M. 1964. *Understanding Media: The Extensions of Man*. New York: Mentor, [reissued 1994, MIT Press, with an introduction by Lewis Lapham]; http://www.marshallmcluhan.com/main.html.

Macrae, N.C., Stangor, C. and Hewstone, M. 1996. *Stereotypes and Stereotyping*. New York: Guildford Press.

Nisbett, R. 2003. *The Geography of Thought*. New York: Free Press.

Nishiyama, K. 1971. 'Interpersonal persuasion in a vertical society: The case of Japan', *Speech Monographs*, 38 (2), pp. 148–54.

Plomin, J. 2001. 'Government told to celebrate diversity of language', *Guardian*, 2 October; http://www.guardian.co.uk/education/2001/oct/02/languages.highereducation

Rotter, J. B. 1954. *Social Learning and Clinical Psychology*. New York: Prentice Hall; http://psych.fullerton.edu/jmearns/rotter.htm.

Samovar, L. and Porter, R.E. 1999. *Intercultural Communication: A Reader*. London: Thomson Learning.

Strawson, P.F. 1969. 'Intention and convention in speech acts'. In K. T. Fann (ed.), *Symposium on J. L. Austin*. New York: Humanities Press, pp. 380–400.

Taylor, F.W. 1911. *The Principles of Scientific Management*. New York: Harper & Row.

Taylor, S.E. and Crocker, J. 1981. 'Schematic bases of social information processing'. In E.T. Higgins, C.P. Herman and M.P. Zanna (eds), *Social Cognition*. Hillsdale, NJ: L. Erlbaum Associates.

Treviño, L.K., Webster, J. and Stein, E.W. 2000. 'Making connections: Complementary influ-ences on communication media choices, attitudes, and use'. *Organization Science*, 11 (2), pp. 163–82; http://orgsci.journal.informs.org/cgi/content/abstract/11/2/163.

UNESCO 1995. *Declaration of Principles on Tolerance*; http://www.unesco.org/cpp/uk/declarations/tolerance.pdf.

Vargas, M.F. 1986. *Louder Than Words: An Introduction to Nonverbal Communication* (Ames, IA: Iowa State Press).

Weber, M.: http://www.sociosite.net/topics/weber.php.

Whitney, L. 2009. 'Web addresses may adopt non-English characters', 26 October; http://news.cnet.com/8301-1023_3-10382873-93.html.

Wittgenstein, L. 1953. *Philosophical Investigations*, translated by G.E.M. Anscombe, 3rd edn. Malden, MA: Blackwell Publishers.

PART TWO

The Second Dimension: Communication at Work

CHAPTER 4

The Micro-Environment of Diversity at Work: Gender Factors and Minority Roles in Workplace Communication

Elizabeth Christopher; Gilles Asselin; Janet Haynes;
Sine Nørholm Just; Robyn Remke

Objectives of the chapter

To study work contexts for diverse human interaction.

Chapter contents

- Outline of chapter
- Gilles Asselin: Transcending the affiliation-achievement dimension of cross-cultural communication
- Discussion points and questions
- Case study: North Korea renews South overture
- Discussion
- Question for classroom discussion
- Janet Haynes: Women and work
- Discussion
- Questions
- Case study: Culture of fear
- Discussion
- Questions
- Sine Nørholm Just and Robyn Remke: Practising workplace diversity – perspectives, pitfalls and possibilities
- Conclusion
- Discussion
- Questions

■ Case study: Individualism in a collectivist culture

■ Conclusion

■ Key points

■ Experiential exercises

■ Recommended reading

■ References

Outline of chapter

The second dimension of communication across cultures, after that of language and communicative acts, comprises the working and problem-solving contexts in which they take place.

Gilles Asselin writes about the achievement and affiliation as respective motivators for task-oriented or relationship-oriented behaviour in work environments. He draws principally on the work of David McClelland (1955, 1961) and Geert Hofstede (1980, 1991) to argue that managers need to understand and mediate between people's different assumptions, implicit expectations and obligations.

Asselin offers two diagrams, one to illustrate two-way communication between people of different cultures, the other to summarise the differences between an achievement and an affiliation orientation. Both are presented with two major objectives. One is to help job candidates tailor their curriculum vitae to the expectations of their prospective employers. The other is to help managers on overseas assignment to recognise both where their values and priorities are 'coming from' and how they have to be adjusted to those of host country nationals.

There are some useful tips on how to combine task-oriented with people-oriented behaviour in the workplace; and important cultural distinctions are drawn between 'promises' and 'commitments'; and on building trust. Asselin leavens his arguments with personal anecdotes and scenarios.

Janet Haynes writes on what she describes as the largely unstudied role of women in the US workplace, particularly of women of colour. Hers is an auto-ethnographic study – based on her own experiences as an African-American woman in the workplace, supported by an extensive literature search.

Sine Nørholm Just and Robyn Remke report on how Westernised organisations define workplace diversity and diversity management practices that enable organisations and groups to achieve a high degree of difference within themselves. Thus a diverse organisation is an entity to which all its members contribute. The authors offer three main perspectives on diversity management, which respectively they call 'discrimination-and-fairness'; 'access-and-legitimacy'; and 'integration-and-learning', and suggest that diversity is a dynamic process continuously re-enacted through organisational practices.

Discussion points and questions are provided after each essay, and illustrative case studies. Key points are summarised and the chapter ends, as usual, with suggestions for experiential exercises to explore its themes; and lists of Internet resources and recommended reading, and chapter references.

TRANSCENDING THE AFFILIATION-ACHIEVEMENT DIMENSION OF CROSS-CULTURAL COMMUNICATION	Gilles Asselin

Introduction

When building or developing relationships across cultures, different assumptions, expectations and implicit obligations come into play. Acknowledging and honouring these culture-related norms significantly influences the amount of trust in a new business partner, a new friend or the stranger on the Internet.

A framework for developing intercultural relations (Asselin and Mastron, 2010)

The accompanying simple, common-sense diagram has two components: cultural self-awareness and other-culture awareness. In the business world few take the time and have the patience to weave relationships based on authenticity about their own cultural values and curiosity about those of others. It is a competitive world where efficiency and speed take precedence over 'human beingness'.

You will notice in the centre of the diagram the arrows retain some of their cultural characteristics. This means that the goal of fruitful intercultural relations is not to become quite like the other, thinking along the same lines and reacting according to the same patterns. It is a matter of being genuine and true to ourselves while honouring this 'truth' in the other and acknowledging that everyone thinks and reacts in a different way, but also that we are of the same stock, so to speak, and that we can successfully work together after establishing a minimum of shared understanding.

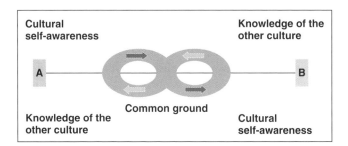

Figure 4.1   Bridging cultural distance

Achievement or affiliation?

The next illustration describes in general terms two major differences in perceptions of 'reality'. One is that life consists primarily of a continuous attempt to achieve tasks and solve problems; the other is that life is 'really' about relationships. These respective world views can be represented along a spectrum, neither of which are at one extreme or the other, but somewhere along it.

Orientations may vary depending on context. You may be more affiliation-oriented in your home, and more achievement-oriented at work, managing people and allocating resources. Nevertheless your primary mode of interaction is likely to be consistent, the difference being one of degree.

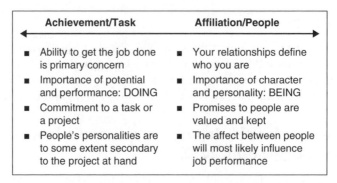

Figure 4.2   Achievement/affiliation orientation

How do you define yourself professionally?

This is a very important question, which influences, among other things, the way you build a resumé. Do you have a tendency to list (and possibly enhance) your achievements; and do you want to tell your prospective employers what you could do for their company? Do you also list personal references that can attest to the quality of these achievements?

Affiliation-oriented recruitment policies are to seek for what employers and candidates have in common. Interviews are set up to learn more about candidates as people rather than as performers. In general terms, an achievement-focused resumé than conveys the message 'Here is what I can do for your company' needs to be redrafted to read 'How I will fit into your company' for an affiliation environment. In this context educational qualifications from the 'right' schools (and therefore including the 'right' connections) are of extreme importance, and they alone might land you the job. What you have accomplished in your career and your aptitudes are important but they might not have as much impact on the final decision.

Doing versus being

The corporate world is driven by concerns of achievement and 'bottom line', and there is indeed a degree of 'achievement' that everyone needs to attain; yet it is possible to successfully combine both achievement and affiliation preferences and enhance the company's performance while also caring for colleagues. Thus one can genuinely want an answer from the colleague of whom you ask 'How are you doing today?' even when under pressure of an urgent deadline (Kingdon and Kuhl, 2007).

Commitments and promises

In affiliation-oriented groups, promises and words of honour are assurances and generally they carry a great deal of weight. The character or reputation of the promise-giver might be at stake, and not being able to keep promises may lead to serious loss of face. On the other hand, in achievement-oriented contexts, promises are vague and don't mean very much; whereas commitments are serious, impersonal and often contractual. Promises are based on affiliation; commitments on achievement. Commitment involves dedicated efforts towards living up to it, usually within a time limit – unlike a promise.

Oftentimes, misunderstandings come from the fact that the words 'promise' and 'commitment' do not always translate well across cultures and languages. It may sound professional to native English speakers when Mexicans, for example, commit themselves to some project; but the nuance of commitment being binding is lost in Spanish. The word is understood in Spanish to imply responsibility and dedication, but no more.

Interaction and trust

How can you trust someone you have never met, and may never even meet? How much do you want to disclose about yourself, your personal preferences, and perhaps your family, knowing this information is going you-don't-know-where? Trust is not something that builds easily in affiliation-oriented cultures. Trust takes time, and you often have to prove that you are trustworthy.

There is an expression in French that expresses just that: you need to show *une patte blanche* (a white paw) in order to be considered trustworthy (Carroll, 1987).

When people are very open about who they are and what they do, they are likely to be more willing to share their personal lives; others are more cautious and inclined to retreat into their own shells. The question arises whether someone can be trusted who shares so much with someone they have never met?

Similarly, can you expect to be invited to a colleague's home after meeting them for the first time? How soon after getting to know them would you invite someone to your home? And what is the meaning in your culture of inviting someone from a different culture to your home for dinner? Is it the beginning of a deep relationship or is it something you would do for just anyone? And how much does personality play a role in this intricate dance, beyond any of the affiliation-achievement tendencies?

These are questions you may have to deal with on a regular basis when working or living across cultures, and even more so if you are leading a team and trying to build a personal relationship with each of your team members. Neglecting this affiliation versus achievement orientation, and assuming we will be 'on the same page' because we are all part of the same 'team' is the surest way to fail while building a team, or starting a new venture in another culture.

It personally took me a long time to understand how American people do business. In the fall of 1995, I was attending a professional tax class in the evening in a community college. During the first class, two people who had never met were casually chatting during recess. At one point, one said to the other, 'We can keep in touch if you are interested in my product.'

I was so flabbergasted that I couldn't believe what I heard: How can two people who've never met, who'd never had any relationship whatsoever, decide after two hours to keep in touch just because of a 'product'? You must be kidding!

It might be a good time to ask yourself how you develop relationships in a virtualised world; and why? How much of 'you' do you share in the open world?

A few vignettes

Here are several scenarios you may want to consider in the light of what we've just discussed. Imagine yourself playing an active role in each.

Email request

You are an external consultant to a US-based company. Over a period of two days, you've trained several expatriate families before their move to Europe, and based on the 'good vibes' you've developed with some of the trainees, you've been able to kept in touch with a few of them. You write to them once in a while, and your discussion is usually centred on professional issues, as well as their adaptation to a new environment.

In order to put together a new training proposal, you need to request some business information to one of those US expatriates you trained. You know, from emailing her a couple weeks prior, that she just spent a week skiing in the Alps with her husband (whom you know as well).

In your email, before addressing the work issue and suggesting a conference call, you write a few words in order to 'warm up the relationship' and ask about her vacation. The response comes back: very brief – barely any greeting and two lines about the business at hand.

Do you interpret this response as

1. Rude and unfriendly (affiliation-oriented);
2. Brief and to the point (achievement-oriented)?

Opening a bank account

You've become acquainted with Anita, an employee of a bank situated in a supermarket. Because of the bank's branch location (you cannot avoid seeing the bank and its employees as you enter the supermarket), it has been easy to stop by, chit-chat and start building a relationship with Anita. Although you haven't been involved in any business endeavours, Anita has been very forthcoming with information and you are starting to like her.

As it turns out, you need to open up a new business account as your relationship with your current bank is turning both sour and expensive. 'What a great coincidence!', you think. 'Let's go see Anita. I'm sure she will be happy to help us.'

You make an appointment and visit Anita on the agreed-upon day. Over the course of the business transaction, you naturally start talking about many different things, some of them quite personal – Anita is married to a person of Chinese descent, Mr Lee, and they decided to name their son Bruce. She also shares with you her cultural background, something you were curious about in the first place. There is in fact some Puerto Rican lineage in her family.

She takes care of all the procedures required for opening the account, including the different identification numbers, a new credit card, and you keep talking about various personal things while waiting for confirmation. In the end, you spend two and a half hours with Anita for a transaction that normally doesn't take more than 60 minutes.

On thinking over this meeting afterwards, you come to the conclusion that

1. It will be a pleasure to bank here (affiliation);
2. It took so long to set up my account I don't think that bank can be very efficient. I shall have to look elsewhere (achievement).

The leisure proposal

You plan to visit Janine, a Chinese-European woman, in Hong Kong, during a five-day vacation trip with your partner. Janine was introduced to you online by a friend and you have had fairly intimate email discussions, especially about Janine's brother who seems to be suffering from a mental affliction. You've showed concern for her brother and tried to reassure her that everything would be fine. You have told her how keen you are to meet her in person and explained that your partner will be with you.

The two of you have excitedly discussed places to visit and things to see in Hong Kong; but three days before your trip Janine sends you a couple of itineraries along with many options and suggestions for what to do in Hong Kong. It is plain she wants to organise your entire stay and accompany you throughout. However, you would also want to spend some time alone with your partner, though the last thing you want to do is to offend Janine. You decide on the following:

1. You and your partner fall in with Janine's plans (affiliation);
2. You stick to your own itinerary, informing Janine of this very politely and inviting her to dinner at your hotel (achievement).

Write your own scenario!

Can you come up with your own achievement-affiliation scenario, perhaps recalling a situation you were involved in?

Affiliation-achievement and other cultural dimensions

The cultural dimension most closely associated with affiliation and achievement is allegiance to the collective (affiliation) versus the individual (achievement). The more group-minded people are, the more they want to build a relationship with group members in order to be accepted and belong. In some cultures, especially those where relationships are tightly woven, affiliation and belonging can take a long, long time.

The time spent to invest into those relationships may appear as incredibly long or as a waste of time to individualists who are used to more flexible networks, and more contextual ways of building relationships. More individualistically minded people don't feel they need to spend ten years in an area to start getting accepted; and moving away from a community or neighbourhood doesn't represent such a tremendous uprooting, it is mainly a fact of life. Time is in flux, people come and go, and so do we.

The belonging factor, and the 'perks' that come with collectivism, such as protection, acceptance, favours, kinship, may come at a fairly high price, which may be seen at times by individualists as loss of autonomy and a forced dependency. Consider the situation of an Asian woman whose well-connected banking father helped her obtain a summer internship in a high-level institution in Singapore. For over ten years, and despite the fact that the connection between the woman and the institution was no longer alive, the father requested his daughter to send a Chinese New Year card to his contact as a way to express her gratitude – and indeed, to maintain his face. Would you have happily moved on after a year and forgotten the contact person at the institution?

Mainstream white US culture is individualistic and achievement-oriented. From an affiliation perspective, something that surprises many visitors is how Americans relate to their families. Consider a social gathering or a religious club in which people come together to carry out some sort of activity. Stephanie and David are the local leaders of such a group, and have two children, Jonathan and Sara. This is a fairly small group and everyone knows them; but David will always refer in conversation to 'my daughter' and 'my wife'.

It is significant that David, a member of an individualistic society, used the word 'my', but the relationship having been established in the group, there is no need to claim this kind of ownership. Everyone would know that Sara is David's daughter and Stephanie his wife.

In societies that truly value affiliation, once connections are established and people know each other, they will speak each other's names on a regular basis. Names relate to human beings and act as identifiers. Names also reinforce connections within the group, and strengthen the power (or 'glue') of affiliation.

Bridging the gap

Questioning ourselves forces us to review the basic assumptions we have about life and people. It allows us to unearth preferences that we often take for granted because they are shared by everyone in our culture and because we have been conditioned to believe it is the proper way to address someone or answer a question. Many people as children learn some version of the golden rule 'Do unto others as you would have them do unto you.' But this may not apply in intercultural relationships, since it is very dangerous to make decisions about another people's preferences based on our own, culturally driven, assumptions. If there's a level where cultures do not cross and communicate well, it is certainly at the hidden level of assumptions. Therefore the 'platinum' rule might be: 'Do unto others as they would like you to do unto them.' Treat them according to their own preferences.

Discussion points and questions

Asselin argues the importance, in communicating across cultures, of sharing thoughts and feelings. A counter-argument is that not everybody wants this degree of self-disclosure, nor do they seek it from others. How do you feel about this? Can you relate your response to a preference for affiliation versus achievement?

Behavioural scientists report that some people have an intense need to achieve, and McClelland (1955) with his associates at Harvard University studied this over a twenty-year period. The research led him to believe that the need for achievement is a distinct human motive. In his *acquired-needs* theory McClelland proposed that individuals' specific needs are acquired over time and shaped by life experiences. He reasoned that most needs can be classified as being for *achievement, affiliation* or *power*, and that people's effectiveness at work or in any other context is influenced by a preference for one of these three (while not excluding the other two). McClelland's theory sometimes is referred to as the *three-need theory* or as the *learned needs theory*.

Asselin has summarised the major differences between orientations towards achievement and affiliation respectively. He does not discuss the motivation of power. However, do you think that perhaps a strong need for achievement is tied up with a need for power, or perhaps control? Thus relationship-oriented people may agree with Asselin on the advantages of self-disclosure in overcoming cultural communication barriers. On the other hand, people with a strong need for achievement, as Asselin indicates, may be more motivated to satisfy their own needs – to get what they want – rather than forming relationships.

Can you think of examples from your own experience that might suggest your preference? And can you suggest some pointers for managers of work teams on how most effectively to motivate individualistic, achievement-oriented and collectivist, affiliation-oriented teams and team members?

Case study: North Korea renews South overture

The following news item is a good example, at a national level, of an Asian government policy (i.e., the policy of a collectivist society) that combines an apparent need both for achievement/power and affiliation. It demonstrates a well-known negotiation tactic: bullying followed by wooing (the 'bad cop, good cop' phenomenon!)

In January 2011 the reunification committee of the government of North Korea made an approach to reopen talks with the South. This was the latest in a series of conciliatory gestures, asking for 'unconditional and early' talks. Earlier in the same week Seoul officials had dismissed a similar offer, deriding it as 'propaganda'; but agreed to review the latest proposals from Pyongyang.

These overtures from North Korea followed the sinking of a Southern warship in March 2010, apparently destroyed by a Northern torpedo, with the loss of 46 lives, though the North denied the attack. In retaliation the South held large-scale military exercises close to the maritime border. Then, on 23 November 2010, the North infuriated the South by shelling one of its islands and killing four people.

However, the following January the North issued no more statements threatening war and retaliation. Instead it made offers of talks and overtures for peace.

News reports around the world quoted the North's Committee for the Peaceful Reunification of Korea as saying: 'The South Korean authorities should discard any unnecessary misgiving, open their hearts and positively respond to the North's proposal and measure.'

The committee suggested talks should take place later in January or early February and that the North would reopen a liaison office with the South at a joint factory complex just north of the demilitarised zone that divides the Korean peninsula. In response, Unification Ministry spokesman Chun Hae-sung told the Associated Press news agency that the statement would be considered, but noted that no formal request had been received.

Sources

'North Korea renews South overture', 8 January 2011; http://www.bbc.co.uk.
'North Korea says it wants to reopen talks with the South', 7 January 2011; http://news1.ghananation.com.

Discussion

An agenda is a plan or list of things to do, based on an order of priorities. The above report begins with what appears to be lowest on the list of priorities for the North Korean government – conciliation – after being accused of sinking a South Korean warship. Top priority seems to have been to deny any involvement. The next, apparently, was to 'save face' – responding to the South's military exercises by shelling one of its islands. Having made this defiant gesture, next on the list was an offer of peace talks – though the offer was worded carefully to imply it was the duty of the South to make a positive response. Only when the Seoul officials described the offer as propaganda did the North Korean government finally ask for 'unconditional and early' talks.

Political agendas and the way the items are put into practice can be compared to workplace agendas drawn up by management in collaboration or conflict with worker representatives, including internal and external politics. Harris and Moran (2007) have identified the following eight categories of cultural systems and subsystems that affect these orders of workplace communication:

1. **Kinship:** The degree of priority given to kinship in employing workers, appointing supervisors, granting promotions, etc. In collectivist countries such as Turkey it is 'natural' to employ relatives; in individualistic countries such as Australia this is seen negatively as nepotism.

2. **Formal and informal education:** The general level of education in the given society will affect the quality of the labour pool. Priorities of recruitment and staffing, levels of pay, provision of training and style of leadership will be set according to this factor. To give just one example, the agenda for firms in developed countries with high rates of pay for skilled workers is commonly to outsource production to less developed economies to gain from the presence of cheap, relatively unskilled labour.

3. **Economy:** The state and conditions of the national economy automatically set priorities for sourcing, distribution, pay and incentives, and repatriation of capital by foreign investors.

4. **Government:** Political constraints on foreign investors are a major factor in their freedom to do business in host countries; and they have to adapt their plans accordingly.

5. **Religion:** Do workers bring religion into the workplace? What priority needs to be given to workers' religious beliefs to maintain and increase motivation and productivity?

6. **Associations, formal, informal:** The extent to which the labour force is unionised will affect employment agendas. For example, in non-unionised workplaces informal leaders may exert a strong influence on their fellow-workers' performance and productivity. It may be a top priority for managers to liaise with these key figures. In strongly unionised organisations negotiations with union representatives will come first on any agenda for change.

7. **Healthcare:** All employers want and need healthy workers. The general standard of health in the given society and the presence or absence of government healthcare programmes come high on the list of factors that affect the cost of local employment. For example, in countries where systemic health problems exist, such as Aids, employers may need to subsidise healthcare. In countries such as the US where public health care is very limited, employers need to offer health insurance to attract employees.

8. **Recreation:** What priority to workers give respectively to work and leisure? Is the local agenda one of 'work to live' as in, say, Mexico, or 'live to work' as in, say, Japan or Germany?

Question for classroom discussion

How do students prioritise these eight factors in their own society or societies?

WOMEN AND WORK	Janet Haynes

Introduction

While the role of white, middle-class women in the US workplace has been widely studied, the literature reveals significant gaps in accounts of the roles of certain women, specifically women of colour, in the fields of organisational behaviour; leadership, management and mentoring. This auto-ethnographic study relates the experiences of an African-American woman in the workplace.

In an auto-ethnographic study, the researcher becomes the data collector. Ethnography is defined as the process of providing a face to fieldwork and culture, with the scholarly conclusion as ethnographic. Ethnography has been described as the capturing, interpreting and explaining the way in which people in groups or alone try to make sense out of their lives, their worlds and their experiences. An auto-ethnographic study, then, would be one person capturing, interpreting and explaining ways in which the world and personal experiences impacts on their life.

Friday, 17 September 2010: how to order lunch

At a 1978 leadership meeting that included management trainees, the waitress came to the table to take what I thought would be 'our' order. She took the order of everyone around me and beside me, ignored me and quickly walked away without saying a word. Five minutes later I tried in vain to get her attention.

I planned to forget about my being hungry and simply drink a Coke. I became more and more frustrated as she delivered drinks, bread and bread plates to the table and all the while continuing to ignore me. Finally, after I thought I would die from a dry throat and suffering through the knowing sympathetic smiles and impotent behaviour of my peers, I turned to the man sitting next to me.

Don was also in the management-training programme and it was rumoured that he enjoyed privilege because his father was a corporate officer. I knew he had privilege because he had no competition for anything including the coveted manager jobs and training assignments as long as he continued to be white and male. I was glad Don was sitting there because I thought we were friends. That is, until he feigned ignorance and forced me to tell him why I needed him to order my Coke.

The insult continued as he chided me painfully because the Coke was the only item I ordered. Who in their right mind would order food in an eating establishment that obviously did not want to serve them? This was 1978, not 1958, and I learnt that my corporate power suit, pearls and briefcase meant I was well dressed for success, but otherwise invisible.

I was reminded of the story of Denny's and the US Secret Service Agents (*Washington Post*, 1993). Twenty-one Secret Service Agents, assigned to detail then-President Clinton's visit to the US Naval Academy in Annapolis, Maryland, went to Denny's Restaurant for breakfast. Six black agents were allegedly denied service. A subsequent investigation by the US Department of Justice found that Denny's waitresses routinely refused to serve blacks. They were often forced to pre-pay for meals, and management also had 'black-out' periods where employees were instructed to limit the number of black customers in the restaurant.

Background to my story

Historically, African-American women entered the corporate workforce in great numbers as a result of Affirmative Action or US federal laws from 1961 mandating certain percentages of minority employees – often affording special funding and business tax consideration as compliance incentives (CRS Report, 2005; Dale, 0000). However, the systems approach that liberalised the workplace also paralysed its progress.

In 1996, there was only one female Fortune 500 CEO. In 1997 the Catalyst Foundation (Catalyst Foundation, 2000) revealed that African-American women were the most underrepresented group in the workplace. Non-white women represented 1.3 per cent of corporate officers in 400 of the Fortune 500 companies, and in 1999 there were still only two women CEOs, in a year in which 46.5 per cent of the working population was female. In 2009 the first African-American woman CEO (Ursula Burns of Xerox) joined 14 women and four African-American men in leadership roles.

In 2010, the *Money Magazine* annual survey revealed there were 15 female Fortune 500 CEOs, with Xerox noted as the only company that replaced a female CEO with another female.

Various analysts note that these 15 female-led corporations produced primarily gender-specific marketed products and services, specifically food and cosmetics. These roles are commonly referred to (along with other stereotypical positions) as the 'pink ghetto', and often advancement opportunities seem to be limited to these areas of soft business rather than areas of high visibility including financial responsibility. Other contemporary questions include why so few women are competing for the top positions at Fortune corporations. There is no lack of qualified female leadership, and one reason why so few women make it to the top may be that men are 'guarding' these top positions for themselves.

The earning gap by gender and race is startling (Conley, 1999). In 1980, 42.6 per cent of the working population was female; 12 per cent of these women were African-American. For every dollar earned by Caucasian men, Caucasian women earned 65 cents, African-American women earned 59 cents and Hispanic women 55 cents. In 1998, for every dollar earned by Caucasian men, Caucasian women earned 78 cents, African-American women 67 cents, and Hispanic women 56 cents.

According to the US Current Population Survey and the National Committee on Pay Equity (AAUW, n.d.), by 2006 the gap had narrowed and women's pay rates increased by 73.5 per cent for Caucasian women, 63.6 per cent for African-American women, and 51.7 per cent for Hispanic women. The 2010 US economy further closed the pay gap as women earned a record-breaking 83 per cent of the median working wage for men. This can be attributed to the high number of jobs lost in the manufacturing and construction industries – typically dominated by men.

Even at the top women are paid exactly 15 per cent less than their male counterparts. This is because their compensation packages – including stock options, cash bonuses and perks – are not equal to those of male executives, although their base pay may be higher. The Paycheck Fairness Act was pending in the 2010 fall congressional session to address loopholes in the Equal Pay Act.

Affirmative action legislation

The actual phrase 'affirmative action' (Sykes, 1995) was first used in President John F. Kennedy's 1961 Executive Order requiring federal contractors to 'take affirmative action to ensure that applicants are employed, and that employees are treated during employment, without regard to their race, creed, colour, or national origin'. In 1967, Lyndon Johnson expanded the Executive Order to include affirmative action requirements to benefit women. Within the next ten years corporations and universities began recruiting earnestly, in order to remain eligible for federal funding, contracts and other monetary awards. By the 1980s, training programmes became the hallmark of corporate America in an attempt to assimilate different groups and to retrain members of old bastions of society who opposed the concept of affirmative action.

Much of the opposition to affirmative action legislation is on the grounds of so-called 'reverse discrimination' and 'unwarranted preferences'. In fact, under the law as written in Executive Orders and interpreted by the courts, anyone benefiting from affirmative action must have relevant and valid job or educational qualifications. However, it has taken decades for some corporations to demonstrate recognition of the law. Their policies result in minimal promotion of minority females, and there continues to be a problem in the hiring, retraining and promoting of African-American women, which suggests that racism still exists in the corporate world.

Research (Insala, n.d.) has demonstrated that employees who have mentors, training and leadership opportunities are promoted more often than those who do not. Unfortunately, African-American women are managed, mentored and treated differently than others in the corporation for a variety of reasons, one of which is stereotyping. For example, senior managers often seem unwilling to assume responsibility for mentoring and networking with women in subordinate positions. Thus, though women may be aware of opportunities to plan their careers they are denied access to informal networks that are routinely created by and for male co-workers.

Thus race clearly affects African-American women in the corporation. It has been defined as a limiting factor to promotional opportunities, pay advancement and a negative factor in interpersonal relationships. Consequently, race affects economic parity, educational opportunities and becomes a limiting factor in daily aspects of contemporary society even as many in the US celebrate the historic first election of an African-American President in 2008.

Leadership

Leadership positions, both in hierarchical and team-based organisational structures, woefully lack the inclusion of African-American women. Corporations have failed until quite recently to classify job types or to pay, promote, train and retain employees in an equitable manner. The result has been a system that inadvertently supports race, class differences, the unequal distribution of wealth and any subsequent legacies from these imbalances.

Gender- and ethnicity-based marginalisation of women and minorities appears to be systemic in US corporations. In 1991, the late attorney Trina Grillo (Grillo and Wildman, 1991; see also hooks, 1995) compared her experience of the medical illness of cancer with her experience of racism as a social illness. She described how her first perceptual filter, through which viewed the world, was of race; but after a diagnosis of cancer, this became her supreme preoccupation. For this reason, Grillo preferred the term 'white supremacy' to describe the perceptual filter through which white people viewed the exploitation of African-Americans and others of colour as the 'only' world view.

Grillo's account of racism is an auto-ethnography. It is a form of autobiographical personal narrative that explores the writer's experience of life, focusing on her subjective experience rather than the beliefs and practices of others. Thus her writings are limited to her perceptions of lived experiences, not drawn from the documented experiences of a wide sample of African-American women in the corporate workplace. While there is considerable evidence that her experiences are similar to those of other African-American women, her data and journal are unique.

Nevertheless it is possible to generalise that the disparity in income between African-American and Caucasian women reflects a societal trend that does not challenge or question the dominant patriarchy. The underlying cause would appear systemic, based on the history of wealth and power in the US. American history and wealth accumulation by race explain the difference in achievement and success between these two groups of women. Family structure is an indicator of wealth transfer, accumulation, and the effect on net worth is a causal role in family structure.

In 1865, African-Americans owned 0.5 per cent of the total worth of the US post-slavery. By 1990, or 135 years post-slavery, African-Americans owned 1 per cent of the total wealth. Further, at every income level, African-Americans have less net income, wealth and assets than Caucasians. Fifty per cent of poor (defined as annual income of $15,000 or less in 1992) African-American families have no assets, compared to less than 23 per cent of Caucasian families.

In 1999, the US Department of Labor reported that for middle-class Americans, as defined by median income of $35,000–$50,000, Caucasians have assets valued at $81,000 and African-Americans have assets at $40,000, or 50 per cent less than Caucasians. In upper incomes, Caucasians average three times the wealth of African-Americans. Explanations are not justifiable by savings patterns because statistical averages indicate that Caucasians saved 10 per cent and African-Americans saved 11 per cent, or no statistical difference.

Median Caucasian middle-class families enjoyed assets of approximately $72,000 compared to $16,000 for middle-class African-Americans. The disparity allows for financial hardship without necessarily requiring the liquidation of assets to survive. In contrast, the majority of assets owned by African-Americans (or the $16,000) are not liquid assets, but necessities that include a home and car.

It is clear that African-Americans have always earned less than Caucasians, and over the years these earnings shortfalls have resulted in fewer savings, less investment and less transfer to the succeeding generations. Over time, less income can result in vast differences in asset accumulation. In addition, however, there is another dimension to the explanation: Social and economic institutions have historically and systematically restricted asset accumulation among African-Americans. Prior to the 1964 Civil Rights Act, many mortgage companies refused to grant loans to non-Caucasians.

According to Conley (1999), it is wealth in the US, not education or occupation, that sustains the greatest inequality. Given the correlation between wealth and race, perhaps it is not surprising that racism has always existed in the US and continues today, often subtly and practised unconsciously by its perpetrators.

Inequality in the media

This hegemony is historical. A Public Service Broadcasting article on the role of women in the Suffrage Movement (n.d.) completely ignored the role of African-American women in this movement, which spanned over seventy years from the early 1830s to 1920s. African-American women had many voices in the movement, including Maria Stewart, Fannie Barrier Williams and others. However, they are not recognised for their participation. Contemporary literature and academic journals offer only footnotes and one-liners regarding the present role of African-American women in the organisation. The lack of reference in contemporary media is representative of the daily experiences of women of colour in and out of the corporation.

Resistance to inequality

In November 1996, Texaco agreed to pay $176.1 million to settle, at that time, the largest race discrimination suit in the history of the United States (Matthews Smith et al. v Texaco, Inc.).

In November 2000, four African-American salaried employees who alleged discrimination in performance evaluations, pay and subsequent promotions, won a settlement of $192 million from the Coca-Cola Company – the largest race discrimination lawsuit ever (Winter, 2000). These four alleged that their Caucasian peers were paid on average $26,000 more annually.

As of December 2010, over 1.5 million current and former female employees were represented in an ongoing class action lawsuit (Dukes v. Wal-Mart) (Maatman and Maechtlen, 2010). This case began on the grounds that women were paid less than men for equal work and promotion policies were inequitable. In the fall of 2010, Wal-Mart petitioned the US Supreme Court for review at an estimated cost of $1 billion. Interestingly enough, Wal-Mart was not appealing on the discrimination ruling but on the grounds that the court's decision should not have included 1.5 million plaintiffs. Subsequent class-action lawsuits have been filed against Abercrombie and Fitch (Leung, 2004), McCormick and Schmick's (Lieff Cabraser, 2008), Walgreen's (Cole, 2007), UPS (SDNN, 2009), Denny's (University of Wisconsin, School of Business, 2001), Target (Disability Rights Advocates, 2006), Costco (Pierce, 2010) and Eastman Kodak (classactionlawsuitsinthenews.com, 2010).

In 2007, one of the largest race-based class-action lawsuits in history was settled in the 9th District US Federal Court (Satchell et al. v FedEx). The settlement was in excess of US$50 million, compensating thousands of FedEx Express employees who were discriminated against by being disciplined, terminated, trained or denied promotional opportunity by this self-styled 'people first' corporation. FedEx was also placed under a four-year monitoring court, scheduled to end in 2011.

Discussion

'Affirmative action' refers to policies for taking into consideration employment factors that include race, colour, religion, gender or national origin. The intention of such policies is to benefit underrepresented groups in the workforce at the expense of majority groups, usually to counter the effects of a history of discrimination. That is, to increase the representation of women and minorities in areas of employment, education, public contracting, health programmes and business from which they have been historically excluded.

Haynes argues persuasively the case for affirmative action in the workplace. To balance her account, some of the arguments against affirmative action include the following:

1. It is unfair to judge applicants on anything other than their merits. Job applicants' racial heritage is not a legitimate factor to take into consideration because it is outside candidates' control. It is impossible for employers to consider every aspect of a candidate's background when making decisions on whom to employ. Why focus on race when there are so many other things that differentiate applicants from one another?

2. Affirmative action does not lead to true diversity – diversity of opinion is important in an organisation, not racial diversity. Affirmative action provides an advantage to some people because of the colour of their skin. This is not an attribute that is relevant to the missions of most companies. Affirmative action gives preferential treatment based exclusively on race, which is a purely external characteristic.

3. In many cases, affirmative action does not achieve its goal of helping disadvantaged minority groups. What it does is perpetuate socio-economic inequalities by making it easy for members of racial minorities from privileged backgrounds to get good jobs while not helping members of the lower classes.

Haynes describes her report as 'auto-ethnographic'. This kind of qualitative research, in which data are gathered from the researcher's own experience, is a valid form of research and yields a rich harvest, especially when combined, as here, with references to other, more quantitative studies. As an African-American woman, Haynes reports her experiences and those of others in the US workplace.

Questions

1. Can you think of any experiences you have had, in school, at university, in social situations or in the workplace, that you feel disadvantaged you? If so, how do you explain this? Did the incident concern you individually or as a representative of a nation, a race, a religion, or other group?

2. Are you in favour of affirmative action programmes as discussed above and by Haynes? Why? Why not?

Case study: Culture of fear

The following report is of another kind of workplace discrimination, against practices that might lay managers (in this case teachers) open to charges of assault against subordinates (or students). As the report testifies, 'unacceptable' behaviour in such cases may be a matter of debate, and proven acts of assault or indecency by teachers may lead to overreaction by those who have teachers' best interests at heart. The result may be that the innocent – teachers and pupils – are (unnecessarily?) disadvantaged.

In 2010 the Musicians' Union in the UK issued a training video for music teachers. One piece of advice was that touching pupils during a music lesson could expose tutors, who often teach in one-to-one sessions, to charges of inappropriate behaviour. The video advised teachers to avoid all physical contact with their pupils.

The Education Secretary, Michael Gove, responded indignantly in letters to the union's general secretary, John Smith, and other youth and music bodies. In part he wrote:

> By telling your music teachers that they should avoid any physical contact with children, it sends out completely the wrong message. It plays to a culture of fear among both adults and children, reinforcing the message that any adult who touches a child is somehow guilty of inappropriate contact.

In an interview the Education Secretary said that teachers, students and parents should move away from this presumption and that the Department for Education was taking steps to restore common sense to the whole topic. He insisted that there are many occasions when it is appropriate and indeed necessary for music tutors to be in physical contact with their pupils, and to feel confident they can demonstrate adequately how to play an instrument and how to control and improve pupils' technique.

> Whether it's adjusting the position of a violin or demonstrating how to handle drumsticks, showing how a trombone slide should work or introducing new subtleties in oboe playing, teachers should be trusted to touch children without feeling they are somehow transgressing the rules of appropriate conduct.

He added that the Government was publishing shorter, clearer guidance on the subject and changing the way allegations of abuse against teachers are dealt with.

But the Musicians' Union was unrepentant, reporting that careers have been ruined by false allegations and that instrumental music teachers were particularly vulnerable as they are often alone with pupils when they give lessons and they should find alternatives to touching. Diane Widdison, national organiser for teaching at the Musicians' Union, said the union existed to protect its members' careers and the children they teach:

> When allegations are made against music teachers they are suspended immediately while an investigation is carried out and their careers are damaged or ruined even if they are declared innocent. In one recent case the parents of a child learning the guitar complained that the teacher had touched their child's finger to pluck a guitar string.

She added that it should not be necessary to touch children to teach them how to play an instrument.

> In many cases having to be more creative and find alternatives to touching reinforces the learning process because it ensures that children are thinking for themselves. This is a more effective way of teaching and means that children remember the correct posture and positions when they are practising alone.

Sources

BBC News 2011. 'Musicians Union: "No-touch rule protects music teachers"', 7 January; http://www.bbc.co.uk/news/education-12140281.

Harrison, D. 2010. 'Don't touch pupils' fingers, music teachers are told', *The Telegraph*, 12 December; http://www.telegraph.co.uk/education/educationnews/8196276/Dont-touch-pupils-fingers-music-teachers-are-told.html.

Shepherd, J. 2011. 'Michael Gove condemns charities' "don't touch" warning to teachers', *Guardian*, 7 January; http://www.guardian.co.uk/education/2011/jan/07/michael-gove-charities-warning.

Discussion

The above news report is an example of what US sociologist Frank Füredi argues is a much wider 'climate of fear' (2002, 2007). He argues that fear has become a common experience for people in the Western world. He suggests that they live in terror of disease, abuse, 'stranger danger', environmental devastation and terrorist attacks. They are bombarded with reports of new concerns for their safety and that of their children, and urged to take greater precautions and seek more protection.

But compared to the past, or to the developing world, people in contemporary Western societies have much less familiarity with pain, suffering, debilitating disease and death. They actually enjoy an unprecedented level of personal safety. When confronted with events like the destruction of the World Trade Center, fear for the future is inevitable. But the greater danger in Western culture is the tendency to fear achievements that represent the constructive nature of humanity, such as genetically engineered food, genetic research, the health dangers of mobile phones. Facts, however, often fail to support scare stories; and obsession with theoretical risks distracts from dealing with the old-fashioned dangers that have always threatened humanity. Füredi describes this as a loss of 'cultural nerve' and identifies the following five trends in the rise of risk aversion in Western cultures.

First, there is a shift in moral reaction to harm. People no longer believe in natural disasters or acts of God but suspect that someone is behind a disaster – an irresponsible corporation or a cowardly bureaucrat. Accidents have been redefined as preventable injuries. For example, when a teenager dies in a car crash, media reports do not regret that bad things randomly happen to good people, but that local roads don't have enough guard rails, or that laws should prevent teenagers driving with friends. Füredi sees this kind of thinking as a superstition that every event has a deeper meaning. In earlier centuries acts of God or the work of the Devil were explanations for misfortune. Today political and corporate conspiracies are to blame for every catastrophe.

A second contributor to a culture of risk aversion, according to Füredi, is that harm is represented in increasingly dramatic fashion. People are no longer expected to rise above adversity or encouraged to get on with their lives after they experience a hard knock. They are portrayed in the media as suffering victims in need of counselling.

Even the timescale of disaster has expanded. According to chaos theory, anything that happens now produces consequences that cannot be predicted; and even the flapping of a butterfly's wing may eventually cause a tornado (Stewart, 1989). Thus people should worry not only about what they do today but what might happen decades down the road; but treating people as permanent victims and constantly speculating about possible future harm can end in social and economic paralysis.

Füredi's third factor is fear that actions like inventing new medicines, chemicals and energy sources might have unknowable, irreversible and ultimately catastrophic effects. Though more people are living longer and healthier lives, life is perceived as very dangerous and worst-case scenarios proliferate: What if an asteroid hits us? What if biotech wheat gets out of control? What if Iran is giving weapons of mass destruction to terrorists? Worst-case thinking decreases cultural capacity to deal with uncertainty. Risk becomes something to avoid, not an opportunity to be seized.

The fourth trend that Füredi opposes is the treatment of safety as a moral principle, as in the phrases 'safe spaces', 'safe medicine' and 'safe sex'.

He identifies a fifth trend in an emerging redefinition of personhood: that people no longer believe they have the capacity to cope and to act with individual autonomy. They are increasing represented as helplessly addicted to sex, alcohol or shopping. More and more groups – children, women, minorities – are described as 'vulnerable'. Public policies are focused on reassuring and supporting people, and risk-taking is stigmatised.

Finally, Füredi makes the point that though there are many creative entrepreneurs working hard today in innovative and positive ways to create new technologies, nevertheless in their personal lives they are very precautionary. They insist on eating pesticide-free products, condemn cigarette smoking, drink alcohol very moderately, and wear helmets, knee and elbow pads to go bike riding.

Questions

How does all this relate to the international communication management? One answer can be found in corporate advertising, which is seldom openly about business or profits. Instead, advertisements show blue skies and an interracial mixture of babies playing happily together. Corporations find it difficult to affirm culturally what they are really doing, that is, creating products, providing services and making profits. To be called a risk-taker used to be considered a compliment; it now carries generally negative connotations.

What might be some lessons here for international managers? It is all very well to diagnose a contemporary culture of fear, but suggestions are needed for restoring people's belief in progress and the power of human creativity.

PRACTISING WORKPLACE DIVERSITY – PERSPECTIVES, PITFALLS AND POSSIBILITIES	Sine Nørholm Just and Robyn Remke

Introduction

Across the globe, workforces and organisations are changing for many reasons. For example, women are entering the labour market for the first time in some countries and positioning themselves as equal to men in other contexts; many countries are experiencing increased population diversity; some workforces are aging, others cannot find room for large groups of unemployed young people. Some countries are facing the effects of outsourcing, while others deal with a so-called brain drain.

This report focuses primarily on how organisations in 'Western' or 'developed' countries have defined diversity and what practices help not only to cope with, but also to benefit from, diversity as an ongoing process.

What is diversity?

As described in the preceding section, the concept of diversity originated in the US in the form of affirmative action programmes that were created in response to federal mandates to reduce racial and later sexual discrimination in the workplace (Johnson and Packer, 1987). Though affirmative action was later supplemented by or replaced by the label 'equal opportunities', the concept of diversity was quickly picked up by British scholars and practitioners. It is now used globally to describe organisations or groups that have achieved a high degree of difference within themselves – and is also a useful concept for organisations that see internal difference as a prudent and morally good objective.

The term diversity is used to define individuals based on a specific identifying feature (e.g., race, sex, religion, physical and mental ability) as well as link them to larger marginalised groups (e.g., women, elderly, Muslims).

Initiatives to hire more women or ethnic minorities are often called diversity initiatives because they focus on the hiring of individuals who represent and are tied to larger marginalised groups. Diversity has even been used to describe individuals' working or communication styles because everyone's is unique in some way.

We often associate diversity with the managerial phrase 'diversity management', a strategy for managing the changing demographic of employees and customers and balancing inequalities in the workplace. Thus diversity management may be defined as a proactive attempt to realise the potential benefit to the organisation of recognition and respect for the diversity of its employees.

Perspectives defining diversity

Diversity can be defined and explained in a number of different ways. For instance, Jewson and Mason (1986) differentiate between equality of opportunity (a liberal view) and equality of outcomes (a more radical view). That is, should all employees be treated equally in order to have the same chance of succeeding or should it be ensured that everyone has the same success?

The liberal view argues that equality of opportunity 'exists when all individuals are enabled freely and equally to compete for social rewards' (Jewson and Mason, 1986: 313). From this vantage point, it is the role of managers and policy makers to remove all systemic barriers that prevent workers access to equal opportunity.

In contrast, from the radical perspective, measures of success are politically situated within white, heterosexual male norms. Therefore, merely working with individuals to achieve equality, as defined through organisational normative measures, will never suffice as a diversity management strategy. Intervening practices that dismantle organisational discrimination such as the use of hiring and promoting quotas are important for achieving diversity.

Rejecting the radical/liberal dichotomy, Cockburn (1989) argues for approaching equal opportunity strategies (diversity) from a linear perspective, suggesting a short-term approach (equality of outcomes) accompanied by long-term organisational cultural change (equality of opportunity). She proposes a middle ground between the desire to implement forced diversity and the need for it to be rooted in the organisational culture.

Beginning from this first division, organisations define and experience diversity in many different ways. Ely and Thomas (2001: 266), for instance, identify three different perspectives, as follows: discrimination-and-fairness; access-and-legitimacy; and integration-and-learning.

The discrimination-and-fairness model

Like the liberal model, the discrimination-and-fairness paradigm is based on the premise that systemic discrimination has prevented the advancement and equal treatment of certain groups. In light of governmental mandates and cultural pressures, organisations are forced to address systemic discrimination and create organisations that foster equal opportunity and fair treatment. Unlike more traditional affirmative action or quota-based policies, which address systemic discrimination with strict hiring and promoting practices (sometimes labelled reverse discrimination), the discrimination-and-fairness model addresses issues of diversity through organisational and cultural initiatives such as mentoring and training programmes.

While this model is designed to grant access to diverse employees, it contains the risk that, in an effort to treat all employees equally, organisational members often fail to make use of the diversity of the organisation, choosing, rather, to be colour- and gender-blind and thus not seeing 'how differences can be used as sources of individual and organisational effectiveness' (Thomas and Ely, 1996: 82).

A diverse organisation is, in this context, a more just and fair organisation, but not necessarily a more effective or creative one. This paradigmatic perspective also tends to constrain or close down conversations about more subtle and nuanced forms of discrimination.

The access-and-legitimacy model

While organisations adhering to the discrimination-and-fairness model tend to downplay difference in an effort to create fair and just workplaces, an access-and-legitimacy policy model is based on a different orientation. It assumes that different demographic groups think and experience the world differently. Therefore minority employees are hired because of their perceived difference from 'traditional' or 'normal' employees.

This strategy has its benefits: it helps organisations target and serve specific groups more accurately. However, it can also lead to discrimination in the workplace, namely, tokenism or 'tracking' employees into certain positions that then become less valued in the organisation. Even worse, some employees can feel exploited because of their identity and connections to certain communities and not for their talent as a worker.

The integration-and-learning model

Finally, organisations who adopt the integration-and-learning perspective view diversity as a 'potentially valuable resource ... not only at its [the organisation's] margins ... but at its core' (Ely and Thomas, 2001: 265). This perspective highlights the unique contributions of diverse members but does not constrain them to the margins of the organisation. Integration, not assimilation, and learning, not access, are the primary goals. While these goals are laudable, organisations must intentionally foster this framework in order to benefit from a diverse membership.

Further, the mere presence of difference within an organisation is not sufficient for an organisation to be diverse. Organisational demography, or the power structures of the organisation, must promote an integration-and-learning perspective for the difference to be experienced as diversity.

There are convincing critiques of the underlying assumptions about diversity that is shared by all perspectives. In particular, Nancy Fraser (1992) argues they create a false dichotomy between market and culture. She argues that equality will materialise only when the interdependent relationship between the economic and social spheres is reflected within organisational practices.

Nevertheless, the perspectives provide a first insight into the diversity of the very notion of diversity and also indicate that different organisations and their members practise and think differently about diversity.

Who is diverse?

In the English-language literature on the topic, diversity includes anyone considered a minority based on identity characteristics such as race, ethnicity and gender. The European Union is empowered to take legal action against acts of discrimination based on sex, racial or ethnic origin, religion or belief, disability, age and sexual orientation (EU Treaty, 2002, article 13). The fixedness of these characteristics is contested by some scholars (see Prasad et al., 2006), and some diversity management strategies now include other identity characteristics such as sexual orientation, religion, national heritage and ability. Even when the list of characteristics is expanded, however, it tends to divide employees into those who are diverse and those who are not.

While classifications of diverse individuals depend on specific organisational contexts, definitions of who will qualify as diverse also correspond with social composition. As demographic compositions of nations and regions change in light of immigration and population shifts, organisations will have to reflect those changes. For example, Risberg and Söderberg (2008) argue that many Danish organisations reflect the rather homogenous population of Denmark. However, in response to an influx of immigrants from Asia, Africa and the Middle East, some Danish organisations have taken initiatives to hire and promote workers from these regions. Similarly, some organisations in Western countries have workplace policies and strategies that enable employees to continue working as they age to help reduce the impact of the 'baby boom' generation retiring.

Why diversity?

Nearly all Western organisations today have a diversity strategy, perhaps because of government mandates and pressure from advocacy groups. Organisations tackle the challenge of diversity in different ways. Most agree tacitly that diversity is a good thing, though some view it as something they must address because their cultural environment has become more diverse, independent of external pressures or agendas. While the tacit acceptance of the need for diversity does not provide any further arguments, the opinion that diversity requires response may be proposed, as in the following section.

Diversity as an organisational reality that requires response

For those who take the former position, diversity is the recognition that society is now different and our workplaces should reflect this difference.

We can credit at least three influences that have helped to foster social change. First, civil rights and other labour movements have opened employment doors to traditionally marginalised individuals. Second, increased immigration to industrialised nations has diversified society and the pool of workers from which organisations hire. Therefore, it makes sense that organisations reflect the demographic changes occurring in their societies. Finally, as organisations grow and become more international, organisations desire to have their workforce reflect their global identity.

Organisational leaders who subscribe to this perspective may also assume that diversity will 'naturally' happen as more minority workers are hired and promoted in the organisation. This rationale is often used to resist proactive diversity management programmes, calling them unnecessary and intrusive. While there is certainly evidence that minority workers are gaining in organisational representation and status, the growth is often uneven, with certain occupations representing disproportionate numbers of minorities. The amount of time needed for most organisations to accurately reflect society in its diversity is, therefore, too long.

This position, moreover, fails to address the systemic barriers that minority workers face in the hiring and promotion process, wherefore it may ultimately result in more subtle forms of organisational discrimination. Even with governmental regulations encouraging diversification and equal opportunity in the workplace, multiple barriers still impede the achievement of minority workers and therefore limit organisational diversity. Specifically, because it is no longer legal in many countries to overtly discriminate on grounds of identity, much organisational discrimination takes a much more subtle and covert form, making it more difficult to address.

Diversity as an organisational possibility

Organisational leaders cite several other reasons for encouraging diversity. For many, the business argument is the most persuasive (Litvin, 2006). It stresses the benefits of diversity to the economic bottom line, as a way of reaching larger employee and customer bases; and gaining competitive advantage through increased creativity and innovation.

That said, much research suggests that forcing diversity in an organisation without supporting it culturally yields little success. Organisational leaders must consider the distribution of power and social dynamics within the organisation.

Some diversity strategies stem from a social justice rationale: a moral obligation to protect individuals' right to equal employment. In particular, some European organisations frame their diversity strategies within a corporate social responsibility (CSR) discourse Boxenham, 2006).

Barriers to organisational diversity

The glass ceiling, mommy track, sticky floor, leaky pipeline, on- and off-ramps and labyrinth are all metaphors used to explain why, even in the age of sophisticated diversity management strategies, minority workers have not gained organisational equality. Each illustrates how minority workers, particularly women, have difficulty in achieving management and leadership positions in organisations. The oldest metaphor, the glass ceiling, highlights the invisible barrier that many women in management or career-track positions experience as they are passed over for promotion. Similarly, the sticky floor metaphor describes the ways in which minority workers are stuck in lower organisational positions, unable to move upwards in the organisation.

More recently, Eagly and Carli (2007: 64) have used the term labyrinth to describe the 'complex journey towards a goal worth striving for'. While many would describe their career as a journey with twists and turns, the labyrinth describes a journey that is difficult (because of systemic discrimination) but not impossible to navigate. This metaphor is slightly more optimistic, but organisations can still make the labyrinth less complicated and difficult through effective diversity management programmes.

The mommy track metaphor (Schwartz, 1989) speaks to the subtle ways in which workplace norms foster and maintain discriminatory practices. It highlights the ways in which managers track female employees into organisational positions that are considered more 'mommy friendly,' often regardless of whether the workers have children or not. Often these positions are also less prestigious and have less potential for organisational promotion. They are 'ghettoized second-class jobs' for women (Kim, 2010). What is essential to understand about this type of discrimination is that female employees do not necessarily ask for these positions – the workers are tracked without their consent, and often with little proof or evidence that they needed this tracking.

While logistical reasons are often cited for the reduction of a female worker's position ('This promotion requires additional travel that you cannot perform because you have children'), it is more likely that employees are tracked because they violate traditional expectations for a particular position. Professionals are supposed to have a particular identity; they should look and sound in a certain way that does not include members of most minority groups. Professional people traditionally are controlled, disciplined, healthy, androgynous and rational (Trethewey et al., 2006). Women, persons of colour, those who speak with an accent or are disabled, have in the past not been considered professional and must not only prove their worthiness on a par with everyone else in the organisation, but must also secure their right to participate in the first place.

Finally, organisational leaders often state that they do not need diversity strategies because they do not consider identity when hiring or promoting; they only hire or promote based on qualifications. This claim is problematic because employers often define employee qualifications in very narrow terms, often tied to educational and networking opportunities based on identity and relationship to specific social groups.

Managers tend to associate with and promote workers similar to themselves and consider these similarities as personal qualifications. These are skills and traits that are not necessarily learnt in college or training programmes, but are considered very important when hiring and promoting. Qualities such as being a team player are important social skills, but can reflect a rather narrow normative working style that is not necessarily better than other working styles. Minority workers with less familiarity with traditional workplaces may not know the unwritten rules that govern the organisational culture and therefore do not foster or display the 'qualifications' that are necessary for promotion.

These unwritten rules are learnt through 'old boys' networks (which besides being single-sexed are often also homophobic and single-raced). Even more legitimate networks – such as university alumni groups, fraternities and professional organisations – cater to the typical male worker, which limits women and other minorities from enjoying full equality in their workplace.

Typical networking events such as meet-and-greets at expensive cocktail bars are usually scheduled during evening hours or weekends, and thus exclude many minority workers who cannot attend because for lack of money or time (or both!). Initiatives meant to increase diversity must include events that cater to a larger group of workers who may have different limitations or family expectations as well as mentor minority workers to help them learn the unwritten rules of the organisation.

Critique of diversity management

As a set of managerial practices, diversity management has been beneficial to many organisations – and as experience is gathered, the practices are becoming more and more sophisticated. Yet scholars have voiced concern about the theoretical underpinnings of these practices and called for stronger theory-building in the field (Nkomo and Cox, 1996).

A main reason for this call lies in the tensions that arise from the different perspectives on diversity as well as inconsistencies between the underlying notions of equal opportunities and affirmative action. It is possible to resolve many of these dilemmas by either opting for one perspective or the other or by exploring how they can be combined. But a more fundamental contradiction between the very notions of diversity and management persistently hampers the field (Kirby and Harter, 2002; Martin, 2000). The basic theoretical concern is that '... the institutionalization of managing diversity threatens to position individuals and structure work relations in potentially alarming ways' (Kirby and Harter, 2002). Or stated directly, management implies control and regulation, and thus seems ill-suited to create diversity.

The admonition that diversity must be managed, if it is to be beneficial, under-writes most diversity initiatives (Von Bergen et al., 2002). This could, however, be read as saying that diversity must be regulated and curbed, rather than allowed to run wild and free, if it is to do the organisation any good.

Diversity management, in sum, offers up a particular image of what diversity is for the involved individuals and groups to emulate; it offers a limited set of opportunities for practising diversity rather than the open field that is its ostensible goal (Litvin, 2006).

In trying to overcome this critique it is important to recognise the impossibility of escaping constraint in the general sense. Yet specific constraints may be dealt with, suggesting the need to keep trying to find new and more inclusive managerial practices. Moreover if conditions for individuals and groups are to be transformed, organisational structures and cultures cannot remain unchanged. Diversity management, then, becomes an all-encompassing and ongoing process rather than a specific set of means to a goal that can be accomplished.

Communicating diversity

Diversity management is about creating policies and taking initiatives that will promote diversity in organisations. Organisations must raise awareness about and support for their diversity programmes externally and internally. They must communicate diversity.

External communication of diversity

When organisations take on diversity initiatives, it is essential that potential employees with untraditional backgrounds are attracted to the organisation. Therefore, many organisations begin with special recruitment initiatives such as training sessions or internships targeted at specific groups of prospective employees (Barak, 2005: 211).

This strategy may be exemplified by initiatives taken by the Danish insurance company Tryg when the company first took up diversity management. Danish society is marked by a large degree of ethnic homogeneity, but the make-up of the population was changing rapidly in the 1980s and 1990s (Danmarks Statistik, 2009:13). However, during that period Tryg did not change the profile of its employees or its customer targets, thus missing out on both talent and business. Then Tryg managers realised that reaching out to new employees might entail an appeal to new customers. In 2003 the firm set up a special educational programme, 'The integration education', that included language classes and training in cultural competencies as well as the traditional training of an insurance consultant. The participants were recruited via local job centres, and they were all resourceful immigrants (e.g., people who had completed an education in their country of origin) who nevertheless had difficulties in using their resources as a means of securing a job in Denmark.

At the same time, the company sought to recruit more people with minority backgrounds for its regular trainee programme, targeting this group by means of posters with messages of diversity. Difference was revalidated as a positive trait, even a necessity, for prospective employees (the main text of the poster says: 'At Tryg there is room for everyone. But you have to be special anyway') and this message was emphasised by the accompanying picture of 'Oriental' tea glasses in different colours and sizes.

Tryg's initiatives not only resulted in more applicants and employees with ethnic minority backgrounds, but also provided Tryg with a platform for commenting on Danish social and political issues. Thus, the now former company CEO, Stine Bosse, publicly advocated a stronger political and social focus on the inclusion of ethnic minorities and has suggested that companies should take the lead in facilitating the inclusion process. Furthermore, the initiatives formed the basis of integrating diversity more fully into the overall strategy of the company.

When communicated externally diversity draws near to the public communication of corporate social responsibility (CSR) initiatives. That is, to most organisations it makes little sense to do good if no one knows about it. Both practices of CSR and diversity management may be beneficial to organisations in and of themselves, but they are often dependent on public recognition for paying off in full. Here, diversity management also comes to look like CSR in the sense that it is typically framed as a matter of the company acting in a socially responsible way, which ensures a sound and sustainable business.

The external communication of diversity management, then, is not just about recruiting for diversity; it is also about projecting an image of the organisation as a promoter of diversity to the public. The communication may serve direct purposes of making the company more diverse by attracting a more varied group of employees, and it may also – more or less indirectly – raise goodwill for the company that becomes known for its diversity policies and practices.

The external communication of diversity management, then, is not just about recruiting for diversity; it is also about projecting an image of the organisation as a promoter of diversity to the public. The communication may serve direct purposes of making the company more diverse by attracting a more varied group of employees, and it may also – more or less indirectly – raise good-will for the company that becomes known for its diversity policies and practices.

Internal communication of diversity

External communication of diversity may be vital in terms of recruitment and important for raising public awareness, but without internal communication of diversity policies and practices these will never succeed.

It is often stated that diversity policies and practices should emanate from and be endorsed by top management (European Commission, 2005: 17). Such communication may take the form of articles on the intranet or in the company magazine, speeches at briefings and so on. Another important aspect is active involvement, for instance, by mentors or colleagues of new employees who are different from traditional members of the organisation.

Meetings in small groups and special training sessions are needed to ensure that all involved employees are fully prepared for participating in the initiatives. Communication should be located at the levels of implementation, that is, in taskforces, councils or with the individual employees.

Internal diversity communication may perform one additional and very important function: creating cultural change. It is often argued that diversity management at its best and most effective is not about specific initiatives of hiring and maintaining non-traditional employees, but rather about changing the general attitude and culture of the organisation. Such communication is directed at creating a culture of inclusion and tolerance where everyone feels secure in contributing unique experiences and points of view. Possibilities include the creation of a diversity council that arranges open meetings and other activities. Others are internal employee blogs, chats with different employees on the intranet and debate forums.

A practical approach to communicating diversity

The notion of communication as practice – or praxis to employ the more technical term – represents a shift from the transmission model of communication; that is, from thinking of communication as means to an end to thinking of it as a goal in itself.

In the transmission model, meaning exists outside of any one act of communication and is merely transferred from sender to receiver. The idea of communication as 'praxis' contradicts this view and begins from the presupposition that meaning arises in and through the process of communication (Smith, 1972).

The understanding of communication as praxis corresponds with two important developments in twentieth-century social science. First, there is the linguistic argument that makes communication central to the formation of individual and social identities (Habermas, 1981, 1989). And second, there is the idea of communication as the basis of social reality. The act of interpersonal communication enables individuals not only to act within and reproduce pre-existing norms and expectations, but also potentially to alter them (Bourdieu, 1977).

Thus it can be argued that differences between groups and individuals do not exist independently of their communication, but rather are established, reconfirmed or overcome in and through communicative processes. Therefore a view of diversity communication as praxis suggests that diversity management should be based in cultural change, and that communication is the means of creating such cultural change.

Even if the idea of communication as praxis is most easily illustrated through examples of interpersonal communication, it nevertheless applies to all types of communication. Even campaigns to promote an image of the organisation as a diverse and socially responsible workplace may be viewed as a praxis of meaning-formation in which a particular image of the company is only realised if its receivers participate actively in creating it. Messages cannot be viewed in detachment from their interpretation.

Therefore diversity communication should be viewed as process or praxis rather than transference. In order to understand this praxis we may analyse it at three levels: the specific situation in which communication/interpretation occurs, the specific cultural and personal backgrounds of communicators/interpreters, and the general norms to which all participants in the communication/interpretation arguably adhere.

If they are to succeed, all practices of diversity must be interpreted positively by the people who engage in or are affected by them. In this sense, all diversity practices are communications as well as actions.

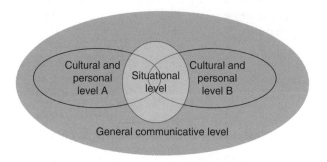

Figure 4.3   Model of diversity communication

Practices of diversity

Recruitment

Recruitment of workers from underrepresented minority groups is at the heart of many diversity programmes, although it is not the primary focus any more (Pitts, 2006). Creative human resource directors use a multitude of strategies to recruit (and retain) qualified minority workers that go beyond traditional methods like quotas or earmarked positions.

Organisations are investing in education and training as a way to prepare minority workers for employment. IBM, for example, faced with the challenge of recruiting women and minority workers trained in mathematics and science recently launched a new programme to encourage young girls to study technology. EXITE (Exploring Interests in Technology and Engineering) is a programme sponsored by IBM and managed by female employees. The programme includes camps where girls, especially minority girls, from around the world learn about 'science and math in a fun, interactive way from female IBM employees' (Thomas, 2004). The girls are then assigned a female IBM employee mentor for the next year. This is just one of many corporate or university funded educational programmes meant to reach minority students who may not otherwise consider continuing their education in mathematics, science, technology or business.

Mentoring

Mentoring can take many forms: formal/informal, open to all employees/open to select employees, task-specific/general career advancement. Specifically, mentoring has become a focus of diversity management professionals because it is viewed as a tool to help minority workers acclimate to organisational culture and perform well within the organisation. Mentoring uniquely addresses both individual questions and issues and simultaneously helps achieve organisational diversity goals.

Informal mentoring was commonplace in traditional organisations; senior executives would often 'show favour' to junior executives and help them with their career development by explaining the unwritten rules and granting them access to opportunities that were particularly fruitful. However, informal mentoring often meant that minority workers were left without mentors. Therefore, many organisations now have formal programmes, some specifically targeting minority workers, which assign mentors with mentored. In good programmes, the organisation also provides additional incentives and support in the form of administrative assistance, and even bonuses or other rewards for the time and effort spent mentoring.

Good mentoring is often very useful, but it is hard to achieve and it is rarely sufficient to support organisational diversity initiatives. Dinolfo and Nugent (2010) argue that mentoring must be part of a larger diversity strategy that includes informative performance evaluations/coaching, support for organisational policies and practices (like family leave), and training and development opportunities.

Work/family management

These practices include on-site child-care facilities, concierge services to assist with shopping and banking, on-site gyms, flexible work time, telecommuting, family leave and even job sharing.

In particular, work/family management programmes aim to help stop the leaky pipeline of women leaving competitive management positions or the workplace entirely to raise young children. Numerous studies across industries suggest that the lack of support for balancing work and family responsibilities is one of the primary reasons why there are still few female organisational leaders. The implementation of such support has yielded some organisational and individual change, although not as much as some had hoped (Bennhold, 2010).

Perhaps the most substantial work/family management practice is family leave. This is the time parents take away from their workplace for the birth or adoption of a child. Much research focus has been dedicated to family leave policies. For example, Kirby (2000) found that even in organisations with a clear policy, its implementation depended on the willingness of supervisors and managers. A recent tendency indicates that fewer women and men in countries with progressive maternity leave policies are taking their full leave – essentially declining free income – for fear that a lengthy leave will jeopardise their organisational standing. In addition, some managers and workers come to resent colleagues who take lengthy leaves because of the strain placed on other organisational workers and the organisation's budget.

Conclusion

Diversity and diversity management are too broad and fractured fields to be covered in full in any one report. Nevertheless it is possible to make some main distinctions. For instance, it is possible to define diversity in a narrow sense as indicating certain identity characteristics. In effect this points to the existence of minority groups who inhabit unprivileged or underprivileged social positions because of their gender, race, religion, etc. Alternatively, it is possible to broaden the term so as to cover the sum of all the differences that are present in an organisational or social setting. That is, 'diversity' may be a label that can be placed on certain individuals or groups who are different from the norm, or it may be something to which all organisational members contribute.

Furthermore, it is possible to distinguish various perspectives on organisational diversity: discrimination-and-fairness, access-and-legitimacy, integration-and-learning – and the practice-based perspective that may deal with the inherent short-coming of the notion that diversity is something that can be managed – with the ideas of 'fixing', 'solving' and 'regulating' that the managerial language implies. Diversity is not something that can be achieved or that the organisation can be done with, but rather a dynamic process that disappears if it is not continuously acted and re-enacted through the many specific and sustaining organisational practices.

Contrary to the more static notions of diversity that identify it with the demographic make-up of an organisation, it can be contended that boasting a diverse workforce does not, in and of itself, make the organisation diverse. Only practising diversity in its myriad subtle ways will ensure that diverse employees remain within the organisation – and that they remain diverse within the organisation rather than adapting to the organisational norm.

Discussion

Just and Remke reject the notion of diversity as narrowly indicating certain identity characteristics of minority groups who are disadvantaged in society because of their gender, race, religion or whatever. They broaden the term to include all human differences in organisational settings. In this view, diversity is seen as 'something to which all organisational members contribute'. They argue that diversity is a dynamic, endlessly acted and re-enacted in organisational practices. However, just because a particular firm can boast a diverse workforce, it is not necessarily a diverse organisation. It can only be so if the people who make it up retain their heterogeneity rather than undergoing an organisational socialisation that persuades them to adapt to a pre-existing set of behavioural norms.

In 1990 Peter Senge, from the Massachusetts Institute of Technology, published *The Fifth Discipline: The Art and Practice of the Learning Organization*. According to Senge (1990: 3), 'learning organizations' are:

> ... *organizations where people continually expand their capacity to create the results they truly desire, where new and expansive patterns of thinking are nurtured, where collective aspiration is set free, and where people are continually learning to see the whole together.*

His rationale is that in situations of rapid change only those institutions that are flexible, adaptive and productive will excel. For this to happen, organisations need to 'discover how to tap people's commitment and capacity to learn at *all* levels' (ibid.: 4).

Senge's argument is that while everybody has the capacity to learn, the structures in which they function are not always conducive to reflection and engagement; and may lack the tools and guiding ideas to make sense of the situations they face. Organisations need continually to expand their capacity to create their future; but to do so requires a fundamental shift of mind among their members.

Questions

Just and Remke offer their own, original, views on essentially the same theme as that of Senge: that human diversity in the workplace must be encouraged, not stifled. Can you think of any collective you know of, where this can be shown to hold true? Was diversity approved or condemned in your family, neighbourhood, school, peer groups, places of employment? Perhaps only those of us who have been fortunate enough to have our diversity valued can know how much this stimulates personal creativity.

Case study: Individualism in a collectivist culture

The following case of diversity management – or mismanagement – illustrates a tug-of-war between convergence of national cultures towards a more individualistic global society and national divergence from individual diversity in an attempt to retain traditional collective values.

Turkish academics sacked over porn dissertation project

BBC News reported in January 2010 that three academics had been dismissed from one of Turkey's top universities, following a scandal over a student being allowed to present a pornographic film as his dissertation project.

As a result, not only did Bilgi University in Istanbul shut down its entire film department but police investigated the possibility of criminal charges being brought against it. A number of non-involved academics protested against such a drastic outcome, but the incident has drawn attention to the clash between traditional values and the diverse and sometimes experimental arts and lifestyles practised in Istanbul.

When film student Deniz Ozgun first broached his idea for a dissertation project with his professors, they were hesitant. He claimed his intention was to reveal how synthetic are the sexual scenes in pornographic films. He was given permission to go ahead with the project but warned of the need for strong intellectual rigour in this, as in any other, academic work. Apparently he did not heed the warning sufficiently, and failed his dissertation.

None of this caused a stir until the disappointed student gave an interview to a news magazine and described the kind of film he had been allowed to make on campus. The news report caused an uproar among parents, who demanded to know what other dubious projects were carried out at Bilgi, one of Turkey's most prestigious private universities, in the name of academic research.

It was rumoured among academics that the Board of Education put pressure on the university to dismiss the three relevant academics – who were investigated by the police – and to close the entire Communications Faculty. Deniz Ozgun, and a former student who starred in his film, went into hiding. Neither the university nor the government would make any comment.

Bilgi has a reputation as one of the most liberal universities in Turkey – it was among the first to ignore the ban on Muslim women wearing headscarves on campus – but this affair clearly touched a nerve. In much of the country people still adhere to strict moral codes by which alcohol is banned, clothing is conservative and sex is never openly discussed. Politicians in the governing Justice and Development Party (AKP) largely subscribe to this view.

However, people from different walks of life in Turkey now hold strikingly divergent values. In Istanbul many citizens have very liberal attitudes to sex, alcohol and the arts. Some films, plays and art exhibitions are as provocative and experimental as in any other European city. But in September 2010 guests attending new exhibitions at art galleries in central Istanbul were attacked by local residents, enraged by the sight of them drinking alcohol on the street outside.

They might have been even more enraged had they seen the content of the exhibitions, which challenged a number of taboo topics. A publisher who translated erotic European literature was also put on trial last year, but eventually acquitted. Turkey is now the world's fifteenth biggest economy; its people are more prosperous and more exposed to outside influences than ever before. Boundaries are constantly being tested. But when they are, sometimes there is a powerful reaction.

Sources

Anon. 2011a. 'Turkey Bilgi Uni shuts its film dept over porn, 3 academics sacked', 9 January; http://www.whatsonningbo.com/news-1229-turkey-bilgi-uni-shuts-its-film-dept-over-porn-3-academics-sacked.html.

Anon. 2011b. 'Turkish academics lost jobs after scandal porn film', 10 January; http://blog.cytalk.com/2011/01/turkish-academics-lost-jobs-after-scandal-porn-film/.

Anon. 2011c. 'Bilgi in decline?', 3 January; http://mustmakecomments.wordpress.com/tag/porn-scandal/.

AOL News 2011. 'Justin Vela: Student's porn film project sparks controversy in Turkey', 10 January; http://www.aolnews.com/tag/bilgi%20university/.

Arslani 2011. 'Turkish academics fired over porn dissertation project', 8 January; http://www.allvoices.com/contributed-news/7832309-turkish-academics-fired-over-porn-dissertation-project.

Head, J. 2011. 'Turkish academics sacked over porn dissertation project', BBC News, Istanbul, 8 January; http://www.bbc.co.uk.

Öğret, Ö. 2011. 'Response to "porn scandal" by Istanbul's Bilgi University violated academic freedom', Hürriyet Daily News, Istanbul, 10 January; http://www.defence.pk/forums/turkey-defence/88361-response-porn-scandal-istanbuls-bilgi-university-violated-academic-freedom.html.

Turkish Digest 2011. 'Response to "porn scandal" by Istanbul's Bilgi University violated academic freedom, protesters say', 10 January; http://turkishdigest.blogspot.com/2011/01/response-to-porn-scandal-by-istanbuls.html.

Conclusion

Everybody feels a need for achievement (task) and for affiliation (relationship), but some people will be more motivated by one than the other; and some will seek power over either. When work is to be done, competent managers learn to understand workers' different needs and create teams by combining task, relationship and control. Moreover they know the difference in cross-cultural contexts between 'promises' and 'commitments'; and how to build trust. Women and members of minority groups are underrepresented in many organisations, and diversity management is an essential part of organisational practice and policy.

Key points

1. Everybody has unique needs and motivations; yet they can be classified to some extent into groups, for example, a primary need for achievement, or affiliation or power. Depending on preference, people will communicate and perform differently in workplace settings and will expect different rewards.

2. Another classification is that cultural values tend to be mainly individualistic or collectivist, therefore to some extent all members of a culture will subscribe to one set or the other. They bring these values to the workplace, and their expectations and behaviours will differ accordingly.

3. Organisations develop their own internal cultures. Successful management requires harnessing individual strengths to organisational tasks.

4. Discrimination in employment against women and members of social minorities has a long history. The aims of affirmative action programmes are to create a 'level playing field' on which all employees can achieve their potential and make their unique contributions to the corporate whole.

5. A diverse organisation is an entity to which all its members contribute. To grow and sustain a healthy corporate body, managers need continuously to seek, encourage and promote the unique individuality of all that it comprises.

Looking ahead

Having taken a macro-view in this chapter of the reconciliation needed between the different agendas of organisational members, we continue the theme in microcosm in Chapter 5 by looking at factors that make for individuals' success or failure when living and working in host cultures. The characteristics of so-called 'culture shock' are described and examples provided of the kinds of behaviour change that foreign managers need to make when working in host countries.

Experiential exercises

1. **Affiliation versus achievement?**

   This is a game to identify which seems to be more important to players, task or relationship. It will take about 40–60 minutes and requires at least six players and preferably more multiples of three (though 'extras' can be included). No materials are required.

Divide the group into triads each consisting of two players and one observer. The game is that the two players in each group will take it in turns to teach each other something. It doesn't matter what (a song, a simple skill, a few words in another language....). Each player has 10 minutes. Observers are instructed privately to watch and take notes on the behaviour of each 'teacher' and 'learner' as the players assume these roles. Do they seem more interested in the process of teaching or learning (i.e., enjoying the activity for its own sake) or the end-product (teaching or learning the task as well as possible)? Give observers the following measurements:

Laughter

Often	Occasionally	Seldom

1---------2-----------3-------------4----------5

Attention

Easily distracted	Fairly focused	Focused

1---------2-----------3-------------4----------5

Chat (talk not relevant to the task)

Much	Little	None

1---------2-----------3-------------4----------5

Learning/teaching

Poor	Moderate	Good

1---------2-----------3-------------4----------5

After 20 minutes call a plenary session and ask all observers to tot up their scores. Players who scored at least an average of 3–5 points seem to be relatively task-oriented. Players who scored less may have enjoyed the game without worrying too much about the task!

2. **I speak more than three languages**

The object of the game is to identify and honour diversity in the classroom. The more players the merrier. Allow about 20 minutes for the game, then about 20 minutes for discussion. Give each student one of the matrices below. The instructions are self-evident. After 20 minutes, give a small prize to the player with the highest score.

The object of this game is to identify the diversity of the class. Find somebody (you can include yourself) who can truthfully reply 'yes' to ONE of the statements below. Ask them to initial the relevant box and then move on. The winner will be the player whose paper has the most signatures. You have 20 minutes to complete this exercise. Good hunting!

I speak more than three languages	I have worked in more than two countries	I have friends from many different backgrounds	I like to watch foreign films
I have been arrested by the police	I like to listen to foreign music	I have experienced discrimination	I belong to a political party
I have taken part in a protest demonstration	I belong to a minority religious group	I had never seen the sea (or the snow) until I left home	My European country is not a member of the EU
My country is a member of ASEAN	My country is signatory to NATO	I have climbed a high mountain and/or been deep sea diving	I think same-sex marriages should be legal
I think personal use of recreational drugs should be decriminalised	I think there is no such thing as 'society'; only individuals	I think society is more important than individuals	I listen first and speak last
I judge by first impressions	I take a long time to make up my mind	I ask family and friends before major decisions	I speak first and listen afterwards
I believe 'older is wiser'	I live in the present	I look to the future	I believe in myself
I like to travel	Home is best	I am open to new ideas	I am cautious about change

Figure 4.4   I speak more than 3 languages

Recommended reading

Books

Barak, M.E.M. 2005. *Managing Diversity: Toward a Globally Inclusive Workplace.* Thousand Oaks, CA: Sage

Bourdieu, P. 1977. *Outline of a Theory of Practice*, translated by Richard Nice. Cambridge: Cambridge University Press.

Conley, D. 1999. *Being Black, Living in the Red.* Berkeley, CA: University of California Press.

Dinolfo, S. and Nugent, J.S. 2010. *Making Mentoring Work.* New York: Catalyst.

Habermas, J. 1981. *The Theory of Communicative Action*, vol. I: *Reason and the Rationalization of Society*, translated by Thomas McCarthy. Boston, MA: Beacon Press.

—— 1989. *The Theory of Communicative Action*, vol. II: *The Critique of Functionalist Reason*, translated by Thomas McCarthy. Oxford: Polity Press.

Hofstede, G. 1980. *Culture's Consequences: International Differences in Work-Related Values*. Beverley Hills, CA: Sage.

—— 1991. *Cultures and Organizations: Software of the Mind*. New York: McGraw-Hill.

Johnson, W.B. and Packer, A. E. (1987) *Workforce 2000: Work and workers for the 21st. century* (Indianapolis, IN: Hudson Institute, Inc.).

McClelland, D.C. 1955. *Studies in Motivation*. New York: Appleton.

—— 1961. *The Achieving Society.* Princeton, NJ: Van Nostrand.

Prasad, P., Pringle, J.K. and Konrad, A.K. (eds) 2006. *Handbook of Workplace Diversity.* London: Sage.

Trethewey, A., Scott, C. and LeGreco, M. 2006. 'Constructing embodied organizational identities'. In B.J. Dow and J.T. Wood (eds), *Sage Handbook of Gender and Communication*. Thousand Oaks, CA: Sage, pp. 123–41.

Journals

Administrative Science Quarterly
American Behavioral Scientist
Electronic Journal of Communication
Gender in Management: An International Journal
Harvard Business Review
Industrial Relations Journal
Journal of Business Communication
Management Communication Quarterly
Review of Public Personnel Administration
Slate Magazine
Sociological Review

References

AAUW (American Association of University Women) (n.d.) 'Pay equity statistics'; http://www.aauw.org [accessed 3 January 2011].

Asselin, G. and Mastron, R. .2010. *Au Contraire! Figuring out the French*, 2nd edn. Boston, MA: Intercultural Press.

Barak, M.E.M. 2005. *Managing Diversity: Toward a Globally Inclusive Workplace*. Thousand Oaks, CA: Sage.

Bennhold, K. 2010. 'In Sweden, the men can have it all'. *International Herald Tribune*, 10 June.

Bourdieu, P. 1977. *Outline of a Theory of Practice*, translated by Richard Nice. Cambridge: Cambridge University Press.

Boxenbaum, E. 2006. 'Lost in translation: The making of Danish diversity management'. *American Behavioral Scientist*, 49 (7), pp. 939–48.

Carroll, R. 1987. *Cultural Misunderstandings: The French–American Experience*, translated by Carol Volk. Chicago: University of Chicago Press.

Catalyst Foundation 2000. 'Women in corporate leadership'; http://www.catalystwomen.org/.

Classactionlawsuitsinthenews 2010. 'Eastman Kodak class action settlement of race discrimination class action lawsuit', 7 September; http://classactionlawsuitsinthenews.com.

Cockburn, C. 1989. 'Equal opportunities: The short and long agenda'. *Industrial Relations Journal*, 20 (3), pp. 213–25.

Cole, C. 2007. 'Class action lawsuit filed against Walgreens', 8 March; http://wichita.injuryboard.com/.

Conley, D. 1999. *Being Black, Living in the Red*. Berkeley, CA: University of California Press.

Dale, C. V. 2005. *Federal Affirmative Action Law: A Brief History.* CRS Report for Congress, received through the CRS Web, 13 September, Order Code RS22256.

Danmarks Statistik 2009. *Indvandrere i Danmark 2009*. Copenhagen: Danmarks Statistik.

Dinolfo, S. and Nugent, J.S. 2010. *Making Mentoring Work*. New York: Catalyst.

Disability Rights Advocates 2006. National Federation of the Blind v. Target, 6 February; http://www.dralegal.org.

Eagly, A.H. and Carli, L.L. 2007. 'Women and the labyrinth of leadership'. *Harvard Business Review*, 85 (9), pp. 62–71.

Ely, R.J. and Thomas, D.A. 2001. 'Cultural diversity at work: The effects of diversity perspectives on work group processes and outcomes'. *Administrative Science Quarterly*, 46, pp. 229–73.

European Commission 2005. *The Business Case for Diversity: Good Practices in the Workplace*. Luxembourg: European Communities; http://.www.equalrightstrust.org.

Fraser, N. 1992. 'Rethinking the public sphere: A contribution to the critique of actually existing democracy'. In C. Calhoun (ed.), *Habermas and the Public Sphere*. Cambridge, MA: MIT Press, pp. 109–42.

Füredi, F. 2002. *Culture of Fear: Risk-Taking and the Morality of Low Expectation*. London: Continuum.

—— 2007. *Invitation to Terror: The Expanding Empire of the Unknown*. London: Continuum.

Grillo, T. and Wildman, S. M. 1991. 'Obscuring the importance of race: The implication of making comparisons between racism and sexism (or other -isms)'. *Duke Law Journal*, 2, pp. 397–412; http://www.jstor.org.

Habermas, J. 1981. *The Theory of Communicative Action*, vol. I: *Reason and the Rationalization of Society*, translated by Thomas McCarthy. Boston, MA: Beacon Press.

—— 1989. *The Theory of Communicative Action*, vol. II: *The Critique of Functionalist Reason*, translated by Thomas McCarthy. Oxford: Polity Press.

Harris, R.T. and Moran, S.V. 2007. *Managing Cultural Differences: Global Leadership Strategies for the Twenty-First Century*, 7th edn. Oxford: Butterworth-Heinemann.

Hofstede, G. 1980. *Culture's Consequences: International Differences in Work-Related Values*. Beverley Hills, CA: Sage.

—— 1991. *Cultures and Organizations: Software of the Mind*. New York: McGraw-Hill.

hooks, b 1995. *Killing Rage: Ending Racism*. New York: Henry Holt.

Insala n.d. 'Benefits of mentoring programs'; http://mentoringtalent.com/ [accessed 6 January 2011].

Jewson, N. and Mason, D. 1986. 'The theory and practice of equal opportunities policies: Liberal and radical approaches', *Sociological Review*, 34 (2), pp. 307–34.

Johnson, W.B. and Packer, A.E. 1987. *Workforce 2000: Work and Workers for the 21st Century*. Indianapolis, IN: Hudson Institute, Inc.

Kim, A. 2010. 'The mommy track turns 21: Why it no longer deserves a bad rap from feminists'. *Slate Magazine*, 31 March; www.slate.com/id/2249312 [accessed 1 August 2010].

Kingdon, K. and Kuhl, D. 2007. *The Matter of Mind: An Explorer's Guide to the Labyrinth of the Mind*. Flagstaff, AZ: Light Technology Publishing.

Kirby, E.L. 2000. 'Should I do as you say or do as you do? Mixed messages about work and family', *Electronic Journal of Communication/La Revue de Electronique de Communication*, 10 [accessed 22 June 2004].

Kirby, E.L. and Harter, L.M. 2001. 'Discourses of diversity and the quality of work life: The character and costs of the managerial metaphor'. *Management Communication Quarterly*. 15 (1), pp. 121–7.

—— 2002. 'Speaking the language of the bottom line: The metaphor of "managing diversity"'. *Journal of Business Communication*, 40 (1), pp. 28–49.

Leung, R. 2004. 'The look of Abercrombie & Fitch: Retail store accused of hiring attractive, mostly white salespeople'. 24 November; http://www.cbsnews.com.

Lieff, C.. 2008. 'McCormick & Schmick's; issue: Race discrimination. Result: $2.1 million settlement'; August; http://www.lieffcabraser.com.

Litvin, D.R. 2006.'Diversity: Making space for a better case'. In A.M. Konrad, P. Prasad and J.K. Pringle (eds), *Handbook of Workplace Diversity*. London: Sage, pp. 75–94.

Maatman Jr, Gerald L. and Maechtlen, L. 2010. 'The Supreme Court accepts cert in Dukes v. Wal-Mart – final word is coming on key class certification issues', 6 December; http://www.workplaceclassaction.com/class-action/post/.

McClelland, D.C. 1955. *Studies in Motivation*. New York: Appleton.

―― 1961. *The Achieving Society*. Princeton, NJ: Van Nostrand.

Martin, D.M. 2000. 'Re-examining diversity paradigms: The role of management communication'. *Journal of the Northwest Communication Association*, 29, pp. 12–31.

Matthews Smith et al. v Texaco, Inc. (2001) 263 F.3d 394 (5th Cir. 2001), No. 00-40337; United States Court of Appeals, for the Fifth Circuit, 22 August: http://ftp.resource.org/courts. gov/c/F3/263/263.F3d.394.00-40337.html.

Nkomo, S.M. and Cox, T. 1996. 'Diverse identities in organizations'. In S.R. Clegg, C. Hardy and W.R. Nord (eds), *Handbook of Organization Studies*. London: Sage, pp. 338–56.

Pierce, S. 2010. 'Costco workers proceed with overtime class action', 17 December; http://www.legafi.com.

Pitts, D.W. 2006. 'Modeling the impact of diversity management', *Review of Public Personnel Administration*, 26 (3), pp. 245–68.

PBS n.d. 'Battle for suffrage, 1848–1920'; http://www.pbs.org [accessed 6 January 2011].

Prasad, P., Pringle, J. and Konrad, A. 2006. 'Examining the contours of workplace diversity: Concepts, contexts, and challenges'. In P. Prasad, J. Pringle and A. Konrad (eds), *Handbook of Workplace Diversity*. London: Sage, pp. 1–22; http://www.sage-ereference.com/ hdbk_workdiversity/article_n1.html.

Risberg, A. and Søderberg, A. 2008. 'Translating a management concept: Diversity management in Denmark', *Gender in Management: An International Journal*, 23 (6), pp. 426–41.

Satchell et al. v. FedEx (n.d.) http://www.schneiderwallace.com/representative_success_detail. php?id=14 [accessed 14 April 2011].

Schwartz, F. N. 1989. 'Management women and the facts of life', *Harvard Business Review*, 67 (1), pp. 65–76.

Senge, P.M. 1990. *The Fifth Discipline: The Art and Practice of the Learning Organization*. New York: Doubleday.

SDNN 2009. 'San Diego firm files class-action suit against UPS', City News Service, 19 August; http://www.sdnn.com.

Smith, D.H. 1972. 'Communication research and the idea of process'. *Speech Monographs*, 39 (3), pp. 174–82.

Stewart, I. 1989. *Does God Play Dice? The New Mathematics of Chaos* (web publication by Mountain Man Graphics, Australia).

Sykes, M. 1995. 'The origins of Affirmative Action'. *NOW Times* (National Organization for Women), August; http://www.now.org.

Thomas, D.A. 2004. 'Diversity as strategy', *Harvard Business Review*, 82 (9): 98–108.

Thomas, D.A. and Ely, R.J. 1996. 'Making differences matter: A new paradigm for managing diversity'. *Harvard Business Review*, 74 (5), pp. 79–90

Trethewey, A., Scott, C. and LeGreco, M. 2006. 'Constructing embodied organizational identities'. In B.J. Dow and J.T. Wood (eds), *Sage Handbook of Gender and Communication*. Thousand Oaks, CA: Sage, pp. 123–41.

University of Wisconsin, School of Business 2001. 'Denny's & racism: These issues will not go over easy', 3 June; http://instruction.bus.wisc.edu/obdemo/suplmnts/dennysgbu.htm 6/3/01.

Von Bergen, C.W., Soper, B. and Foster, T. 2002. 'Unintended negative effects of diversity management'. *Public Personnel Management*, 31 (2), pp. 239–51.

Washington Post 1993. 'Secret Service Agents allege racial bias at Denny's', May; http:// garnet.berkeley.edu.

Winter, G. 2000. 'Coca-Cola settles racial bias case', *New York Times*, 17 November; http:// query.nytimes.com.

CHAPTER 5

'I Don't Like it Here': Culture Shock and Adjustment

Elizabeth Christopher; Hannah M. Mugambi; Dharm P.S. Bhawuk; Kathryn Anbe; Anna Reid; Peter Petocz

Objectives of the chapter

- to study factors that make for successful communication across cultures over a range of contexts, economic, political and social;
- to discuss the advantages and disadvantages of living and working in host cultures;
- to identify the characteristics and phases of so-called 'culture shock';
- to acknowledge the importance of cross-cultural sensitivity;
- to find examples of the kinds of behaviour change that foreign managers need to make when working in host countries;
- to provide an illustration of poor cultural adjustment.

Chapter contents

- Further reading
- Discussion points and questions
- Conclusion
- Key points
- Experiential exercise
- Further reading
- References

Outline of chapter

Following Chapter 4 on workplace diversity, Hannah Mugambi discusses workplace communication between members of monochronic and polychronic cultures respectively, as defined by Edward T. Hall. Her setting is that of Northern Nigeria, but her observations can be applied to any cross-cultural setting. Against a historical backdrop of British colonial domination, she sets the scene for modern cultural conflict between expatriate members of Western firms and native Nigerian companies.

Her argument is that a major reason for expatriate failure is lack of cross-cultural competence, resulting in high turnover of expatriate employment. She suggests that more mutually positive attitudes are likely to develop structurally with the creation of more 'horizontal corporations'.

A brief overview is then given of Oberg's stages of shock and subsequent adaptation by foreigners to host cultures. This leads into a summary of a fascinating study by Dharm P.S. Bhawuk and Kathryn Anbe on the 'decline of the majority, rise of the minority: community cultural changes in Hawai'i', which provides a template for behaviour changes needed by foreign managers working in host countries.

Bhawuk and Anbe's account is contrasted with a case of dysfunctional management. The central characters, an Australian and his wife, found it impossible to become accustomed to the lifestyle in Japan or to learn how to function within it. Suggestions are offered for the reasons for their lack of ability to adjust, and how they might acquire more cross-cultural sensitivity.

After that, Peter Petocz and Anna Reid report the results of their investigations of international students' ideas on cross-cultural sensitivity. The findings are based on a series of interviews at an Australian university, and they offer practical suggestions for ways in which students and lecturers might develop intercultural understanding in the context of university business studies.

A brief discussion follows of different cultural views of the importance of further education, with comments on the increasing need internationally for high qualifications in managing communication across cultures.

Further discussion points, questions and case studies illustrate and expand all this material; and after a summary of the key points of the chapter an experiential exercise is suggested for the classroom; a list of recommended reading for further study and chapter references are also added.

'I CAN'T STAND IT HERE': EXPATRIATE EXPERIENCES IN NORTHERN NIGERIA	Hannah M. Mugambi

Introduction

This is a study of cross-cultural communication problems within the setting of expatriate-led international institutions based in Northern Nigeria, West Africa. The largest ethnic group in Northern Nigeria is the Hausa and Fulani, and the dominant religion is Islam. A guiding principle for this analysis of expatriate staff experiences was Edward Hall's concept of monochronic and polychronic cultural systems (Hall, 1959, 1966, 1976, 1983).

Historical background of the relationship between Nigeria and the West

As a former British colony, Northern Nigeria came into contact with Western culture as early as the 1900s. Peter Tibenderana (2003), in discussing Nigerian traditional and Islamic education systems, notes that they ensured social stability and continuity through acculturation. He argues that the British colonial system promoted expatriate bureaucracy to exclude growing numbers of educated Nigerians from administration and governance of their own country. In particular he suggests that Africans were denied education in the English language to keep them in ignorance of their democratic rights. Instead they were given technical education that would ensure their placement in low-status jobs.

A recent USAID report (2010) attests that there is a high level of illiteracy in Nigerian schools, and Tibenderana attributes this to the rejection of Western education by Northern Nigeria, resulting from perceived negative Western influence on Islamic children. Muslims consider Western education to be morally harmful to their children and a means of converting them to Christianity. The British in response left education out of their development agenda for Northern Nigeria. Today, however, North America, Britain, Canada and Australia invest heavily in international aid and soft loans for the education sector in Northern Nigeria. With these investments donor countries send large numbers of expatriate teachers to Northern Nigeria (USAID, 2010).

In general the use of expatriate teaching professionals probably is not the best solution to problems of Northern Nigeria's education since Nigeria now has a large population of internationally recognised professionals. However, the use of expatriates does allow Nigerian youth to experience both positive and negative impacts of cultural change and globalisation.

Cultural differences, conflicts and misunderstandings are a stumbling block to the success of many international organisations around the world (Doremus et al., 1998), including those in Nigeria. Expatriates and nationals therefore need education on cross-cultural communication management in order to overcome cultural barriers (Seneghaas, 2002).

Expatriate failure in foreign-based institutions

Several studies have shown that many foreign-managed companies close down early owing to the failure of expatriates and their home countries to adjust to, cope with and understand the cultural challenges and demands of the international business environment (Samovar et al., 1997). Those cultural challenges occur not only in direct interaction between nationals and foreigners but also in the more complex workings of local economic, political and socio-cultural systems of the host country (Black et al., 1991).

A major reason for expatriate failure is lack of cross-cultural competence, defined as 'the ability of individuals to draw on a set of knowledge, skills and personal attributes in order to work successfully with people from different national and cultural backgrounds at home or abroad' (Johnson, Lenartowicz and Aupud, 2006). Lack of such competence is observable within Northern Nigerian foreign-led institutions where turnover of expatriate employment is high, with the given reason that foreign nationals 'can't stand it here'.

'I can't stand it here!' Expatriate experiences with Northern Nigerian culture

Edward T. Hall (1981) declared that institutions and cultural patterns determine people's behaviour. This observation helps to explain why US Americans, other Westerners – and indeed non-West Africans – may feel they 'can't stand it here'.

For example, when first visiting a local market in Northern Nigeria I was confronted with a huge crowd speaking a language I didn't understand, with sporadic outbreaks of knife fighting, and with prices that soared depending on how foreign the customers looked and sounded. There were swarms of flies, non-hygienic water drainage, rotting meat, smelly fish, narrow paths, (*achaba*) motor bikes carrying three passengers and even a goat racing past buyers and sellers on narrow paths crowded with cars as well as people. I thought it was all crazy.

Monochronic and polychronic systems: Cultural conflict and misunderstanding

Although Westerners may describe the Hausa market as chaotic, in Hausa and non-Western views many of the ways in which Western institutions function seem constrained and restraining. Hall (1981) explains how members of Western and non-Western cultures organise themselves around time and space. He refers to them respectively as 'monochronic' and 'polychronic'.

In monochronic cultures, such as those of Europe, Australia, New Zealand and North America, most people expect to take on one task at a time and to stick to a well-organised schedule. Those who do not are generally seen as being disorganised. Therefore when Westerners and non-Westerners are put to work on the same project they are bound to come into cross-cultural conflict.

One expatriate manager of a roads construction company had a lot to say about the 'chaotic' (and therefore non-acceptable) behaviour of Hausa workers in Northern Nigeria. As a Christian he found the Muslim culture difficult to fit with his own monochronic ideas of the way tasks should be organised. It seemed to him that the Hausa reported to work at whatever time they pleased, took nine breaks a day to pray, employed their own relatives to work with them, and made all manner of excuses related to the death of relatives to absent themselves from work. All this infuriated the expatriate, who found himself unable to complete his projects on time, which meant his company lost money and business opportunities.

Hall explains that monochronic (M-time) and polychronic time (P-time) represent two kinds of use of both time and space. Space is included because the two systems (time and space) are functionally interrelated. M-time emphasises schedules, segmentation and promptness while P-time systems accommodate several things happening at once, involving several people, including extended family, friends and associates. To Westerners, understanding of P-time culture is difficult and dealing with it is confusing.

According to most Westerners, managing time through planning and time-tables allows for equal attention to, and opportunity for, all aspects of business transactions (Hoecklin, 1995). However, in P-time systems, as operated by Hausa, planning, making and keeping appointments are no guarantee that clients will get service. It often happens that one will make an appointment for a particular date, time and place, with a particular officer, only to be kept waiting for hours. Westerners find this behaviour disrespectful and annoying.

At international institutions in Northern Nigeria a blend of M- and P-time seems to have emerged by which participants in both systems try to adapt to each other. The attempt represents the will to succeed, but it can be subverted. For instance, students in West African educational institutions may make appointments to see their foreign professors (particularly if the students anticipate poor grades). They then trick the professors into missing the appointment so they can lay the blame on them for irresponsibility.

One way in which people in P-time systems prioritise service to clients is on the basis of 'who knows who' – a method that is unacceptable for most Westerners, though it may act to their advantage. In P-time cultures such as that of Northern Nigeria white European or US foreigners are known and easily identified in banks, hotels and public institutions, and are accorded special services. They enjoy privileges and are often given priority, followed by less prestigious expatriates and lastly by the locals. Of the last group, the rich, politicians and military officers get priority over the poor and ordinary Hausas. The result is that some Hausa families remain in poverty and are denied opportunities that would raise their socio-economic status.

However, even though valued foreigners get priority treatment they are still regarded as 'outsiders'. There are certain rights reserved for 'insiders' in P-time organisations that makes it impossible for M-time expatriates to keep abreast of events, and they may not even be sure that the decisions they make in their business with P-time counterparts will not be reversed without their knowledge and approval.

There are positive and negative aspects in both systems. P-time systems may exclude outsiders but they are built around context and relationships with other people. P-time organisations work at the convenience of the insiders and tend to be inwardly focused. M-time systems compartmentalise work and take insufficient account of context; but scheduling is another way of setting priorities, of deciding orders of importance in work and the goals that will be met within particular limits of time. Like P-time, M-time systems also are vulnerable to abuse, for example, through favouritism and racism.

Gift giving is common in the P-time system of Northern Nigeria, and, unlike M-time organisations, P-time people interact with several others simultaneously and are continually involved with each other. Gift giving and receiving capture the attention of those in authority. M-time people also give gifts, but usually to friends, not particularly as a means to seeking favours or undue advantage in business. However, gifts in P-time cultures are used to seal deals, and given even in anticipation of favours to come. Most P-time bureaucracies are managed by insiders, relatives, friends and associates, with 'outsiders' excluded. However, excluding 'outsiders' is a disadvantage to P-time organisations, for being mostly inward-looking, these organisations may be unable to handle large volumes of business, or deal with problems with foreigners.

For example, the retail sale of petroleum in Northern Nigeria is a popular business, and gas stations are operated mostly by wealthy Hausa Muslims. Petrol shortages are frequent, and the rich are served last. Privately owned vehicles are ignored while roadside fuel vendors get priority. Most of these vendors are small businesses owned by relatives, friends or associates of the gas station managers. Vendors sell their fuel at triple the pump price. Motor bikes serve as a means of local public transport, and can therefore afford to pay a higher price and charge the excess to the customer. Anyone who is willing to pay a higher price or to bribe the gas station attendants can get served first. Gas stations close at 5:00 pm, and everyone else has to buy petrol from the roadside vendors.

Foreigners find this difficult and stressful. Being white is a disadvantage because the privileged pay the highest price possible for their fuel and they do not get served first. Hausa drivers will often act on behalf of foreigners to buy fuel at the station in exchange for money for the service.

Because opportunities in P-time organisations are so dependent on personal relationships many families live and die in poverty, while many more depend on wealthier families for their livelihood. Begging is integral to the culture, and some families and indeed clans or tribes are referred to as 'slaves' to other wealthier families and clans. Some groups become what are called lifetime 'praise singers', beggars and dependants of other groups; this dependency is perceived as 'good' and is expected. (This kind of relationship is not unique to Africa. For example, Du Bois (1996), writing in 1899, argues that to some extent it applies to 'the Philadelphia negro').

The rich use the poor to shop, clean, cook, wash laundry, iron and drive, paying meagre wages. Foreigners are regarded as wealthy and expected to be generous to the poor and to the community as a whole by employing locals, giving gifts and alms to the poor, and paying higher prices for goods and services.

Culture is not innate, it is learnt, and people can 'unlearn' some unjust aspects, perhaps to make way for multiculturalism, but in general differences between people stem from the particular culture of their society. Because acculturation begins from birth to accustom people to do things in certain ways, they believe their culture is 'true,' or 'innate'; it becomes part of their unconscious, and it seems natural, while any other culture or way of doing things seems abnormal.

Cultural change (Kegan and Lahey, 2001): Inclusion of minority cultures

Wendy Griswold (2004) discusses why people do not change or discard their traditional beliefs and cultures in this post-modern globalised world. She believes that when a group's cultural boundaries are threatened by outside pressure, the group reasserts traditional beliefs instead of succumbing to change. Members see new ways as intrusive and threatening to their identity and existence. For example, when Christian expatriate managers ask Muslim workers to report to work on time and to follow an M-time system, the workers may feel even their religion is threatened. Sometimes this leads to violent protest – as in Northern Nigeria, which has had its share of conflict between Christians and Muslims.

Xanthaki (2010) explains that in order to promote justice among groups, some managers try to make decisions that are culturally inclusive and impersonal, as a means of respecting all citizens and their cultural beliefs and ensuring the success of their companies. However, Xanthaki believes it is not possible for authority to be so neutral:

> ... *in the face of unequal opportunities and unequal treatment between the majority and minorities, state neutrality is in effect an affirmation of the way of life, the choices, and the ideas of the dominant group within the state. The neutral state does not promote justice; rather, it maintains the status quo. Members of minority cultural groups do not have the same opportunities to live and work in their own culture and make their own choices to the same degree as the members of majority cultures.*
> (Xanthaki, 2010: 28–9)

In Northern Nigeria the dominant culture and religion is Islam, and the Muslim community makes most state decisions, which often favour the Muslims. Resistance against Christianity and Western education reinforces this domination by Northerners' control of Nigerian politics. Thus Muslim authorities perpetuate cultural hegemony by institutionalising social and political control of the country under which Christian minorities struggle to maintain their own culture and identity.

For the sake of social stability it is important to allow minority cultures the right of members to practise their beliefs freely and to permit them some cultural autonomy. All individuals are affected to some extent and on a daily basis by other cultures, so they need a secure cultural framework from which they can respond to outside influence, and from which they can make choices (Xanthaki, 2010: 28). Although tolerance of cultures is a starting point for achieving cross-cultural competence, globalisation and communication technological advancement pose new challenges in attaining cross-cultural competence particularly for international business (Barkema et al., 1997).

Information in general tends to be censored and limited in both M-time and P-time systems. With technological advancement information ought to reach all employees easily and speedily, yet in many organisations, particularly those with P-time systems, this right is not respected. P-time cultures tend to rely heavily on informal channels of communication, and since formal channels are often closed to the majority, rumours replace formal communication channels.

Northern Nigeria is not well connected with modern communication technology, but even the limited availability of Internet and cell-phones has brought greater flexibility and collaboration among employees, particularly in international businesses. The result is to reduce hierarchies and allow the formation of flatter organisations, or 'horizontal corporations' (Hinds and Kiesler, 1995).

Flat organisations help to counter excessive dominance in both M- and P-time systems, though hierarchies are still respected. For example, in the P-time systems of Northern Nigeria, honorifics are still used when addressing higher-status individuals, such as 'Sir', 'Oga' or 'Madam'. By contrast members of US-owned M-time companies prefer first names regardless of status as a way of treating everybody with the same degree of respect. Unfortunately, use or non-use of honorifics determines Northern Nigerian assessment of the levels of politeness shown to them by expatriates and other employees. This becomes a point of cross-cultural conflict as politeness accounts for employee's attitudes towards each other, and can affect intercultural interaction negatively.

Resolving cross-cultural conflict

Westerners often underrate P-time behaviour in favour of M-time, mainly owing to historical Western colonisation of other cultures. But most cultural conflict is not geographic but socio-economic. Therefore any resolution must occur through reduction in undermining behaviour, discrimination and disrespect that foreigners are seen to display towards members of those cultures they plan to exploit economically.

One aspect of organisational disrespect is that shown by members of M-systems to those who prefer P-systems. The finding of this study is that flatter organisational structures ('horizontal corporations') seem to promote more liberal views in that organisational communication becomes less formal, less hierarchical and more personal. As a result, more positive attitudes seem to develop between people who own very different cultural views.

Conclusion

This study suggests that successful cross-cultural communication in economic, political and social cultural fields depends on development of positive attitudes towards foreign cultures. The study is limited to aspects of foreigners' working experiences in Northern Nigeria, of communication barriers between monochronic and polychronic systems. Nevertheless the findings can be generalised to other environments in which M-time and P-time has to be connected; and more research is needed along these lines.

Discussion questions

1. A disadvantage of employing expatriate teaching professionals in developing economies is that the practice overlooks emerging numbers of competent local teachers. The positive view is that under foreign teachers local young people gain more knowledge of cultural change and globalisation. What is your opinion on the debate between employing foreign or native teachers?

2. Turnover of expatriate employment is high when foreign nationals feel they 'can't stand it here' in the local environment. Have you experience of 'culture shock'? Read the overview, 'Culture shock', in this chapter and discuss it.

3. Do you belong to a 'monochronic' or a 'polychronic' culture? One way of answering is to think back to when you were a child. Did your parents tell to 'finish one thing before you start another?' and 'Don't get distracted, stick to the job in hand'? Or were they more likely to say: 'Drop what you're doing, this is more important!' and 'Stop doing that and come and say good evening to our guests!'

OVERVIEW: ACCULTURATION BY DEGREES	Elizabeth Christopher

Culture shock was first defined in the 1950s by Dr Kalervo Oberg (1951), an anthropologist. He stated that culture shock is initiated by 'the anxiety that results from losing familiar signs and symbols of social intercourse'. He defined six aspects:

1. Strain of making necessary psychological adaptations.
2. Loss and deprivation of old friends, family, status, career and possessions.
3. Being rejected by and/or rejecting members of the new culture.
4. Confusion in role, role expectation, values, feelings and self-identity.
5. Surprise, anxiety, indignation, even disgust for cultural differences.
6. Powerlessness in a new environment.

Oberg developed a model of activities, attitudes, emotions and physical responses in a six-month time frame of adjustment to a foreign culture, although it can be repeated at any time with a variety of reactions and time periods. The following is Oberg's model as adapted by Elizabeth Christopher (October 2010):

Pre-departure: excitement, anticipation and enthusiasm;

First month: honeymoon: still filled with the excitement of travel and newness of food, culture and environment; learning the language; making new friends;

Second and third month: homesickness, hostility: awareness of differences as unpleasant; inconveniences in accommodation, not speaking the language well enough to be understood; lack of familiarity of foods, shops, surroundings and social behaviour;

Fourth month: humour: acceptance of differences, return of enthusiasm and enjoyment of new foods, new ways of doing things; improvement in language skill;

Fifth month: honour: genuine appreciation of new friends and host country values and beliefs; emotions steady and confidence regained;

Sixth month: home: normal lifestyle, established routines and social life; travelling, helping other newcomers; genuine distress when time comes to leave 'second home' and possibility of culture shock on return to own culture.

Causes of culture shock: being cut off from cultural signals; living or working in ambiguous situations; having personal values questioned (previously considered absolutes); being expected to function but in a situation in which rules have not been explained.

Signs of culture shock: homesickness; withdrawal; excessive home nationalism; stereotyping host nationals; tiredness; stress; inability to work.

Dealing with intercultural stress and shock: Get to know the place and people; travel locally, enrol in a language class, join a club; don't criticise; find a friend as your 'cultural informant' to introduce local life and practices; laugh at yourself and strange situations; avoid self-pity; get enough rest; eat healthy food; take some cultural risks; ask for help; keep involved, don't withdraw. Record your experiences, insights and frustrations in a journal (who knows, you may publish it!). Try to see things as 'different' instead of 'good' or 'bad', 'right' or 'wrong'. Be open and flexible to change as much as possible, but accept that everything cannot be assimilated all at once.

The following commentary by Bhawuk and Anbe illustrates the importance of such behaviour.

DECLINE OF THE MAJORITY, RISE OF THE MINORITY: COMMUNITY CULTURAL CHANGES IN HAWAI'I: SUMMARY OF A STUDY OF ACCULTURATION TO A HOST COUNTRY	Dharm P.S. Bhawuk and Kathryn Anbe

To identify how people adjust when moving from one culture to another, culture can be viewed as a repertoire of behaviours, collection of frames, or inventory of scripts that people carry in their mind: learnt through enculturation or natural socialisation. Triandis (1972) calls this the subjective culture.

Acculturation refers to changes in attitude and behaviour by individuals while living in a culture to which they were not born. Triandis suggested that the greater the perceived differences in subjective culture, the greater will be the affective reaction. The more individuals perceive their culture to be different from the host culture the more anxiety they will experience, both in simple interactions and in trying to bridge the gap.

At the extreme, a large perceived difference might lead to a form of paralysis or culture shock in which individuals see the two cultures as impossibly different. They might be inclined to give up, because the required personal change is too large to make the effort worthwhile. The possibility of failure is also likely to be a strong deterrent.

Ward (2004) found that cultural distance and psychological disturbance are interrelated. Depending on perceived cultural differences, sojourners are likely to experience separation (i.e., refusal to integrate with the host culture) or marginalisation (i.e., a dysfunctional relationship with the host culture) if the cultural difference is immense. If the culture difference is not perceived as large , they are likely to develop assimilation or integration strategies.

Triandis suggested that both the ecology and the history of people in a certain region shape culture. Culture in turn shapes human personality through the process of socialisation, which is often unique to a culture. And finally, personality determines human behaviour. This is not to rule out individual differences, nor to present culture as a tyrannical force since humans shape culture, albeit slowly, as much as culture shapes humans.

For example, Hawai'i has gone from being an independent country to being a state of USA, and clearly this history has shaped the behaviours of people on the islands. The following is a summary of a study in Hawai'i consisting of interviews and focus group discussions to evaluate the impact of acculturation on the daily behaviours of the people concerned. The findings were that Hawai'ian culture has impacted the attire of the respondents (including the use of leis or floral garlands in daily interactions), their communication, use of Hawai'ian words in English (for instance, when asking for directions) and also on other cultural aspects such as food menus, music and dance.

Attire

With the tropical weather and the laid-back atmosphere many participants felt that the style of attire in Hawai'i is relaxed. 'Aloha' attire was described as being a floral printed shirt or dress, usually with multiple colours. Aloha attire began in the late 1920s and 1930s as custom-made clothing, which became very popular with tourists (Steele, 1984). It was not until the late 1940s that aloha shirts became appropriate, even expected, work attire for men; due in large part to the hot and humid weather that made wearing a suit and tie uncomfortable. One of the focus group said:

> *I think because of the laid-back atmosphere, in Hawai'i a suit and tie just doesn't work. Here it's too hot, and it's just not the way we function here. Hawai'i is a lot slower than [the mainland]. [Aloha attire] is our dress up, it's our business casual.*

Typical business attire for men on the US mainland is a long-sleeved button-down collared shirt and tie; but in Hawai'i this may be seen as 'intimidating' and can make co-workers 'nervous' with its formality. However, 'aloha' dress is categorised into work and casual wear. For work the colours are more neutral or limited to only one or two shades, and the prints are smaller and less visible, whereas a casual aloha shirt is colourful or 'loud', with big prints, as favoured by tourists.

Giving leis is a popular custom in Hawai'i. Everyone interviewed had received a lei since coming to the islands. This custom dates back to the native Hawai'ians who wore these woven garlands made from feathers, shells, flowers, seeds, bones, nuts, and stones, often with spiritual significance. Specific leis were woven to honour specific Hawai'ian deities: for example, the twisted *maile* vine was worn to represent the hula goddess, *Laka*, or the kukui nut lei is worn to represent the pig god, *Kamapua'a* (Alameida, 1997). In the past lei-giving held a special meaning for the lei was hand-made specifically for the receiver. Today leis are often purchased from flower stores; and even large grocery stores and big stores like Wal-Mart carry leis.

The tradition of lei-giving took off during the 'Boat Days' in the early twentieth century when visitors to the islands were greeted at the docks with leis, hula and song (McDonald, 1995). Today the lei is still given during special occasions, such as birthdays, graduations, ceremonies and as a welcome or parting gift of aloha. The participants remarked when going lei-shopping that they were often told which type of lei to buy, shell or nuts for men and flowers for women, while the native Hawai'ians did not make such a distinction:

> And even when I was buying leis for graduation, I didn't know what kind of leis I wanted to get … [I wanted] something nice, and they said well these are male leis and they had a section of those leis. … And just by the look of some leis you can tell it's not girly, but you know you can give a guy like carnations or orchids. Kukui nuts are for guys, I have never seen a girl wear one. … In Waikiki I see the tourists wearing them, like a husband and wife, and it's weird. Or, it's trendy to do.

Communication

When people come to Hawai'i, one of the first things they notice is the dialect spoken by the local population. The participants in the survey called this Pidgin English and commented also on its speed of delivery, use of shortened sentence structure and abbreviations.

Language in Hawai'i has been impacted by the different immigrant groups that came to the islands. The origin of Pidgin English is in the plantations where the different immigrant groups created a mixture of English, abbreviated words, Hawai'ian and other native tongues to create a common form of communication. In linguistics 'pidgin' is considered to be a shortened, abbreviated version of words, often spoken quicker than normal speech, and ending with a 'yeah?' in the form of a question, with the intonation rising at the end of the sentence.

When asked for examples of Pidgin English, half of the participants stated it was spoken in casual conversation among friends, and gave the following examples:

> 'you come, stay go?'; 'Get chapter three yeah?'; 'Eh brah, try come?, da kine.'

The interviewees stressed the point that many who continue to speak Pidgin English are those from 'certain areas', typically categorised by lower economic status and less education. It was even suggested that Pidgin English presents a glass ceiling for local people as there are negative connotations associated with it. However, it was generally agreed that speaking in Pidgin did not necessarily imply intellectual inferiority and that some people chose to speak in Pidgin at times because the casual lifestyle of Hawai'i is emphasised in its use.

When asked if the participants could say a few words in Hawai'ian, 13 out of the 17 participants chose to say *mahalo* and *aloha* ('Thank you' and 'Greetings'). When asked to name Hawai'ian words, some participants had difficulty recalling any. Some participants also spoke of the local language as a difficulty in conversing with local people because of the use of Pidgin English and Hawai'ian words in everyday speech. One of the participants stated that a popular misconception is that *mahalo* means trash or rubbish to foreigners because the word is written on the trash cans all over the city, especially in Waikiki. Of course, the sign is meant to thank people for not littering and for using the trash cans.

In the focus group also people discussed how the Hawai'ian language is not understood by newcomers, who miss the deeper cultural meaning associated with 'aloha':

> *The tourists see it as ... only a commercial tool ... for commercial purposes and used so lightly ... when you say aloha you are supposed to mean it from the bottom of your heart.*

Today the impact of the Hawai'ian language is seen in the everyday words such as *aloha, mahalo, pau (are you pau* means 'are you done?', and people say *I am pau* when they are done), *haole,* or *hapa* as well as in the Hawai'ian street names, places of business and companies in Hawai'i. These words have also been incorporated into the creole language of the islands, or Pidgin English.

Giving directions

The participants unanimously agreed that giving directions was different in Hawai'i compared to mainland USA – not only in choice of words but also owing to the geography or island nature of the place. Of the 17 participants 15 stated that people use *mauka, makai, ewa* and Diamond Head to denote north, south, west and east. One participant thought that people have to use landmarks for giving directions since Hawai'i is not situated on the grid system. He also noted that Honolulu is a relatively small town, and one can go to most places within 30 minutes. For this reason, directions needed to be given with mountains, the ocean and restaurants as landmarks.

Participants also noted that many of the streets in Hawai'i have Hawai'ian names, which makes it difficult to give directions orally. One story was of the experience of looking for the 'Likelike Highway' instead of the Like Like Highway (the first is pronounced as one word 'like-like' and the second as two words, pronounced 'leekie leekie'). Highway and street names highlight the use of Hawai'ian words and language in everyday speech, This, as well as difference in pronunciation, may make it very difficult for someone to get around who is not familiar with the language.

Food

The participants were unanimous that Hawai'i's local cuisine or 'local *kine grindz*' is represented by the plate lunch. They also agreed that a plate lunch consisted of rice, macaroni salad and some type of meat or main dish. The main dish was not specific to any cultural cuisine, with main dish items ranging from Japanese dishes to traditional Hawai'ian food.

> *When I think of Hawai'i the first thing I think of is plate lunch. So you have your main dish, like chicken katsu, and then you have your two scoops of rice and a scoop of Mac salad. And for the mainland it would probably be a burger.*

When tourists come to Hawai'i their experience with local food may be in the form of a *lu'au.* The *lu'au* (pronounced 'loo-ow') is a Hawai'ian tradition – a feast to celebrate accomplishments, honour important people and commemorate great events. In old Hawai'i a *lu'au* meant a lavish food extravaganza to fete royalty, foreign dignitaries, powerful chieftains, or hundreds of guests at important weddings, christenings or birthdays. *Lu'aus* often lasted for days and required an incredible amount of preparation. Guests sat on mats on the ground, with food piled high in calabash bowls in front of them. They ate a bit, danced a bit, drank a little and sang a lot; it was a feast of *aloha*.

It was pointed out by many participants that while Hawai'ian food may be considered local food the reverse was not true:

> *Actually Hawai'ian food can be local food but local food can't always be Hawai'ian food. Chicken katsu would be local food but not Hawai'ian food, kalua pig is both local food and Hawai'ian food.*

One participant went as far as to describe Hawai'ian food as being in two categories: the '*Hawai'ian Hawai'ian*' food, which is traditional Hawai'ian food, and '*Hawai'ian*' food, which would be the contemporary Hawai'ian food such as kalua pig and cabbage.

The participants stated that there were more varieties of ethnic foods in Hawai'i as compared to the mainland USA. They noted this difference as one of variety versus choice: whereas on the mainland there are many restaurants to choose from, in Hawai'i one could have a variety of ethnic foods such as Japanese, Chinese or Korean, or the plate lunch. The choice of food offered even in fast food restaurants in Hawai'i is different as compared to the mainland. For example, McDonald's in Hawai'i offers breakfast choices such as Portuguese sausage or spam, eggs and rice, or teriyaki burgers, taro pies or saimin (ramen noodles), which one would not find on the mainland.

The participants also spoke about the differences in food choices in the supermarket, where it may be easier to find Asian food products in Hawai'i than on the mainland, in large part in response to market demand.

One participant said the atmosphere in local restaurants is more relaxed and inviting than on the US mainland.

Food taste, variety, and selection were discussed with the participants, who agreed that the food in Hawai'i has been strongly influenced by both the immigrant populations as well as the native Hawai'ian culture:

> *Asian food, lots of Asian food, you can order all kinds here. And we have the real thing here, we have Chinese people cooking Chinese food. Take what I have been eating the past few days, I had Asian food all day today, Subway for lunch, Hawai'ian food for dinner last night and Korean food for lunch yesterday, and American food, pancakes for breakfast. Oh that's another thing with the Hawai'ian food – it's made by the Hawai'ian people.*

Music and dance

The dances presented at the *lu'aus* have been misunderstood as Hawai'ian dance. Oftentimes *lu'aus* have Tahitian dances, fire dancers and knife dancers.

This is part of the Pacific Island traditions, but these dances are not part of the Hawai'ian tradition. This is a problem because while they may be called Tahitian and Samoan, tourists often lump them together as Hawai'ian, diluting the meaning of what is traditionally Hawai'ian. The atmosphere in places like Waikiki, which one participant aptly called 'the tourist part of the island', is quite different.

A participant suggested that what the tourists see as Hawai'ian culture is really second-hand knowledge packaged specifically for tourists.

Summary

Aspects of traditional Hawai'ian culture are used commercially to present the islands as an exotic destination for tourists, particularly from the US mainland. They are welcomed with leis, a few Hawai'ian words like *aloha* and *mahalo*, and Hawai'ian tunes played on a ukulele. The objective is to make them feel they are not in the USA, though they do not have to apply for a visa, can still drive on the freeway as they do at home, and the only document they need is their driver's licence.

These 'touristy' aspects of Hawai'ian culture and the Waikiki atmosphere may give visitors a taste of the culture but they are not authentic. It is to be questioned whether such colonisation of the native culture does justice either to the culture or its original members; or whether in effect it serves to further marginalise them.

Discussion

How might the above be generalised to situations where managers are sent on tours of duty to countries or regions where they have to learn to live and work in cultural environments very different from their own? This study of life in Hawai'i offers a number of 'helpful hints':

1. 'Culture' can be summarised usefully as a subjective 'repertoire of behaviours' learnt through acculturation and socialisation. Sojourners (people who live and work for extended periods in a foreign culture) need to identify and accommodate themselves to important aspects of this repertoire. Otherwise they will be regarded as insensitive and ignorant foreigners. This will make it very hard for them to gain and keep the respect they need to carry out their responsibilities.

2. Acculturation refers to changes in attitude and behaviour by individuals while living in a culture to which they were not born. Cultural distance and psychological disturbance are interrelated. The more individuals perceive their culture to be different from the host culture the more anxiety they will experience. Some people in this situation find it too difficult to adapt; and this is one reason why expatriate managers fail to complete their assignments. Another is that they become marginalised, that is, they form a dysfunctional

relationship with the host culture. They see themselves, and the local people see them, as 'foreigners'. However, if expatriates can accept that the cultural difficulties are not so insurmountable they are likely to develop integration strategies for social and work interactions.

3. One tactic, as part of this strategy, seems to be to dress in accordance with the local social norms, even if they are quite different from those back home.

4. Another tactic seems to be to learn the local ways of gift giving, which are not always as simple as they might appear. The writer well remembers witnessing the humiliation of a US manager assigned to a firm in Japan who thought he understood that all new employees were presented with the company emblem in the form of a pin to be worn on suit or dress. Proudly he gave this pin to his newly appointed Japanese assistant, who was plainly embarrassed by the gift. When next day she was not wearing it, he assumed she had lost it and gave her another. She was obviously so distressed that finally he had the sense to ask the advice of a senior Japanese colleague, who informed him that these pins were presented to new recruits during formal welcoming ceremonies. The gift was considered a privilege, never handed out casually, and indeed to do so would be a form of insult.

    In the study above, the example of gift giving is that of garlanding recipients with floral leis, and information is given about who should receive them, when and why. Thus, whether in Japan, Hawai'i, China, Australia, the UK or Finland, expatriate managers should learn the rules.

5. Sojourners need some knowledge of the local language, even if only a few words of greeting or farewell. Another example from the writer's experience is that residents and locals in Hawai'i feel a certain contempt for visitors who insist indiscriminately and frequently on saying 'A-lo-ha!' loudly with the accent on the third syllable. As the participants in the above study confirm, this Hawai'ian word of special greeting or farewell was traditionally reserved for special occasions, and was heartfelt. Moreover, when spoken the accent is evenly distributed over all three syllables. Thus, to generalise from this particular example, sojourners should make sure they 'get the words right' if they are not to make fools of themselves. The best way to do this is to find a friendly local informant to mentor them.

6. Finding one's way about can be really difficult in a foreign place. Even the street signs may be written incomprehensibly. Sojourners need a crash course in the local geography, landmarks, important buildings, street names, names of popular local restaurants and cafés.

7. Local food may be very different from the common cuisine at home. Advice for sojourners is to develop as broad a taste palate as possible. Formal dining, such as business functions and social events, often includes dishes that are not usually offered on everyday menus. The example above is that of the *lu'au*, a local banquet at which very local dishes are served. Sojourners are well advised in such situations to 'shut up and eat up', however strange the appearance of the food and however mysterious

its provenance: though, of course, religious and other dietary restrictions should be respected.

8. Shopping in the local supermarket or equivalent can be tricky. Some Asian packaging, for example, displays no words of English so Westerners may not be able to read what it contains. Again, local informants are essential if the poor sojourner is not to end up eating dried sardines instead of cereal. The same suggestion applies to eating in local restaurants. The writer's advice is to invite a local to eat with you and be prepared to pay for two meals instead of one for at least a month after arrival. Take careful note of what your companion orders so you can do the same later on your own.

9. Social events need to be handled with care until the newcomer gets used to the way the locals relax and enjoy themselves. Where they go to 'party', what they eat and drink, what kind of music they like, what kind of singing and dancing – all these activities are part of the local culture, innate to the locals but foreign to newcomers who have to learn how to do them.

10. Finally, if sojourners don't want to be regarded as ignorant foreigners – or, worse, as tourists – for the length of their stay, they will learn to identify and respect the authentic culture of their hosts and their country. Otherwise they will remain separated and marginalised.

Questions

Students with international experience of living, working and studying in more than one country might become a resource for this exercise. They might be asked to form a brains trust, seated along a high table in front of their classmates as audience, who would ask them questions about their experiences. This activity may be planned in advance – in which case questions can be submitted to the panel ahead of time – or set up spontaneously in class time. Suggestions for questions include:

1. Have you ever found an international experience more than you could handle and been compelled to cut it short? If so, why?

2. Have you ever found an international experience so unpleasant that you formed a dysfunctional relationship with the host culture by refusing to have anything to do with it?

3. Did you behave differently from back home in order to fit in with the local people? In what you wore? In giving gifts? In speaking as much as possible in the host country language?

4. Did you find local people who would help you to learn what to do, how to get around, what food to buy, what restaurants to eat in?

5. Did you make friends and build a social life?

6. Did you learn to respect the local culture?

Case study: Developing global managers: Poor old Bruce; he couldn't cut the wasabe

Bruce gazed out of the window of his 24th floor office at the tranquil beauty of the Imperial Palace amid the hustle and bustle of downtown Tokyo. It was only six months since he had arrived from Sydney with his wife and two children, with high hopes for this three-year assignment as the director of the Japanese office of North Ryde and Associates. Now he was unhappily trying to decide whether to pack up and go home or persuade his wife to stick it out.

They hadn't had much warning of the posting, and they knew nothing about living in Japan. But the proposed salary was so good, plus it was such a career opportunity for Bruce, that Sheila decided to quit her teaching job in order to tackle this exciting new challenge.

After the eight-hour flight, and the long journey from the airport to Tokyo (in a chauffeur-driven limousine, accompanied by a young Japanese employee who spoke very little English), they were exhausted and the children were fretful. An apartment had been rented for them but they were dismayed by how small it was (and horrified by the amount of rent): two tiny bedrooms, a small sitting room plus kitchen and a minute bathroom. However, everything was spotlessly clean and beautifully – though simply – furnished and decorated.

They spent a day settling in, then Bruce went to the office to meet his new staff and colleagues – all Japanese, except for one of the accountants, Peter, who was Australian. Bruce called a general meeting and asked everybody to identify themselves and tell him what their position and duties were. They seemed to find this difficult and gave very vague and general answers. He got the impression nobody really knew exactly what they did!

However, he thought this might be due to language problems, though most of them spoke English reasonably well, if sometimes with a strong accent. Over the next few weeks he discovered that everybody appeared to work efficiently. He made it his business to talk individually to each staff member and tried to discuss their job with each of them, but found it really hard going.

Meanwhile Sheila was complaining that all the laundry had to be taken to the local laundromat because there was no laundry in the apartment. She found it difficult and expensive to buy the kind of groceries she wanted – potatoes and salad vegetables, fresh bread, meat and dairy products. The kitchen was so small it was impossible to cook the kind of family meals she was used to in Australia, which meant lots of meals at local restaurants. The children, Bev and Tim, wouldn't eat Japanese food at first, but thank goodness there was a McDonald's nearby.

Bev and Tim settled fairly well into an English-language school where about half the students were expatriates like themselves, and made friends with American, English and European young people as well as fellow Australians. There were also many Japanese students, and Japanese was taught in school. It wasn't long before Bev and Tim at home were using Japanese words, phrases and even whole sentences of Japanese mixed up with English. They also started asking for rice at dinner instead of bread, and fish instead of meat, much to their mother's frustration.

Also she was seriously upset when she went to pick them up from school one day and saw her son bowing to his teacher. 'You're not his servant,' she scolded. 'Australians don't bow!' Tim, resigned to his mother's ignorance, just replied, 'Oh, *Mum!*'

Bruce was feeling equally frustrated by his inability to understand his Japanese staff and clients. He fixed up an important meeting with a client company and made what he thought was a great sales pitch, but the Japanese clients were very slow to respond and he only heard later, in a very roundabout way, that they thought his quotation was too expensive. 'Why didn't they say so, straight out?' he demanded, but got no answer.

He confronted Mr Tanaka, the head of the client's negotiation team, with the question, only to receive the reply: 'There are many matters we need to discuss further before we can proceed.' When Bruce asked what these were, Mr Tanaka answered: 'We will discuss them when the time comes.' 'Well, I'll wait to hear from you, then,' said Bruce, but he heard no more.

He found his own people equally infuriating. He asked his assistant manager, Tsuyoshi, to prepare a report on another potential client, but Tsuyoshi replied: 'That will be difficult.' 'Well, do your best, I'm sure you'll find a way to get the information you need,' replied Bruce. After a week, he asked for the report and was told it was not ready. 'Why not?', he asked, and was again told that it was 'difficult'. 'I don't pay you to make difficulties!', shouted Bruce, now entirely out of patience and forgetting how public everything was in the open-plan office. He was aware several staff members were listening and he sensed their disapproval. He assumed they shared his annoyance at the delay.

Later, one of them, Yoshiko, mentioned, apologetically, and in a very general way, that some information about corporations that might be on public record in a country like Australia might not be so easy to obtain in Japan. Bruce assumed she was trying to defend the assistant manager, and thought no more about it.

Brian took Peter out for lunch one day and described his frustrations. 'Nobody every answers a question directly,' he complained. 'All they do is look at each other and then murmur something meaningless! I have no idea what they are thinking.'

'Do you ever go out to a bar for drinks with a group of them after work?', asked Peter. 'Well, no', replied Bruce. 'I try to get home as early as I can to keep Sheila company. She doesn't seem to know anybody who speaks English and hasn't made any friends. Even the kids seem to speak more Japanese now than English.'

In fact when he got home that night, Sheila burst into tears, and said she'd had enough. She wanted to go home. Bruce tried to comfort her but felt pretty much the same way himself. Now he was sitting in his office wondering what to do.

Source

Based on Deresky, H. and Christopher, E. 2008. *International Management: Managing across Borders and Cultures.* Frenchs Forest, NSW: Pearson Education Australia, Ch. 9.

Questions

1. What were the major reasons why Bruce and Sheila found it so difficult to adjust to living in Japan?
2. Which of the following explanations is the most likely one for Bruce's first impression of his Japanese staff as being unable to explain their jobs?
   - They didn't speak English well enough and couldn't explain exactly what their duties were.
   - Japanese culture is one of modesty rather than self-aggrandisement. When confronted with a demand to explain what their job is, they are much more likely than Australians to 'play it down'.
   - Bruce was still suffering from jet lag and couldn't concentrate on what people were telling him.
   - Japanese describe positions in the organisational hierarchy in different terms from Australians and therefore Bruce couldn't understand the information they gave him.
   - The Japanese staff were hostile towards Bruce, as a foreigner in charge of them. They wanted a Japanese manager and were being difficult out of resentment.
3. What were the likely causes for the communication problems between Bruce and Mr Tanaka, representative of the client company with which Bruce was negotiating? What did Tsuyoshi mean when he said it would be 'difficult' to comply with Bruce's request? How might Bruce help Sheila to become more acculturated in Japan?

The following report begins with a definition of the kind of cross-cultural sensitivity needed to avoid unfortunate situations such as those experienced by Bruce and Sheila. Reid and Petocz (below) describe it as one of a group of high-level dispositions, in which people interact with others from different cultural backgrounds.

Another version is by Kishan Rana (2002), who writes that to cultivate cross-cultural skill is to develop an understanding of the other culture, through a study of its history, its value system, and other factors that identify and differentiate it. Without losing pride in one's own heritage, xenophobic notions have to be abandoned – though this is more difficult in practice than in theory. Genuine curiosity and a desire to learn are helpful attitudes; and acceptance that different societies and peoples have evolved their own distinct qualities, which are neither superior nor inferior to others. Diversity is what human society as a whole celebrates, and the factors of commonality are more profound than surface differences.

BUSINESS STUDENTS' CONCEPTIONS OF CROSS-CULTURAL SENSITIVITY	Anna Reid and Peter Petocz

Introduction

In contemporary higher education, various dispositions or ways of communicating with the world are increasingly seen as important aspects of the behaviour of successful graduates. Cross-cultural sensitivity (CCS) refers to the way in which people interact with others from different cultural backgrounds: it can be regarded as one of a group of high-level graduate dispositions. When students move into professional work, their employers will expect them to demonstrate *creativity* in finding and solving problems, to have a well-developed *ethical stance*, to be able to contribute to their company's position on *sustainability* and *sustainable development*, and to display a high level of *cross-cultural sensitivity* and understanding. All these attributes can be viewed as cross-disciplinary or 'generic' capabilities from the point of view of the university, to be included as part of every student's learning programme.

There have been various approaches to definition and exploration of cross-cultural sensitivity – and what is sometimes called cross-cultural or inter-cultural competence. One prevalent idea is that CCS is a stable personal characteristic that can be evaluated through the use of various tests, for instance, the Multicultural Personality Questionnaire (Van der Zee and Van Oudenhoven, 2000), devised to predict the cultural effectiveness of employees preparing for overseas work. Another perspective is to study candidates' perception of 'home culture' as an indicator of how well they might adjust to different cultural experiences. Yet others are to investigate how CCS seems to lead to personal transformation through critical reflection on novel cultural experiences; and the various factors that lead to successful inter-cultural communication, including cultural self-identity. Yet other investigations have looked at the learning styles of students from different cultural backgrounds, and the different learning support that is most effective for each of them.

The empirical evidence

The data on which this article is based were collected at Macquarie University in Sydney, Australia as part of a study investigating domestic and international students' views of professional aspects of communication that they develop through their studies in preparation for their future workplaces.

The students were all undertaking a business degree either on the main campus in the Faculty of Business and Economics (at that time called Division of Economic and Financial Studies, EFS) or at the International College of Management, Sydney (ICMS), an independent institution with links to Macquarie University and teaching business courses from the same curriculum – and sometimes with the same lecturers.

Interviewed students were somewhere in the middle of their degree, rather than those in their first or last years of studies. Most of the international students were from countries in the Asia-Pacific region, though some were from Europe and the United States. The domestic students were equally diverse, and many of them were from Asian backgrounds. Students were offered the opportunity to participate via advertisements in student newsletters and noticeboards, and announcements in large lectures. The details of the study were approved by the appropriate ethics committee, and each student gave their informed consent to participate. A total of 44 students were interviewed; about one-third of them were female and two-thirds male, half of them domestic and half international students, around half from the main campus (EFS) and the others from ICMS.

Students were given the option to participate in an interview using email, and about a quarter of them took this option; another quarter of the group were interviewed face to face individually, and the others were interviewed face to face in groups of two to four. In such group interviews, each student was asked the same questions in turn, including any follow-up questions, so individuals' views could be distinguished – although, of course, they could be influenced by other participants in their group. Over 88,000 words of transcript were recorded and email records. Here the focus is specifically on what respondents said in answer to the questions: 'How do you understand the idea of cross-cultural sensitivity?' and 'What role do you think cross-cultural sensitivity will play in your future professional work?'

Theoretical approach

The research objective was to investigate students' views of cross-cultural sensitivity, so an obvious approach was to ask them directly, allowing them to come up with their own definitions of the term, rather than supplying a definition from the literature or the views of the researchers.

Phenomenography is an appropriate theoretical approach for investigating the different ways in which people view a particular phenomenon, in this case, CCS. It was developed in the 1970s by Ference Marton (1975a and b) and colleagues in Sweden, initially as a way of describing the process and outcomes of learning from the view of the learners themselves. More information about phenomenography can be found in Marton and Booth (1997). However, the following brief description will be sufficient for the purposes of this report.

Many phenomenographic studies have shown that when a group of people experience a particular situation they will view it in a small number of qualitatively distinct ways. Some people will share a particular way of looking at the situation, while others will look at it in other quite distinct ways. This unexpected finding has been one of the important contributions of the approach.

Phenomenography focuses on identifying and describing these different approaches, called conceptions, and the relationships between them. It often happens that the conceptions can be arranged in a hierarchical and inclusive relationship, with the narrower and more limiting views contained in the broader and more inclusive views. Evidence for such a structure can be obtained either logically, from the definition of the categories, or empirically, by looking at the various statements made by participants in the investigation.

People who seem to hold the broadest conceptions of a phenomenon such as CCS seem to be aware of the narrower conceptions, and can make use of them if they are needed. However, those people who seem to hold the narrowest conceptions do not seem to be aware of any broader ones. This implies a view of learning as a process of changing from narrower to broader conceptions. It also explains why educators favour the broader, more inclusive conceptions over the narrower, more limiting conceptions.

Conceptions of cross-cultural sensitivity

The phenomenographic analysis of data from the student interviews revealed three qualitatively different conceptions of cross-cultural sensitivity. These were labelled respectively as *Awareness, Knowledge* and *Respect*, from the narrowest and most limited to the broadest and most inclusive of interpretations.

When students discussed CCS, it was sometimes in the context of their daily life experiences, and sometimes in the context of their business studies and their future professional work in the world of business. This context is an important aspect of the results: people in a quite different context (maybe a secondary school or a large multinational workplace) could have quite different views about CCS.

1. *Awareness:* students talked about CCS in terms of being aware of the 'otherness' of different people and groups (and also of how easy it is to give offence). This awareness was based heavily on proximity in the specific context – an Australian university with large numbers of overseas students studying with local students, many of them of overseas cultural backgrounds. While this is the narrowest conception identified, it was most often (though not always) seen as a component of other, broader views.

   Two respondents, Hercules and Bruce, identified specific instances of 'otherness', while another, Janine, made a more general statement.

   > Hercules: *Especially this industry because as the person working in a hotel, when you meet different people from all over the world, and then he may come and tell you I would like, I don't know, meat dipped in some strange sauce you know, and for you it's really strange. You know, you shouldn't have any reaction and you just have to understand that that's the way he eats maybe or she eats.*

   > Bruce: *He at one point wanted to joke with a, one of the Asian students and ran up and accidentally hit him a little bit light on the head, on the back of the head, which created quite an issue because the back of the head is very important for some people. So the problem wouldn't have happened if he would have smacked him on the shoulder, for instance.*

   > Janine: *The world is made up of people from many different cultures. They have different ideas about the same subject. Such as in the university or in my future work or company, people, we have to work with different kind of people, we can't think the same way they think as us. So, try to communicate with them and learn something about their culture. You know in some country, when they think it is right it is wrong. So, when we meet these kind of things, we will feel confused.*

2. *Knowledge:* students built on their awareness of difference and focused on CCS in terms of their knowledge of other people's and groups' different beliefs, approaches and cultures. This was often linked with the notion of

expedience – using knowledge about others' cultural differences as a way of managing them in a business situation. This intermediate conception was the most common. Some students, for example, Sid and Tim, talked about the knowledge they needed in general terms, while others such as Erica talked about specific knowledge – in her case about Japanese customs.

> Sid: *People expect you to go somewhere, to go from here to Asia and do business there and come back. You know, and do business properly, in order to go there and do business, you gotta understand the culture as well, so [it] plays [a] very important role because businesses, they are consolidating, they're integrating their operations.*

> Tim: *I think if we can't be aware of people's different ideologies and different beliefs, where they're from, their background, then we're losing out. You know, because it, it's very interesting in the end. [...] There's wealth in understanding different people's backgrounds and where they come from. [...] So being able to communicate with people and look at things from their level as well as my level, as well as different stakeholders' level, will be very important in coming up with effective solutions on, on different issues.*

> Erica: *I don't know that much about Japanese people as such but, just ideas of eye contact, a level of eye contact, whether you shake hands or whether you bow, what, how do they deal with orders and things, or do they prefer to be left alone to manage themselves, that kind of thing.*

3. *Respect:* added to an awareness of difference and a knowledge of other people's beliefs and cultures is the notion of respecting others' beliefs and changing one's actions, and maybe even one's own beliefs, in response to them. Though this was the most inclusive conception, it was only articulated by a few students. Xena introduced the notion of modifying one's behaviour to reduce conflicts or solve problems, Casey pointed out that such acceptance and change needs to be a 'two-way street' – mutual respect as a basis for CCS – and Henry discussed the need for such respect and compromise, and then returned to the important role of knowledge about difference.

> Xena: *I guess cross-cultural sensitivity is the fact of respecting and understanding that there are differences between different cultures and nations, and that you can't just gloss over them. You have to be respectful of them and try to understand them and understand the differences and respect those differences. And in the workplace that affects it a lot. [...] And so then that's where clashes arise, and for a manager it's really important to understand that there are different cultures and different ways to look at stuff so that you can mediate between them. [...] Especially in the hospitality tourism industry. Not only because you're dealing with visitors from other countries but your staff is usually made up of people from other countries as well.*

> Casey: *I think definitely when you do put all of different cultures together you do have to be sensitive to the fact that people do have different beliefs, do have*

different values, different way of doing things. [...] I think is definitely I have to understand their beliefs and their understandings for me to actually be able to be sensitive to the fact if I want to work for them I have to understand and be, you know, and work in the way that they are happy for me to work with them. Obviously it has to be, has to be a two-way street. They have to understand my culture as well.

Henry: *So unless and until you are sensitive to other cultures and listening to you are able to appreciate other cultures, you'll, you'll not go anywhere. You should be able to appreciate other cultures. Well, and if you are able to mould yourself into their culture, well and good. But if you want to stay back and still follow your own culture, yes do it, but you should have the eye and patience, you should have that sense of appreciation, sense of acknowledging other cultures; if you can't do it, I don't think you can be successful, at least in this globalised world. [...] So you need to be aware of so many cultures, you need to know how different cultures react when you're speak in some sort of fashion. So I think cross-cultural sensitivity is pretty much [an] important topic for every discipline. Just not business. Any graduate from any discipline should have an idea, should learn it like people are learning English today.*

Summary and conclusion

What are the pedagogic lessons from these results for university students in business (and other) courses and for lecturers in such courses, for helping students with their learning? An obvious first step is to become aware that not all students think about cross-cultural sensitivity in the same way. Some of them are simply aware that their fellow students are different in various ways – and in most classes in higher education this is fairly obvious.

Other students will think about CCS in terms of their knowledge about different groups, and sometimes, particularly in business classes, in terms of how that knowledge can be used in order to work better with them in current study assignments or even future workplaces. Yet other students will be aware of the need to respect their colleagues and to modify their actions and even their beliefs to show that respect. Reading, thinking about and explicitly discussing views of CCS with other students is a powerful way of moving towards the broader and more inclusive conceptions.

Lecturers who have the opportunity of setting the agenda in their classes and deciding on the particular ways of achieving their pedagogical aims could consider that the way they carry out their teaching can have a strong influence on the way their students go about their learning. Asking students to work in groups will allow them to become aware of the cultural diversity of their colleagues, particularly if this is preceded by explicit discussion about such diversity and its potential benefits, and accompanied by development of appropriate skills for working with people from different cultures.

Ramburuth and Welch (2005) give an interesting discussion of a range of common strategies, including cross-cultural group work, cross-cultural case studies and even international exchanges; they add to these their own approaches such as diversity audits, cross-cultural awareness tools and student-generated case studies. Their basic idea is to not only accept but to actively utilise the cultural diversity that is usually found in contemporary business classes.

Petocz and Reid (2008) present other examples in the context of several case studies of 'internationalised' pedagogy in Australian university classes, while Gordon et al. (2010) investigate the ways in which some educators view student diversity as a resource for learning in the classroom and lecture theatre.

Although the previous paragraph is directed to lecturers, students should be aware that they often have a large degree of autonomy in terms of how they go about the process of their learning. There is nothing to stop students forming assignment groups with colleagues from different cultures and benefiting from their diverse points of view – and if group assignments are not common, they can set up cross-cultural study groups.

If students are given the option to select their own case for study, with international aspects, this can allow investigation of different cultural viewpoints. Learning the facts about a particular topic is a fairly narrow form of learning; developing an appreciation of different ways of looking at a situation, and the personal change that accompanies such awareness, is a much deeper and more essential form of learning.

Acknowledgement

This research was initially funded by a grant from the World Bank/Global Development Network's Asia-Pacific Education Policy Research Initiative administered by the Korean Educational Development Institute (see http://eng.kedi.re.kr).

Further reading

Petocz, P., Reid, A. and Taylor, P. 2009. 'Thinking outside the square: Business students' conceptions of creativity'. *Creativity Research Journal*, 21 (4): 1–8.

Reid, A., Petocz, P. and Taylor, P. 2009. 'Business students' conceptions of sustainability', *Sustainability*, 1 (3), pp. 662–73; http://www.mdpi. com/2071-1050/1/3/662.

Reid, A., Petocz, P., Braddock, R., Taylor, P. and McLean, K. 2006. *Professional Formation: Exploring Students' Understanding of Creativity, Sustainability, Ethics and Cross-Cultural Sensitivity*, report prepared for AP-EPRI KEDI; http://eng.kedi.re.kr.

Reid, A., Taylor, P. and Petocz, P. 2011. 'Business as usual: Business students' conceptions of ethics', *International Journal for the Scholarship of Teaching and Learning*, 5 (1): ISSN 1931-4744; http://www.georgiasouthern.edu/ijsotl.

Discussion points and questions

Consider the questions the researchers asked in this study:

1. How do you understand the idea of cross-cultural sensitivity?
2. What role do you think cross-cultural sensitivity will play in your future work?

Write down a short answer for each of these questions. Then discuss your answers with the other members of your group. Did they have similar ideas or were they quite different?

The study was of international business students' ideas on sensitivity in cross-cultural communication. Respondents were asked for their thoughts on awareness, knowledge and respect as factors in demonstrations of cross-cultural sensitivity. Granted that your context may be different from that of the students in the survey, to what extent are you aware of the 'otherness' of different people and groups? Do you think it is easy to give and take offence in cross-cultural encounters (the example in the study was of someone being very offended at being given a playful blow to their head whereas they would not have objected to it being to their shoulder)?

In what circumstances would you need specific, as opposed to general, knowledge of another culture?

To what extent do you agree that out of respect for another culture you should modify your behaviour to reduce conflicts or solve problems? Do you agree with Casey that such acceptance and change needs to be a 'two-way street'?

Conclusion

This chapter dealt with the general topic of learning how to live and function in a host culture very different from one's own. General principles were illustrated first by Mugambi in her account of cultural conflict between expatriate members of Western firms and native Nigerian companies. The accompanying commentary was of Oberg on 'culture shock'. Bhawuk and Anbe reported on acculturation to local culture and the kinds of behaviour change that foreign managers need to make when working in host countries. The case of 'poor old Bruce' was a study of the unhappy results of not learning how to do so. Reid and Petocz discussed the importance of cross-cultural sensitivity from the context of university business studies, followed by a discussion of the importance of higher education in the creation of an educated and skilled society.

Key points

1. There are major differences between culture-based sets of assumptions in different countries and communities. One is between the respective viewpoints of members of monochronic and polychronic cultures as defined by Edward T. Hall and discussed also in Chapter 1.

2. 'Culture shock' is almost always experienced by people who move from one cultural environment to another. This seems to run through several levels, from unreasonably optimistic expectations of the new culture, to reactions of resentment and hostility, then gaining a sense of proportion, learning to value at least some aspects and finally feeling 'at home'.

3. It is important for everybody who works and lives in a cross-cultural environment to develop a cultural sensitivity to the feelings and values of others.

4. Experience seems to support the view that comparatively flat organisational structures aid and support cross-cultural communication.

5. Studies show the importance of higher education for management of communication across cultures.

6. Foreign managers may need to make a number of major changes in their accustomed verbal and non-verbal communication media when working in host countries. One example is mode of dress; another is forms of address.

7. Lack of preparation for, and knowledge of, overseas assignments increases the risk of their failure.

Looking ahead

This chapter has been concerned essentially with the kind of behaviour people need when communicating across cultures; and the changes people may have to make to their usual styles to accommodate to cross-cultural interaction. Since a pragmatic definition of learning is behaviour change, Chapter 6 expands on this theme by studying theoretical and practical similarities and differences in teaching methods, learning and problem-solving styles over time and place.

Experiential exercise

A very good exercise in experiencing culture shock is for lecturers to organise a field trip for students between one class and the next to some location where they will almost certainly find themselves in unfamiliar territory. This can be arranged on an individual or a group basis (i.e., students can be asked to do this by themselves or the lecturer can escort a group). Examples might be a football game for students who have never attended one; a visit to a horse racing track; a job centre for the unemployed; a night soup kitchen run by volunteers for street people; a church, synagogue or temple. Students should be asked to write a brief account of their feelings about the experience, commenting on specific aspects they found strange, different, disturbing, interesting and attractive; and why. Then during the class following the outing, they can be asked to read their comments aloud to the class. If classes are large, this feedback can be spread over several weeks.

Further reading

Books

Doremus, P. N., Keller, W. H., Pauly, L. W. and Reich, S. 1998. *The Myth of the Global Corporation*. Princeton: Princeton University Press.
Hall, E. and Hall, T. 1959. *The Silent Language*. New York: Doubleday.
—— 1966. *The Hidden Dimension*. New York: Doubleday.
—— 1976. *Beyond Culture*. New York: Doubleday.
—— 1983. *The Dance of Life: The Other Dimension of Time*. New York: Doubleday.

Samovar, L.A., Porter, R.E. and McDaniel, E.R. 1997. *Intercultural Communication: A Reader*, 8th edn. Boston, MA: Wadsworth.

Senghaas, D. 2002. *The Clash within Civilizations: Coming to Terms with Cultural Conflicts*. London: Routledge.

Triandis, H.C. 1972. *The Analysis of Subjective Culture*. New York: Wiley.

Online

Oberg, Kalervo: see http://www.mnsu.edu/emuseum/information/biography/klmno/oberg_kalvero.html.

Journals

Academy of Management Journal
European Journal of Personality
Harvard Business Review
Human Rights Quarterly
Journal of International Business Studies
Journal of Teaching in International Business
Organization Science

References

Alameida, R. 1997. *Stories of Old Hawaii*. Honolulu, HI: Bess Press.

Barkema, H.,G., Shenkar, O. and Vermeulen, F. 1997. 'Working abroad, working with others: How firms learn to operate joint ventures'. *Academy of Management Journal*, 40 (2), pp., 426–42.

Black, E., Abney, S., Flickinger, D., Gnadiec, C., Grishman, R., Harrison, P., Hindle, D., Ingria, R., Jelinek, F., Klavans, J., Liberman, M., Marcus, M., Roukos, S., Santorini, B. and Strzalkowski, T. 1991. 'A procedure for quantitatively comparing the syntactic coverage of English grammars'. *Proceedings of the DARPA Workshop on Speech and Natural Language*. Pacific Grove, CA: Morgan Kaufman, pp. 306–11.

Doremus, P.N., Keller, W.H., Pauly, L.W. and Reich, S. 1998. *The Myth of the Global Corporation*. Princeton, NJ: Princeton University Press.

Du Bois, W.E. Burghardt 1996. *The Philadelphia Negro: A Social Study*. Philadelphia, PA: University of Pennsylvania Press, first published in 1899.

Gordon, S., Reid, A. and Petocz, P. 2010. 'Educators' conceptions of student diversity in their classes'. *Studies in Higher Education*, 35 (8), pp., 961–74.

Griswold, W. 2004. *Cultures and Societies in a Changing World*, 2nd edn. London: Sage.

Hall, E.T. 1959. *The Silent Language*. New York: Doubleday.

—— 1966. *The Hidden Dimension*. New York: Doubleday.

—— 1976. *Beyond Culture*. New York: Doubleday.

—— 1983. *The Dance of Life: The Other Dimension of Time*. New York: Doubleday.

Hinds, P. and Kiesler, S. 1995. 'Communication across boundaries: Work, structure, and use of communication technologies in a large organization'. *Organization Science*, 6 (4), pp., 373–93.

Hoecklin, L.A. 1995. *Managing Cultural Differences: Strategies for Competitive Advantage*. Reading, MA: Addison-Wesley.

Johnson, J.P., Lenartowicz. T. and Aupud, S. 2006. 'Cross-cultural competence in international business: Toward a definition and a model'. *Journal of International Business Studies*, 37, pp., 525–43.

Kegan, R. and Lahey, L.L. 2001. 'The real reason people won't change'. *Harvard Business Review*, pp., 84–92.

McDonald, M.A. 1995. *Ka Lei: The leis of Hawaii*. Honolulu, HI: Ku Pa'a Publishing.

Marton, F. 1975a. 'What does it take to learn? Some implications of an alternative view of learning', paper presented at the Council of Europe symposium on 'Strategies for Research and Development in Higher Education', Göteborg, 7–12 September 1975; also in Marton, F., Entwistle, N. and Hounsell, D. (eds) 2005. *The Experience of Learning*, 2nd edn. Edinburgh: Scottish Academic Press; http://www.research.lancs.ac.uk.

—— 1975b. 'On non-verbatim learning. I: Level of processing and level of outcome'. *Scandinavian Journal of Psychology*, 16, pp., 273–9.

Marton, F. and Booth, S. 1997. *Learning and Awareness*. London: Routledge.

Oberg, K. 1951. 'Culture shock' [panel discussion at the first Midwest regional meeting of the Institute of International Education, Chicago, 28 November]; see also Oberg, K. 1960. 'Cultural shock: Adjustment to new cultural environments'. *Practical Anthropology*, 7 pp., 177–82.

Petocz, P. and Reid, A. 2008. 'Evaluating the internationalised curriculum'. In M. Hellstén and A. Reid (eds), *Researching International Pedagogies: Sustainable Practice for Teaching and Learning in Higher Education*. Dordrecht: Springer, pp. 27–43..

Ramburuth, P. and Welch, C. 2005. 'Educating the global manager'. *Journal of Teaching in International Business*, 16 (3), pp., 5–27.

Rana, K. S. 2002. *Bilateral Diplomacy* (Malta: Diplo Projects) [see especially Chapter 12, 'Cross-cultural sensitivity']; http://www.diplomacy.edu/

Samovar, L.A., Porter, R.E. and McDaniel, E.R. 1997. *Intercultural Communication: A Reader*, 8th edn. Boston, MA: Wadsworth.

Senghaas, D. 2002. *The Clash Within Civilizations: Coming to Terms with Cultural Conflicts*. London: Routledge.

Steele, H.T. 1984. *The Hawaiian Shirt*. New York: Abbeville Press.

Tibenderana, P.K. 2003. *Education and Cultural Change in Northern Nigeria, 1906–1966: A Study in the Creation of a Dependent Culture*. Kampala: Fountain Publishers.

Triandis, H.C. 1972. *The Analysis of Subjective Culture*. New York: Wiley.

USAID 2003. 'Northern Assessment Report', *Strategic Assessment of Social Sector Activities in Northern Nigeria*, Abuja; http://www.usaid.gov/ng/downloads/rfa/usaidnorthern assessmentreport1.pdf [accessed 25 June 2010].

Van der Zee, K.I. and Van Oudenhoven, J.P. 2000. 'The Multicultural Personality Questionnaire: A multidimensional instrument of multicultural effectiveness'. *European Journal of Personality*, 14, pp., 291–309; http://www.tamas.com/samples/source-docs/mpq.html.

Ward, C. 2004. 'Psychological theories of culture contact and their implications for intercultural training and interventions'. In D. Landis, M. Bennett and J. Bennett (eds), *Handbook of Intercultural Training*, 3rd edn. Thousand Oaks, CA: Sage, pp. 185–216.

Xanthaki, A. 2010. 'Multiculturalism and international law: Discussing universal standards'. *Human Rights Quarterly*, 32 (1), pp., 21–48.

CHAPTER 6

Learning and Teaching across Cultures

Elizabeth Christopher; Suman Mishra; Adriana Medina-López-Portillo; Laura Rutter Strickling; Joan Kang Shin; Illysa Izenberg

Objectives of the chapter

- to contrast and compare Western and Asian teaching methods and learning styles;
- to summarise some theories of learning and teaching;
- to illustrate differences in individual learning and problem-solving styles;
- to suggest ways of improving classroom and online teaching.

Chapter contents

- Outline of chapter
- Suman Mishra: Asian learning and teaching styles: Tradition and modernity
- Conclusion and discussion
- Discussion
- Questions
- Case study: UK universities raise student fees
- Discussion points and questions
- Discuss the following points with your classmates
- Adriana Medina-López-Portillo, Laura Rutter Strickling, Joan Kang Shin and Illysa Izenberg: Learning and teaching across cultures
- Conclusion
- Questions and discussion
- Conclusion
- Key points
- Experiential exercise
- Further reading
- References

Outline of chapter

The chapter follows the content of Chapter 5 – a study of factors for effective communication when working across cultures – by examining differences between traditional Western and Asian teaching methods, learning and problem-solving styles.

The central argument is that Western teachers and trainers can and should learn from Asian teaching traditions the value of a holistic approach to learning, the importance of reflective and repetitive learning, the crucial role of the teacher–learner relationship in formal learning environments, and learners' need for hard work and self-discipline if high standards of knowledge are to be attained and retained. From Asian perspectives there has been much learning from Western teaching methods, particularly in teaching the sciences, technology and engineering, and business management.

Recognition is given to the difference between intrinsic and extrinsic motivation to learn; between collective and individual teaching methods; and between form and content in learning.

The case chosen to complement this report is an account of university fees increases in the UK, in stark contrast to India, for example, where the government heavily subsidises higher education.

The next section of the chapter deals with the different ways in which people process information, and how these are connected to culture. A number of instruments are described for assessing individuals' preferred learning and problem-solving styles, including the Myers-Briggs Type Indicator, the Mind Styles Model and the Learning Styles Model. Reference is made to the difference between topic-centred and topic-associative teaching methods; to differences between individual and collaborative study; verbal and non-verbal communication; and different views of time management and risk in acquiring new knowledge. The questions and discussions that follow deal with key variables in appropriate and effective communication and negotiation across cultures, including e-learning contexts.

The case study that follows is of robots who learn, and the chapter ends with a lengthy but worthwhile simulation game to raise players' awareness to learning style differences.

No one chapter on teaching methods and learning styles can cover all the research; but the key findings are here; and there are many recommendations for further reading, along with the chapter references.

ASIAN LEARNING AND TEACHING STYLES: TRADITION AND MODERNITY	Suman Mishra

Introduction

Nineteenth- and early twentieth-century Western scholars believed the persistence of traditional cultural values impeded modern social and economic development in Asian countries such as China, India and Japan. However, in more recent decades it appears that many of the best and brightest minds are being cultivated in these countries.

The effectiveness of Asian learning styles can be measured in terms of international test scores for mathematics and science at K-12 school levels and by the large numbers of students from these countries at undergraduate and graduate schools enrolled in engineering, chemistry and mathematics in the US, the UK, the countries of the EU and Australia. It can also be seen in the obvious social and economic transformations within these and similar Asian societies. In China, Japan and India, education has been and continues to be the engine that has transformed these nations into economic powerhouses: hence the paradox of once-traditional societies with powerful entrenched educational institutions developing into modern societies and economies.

'Traditional' Asian learning styles: Commonalities and differences in three Asian societies

The traditional Asian learning style, strongly influenced by religious and philosophical concepts ranging from Confucianism to Hinduism, is often described as a system in which students passively receive knowledge and information. It is perceived to involve rote learning in large classrooms as a laborious process under authoritarian teachers (Chan, 1999; Kennedy, 2002; Song, 1995; Watkins and Biggs, 2001; Zhengdong, 2009). This strongly contrasts with Western learning through discussion, spontaneous comment, argument, analysis, reasoning and questioning from friendly teacher participants.

However Watkins and Biggs (2001: 6) and Marton et al. (1996) argue that Western scholars apply the term 'rote learning' to what is in effect repetitive learning that helps in forming deep impressions, resulting in better recall and enhanced understanding through discovering new meanings. In traditional Asian learning style emphasis is given to *effort*. The belief that educational success directly and positively correlates to effort has its roots in Confucian philosophy (Yu, 1992). Dahlgaard-Park (2006) points to two old Chinese written characters that represent learning. The first means 'to study' and the second means 'to practise repeatedly'. According to Dahlgaard-Park, the two characters emphasise mental (cognitive and intellectual learning) and physical (endless physical practice).

This traditional belief that putting in effort and hard work will help achieve academic success is still very strong among Asian students and teachers (Watkins and Biggs, 2001). It is not, however, uniform across the Asian region. For example, the belief is stronger among Chinese and Japanese students, teachers and parents than it is among Indians. Indians do believe in effort but also in an individual's innate ability to learn.

The more distinctly East Asian belief that working hard is the only way to achieve academic success has resulted in students spending more time studying, mastering the material and getting better test scores. Such benefits, however, come at a cost. They have resulted in tremendous pressures on students and deep disappointment at not being able to be successful despite working hard. The resulting stress has contributed to in increasing suicide rates among Chinese and Japanese students (Curtin, 2004; Watts, 2005).

It is also important to acknowledge that China, Japan and India are countries with large populations and limited resources, and that both factors add to the intensity of educational competition. Since education is believed to be *the* means to achieve success in life, when this success is not achieved, it can become life-shattering.

Motivation is considered very important part of learning. Watkins and Biggs (2001) suggest that Western students are usually intrinsically motivated while Asian students are usually extrinsically motivated. They contend that the Chinese students' motivation in learning comes from personal ambitions, saving the family's 'face' and material rewards. In contrast, the Western students' motivation for learning is said to come from personal rewards such as a sense of mastery and self-fulfilment.

It should be noted that there is a danger of oversimplification in such sweeping characterisations even within a single society and culture. For example, Indian learners seem to be both intrinsically and extrinsically motivated, driven by personal ambition and also by rewards and recognition, particularly improved social standing. On the other hand, the extrinsic motivation in Chinese students suggested by Watkins and Biggs is in sharp contrast to traditional Confucian ideas of intrinsic motivation. Confucius (active circa 550 BC) believed that self-motivation, self-respect and joy in learning were important characteristics for a student to have in order for them to learn (Dahlgaard-Park, 2006). He believed that not everyone could be a good learner but only an individual with genuine desire for knowledge and possessing enthusiastic eagerness could achieve this goal (ibid.).

Another major difference often cited by researchers between the East and the West is that students in the East learn collectively and students in the West individually (Watkins and Biggs, 2001). In some Asian cultures, particularly those of China and Japan, there is emphasis on collective learning under the main authority of the teacher. Important aspects are that students collaborate in class and outside, that there is peer tutoring and strong classroom relationships (Watkins and Biggs, 2001; Wu, 1999. However, this is not common in India, where students learn individually.

The teacher's place in 'traditional' Asian learning styles

Traditional teaching in Asian contexts is said to be authoritarian (Ho, 2001). China, Japan and India are cultures with high power distance (Hofstede, 2001), that is, their values accept and expect differences in power among different members of the society. In formal learning, teachers and learners understand the hierarchical nature of their relationship. Traditional teachers maintain a strict demeanour – friendliness with the learners, smiling and laughing with them, are considered counterproductive to class control (Salili, 2001), whereas in the West such authoritarian behaviour is likely to be considered cold and unfriendly.

However, according to Biggs (1996), this Western perception is inaccurate and a simplification of the complex student–teacher relationship that functions in a traditional Asian setting. Both Biggs and Salili (2001) observe that though traditional teachers do maintain a distance between themselves and their students, this is to promote learning; and outside the classroom they show more warmth and engage in informal discussions and activities.

The boundary between personal and professional behaviour is acknowledged and maintained by teachers in the West, but this is not the case in Asia (Salili, 2001).

Traditional teachers in Asia tend to believe that direct praise may only lead to students becoming arrogant. Students may also become complacent and fail to make the effort needed to maintain academic performance (Salili, 2001;

Salili and Hau, 1994)). As a result teachers are more prone to criticise than to praise and encourage. This contrasts with Western educational thinking where praise and encouragement for even mediocre performance are given to motivate students and build 'self-esteem' (Salili, 2001).

China: Confucius trumps Mao and the 'master' in the classroom

During the years of the Cultural Revolution from 1966 to 1976 – which scholars sometimes consider educationally a lost decade – classroom authority based on age and superior credentials was overturned in favour of learning from young people and the masses. Teachers, particular older people and those believed to be politically conservative, were hounded, lost their positions and forced to recount their counter-revolutionary sins. Confucius, the ultimate master teacher, was condemned as a class enemy in national campaigns.

Confucius today has made a dramatic comeback. In fact, the Chinese central government uses his name for their global undertaking to promote Chinese language and culture. This reversal represents the resurgence of what might be called the Chinese form of authoritative teaching and acceptance of an appropriate attitude towards learning. The common features of the current model of what might be called a typical Chinese learning style (Chan, 1999; Kennedy, 2002; Song, 1995; Watkins and Biggs, 2001; Zhengdong, 2009) include acceptance of the importance of the teacher as the central dispenser of essential information and knowledge; emphasis on memorisation and repetitive learning; a teacher-dominated two-way flow in classroom activities; and a comparatively quiet classroom in that students' participation is secondary, with emphasis on book (and increasingly IT-delivered) information and knowledge over problem-solving by group discussion, team projects and experiments.

These characteristics are not usually considered by Western educators to encourage creativity and innovation. Nevertheless, they may be applicable to new disciplinary subjects such as mathematics, engineering, foreign language study and business administration.

Japan: The *'kata'* approach of mastering form to master content

Features of the Japanese learning style in many respects parallel the Chinese model. But just as the paths of educational history and economic modernisation have differed in these two nations so have classroom practices and attitudes among teachers and students.

Historically, one salient feature has been that the Japanese quickly eliminated any explicitly ideological or pedagogical loyalty to Confucianism. This is not to assert that the central role of the teacher was diminished in Japan. In fact, the authority of that role was strengthened between the 1870s and 1945 as teachers were made public officials charged with cultivating patriotism as well as practical knowledge. But their efforts were towards propagation of Western learning in mathematics, science and economics as well as the humanities, decades before these subjects became incorporated into the Chinese curriculum.

The modern approach to learning before or after World War II obviously did not do away with traditional approaches in Japan. One of the most predominant has been the concept of *kata* or the idea of first mastering *form* as a preparatory process to mastering *content*. The idea is evident in the martial arts derived from samurai warrior traditions as well as other visual arts (pottery) and cultural pursuits (tea ceremony). It requires working closely with a master teacher as a disciple or apprentice and learning through graduated steps until the art – or body of knowledge – is mastered.

The *kata* approach, however, is more than learning without understanding. It more resembles repetitive learning, creating deep impressions that make for superior recall and mastery that enables the learner to discover new meanings through refining understanding (Marton et al., 1996; Watkins and Biggs, 2001).

There are obvious similarities that this Japanese learning style shares with the Chinese approach. The teacher remains the centrally important person in the classroom. Memorisation and mastery of texts are also essential, as is the notion that the students learn, not from one another, but from authorities, the teacher and the text, and that the pupil's place is secondary in this process.

In the years before and after World War II, the traditional approach was used in classrooms from pre-school to university level. Entrance examination competition is considered more egalitarian than elitist, and although the educational system may rely on traditional methods it is meeting requirements to support a modern industrial economy and works as the basis of Japan's affluent society.

India: Understanding the culture of formal education from *guru–gurukul* to modern classrooms

There are common features of both the Chinese and Japanese learning and teaching styles in modern Indian education with a traditional focus on textbooks, assessments, memorisation and lecturing. However, Western student-oriented teaching and learning methods are being adopted, and the Indian system today has been influenced not only by traditional Indian educational values and beliefs but also by colonial British educational policies and some progressive ideas from America (Gupta, 2007). Thus it does not correspond exactly with the major East Asian states. The success of the education system in producing engineering, science and maths graduates has renewed interest of the West in Indian culture and social environment, history, educational beliefs and practices.

Culture and social environment

The importance of education and educational institutions can be understood through the ancient tradition of *guru* (master) and *gurukul*. *Gurukul* is a place where the guru resides with his *shishya* (pupils). In Sanskrit *kul* refers to domain, which is derived from *kula*, meaning extended family. The students or disciples in this traditional set-up were treated like a family member. They stayed with the guru and learnt various skills. In the *gurukul*, children of kings, nobility and ordinary people were all treated alike. They all followed the strict rules and decorum set by the guru and lived a very structured life (Gupta, 2007).

This ancient tradition of resident schools kept students away from distractions and helped them focus on learning. Since education was not considered a commercial venture, students did not pay any money for their stay and education but helped the guru with the household chores. Knowledge was considered as something to be passed on for free or donated – *vidya dan*. Culturally, this is at the heart of not attaching profits to education. Today, educational institutes in India, in spite of adoption of Western models of for-profit education, have remained comparatively accessible and more affordable than in the West. The government heavily subsidises schools and universities, and this has helped in building a large educated workforce in India.

The success of learning in mathematics, science and engineering can also be attributed to the high cultural value that Indians place on education as *the* path to success and getting out of poverty. Indians believe in scientific enquiry and science as a means to solve problems; also there is more opportunity for employment for science and engineering graduates in India than in commerce and the humanities; and there is more prestige attached to them.

History and the education system

During colonial times, the British found the traditional Indian education system inadequate and outdated. To educate the natives and bring them into the modern world, colleges and universities were set up, modelled on British universities. This marked the beginning of the Westernisation of Indian education (Gupta, 2007). The colonial British rule introduced an education system that was textbook-centred and exam-oriented. Local people had to learn English and pass various exams to get lower-level British government jobs. In the post-colonial era, many top politicians, especially those who were in charge of setting up the educational policy in India, were educated in the West. For India to progress, grow and compete in the global world the policymakers realised that they needed an educated workforce, especially in engineering and medical sciences, and thus began the emphasis on these professions. The well-known Indian Institute of Technology (IIT) was established in order to fulfil the need for engineers in the newly industrialised nation to build dams and other industrial machinery. Thus engineering became a very sought-after profession as it guaranteed job, money and success – more so than in any other profession.

The Indian education system involves traditional Asian teaching and learning methods. Memorisation, rote learning, lecturing and exams are the norm: but memorisation is not devoid of conceptual understanding. India has a very exam-centred and assessment-oriented educational system. Apart from regular exams in the class, students prepare for national board exams. In addition they take special tests administered by individual colleges and universities to get into engineering, medicine and other programmes. There are also highly competitive exams to gain admission to various private and public sector jobs.

The preparation for getting into engineering and medical colleges is quite intense as these exams are seen as life-changing. As a result many students joining undergraduate or graduate programmes in Western universities realise that they have already learnt the material taught in the classes. However, since specialisation starts earlier than in many Western education systems, if students have not acquired reading and writing skills and a good general education by their mid-teens, the narrow focus on sciences at senior school level provides fewer opportunities for further development of these skills in a formal educational setting. Thus, even though many adult Indian graduates excel in the sciences, they sometimes lack creativity and communication, reading and writing skills.

Melding of learning styles: Cross-cultural applicability of Asian learning and teaching styles

A reasonable approach to getting the most from a variety of learning styles is suggested by Smith (2008), who posits that it is not necessary for the West to completely adopt Asian methods or vice versa. It is more pedagogically effective to benefit from the advantages inherent in a variety of systems; and the following are areas where valuable adaptations might take place in traditional Western teaching and training:

Holistic learning: The tradition of the West to focus on separation, measurement and analytical thinking (Biggs and Watkins, 2001) misses the holistic aspect of Asian learning that introduces complexity and interwoven concepts. It would be benefit Western students to learn to explore ways to look at larger pictures instead of focusing on small pieces of puzzles. This kind of learning will help students be better prepared to solve real-life problems, which are often complex.

Emphasis on reflection: Western students are encouraged to argue and discuss. This method helps them to develop verbal skills and quick thinking, but not to pause and reflect. Developing reflective sensibilities – common in most Eastern philosophy – will help Westerners break the cycle of what Smith (2008) calls hyperverbalism (over-emphasis on verbal communication).

Collaborative learning: Another aspect of Asian learning that can be successfully incorporated with Western-style teaching and training is that of collaborative learning. Studies show that regardless of the subject matter, collaborative learning helps student retain information longer; and students' satisfaction has also been found to increase when they work in collaborative groups (Beckman, 1990; Chickering and Gamson, 1991; Davis, 1993). This practice has been recommended by professionals in the West (Chickering and Gamson, 1991; Davis, 1993), but used by few teachers because Western cultures value individualistic learning, and therefore to work in groups is a challenge. However, designing courses and assignments that encourage students to work in groups and learn from each other will help them learn not only cooperative skills – as required for many jobs – but also to help them learn the material well.

Setting higher standards: In China, Japan and India the expectation and standards set by teachers are high. Students work hard to meet them, and in so doing they improve their own standards. Western teachers seem to expect less and less from their students, and to accept that their responsibilities are to motivate and entertain while they teach. Students come to classes with the expectation to learn without much effort. Effort in learning is stressed too much in Asian traditions and too little in Western tradition. Expecting higher performance and hard work is likely to help students become more self-motivated and raise their standards.

Conclusion and discussion

Globalisation has inextricably linked regions of the world together. Asian countries are investing in teaching English (Ostler, 2008) and other languages that will help their citizens to be globally competitive. In India, most students learn English, the local language of the state or Hindi, and a third language of their choice. In a global economy these language skills provide benefits: but in the West, particularly in the US, students are not being adequately prepared to join the global workforce or to compete on a global scale.

Since 9/11 and the recession in the US there seems to less openness and greater awareness of 'us' versus 'them'. This mindset is likely to hinder learning. Today there is greater need to understand and learn about different people and cultures, and to understand the complexity of the world; but business and politics have become battlegrounds for fear and prejudice. Personal attacks and criticism of language learning programmes such as Spanish and Chinese are often referred to as 'indoctrination' or unnecessary or unAmerican (Fox News, 2010; Mei, 2010; Park, 2002). This is likely to cause problems for American management trainees who will be expected to be active leaders of global workforces and thus need to be prepared for the task.

In China, Japan and India there is tremendous value placed on formal education, and parents are very involved in their children's education and learning in general. Thus Asian children grow up with a sense of the importance of knowledge and learning. In the West teaching children is assumed to be largely the teachers' responsibility; parents are involved minimally and teaching takes place in school rather than in the home. This disengagement of parents hinders the continuous learning into adulthood that many Asian students enjoy and share.

In addition Western cultures, particularly US culture, value individual and self-learning, and thus formal education is not considered as useful as it is in many Asian countries: one can be successful without formal learning. This mindset works for a very few extraordinary people, but not for most. Most people have to put in the effort in order to learn and be successful. Thus if Western training is to improve success in science, mathematics and engineering, maybe there needs to be some adoption of Asian teaching and learning models; but there also needs to be some cultural shifts in how formal education is viewed by society in general.

Discussion

The writer's thesis is that modern social and economic development in Asian countries such as China, India and Japan is due in large part to teaching methods and learning styles that actively promote acquisition and retention of knowledge in fields such as engineering, chemistry, mathematics, foreign language acquisition and business management. The distinction is made, as elsewhere in this book, between collectivist and individualistic values; and the advantages and dis-advantages are summarised of collaborative versus individual study. The writer's argument is that Western assumptions of what is 'good' teaching and training might usefully be reviewed in light of the success of Asian methods.

In particular, Asian stress on hard work and effort as the means to achieve success in life – though it can be overdone – contrasts with a Western notion that education should be 'fun'. Also there is the suggestion that Western students are usually intrinsically motivated (i.e., by the need for 'self-fulfilment) while Asian students are usually motivated extrinsically (i.e., by desire for economic and social success). However, too narrow a focus on prestigious areas such as science, engineering and business management may lead to neglect of basic reading, writing and communication skills.

The student–teacher relationship is quite different in Asia and the West. In Asian educational environments teachers are dispensers of wisdom, and students are to be criticised rather than praised for their comments for fear of them becoming arrogant. The concept of learning 'form' before 'content' ('how to learn' before 'what to learn') comes from Japan, to promote learning with understanding. Thus culture and social environment shape the way adults acquire and retain knowledge.

The writer concludes that Western teaching can acquire from Asia a sense of the importance of holistic ('big picture') learning; of reflection before action; of collaborative learning; and of the need to set high standards.

Questions

1. How do you think about learning? In general do you expect it to be more effort than enjoyment; more work than pleasure? However you regard learning, to what extent do you think your views are based on cultural assumptions about the nature of the teacher–learner relationship?

2. Do you regard learning as a lifetime activity or as something finite, for example, to acquire specific skills or qualifications?

3. Do you think your motivation to learn is intrinsic (primarily for your own satisfaction) or mainly extrinsic (to promote your career, income and social standing)?

4. In the management of people at work, how important do you think it is that employers should provide a wide range of training programmes even if they have nothing directly to do with the work of the firm?

Case study: UK universities raise student fees

The following report, compiled from a number of news sources, offers a stark contrast to Dr Mishra's observation that Western teaching should benefit from Asian perspectives – for example, that of the Indian government, which heavily subsidises schools and universities with the resulting creation of a large educated workforce in

India. Moreover the Asian view is that education should encourage high standards of reflective 'big picture' learning.

In February 2011 senior managers at Oxford and Cambridge universities announced plans for new tuition fees of £9,000 a year, the maximum allowed, though David Willetts, the Universities Minister, had said fees of £9,000 would be allowed only in 'exceptional circumstances'.

MPs voted to raise tuition fees in December 2010, after the Liberal Democrats pledged in their manifesto to scrap fees. The government lends the fee money to students until they graduate and are earning £21,000 a year. Aaron Porter, president of the National Union of Students, said he expected a race by all universities to join the '£9,000 group'; and that it was only a matter of time before the most expensive start asking for the freedom to charge even more.

Details of the government's plan to encourage poorer students to go to university despite the rise in tuition fees were revealed. The National Scholarship Programme would have £50 million to spend in 2011 – half from government and half from universities wanting to charge the highest fees. Having raised the maximum fee level to £9,000 per year, the government said it wanted to ensure that higher fees would not exclude poorer students from university. Ministers said it would be used to offer bursaries, waive fees or cover living costs for students with a household income of less than £25,000. Critics replied it did not go far enough.

All universities were expected to raise fees to at least £6,000. New universities reported they would be forced to raise fees to more than £6,000 because of cuts to teaching funds, and were concerned that students from low-income families would not be able to afford them. For the first time, graduates also face a 'real' rate of interest on loans they take out to cover the costs. Under plans outlined in February 2011 successful graduates would be forced to repay student loans at higher rates of interest than those on low incomes.

Students who had already started their courses when the new regime comes into force would not be affected, but all students starting courses in 2012 will pay the new tuition fees. The news wrecked the plans of thousands of sixth-formers who hoped to enjoy a gap year and also beat the £9,000-a-year fees by applying in 2011 for a deferred entry place.

Deputy Prime Minister Nick Clegg angered students by breaking his pledge to vote against raising tuition fees. In his defence he said that universities who wanted to charge more than £6,000 per year must improve access; and that there was a social crisis of opportunity in the country because universities, the gateways to the professions, were too often acting inadvertently to narrow opportunities rather than widen them. National Union of Students' president Aaron Porter issued an angry response to Mr Clegg, accusing him of living in a fantasy-land if he thought he could become a champion for students.

There were also tuition fee changes ahead for other parts of the UK. In Northern Ireland, a report commissioned by the Department of Employment and Learning (DEL) recommended that fees should rise to a maximum of £5,750. In Wales, students are protected from increases in tuition fees, with the Welsh Assembly Government subsidising the cost of higher fees. In Scotland, students do not pay tuition fees. On the other hand, the Prime Minister, David Cameron, suggested that sharp rises in university tuition fees would make studying in Britain more affordable for overseas students. During a visit to China, the Prime Minister said government plans to lift the cap on fees for British students would mean foreigners could be charged less. British students currently pay significantly lower fees than overseas youngsters who want to take degrees in the UK. However, the cap for British students could be lifted from around £3,000 to a maximum of £9,000 a year under planned reforms.

The Liberal Democrats incurred the wrath of the demonstrators because all of the party's MPs had signed a National Union of Students pledge to abolish tuition fees before the election in May. Under the terms of the Coalition Agreement, the Lib Dems are permitted to abstain over the issue, and a number are expected to rebel when the proposal comes before the House of Commons. As the demonstrations turned into riots, Martin Horwood, Liberal Democrat MP for Cheltenham, was called a 'liar' by angry protesters after coming out to address the crowd. He confirmed that he would not support the new £9,000 tuition fee cap, telling the students: 'You don't know that I've lied about anything.'

Sources

BBC News 2011. 'Scheme to limit impact of tuition fees rise on poor'. 10 February; http://www.bbc.co.uk/news/education-1240942.8.

Clarke, L. 2011. 'Increase in university fees will kill off 2011 gap year as students fail to avoid charges hike'. *Daily Mail*, 10 February; http://www.dailymail.co.uk/news/article-1332206/University-fees-increase-kill-gap-year-students-fail-avoid-charges-hike.html.

Shepherd, J. 2011. 'Oxford and Cambridge to join £9,000 club on fees', *Guardian*, 9 February; http://www.guardian.co.uk/education/2011/feb/09/oxford-cambridge-9000-fees.

Wardrop, M. and Prince, R. 2011. 'David Cameron: "Raising university tuition fees could cut cost for foreigners"', *Daily Telegraph*; http://www.telegraph.co.uk/news/newstopics/politics/david-cameron/8124716/David-Cameron-Raising-university-tuition-fees-could-cut-cost-for-foreigners.html.

Discussion points and questions

Managing communication across cultures includes staff recruitment, selection, training and development. If local employment pools do not stock a needed number of highly qualified candidates, managers will have to fish in international waters, thus disadvantaging even more the already disadvantaged local population. Moreover when they do hire local people they will have to spend time and money training them. For both these reasons, opportunities for further education are essential for young people if they, and the country in which they live, are not to fall behind in an increasingly competitive international marketplace. Moreover in developing and emerging economies such as that of India, education is seen as one of the ways to upward social mobility.

Discuss the following points with your classmates

- Why are you studying in your present institution?
- Were university fees a factor in your decision?

- Was a future need to repay a student loan a factor in your choice of curriculum?
- Would you have chosen a different course of study if student fees had not been a factor?
- Do you plan further studies? If so, where and why?

LEARNING AND TEACHING ACROSS CULTURES	Adriana Medina-López-Portillo, Laura Rutter Strickling, Joan Kang Shin and Illysa Izenberg

As individuals, we all learn differently and have preferred and consistent systems by which we acquire, organise and process new information (Riding and Sadler-Smith, 1997). Understanding how different people perceive the world and take in new information can help us become aware of our own learning styles, as well as those of others. When we develop a variety of learning approaches, we are better equipped to understand how to maximise learning, solve problems, work in teams, manage disagreement and conflict, and improve personal and professional relationships (Kolb, 2007).

Numerous psychology and anthropology studies (e.g., Chen and Ford, 1998; Nisbett and Norenzayan, 2002; Nisbett et al., 2001; Riding and Rayner, 1998) have shown that learning and learning styles are connected to culture. For example, a study by Masuda and Nisbett (2001) found perceptual differences between Japanese and US participants who were shown the same underwater scenes. One result showed that the Japanese participants made 70 per cent more statements about the general environment and 50 per cent more statements about the relationships between the fish and the background than did those from the US.

The researchers concluded that Japanese are more focused on the whole field (the 'big picture') and on relationships, whereas US Americans are more focused on objects (the details) and they detach those objects from the field. The researchers labelled these cognitive differences as holistic versus analytical respectively. This example illustrates the cultural variation in learning styles. Education researchers have developed models for assessing differences between individuals' learning styles; and a well-designed instructional programme for a culturally diverse group of learners takes these into consideration.

The Myers-Briggs Type Indicator (MBTI)

The purpose of this personality inventory (http://www.myersbriggs.org/my-mbti-personality-type/mbti-basics/ [accessed 9 February 2011]) is to make the theory of psychological types, first described by C.G. Jung (http://www.cgjung page.org/ [accessed 9 February 2011]) understandable and useful. The essence of the theory is that most apparently random variations in behaviour are in fact orderly and consistent, based on differences in the ways people use perception and judgement.

World view: Extroverts and introverts (E and I)

According to the MBTI, individuals who tend to focus on the outer world are 'extroverted', whereas those who seem more to focus on their own inner worlds are considered to be 'introverted'. Extroverts are action-oriented and creatively stimulated by being around people. Introverts can be sociable, but they need to 'recharge their batteries' through quiet and reflection.

Information: Sensing and intuitive personalities (S and N)

Individuals receive and process in information mainly in 'sensing' or 'intuitive' ways. Sensing personalities seem to prefer factual information with plenty of detail organised in linear and structured ways. Intuitive personalities appear more to receive and integrate information into a 'big picture': to see patterns and relationships where more 'sensing' learners might only see chaos.

Decisions: Thinking and feeling (T and F)

When making decisions some people seem first to look for logic and consistency ('thinking') while others consider more the people concerned and the surrounding circumstances ('feeling').

Structure: Judging and perceiving (J and P)

Some people seem more to need fixed and firm ideas and beliefs ('judging'); other more to stay open to new information and options ('perceiving').

Sixteen personality types are derived from the above, in what is called a 'type table' (see http://www.myersbriggs.org/my-mbti-personality-type/mbti-basics/the-16-mbti-types.asp#ENTJ for more detail).

The Mind Styles Model

This model (http://gregorc.com/packages.html [accessed 9 February 2011]) provides an organised way to consider how the mind works, and is divided into perceptual quality and ordering ability. Individuals' perceptual quality can be concrete, to register information directly through the senses; or abstract, to visualise and conceive ideas. Everybody has both qualities, but individuals seem to be more at ease employing one over the other. A person whose natural strength lies in the concrete, for example, may communicate in a direct, literal, no-nonsense manner. The person whose natural strength is the abstract may use more subtle ways to get a point across.

The Mind Styles Model also demarcates one's cognitive ordering ability as either sequential or random. A sequential orientation allows one's mind to organise information linearly, or what might be considered the Western traditional approach to organising information, whereas a random orientation allows one's mind to organise information by chunks and in no particular order. When people use the random orientation, they may be able to skip steps or start at the end and work backwards and still achieve successful results. An instructional environment grounded in a sequential orientation may not support the abilities of the random-orientation learner.

Learning Style Inventory

The Learning Style Inventory (http://www.learningandteaching.info/learning/experience.htm [accessed 9 February 2011]), designed and described by David Kolb (1984), identifies four statistically prevalent learning styles: diverging, converging, assimilating and accommodating. According to the model, people with the *diverging-style* view concrete experience and reflective observation from many different perspectives. These individuals perform better in situations that call for generating ideas, such as brainstorming sessions or working in groups. By contrast, people with the *converging-style* favour abstract conceptualisation and active experimentation. These individuals are best at finding practical uses for ideas and theories, and prefer to deal with technical problems rather than with social issues. People with the *assimilating-style* prefer abstract conceptualisation and reflective observation. These individuals work best at understanding a wide range of information and putting it into concise, logical form. They prefer readings, lectures and having time to think things through. People with the *accommodating-style* prefer concrete experience and active experimentation. They favour hands-on experience and, in formal learning situations, tend to test out different approaches when working on a project.

Teaching styles

Instructors develop unique teaching styles based on the cultural underpinnings that influence not only their own learning style, but also their beliefs about what constitutes good teaching and the norms of their particular discipline. Some believe that instruction should be teacher-centred where the teacher is the expert and authority in presenting information. Others take a learner-centred approach, viewing their role as more of a student-learning facilitator.

Social constructivism in Western educational theory

The teaching approaches associated with current Western educational philosophy are based in social constructivism. As Faigley (1999: 137) explains:

> *… most learning is not 'self-taught', not a solitary experience, and […] people learn best learning with other people.*

Based in postmodernism, social constructivism suggests that knowledge and self are socially constructed, and that knowledge 'is not a stable construct of ideas to be passed from teachers who know and participants who learn' (Cooper, 1999: 144). This teaching approach is based on low power distance, which Hofstede and Hofstede (2005) describe as relationships that reflect equality and informality, in this case between instructors and learners. When confronted with more instructor-centred approaches, learners whose culture is rooted in social constructivism may expect more discussion and group work and could question the instructor's ideas and authority.

Teacher-centred approaches in Confucian heritage cultures

Asian countries with Confucian heritage cultures such as China, Vietnam, Singapore, South Korea and Japan have certain characteristics that could create dissonance in a classroom that embraces social constructivism. First, there is high power distance in these cultures, with clear hierarchies and inequality in power in relationships (Hofstede, 1986). In Confucianism the hierarchy between teacher and student is just below 'king and subject' and just above 'father and son'. Karababa (2006: 5) describes the effect of this high power distance:

> There are strong hierarchy rules ... even influencing student–student relationship. Because of the strong need of dependence, Hofstede argues that the educational process is teacher-centered: teachers should always have the right answers to questions asked from students. On the contrary, in Western countries, the student maintains a high level of knowledge whereas the teacher plays the role of a guide, the one who observes the work team and motivates learning.

When learning is highly dependent on the teacher, students from Confucian heritage cultures can find a Western classroom based in social constructivism a challenge to their learning style, resulting in reticence during class discussions, dismissal of other students' opinions and expectations for the teacher to provide the right answers.

Topic-centred and topic-associative expression

The way that ideas and thoughts are organised in written and spoken expression affects learner achievement and communication. Two culturally based discursive techniques are topic-centred and topic-associative expression. In topic-centred discourse, speakers focus on one issue at a time, arrange facts and ideas in linear order, and make explicit relationships between facts and ideas. In this process, cognitive processing moves deductively from discrete parts to a cumulative whole with a discernible closure.

A topic-associative style of discourse is episodic, anecdotal and thematic. More than one issue is addressed at once. Related explanations unfold in overlapping, intersecting loops, one emerging out of and building on others. Relationships between segments of the discourse are inferred rather than explicitly established. Thinking and speaking appear to be circular and seamless rather than linear and clearly demarcated.

For those unfamiliar with it, this communication style sounds rambling and disjointed, as though speakers never end a thought before going on to something else. Topic-associative discourse can be misinterpreted as lack of cognitive ability (Gay, 2000).

Value orientations

Cultural traits can also influence the dynamics of the learning environment. Although to varying degrees and depending on the individual and the context, each culture has preferred and shared ways of perceiving the individual's role in relation to the group, relating to each other, conceiving and managing time, approaching risk-taking, and undertaking tasks and relationships. These themes are called value orientations, and they play a key role in the classroom. When discussing the risk in learning something new at the expense of letting go of outdated but maybe cherished ideas, the great US educator John Dewey wrote (2003: 246):

> *No-one discovers a new world without forsaking an old one; and no one discovers a new world who exacts guarantees in advance for what it shall be, or who puts the act of discovery under bonds with respect to what the new world shall do to him when it comes into vision.*

How individuals perceive themselves in relation to the group refers to their preference to emphasise the individual over the group (individualistic cultures) or the group over the individual (collectivistic cultures). People in individualistic cultures tend to have loose ties to the groups they belong to and are expected to take care of themselves (Ting-Toomey, 1999). They tend to make decisions individually and are comfortable with individual initiative (Peterson, 2004). People in collectivistic cultures have strong ties to their group, protect and take care of each other, and tend to emphasise loyalty (Ting-Toomey, 1999). They also tend to conform to social norms, act cooperatively and make decisions as a group (Peterson, 2004).

The concept of time, so important when working with and managing diverse groups, refers to how flexible, limited or structured people perceive time to be. It also relates to individuals' priorities when it comes to punctuality, nurturing relationships and accomplishing tasks.

Risk-taking refers to how individuals approach conflict (e.g., avoiding it or facing it), their focus on the past or present and future, the amount of rules and regulations they set, their ability to change plans at the last minute, and how innovative they are (Peterson, 2004).

Finally, how individuals approach working in teams or performing tasks and how they develop relationships refers to:

> *the process of putting relationship building and trust first and foremost in doing business as opposed to placing business center stage – and if a personal relationship develops in the process, it's icing on the cake.* (Peterson, 2004: 47)

Relationship-oriented individuals tend to be more interested in who people are more than what they do. They develop personal relationships at work, and attempt to build trust with people they do not know before doing business or working on a project. Therefore, they prefer hiring and working with people they already know and trust. In addition, they also favour family and leisure time over work, thus creating clear boundaries between the two. On the other hand, *task-oriented individuals* tend to be interested in what people do over who they are, keep relationships at work impersonal, feel comfortable getting right down to business even with people they do not know, and favour work over family and leisure time.

Key variables in appropriate and effective communication and negotiation

Another key aspect in learning environments is communication styles. Communicating appropriately (by following the rules) and effectively (by accomplishing a goal successfully) is one of the greatest challenges humans face. We express ourselves using highly sophisticated verbal and non-verbal symbolic systems, most of which make sense within our community. Pragmatic rules guide us to be appropriate in what we say, to whom we say it, how we say it and under what circumstances. Communication styles, 'how we express ourselves' (Saphiere et al., 2005: 6), either help us or hinder us in communicating effectively. They dictate how we deliver our messages and how we interpret those of others. Here are some useful considerations that can affect learning and teaching across cultures:

1. We describe and understand behaviours by using others as a frame of reference. How loudly/quietly, fast/slow, directly/indirectly we speak is determined by how loudly/quietly, fast/slow, directly/indirectly others speak (as individuals and as groups). It is not until we are faced with a different way of behaving and thinking that we are challenged to recognise differences in style.

2. Our choice of communication style is determined by context (Saphiere et al., 2005: 58–9). This means the physical context where the communicative event takes place, the roles of those communicating, and their historical context or shared history. Also to be considered are the perceptions held by each party about the other, the chronology and any previous history of the event, and the language of choice. Other influential factors include the relationship between those communicating, as well as any possible constraints, such as time limits or the communication medium, for example email or face-to-face.

3. Verbal communication consists of several dimensions. A crucial one is low and high context (Storti, 1999). *Low-context* people rely on words over context and look at the speaker as the one responsible for the communication. They see sharing information as a key goal of communication, and they tend to be direct and speak their mind. They also tend to see verbal disagreement as positive. *High-context people* rely on context over words (seniority, age, use of silence, non-verbal communication) and place the responsibility of understanding the message on the listener. They also view developing the relationship to be the main goal of communication, tend to be indirect and avoid direct conflict.

   Other verbal communication dimensions are rhythm and intensity, degree of emotional expressiveness, formality and informality, and use of silence. To be considered also are the amount of self-disclosure, linear/spiral logic, self-credentialing/self-humbling, face negotiation and requesting strategies (Ting-Toomey and Chung, 2005). We are clued to our own preference when we are uncomfortable with another's style, for instance, if we find it to be too loud/quiet, too linear/circular, too passionate/cold, too humble/self-credentialing, disclosing too much/little personal information, etc.

4. Non-verbal communication consists of facial expressions, paralanguage (how we speak: accent, pitch range, pitch intensity, volume, articulation and pace), artefacts, clothing, gestures (hand and body movements) and haptics (touch behaviour). Proxemics (use of space, whether it is personal, physical or psychological) and time management are to be considered also (Ting-Toomey and Chung, 2005). As with verbal communication, our own preferences come to light as we evaluate the other person's choices, which are mostly unconscious.

Cross-cultural misunderstandings often occur because human interaction is deeply rooted in the culture of a society (Hofstede, 1986). Instructors need to use culturally responsive teaching methods that begin with assessment of their own learning styles in relation to those of their students.

Online teaching and learning media: Teaching across cultures and distance

Like face-to-face learning contexts, online teaching and learning environments should take a cross-cultural perspective to serve the needs of diverse learners.

E-learning context

Online distance education often relies on electronic communication that can be based in course management systems like Blackboard, Desire2Learn, Moodle and Nicenet – or conducted through electronic mail.

In most cases, online communication requires files to be transferred from instructors to participants with information about the course subject matter. These documents can be Microsoft Word or PowerPoint, Adobe PDF files, or audio and video files that require software like QuickTime, Windows Media Player or iTunes. Students transfer them back to the instructor, usually as papers and projects completed using the same applications in which they were created.

More recently, online instruction has incorporated use of Web 2.0 technology – like blogs, wikis, social networking sites and video-sharing sites – in order to share information, encourage interaction among course participants, and encourage learner-generated knowledge-sharing. Furthermore, course management systems have incorporated software like Wimba to encourage synchronous communication between teachers and students in a virtual classroom. For asynchronous interaction, these systems provide virtual space for discussion boards and wikis.

Online instructors also make use of webinar software, such as GoToWebinar and Adobe Connect, in order to make presentations to students in real-time and to connect with students with options for interaction through text, audio and visual media. In addition, some instructors make use of other software like Google or Skype to communicate one on one with students through video, audio or text chats.

Since much of the knowledge-sharing between instructor and student is based on the transfer of electronic documents and media, an important aspect of cross-cultural concerns is the design and usability of web pages. Differences in cultural norms for web design are not merely cosmetic. The presentation of multimedia can affect students' ability to navigate the course site and interpret the information on the page, which affects their understanding of course content.

Barber and Badre (1998) coined the term 'culturability' (culture plus usability) to emphasise the effect of culture on the design of web pages. Many studies show that usability of web pages is affected by culture and that people from different cultures have different web design preferences (Sun, 2001; Badre, 2000; Marcus and Gould, 2000; Barber and Badre, 1998; Del Galdo and Neilson, 1996). Cyr and Trevor-Smith (2004) conducted a study on the differences in culture based on interface design with web users from Germany, Japan and the US, and found the following cultural differences to be statistically significant:

1. Representation of language and script, including stylistic elements such as headlines, paragraph and direction of script.
2. Website layout and spatial features, such as placement of banners, location of menu, preference for visuals and search functions.
3. Symbols used, such as currency and time.
4. Content and structural characteristics of websites, such as index features, site map features and type of help available (i.e., online, email, phone).
5. Design preferences for navigation and search, such as types of menus (e.g., drop down, horizontal, vertical), keyword search and preference for text or symbolic links.
6. Number of external links and the functionality of links.
7. Design preferences for multimedia elements and the extent of multimedia, such as animation.
8. Colour choices.

Language and reasoning pattern differentials: Presentation of information

Bentley et al. (2005) outline eight educational value differentials for understanding cultural issues in internet-based learning: these are reasoning pattern; language; high- and low-context awareness; learning style; cognitive style in web page perception; social context; technical infrastructure, connectivity and access to text-based online support; and cultural dissonance with local contexts.

Reasoning pattern

Cyr and Trevor-Smith (2004) found that, in terms of layout and spatial features, German and US sites tend to locate the menu on the left and bottom of the page, which could create navigation confusion to students used to a different layout. In terms of representation of language and script, Japanese users have a strong preference for point form and use of symbols instead of text for links, whereas the German and US sites use paragraph form twice as often and prefer use of text for links. In addition, with regard to hyperlinks, Japanese sites use external links more commonly. These choices in layout, spatial features and representation of language and script show a difference in reasoning pattern.

The Western preference for more text in paragraph form is based on linear communication practices rather than point form that may present information in a non-linear manner. The Japanese use of more external links that take the reader away from the main site can also indicate more non-linear patterns of reasoning since the reader moves away from the central site of information more often. These considerations are important when teaching or designing an online course because students from different cultures may not read web pages in the same way.

Language; high- and low-context, learning style; text-based online support

The choice of text versus point form and symbols on web pages exemplifies differences in high- and low-context communication. As stated above, Japanese sites favour the use of point form and symbols, which denotes high-context communication. On the other hand, the German and US cultures tend to be low-context: they are more verbal and use more text to communicate ideas. In addition, a significant structural characteristic that could affect students' experience in an online course is the expectation for help and support. Ninety per cent of US sites had email support available, whereas two-thirds of Japanese sites provided telephone numbers. Germany had the same amount of email support as Japan, and only one site provided support by telephone.

Japanese students may have a difficult time when online communication is expected rather than face-to-face. Cyr and Trevor-Smith (2004) explain this difference as based on Japan's high-context culture, which has a preference for additional information beyond written text.

Learning style differential: Cognitive style in web page perception

Cognitive styles can be affected by culture. Masuda and Nisbett (2001) found perceptual differences between Japanese and US Americans, who were holistic and analytical respectively when looking at a video scene. A study by Dong and Lee (2008) connected cognitive styles of Chinese, Koreans and US Americans to perceptions of web pages. The study concluded that Chinese and Koreans displayed holistic thought patterns when viewing web pages, whereas US American showed analytic thought patterns.

This means that holistically minded people show a tendency to spread their fixations over the page and follow a non-linear reading pattern, whereas analytically minded people tend to concentrate their fixations while viewing the page and follow a linear reading pattern. With these and previously mentioned differences in learning styles based on different cultures, the design of e-learning needs to be considered with diverse learners.

Educational culture and social context differential: Predominance of social constructivism

Paloff and Pratt (1999: 5) state that

> *key to the [online distance education] learning process are the interactions among students themselves, the interactions between faculty and students, and the collaboration in learning that results from these interactions.*

They explain this to be a result of distance, which does not allow learners to be passive. If they enter the discussion forum and do not post a message, the instructor may consider learners to be absent or not engaged. Therefore to be 'present' in a virtual class means to be an active participant. This approach to teaching, based on student interaction, is grounded in social constructivism.

Given that e-learning is predominantly found in post-secondary education in English-speaking countries, also known as BANA (Britain, Australasia and North America), the global methodology for online teaching is grounded in these countries' educational philosophy (Catterick, 2007). Online education became a regular part of higher education in the mid-1990s, with constructivism as the dominant educational ideology in Western countries, particularly BANA.

According to social constructivist theory founded in the work by Vygotsky (1978), learning is not a one-way knowledge transfer from teachers to students. Knowledge is co-constructed through interactions between instructors and students as well as among students. The foundations of this approach are active and collaborative learning, reflective practice (Kolb, 1984) and autonomous learning (Littlewood, 1999; Ryan, 1991). Therefore the culture of learning in online distance education is embedded in a social context that is collaborative in nature where instructors play the roles of facilitators instead of knowledge givers, and students are active participants in the construction of knowledge.

Because of the difference in power distance, this e-learning approach based on social constructivism can come into conflict with Confucian-heritage other cultures based on traditional teaching approaches. In the Confucian approach, owing to the hierarchy in the relationship between teacher and student, the students listen and do not ask questions. To them, saving face and maintaining harmony is a priority. The teacher takes the responsibility for the transfer of knowledge, and students may not be used to collaborating and being active, autonomous learners.

Technical infrastructure differential: Connectivity and access

For online education settings, the difference in technical infrastructure between less and more developed countries is great, and this technological divide can cause a breakdown in communication that can affect students' performance. The technology can curtail learning because it needs high bandwidth and computers with sufficient memory and power. Thus students who have a dial-up internet connection or lack upgraded software will struggle.

Some online course designers use only text-based communication and avoid using multimedia so as not to disadvantage students from less-developed countries. Furthermore, use of social websites like YouTube and Facebook can be considered culturally inappropriate, and some countries may block the sites.

Global vs local differential: Cultural dissonance with local contexts

Bentley et al. (2005) stress that online instructors and instructional designers should keep in mind the local perspective when designing online courses. They explain that students with a non-US educational background have statistically significant different preferences from those of US students for how they interact with content. Therefore instructors from BANA countries – dominating e-learning globally – should be aware of the cultural orientations of their students from other countries and cultures, and they should consider the local context when adopting the e-learning environment.

Conclusion

Culturally diverse learning environments present challenges to students and instructors alike. All will be better served when they become aware of their own learning (and teaching) styles and cultural preferences. Essential keys to classroom dynamics include value orientations, communication styles, pedagogical approaches, expectations in relating to one another, time management and non-verbal communication. In addition an online educational environment should consider web design, presentation of information, technical infrastructure and local contexts, in order to create equal opportunities for all. To be inclusive, face-to-face and online educational environments should put learners at the forefront and incorporate their various learning styles, teaching styles, communication styles and cultural preferences.

Questions and discussion

1. Behaviour likely to promote effective intercultural communication

Why do we need to work on communicating effectively with others? Why is it challenging? What makes it challenging? What do people need to know about culture?

Some answers you might like to discuss are that culture is complex; that it has patterns; that it has great internal variation (and here you need to think about the dangers of stereotyping); and that uncertainty and violated expectations can cause great cross-cultural conflict.

What do people need to know about themselves? What behaviour is most likely to promote communication between people from different cultural backgrounds? What competencies are needed to create an environment that promotes effective communication? What happens when different team members have intercultural competencies more or less developed than their colleagues?

Milton Bennett's model

Take time to study Milton Bennett's Developmental Model of Intercultural Sensitivity (e.g., visit http://blog.communicaid.com/cross-cultural-training/cross-cultural-theory-developmental-model-of-intercultural-sensitivity/ [accessed 10 May 2010]). The model demonstrates how people can move from feelings of ethnocentrism ('my way is best') to ethno-relativism ('my way and your way can co-exist'). If they begin with *denial* they will refuse interaction with the foreign culture and show disinterest, even hostility, in discovering cultural differences. They may move to feeling a need to *defend* their own culture against all others; but with time they may *minimise* differences and start believing that all cultures share some values. Thus comes *acceptance* of differences and appropriate *adaptation* of behaviour, finally to *integrate* with the other culture.

2. Teaching and learning styles

Not everybody learns in the same way, and learning styles vary between individuals, no matter what their cultural background.

Ronald Schmeck's Inventory of Learning Processes

For example, Schmeck, Ribich and Ramanaiah's 1977 Inventory of Learning Processes (ILP) was revised by Schmeck in 1983 as a self-report inventory to assess learning styles on six scales:

1. Shallow processing (very little or no retention of information once the lesson is over).
2. Deep mental processing of information (i.e., retention of knowledge and ability to recall).
3. Elaborative processing (taking the information further by applying it to different situations).
4. Self-efficacy (taking personal responsibility for one's own learning).
5. Conceptualising (theorising without necessarily looking for practical examples).
6. Memorisation and methodical study.

Benjamin Bloom's taxonomy

Teaching strategies are argued to include active listening, questioning and giving constructive feedback on students' learning on a number of levels. Bloom's (1956) taxonomy of levels of intellectual behaviour in learning has been updated by Lorin Anderson (a former student of Bloom's) and is reported by Overbaugh and Schultz (2010) as behaviour in which students should be able to:

1. Remember: show evidence of recall of knowledge.
2. Understand: be able to explain ideas or concepts.
3. Apply: use the information in new ways.
4. Analyse: distinguish between the different parts of an argument.
5. Evaluate: justify a stand or decision.
6. Create: create new products or points of view.

David Kolb's classification

David Kolb (2010) has been the inspiration for a large numbers of theorists who argue that learners can be identified under four major sets of characteristics:

1. Activists – who are 'hands-on' learners and prefer to 'have a go' and learn through trial and error.
2. Reflectors – who are 'tell me' learners and prefer to be thoroughly briefed before proceeding.

3. Theorists – who are 'convince me' learners and want reassurance that a project makes sense.
4. Pragmatists – who are 'show me' learners and want a demonstration from an acknowledged expert.

Kolb suggests that there are four stages in learning, which follow from each other: *concrete experience* is followed by *reflection* on that experience on a personal basis. This may be followed by the derivation of general rules describing the experience, or the application of known theories to it (*abstract conceptualisation*), and hence to the construction of ways of modifying the next occurrence of the experience (*active experimentation*), leading in turn to the next concrete experience. All this may happen in a flash, or over days, weeks or months, depending on the topic, and there may be a 'wheels within wheels' process at the same time.

Another study suggests people have different distinct ways of acquiring information. Some are spatial/visual learners who learn by seeing. Some are tactile/kinetic learners who learn by doing and/or touching. Others are auditory learners who learn by listening and talking. The rest may be logical learners who learn by thinking.

Howard Garner's Multiple Intelligent Assessment

Garner defined intelligence as the capacity to solve problems or to fashion products that are valued in one or more cultural settings (http://www.infed.org/thinkers/gardner.htm). However, his work was heavily influenced by his own (US) cultural assumptions and these need to be taken into account when reading his findings.

Anthony F. Gregorc's Mind Style Model

Gregorc identifies ways in which the mind works (see http://www.ieslearning.co.uk/mind.html). His fundamental categories are perception and ordering ability:

Perception:

Concrete: dealing with the obvious, the 'here and now', not looking for hidden meanings, or making connections between ideas or concepts;

Abstract: intuition, imagination, looking beyond 'what is' to hidden meanings and connections.

Ordering ability:

Sequential: linear, step-by-step, logical, planned;

Random: skips steps, may start in the middle or at the end and work backwards; impulsive, spur of the moment.

We all have ability in all these ways of ordering but usually we tend to use one more easily and comfortably than the other. For instance, a natural *concrete* thinker will often communicate in a very direct, literal, no-nonsense manner, while a natural *abstract* thinker may use subtle methods such as metaphor to get the same meaning. Conversations between one of each thinking style may contain the seeds of much misunderstanding.

Gregorc proposed four combinations of the strongest perceptual and ordering ability in each individual:

Concrete Sequential (CS)

Abstract Random (AR)

Abstract Sequential (AS)

Concrete Random (CR)

Log on to: http://www.ieslearning.co.uk/mind.html and click on the relevant links to identify your own mind style! There are no right or wrong, bad or good learning ways. It's just about preferences with which people are born and into which they are acculturated. Virtually everybody is capable of learning by any of the above methods; but most people seem to have a preference for one and use it to conduct them through the others. For example, of course visual learners will learn also by talking and listening; but they are particularly good at learning from pictures and images (Ho, 2006).

Neil Fleming's VAK/VARK model

One of the most common and widely used learning style inventories is Neil Fleming's VARK model (sometimes known as VAK), which expanded upon earlier neuro-linguistic programming (NLP) designs (see http://www.vark-learn.com/english/index.asp). NLP is a controversial approach to psychotherapy and organisational change based on the relationship between successful patterns of behaviour and the patterns of thought underlying them. The co-founders, Richard Bandler and linguist John Grinder, coined the term 'neuro-linguistic programming' to indicate a connection between neurological processes ('neuro'), language ('linguistic') and behavioural patterns learnt through experience ('programming').

Fleming found three basic learning style preferences: for visual, auditory or kinaesthetic (tactile) experience. He claimed that *visual learners* have a preference for seeing (think in pictures, visual aids such as overhead slides, diagrams, handouts, etc.). *Auditory learners* best learn through listening (lectures, discussions, tapes, etc.). *Tactile/kinaesthetic learners* prefer to learn via experience – moving, touching and doing (active exploration of the world, science projects, experiments, etc.).

Its use allows teachers to prepare classes that address each of these areas. Students can also use the model to identify their preferred learning style and maximise their educational experience by focusing on what benefits them the most.

Sources

Bloom, B.S. 1984. *Taxonomy of Educational Objectives*. New York: Allyn & Bacon.
Hawk, T.F. and Shah, A.J. 2007. 'Using learning style instruments to enhance student learning'. *Decision Sciences Journal of Innovative Education*, doi:10.1111/j.1540-4609.2007. 00125.x.
Ho, L. 2006. 'Four learning styles'. *Lifehack*, 24 January; http://www.lifehack.org/articles/ lifehack/four-learning-styles.html.
Kolb, D.A. 1984. *Experiential Learning: Experience as the Source of Learning and Development*. Englewood Cliffs, NJ: Prentice Hall.
—— 2010. http://www.learningandteaching.info/learning/experience.htm.
Lewin, K. 1948. *Resolving Social Conflicts: Selected Papers on Group Dynamics*, ed. K. Lewin and W. Gertude (ed.). New York: Harper & Row.
LSQ: http://www.peterhoney.com/content/LearningStylesQuestionnaire.html.
Overbaugh, R.C. and Schultz, L. 2010. 'Bloom's taxonomy', http://www.odu.edu/educ/rover-bau/Bloom/blooms_taxonomy.htm.
Schmeck, R.R. and Grove, E. 1979. 'Academic achievement and individual differences in learning processes'. *Applied Psychological Measurement*, 3 (1), pp. 43–9.
Senge, P. 1990. *The Fifth Discipline: The Art and Practice of the Learning Organization*. Boston, MA: McGraw-Hill.
—— 1994. *The Fifth Discipline Fieldbook: Strategies and Tools for Building a Learning Organization*. Boston, MA: McGraw-Hill.
Sternberg, R.J. and Zhang, L.-f. (eds) 2001. *Perspectives on Thinking, Learning, and Cognitive Styles*. London: Routledge.
Withers, J. 2010. 'VARK learning styles theory', *eHow Contributor*, 9 June 2010; http://www. ehow.com/about_6612058_vark-learning-styles-theory.html.

3. Use of more effective online teaching and learning media

Free tools ('talk and chalk'); commercial and other tools; online discussion boards.

Suggestions:

- Make expectations clear;
- Use time deadlines;
- Require responses to other students;
- Teach students how to write effective postings;
- Watch written chat as well as listen to those who speak online – students in other countries may not have same technology and have to use a cellphone to call in.

Live classrooms:

- Wait for at least 10 seconds before calling on hand-raisers;
- Use a mix of short lecture (no more than 8 minutes) and discussion/ debate;
- Give equal time to all voices.

Podcasts:

- Allow students to listen to recorded lectures several times to be sure they understand them;
- No more than 8 minutes per session;
- Intersperse with required journaling; can be private (wikis, anonymous discussion boards) or public (discussion board, course wiki)

Considerations when working with electronic media in an intercultural environment

- Plagiarism in discussion boards;
- Time differences and conventions (a.m./p.m. vs 24 hour clock);
- Use several methods to communicate requirements/assignments/directions;
- Write directions in simple language;
- Write in linear order;
- Use active not passive voice;
- Choose date convention for deliverables – US: dd/mm/yy; UK: mm/dd/yy; International: yyyy/mm/dd'
- Text-speak allowed/disallowed?;
- Cultural phrases avoided.

Conclusion

The objectives of this chapter are to study teaching and learning methods in Western and Asian settings; to apply this to individual learning styles in the context of teaching and learning theory; and to suggest ways of improving international classroom and online teaching. The general conclusion from the various contributions that make up the chapter is that there should be as little dissonance as possible between teachers' behaviour and students' learning style preferences, derived from culture and individual personality.

Key points

1. Asian and Western teachers and trainers have much to learn from each other about teacher–learner relationships; student motivation to learn; lesson form and content; the importance of overview as well as detail in learning; of reflective as well as active learning; and of the need for effort to achieve high standards of knowledge.

2. People process information differently; and the differences relate both to culture and individual personality. It is the responsibility of teachers, who accept formal responsibility for creating environments most conducive to learning, to cater as much as possible for all learning and problem-solving styles.

3. These are generally taken to include linear versus non-linear reasoning (topic-centred and topic-associative, respectively); experiential versus theoretical behaviour; active experimentation versus reflection; a preference for visual, auditory or sensory input; and for individual or collaborative study.

4. Thus both verbal and non-verbal communication are essential in teaching and learning; and teachers need to use as wide a range of media as possible to appeal to all learning styles.

5. Online teaching is becoming as routine as classroom teaching; and there are many digital media for enhancing and promoting learning.

6. A number of instruments exist for assessing individuals' preferred learning and problem-solving styles, including the Myers-Briggs Type Indicator, the Mind Styles Model, the Learning Styles Model and Fleming's VARK model.

8. Different views of time management will affect the way people choose to learn.

9. Some people are more risk-aversive than others and are reluctant to let go of cherished ideas in order to learn something new.

10. Without heavy investment in education and training by governments and the private sector, nations cannot hope to stock a rich pool of individual and team talents, attributes and skills.

Looking ahead

This chapter has been the last in Part Two, the section dealing with the dimension of communication contexts and following the general content of Part One's 'different voices'. Part Three concerns the global dimension of international negotiations, alliances and networks. It opens with Chapter 7 on 'command and control' of these activities, including negotiation tactics.

Experiential exercise

My worlds

Created by Jon Curwin, Business School Learning Centre, University of Central England Business School. Originally published in Christopher, Elizabeth and Meadows, Dennis (eds), (1999) *Games from Many Nations for Management and Leadership Training* (Japanese Foundation for the Fusion of Science and Technology (FOST)), and reproduced with permission.

This game takes participants on a journey to four 'worlds' and four 'cultures'. In each of them a different problem-solving style is required. Thus players experience and evaluate several kinds of learning role. Each world has its own 'currency', and players need to earn some of it before they can move on to the next world. During debriefing after the game they discuss their own and others' learning style preferences as demonstrated during the game; and how these observations might help them to become more effective problem-solvers. This is a lengthy game, but the results in terms of participant learning make the time well spent.

Objectives

- To identify four different learning behaviours;
- To study some of the consequences of the differences;
- To speculate on implications for the management of organisational change.

Number of players

This game is most effectively played with a fairly large group of players, say at least 20. The maximum is any number the presenter can manage. Large groups will need more than one presenter. However, the game can be played with as few as 12 people.

Materials

1. A room large enough for the needs of the group; sufficient chairs and tables;
2. Writing materials for each player; and somewhere to post results, e.g., a blackboard, whiteboard or flipchart;
3. A copy each of the Handout and the Instructions for each player (see below);
4. Four sheets of cardboard to identify each world;
5. The following game items:

    - a box of dominoes
    - 2 decks each of 52 playing cards
    - 100 sheets of blank paper
    - 6 tennis balls
    - children's scissors
    - a pack of pens
    - a roll of masking tape
    - paper clips
    - a box of crayons
    - a package of plastic drinking straws
    - a map of any town or city.

Time required

About an hour and a half to two hours.

Preparation

1. There should be a desk and chair for each game director at the front of the classroom. Make sure all directors have writing materials.

2. Organise the classroom into four 'worlds' by putting a big table in each corner of the room, with as many chairs as you will need for each playing team (so, if you have a group of 20 players, you will need 5 chairs in each world). Put writing materials on the tables for each player.

3. Fold 4 sheets of cardboard to make 4 nameplates, one to stand on each table. They should display, respectively: TEMPORA; MIRA; RIGOR; PRAGMA.

4. Put a pack of playing cards (52 cards); 3 tennis balls; a set of dominoes on the TEMPORA table.

5. Put a map of any town or city; a deck of cards; 3 tennis balls and a packet of plastic drinking straws on the RIGOR table.

Running the game

1. Give a copy of the set of instructions and tasks to each participant (be sure to keep copies for yourself) and read aloud with them the introduction. Then go through the instructions and rules to make sure everybody understands them. Encourage questions without being diverted into a long discussion. Keep the action moving: you have a lot to get through.

2. Divide participants into four teams, each of 3–7 people. If you have more than 28 players, form more than four teams. It is important that each team be fairly small.

3. Assign each team at random to a different world. If there are more than four teams, more than one team will begin in one or more worlds.

4. Start the game. Keep a general eye on the action. Time activities when asked.

5. Keep a record of all scores and make sure that each team completes at least two tasks in each world. They may wish to attempt all five. (Note: if the group is large you may want to ask one of the participants to help you with this responsibility.)

   Do not enter into debates about scoring. Remind players that your decision is final and that an opportunity to discuss scoring will arise when the game is over. Tell them to enter their scores onto the scoring sheet in their Instructions.

6. Instruct players of TEMPORA TASK #5. DOMINOES how to play the game, if they don't know, as follows:

   Dealer deals out dominoes, one by one to each team member until all pieces are allocated. Player #1 places a domino face up on the table. Player #2 has to line up one end of this domino with one end of their own, e.g., by laying a 4 against a 4. Player #3 follows and so on, until a line of dominoes is patterned on the table. If any player cannot match a number, they lose a turn. The game is over when a player gets rid of all pieces. Players have a total of 10 minutes. Time them and score according to the instructions.

7. The answer to RIGOR TASK #5 is an infinite speed, i.e., the task cannot be done because the driver has already used up all the available time yet has only covered half the required distance.

8. Let the game run for about 45 minutes, then call a halt, finalise and post the total number of Temps, Mirs, Rigs and Pragms that each team acquired. Begin the debriefing. It should run for at least half an hour.

Debriefing notes

Questions to begin discussion:

■ Did some groups or some individuals achieve higher scores in particular worlds?

■ What were the characteristics of each of the worlds?

■ What value is there in travelling from one world to another?

When discussion is established, issue a copy of the HANDOUT to each participant and use this as a basis for further analysis.

MY WORLDS HANDOUT (one copy for each player and one for the presenter)

Theories from the literature:

The authors of MY WORLDS suggest there are two key theories that form a useful background for running this game, namely Kolb's learning cycle and Honey and Mumford's learning styles.

Kolb identified four stages of learning in a continuous, never-ending cycle of *concrete experience and personal involvement, reflective observation, generalisation and theorising,* and *active application of theory to real life.* He further suggested that most people have a preferred learning (or problem-solving) style and a preferred entry-point to the cycle. For example, some people are more 'hands-on' in their approach to problem-solving while others are more inclined first to 'read the instructions'.

Honey and Mumford have built on the work of Kolb to develop a model of learning that identifies four different learning styles: *activist, reflector, theorist* and *pragmatist.*

Thus the world of TEMPORA might appeal more to *activists*, who favour concrete experience and prefer to be involved actively in problem solving, especially in new experiences. Activists are argued to be enthusiastic and to want to get stuck into new tasks immediately. They tend to act first and consider the consequences afterwards. There is an emphasis on activity and doing; they thrive on challenge and will tend to dominate activities they are involved in.

By these arguments, activists and probably pragmatists should thrive in TEMPORA whereas reflectors and theorists might not feel so comfortable. How do participants respond to this? Do any team members report that TEMPORA was their preferred problem-solving 'culture'? Or the opposite? Do any of them recognise themselves in the above description?

On the other hand, *reflectors* are supposed to think before they leap, to want to evaluate alternatives and perspectives. They are assumed to be cautious people who will take their time before they reach a conclusion: thoughtful people who will want to collect lots of different information to put the problem in perspective. Thus reflectors should thrive in MIRA whereas activists might become impatient. Are there group members who recognise themselves as reflectors from their experience of the game?

Honey and Mumford suggest that *theorists* are looking for the logical approach: they think problems through in a vertical step-by-step way. They are keen to find a framework or theory to explain a problem, adopt an analytical frame of mind and are trying to maximise certainty. If so, theorists should thrive in RIGOR, but reflectors might wilt. How do participants feel about this?

Pragmatists are described as practical people who seek out new ways of tackling problems, and are always on the look-out for new techniques and theories to see if they can make them work in practice. This is inclined to infuriate theorists, who tend to be more cautious; and reflectors might see pragmatists as very short-sighted. Pragmatists should thrive in PRAGMA because players who enjoy the tasks in that world usually seem to prefer the pragmatist learning style – perhaps because they need to see obvious practical advantages in what they are doing. They like to try out and practise techniques in the 'real world', but theorists or reflectors perhaps do not. How do group members respond to these suggestions?

Once groups have reviewed their performance they might be asked to move into 'world groups'. Group members move into the world where they feel most comfortable. Like-minded people then discuss the characteristics of their shared world. You could then pool these descriptions and use them as a route into discussion of the concepts underpinning the game.

Honey and Mumford argue that different individuals will learn better from different types of activities because of a tendency to favour a particular type of learning style. However, they believe in self-development and recommend a range of activities to help individuals to become 'all-round' learners. The first stage of this development is self-awareness, and hopefully this game will help participants to be more aware of the different approaches to learning and of their individual learning styles.

Sources

Honey, P. and Mumford, A. 1992. *Manual of Learning Style*; http://www.peterhoney.com/contents/manuals.html [accessed 4 April 2012].

Kolb, D.A., Rubin, I.M. and McIntyre, J.M. 1971. *Organizational Psychology: An Experiential Approach*. Englewood Cliffs, NJ: Prentice Hall.

Pedlar, M., Burgoyne, J. and Boydell, T. 1994. *A Manager's Guide to Self Development*; http://www.mhprofessional.com/ [12 May 2012].

Instructions and rules (one copy for each player and one for the presenter)

Introduction

In MY WORLDS you will explore the argument that an essential task for managers is to continue to learn – that is, to find new ways to solve problems in today's international world where rapid organisational change is becoming the norm.

However, learning is an individual process and most probably you will all have aptitudes or preferences for situations that suit your individual problem-solving strengths.

MY WORLDS takes you on a journey to four 'worlds' and four 'cultures':

- TEMPORA, where time is important and work must be completed;
- MIRA, where observation and reflection are the most important learning behaviour;
- RIGOR, a rigorous world where tasks require a theoretical and logical approach;
- PRAGMA, a practical world where activities need to be planned.

In each of them a different problem-solving style is required. Thus you will experience and evaluate several kinds of learning role by completing various different tasks in each world.

Each world has its own 'currency' and you will need to earn some of it by completing certain tasks before you can move on to the next world.

When the game is over, we will discuss which of the tasks we found, individually, to be more or less easy and comfortable and which we found more difficult or tiresome; and why. We will see if we can relate these observations to ideas about 'learning how to learn'.

Teams may move around the universe of the game and visit the different worlds as often as they please, without overcrowding any one world at any one time. All teams must visit all four worlds and complete at least two tasks in each world. You may complete up to five tasks in any one world.

TEMPORA

The emphasis in Tempora is on action, stimulus, excitement, fun! It is all about working as a team to get things done and achieve set tasks in a given time.

TEMPORA TASK #1: WORDS, WORDS, WORDS

Write down each letter of the alphabet on a separate piece of paper, then make as many words of four letters as possible using each letter only once. You have a maximum of 10 minutes and will be awarded half a temp for each word. You will only get a score for real words. Indicate to the presenter when you begin, so that you can be timed. When you have completed your list, take it to the presenter for checking and to receive your score. Be sure that you record all your scores and that the presenter does so also.

TEMPORA TASK #2: TOWER OF CARDS

You are required to build a tower from a pack of playing cards. You will be given 1 temp for every 10 cards in the tower. You have 10 minutes to build the tower. Ask the presenter to start timing you as soon as you begin building. If you manage to build the tower in less than 10 minutes you will be given a bonus of 1 temp for every minute less.

TEMPORA TASK #:. JUGGLING

You have to pick one of you to be a juggler, who has to demonstrate juggling 3 tennis balls. Temps are awarded on the length of time 3 balls are kept moving by the juggler. The juggler will have 5 minutes to practise, then must demonstrate for the presenter, who will score the performance as follows:

3 balls moving for 5 seconds: 1 temp

3 balls moving for 10 seconds: 3 temps

3 balls moving for 20 seconds: 5 temps

TEMPORA TASK #: TWO EMPTY RUBBISH BINS

You have 5 minutes to write a list of as many uses as you can think of for two empty rubbish bins. None of these uses should include anything to do with rubbish. You will be awarded 1 temp for each 5 uses. Ask the presenter to time you. Make your list, then choose one of the uses you have identified and mime it for the presenter. You will be given 1 temp for every mime the presenter can guess correctly. You have 5 minutes for your mime.

TEMPORA TASK #5: DOMINOES

You have to play a game of dominoes in the least possible time. The presenter will show you how to play the game if you don't know it. If any team member cannot lay a domino, they miss their turn. You have a total of 10 minutes. When your time is up the presenter will inspect the pattern of the dominoes. Scoring will be as follows:

Game completed in 10 minutes: 10 temps

Game completed in 15 minutes: 5 temps

Unable to complete: 0 temps

MIRA

The tasks in MIRA are designed to encourage observation and reflection on activities or experiences. Review and analysis is required rather than immediate action.

MIRA TASK #: WHAT IS A SKILL?

Write down as many different statements as you can, to complete the following. There is no time limit, and you do not have to inform the presenter when you begin this task. Take your list to the presenter for a score when you feel you have played this game long enough.

A skill is …

You will be scored as follows:

0–3 reasonable statements: 0 mirs;

3–8: reasonable statements: 5 mirs;

More than 8: 10 mirs

MIRA TASK #2: A QUESTION OF LEADERSHIP

Consider the following statement: Leaders are born not made.
In two columns, list as many arguments you can for and against this statement. There is no time limit. When you have had enough of the exercise, take your list to the presenter for scoring.

2 or less relevant entries in any column: 0 mirs

3 relevant entries in both columns: 1 mir

4 relevant entries in both columns: 2 mirs

Up to a maximum of 10 mirs for 10 or more relevant entries in both columns.

MIRA TASK #3: SUCCESS?

Analyse any two previous tasks: one that you see your team as a success and one you think you were less successful. List the factors you think influenced your results. There is no time limit. Go to the presenter when you want a score.

Fewer than 3 factors on each: 0 mirs

3–8 factors on each: 5 mirs

10 or more factors on each: 10 mirs

MIRA TASK #4: GROUP REFLECTION

On the results of your completion of Task #3, list your strengths and weaknesses as a problem-solving team. Ask your presenter for a score when you have finished.

2 or less relevant entries in any column: 0 mirs

3 relevant entries in both columns: 1 mir

4 relevant entries in both columns: 2 mirs

Up to a maximum of 10 mirs for 10 or more relevant entries in both columns

MIRA TASK #5: WHAT DOES IT MEAN?

Give 3 meanings to the figure below, and explain how these meanings can help you within the game. There is no time limit. Scores will be awarded for originality and obvious reflection, on a scale of 0–10 mirs. The decision of the presenter is final.

RIGOR

The tasks in RIGOR recognise that many people seem to need to work within a set of rules or to develop a set of rules. Such rules allow consistent individual and organisational approaches that can be replicated when necessary. Such rules need to be seen as providing an effective solution. The tasks in RIGOR are likely to have a structure that can be described in technical terms. Theories can be developed and applied in a systematic way. Mathematics may feature in the solution or provide a means for exploring the problem. Solutions can be given as a set of instructions.

RIGOR TASK #1: ORDERING

In 15 minutes, shuffle a pack of cards and:

1. Order the cards in a consistent way taking account of such factors as numerical value and colour..
2. Devise a set of rules that will allow a particular card to be easily found.
3. Show your ordered pack of cards and set of instructions to the presenter.

Scoring is as follows:

Presentation of an ordered set of cards and a clear set of instructions: 2 rigs Using your instructions the presenter will attempt to find 5 cards. Score 2 rigs for each card.

RIGOR TASK #2: DIRECTIONS

In 15 minutes, given the map of (city), you are to produce a set of directions for a blind person who is at the junction of (Avenue) and (Street) and wants to get to the (Cathedral).

The method of scoring will take account of the level of detail provided and general advice given to the blind person.

Scoring is as follows:

- 2 rigs if instructions are clear and correct
- 2 additional rigs if the instructions include any of the following points:
    - the use of landmarks, e.g., crossing a bridge
    - advice to check critical points along the route
    - a count of turnings passed on the left or the right
- The presenter will use discretion to add to this list of points.
- A maximum of 10 rigs to be awarded.

RIGOR TASK #3: DEVICE

As a group you must think of something that has moving parts (e.g., a toy car, a fan, a paper punch). Produce a set of instructions on how this object could be taken apart and put back together. Score 1 rig for each necessary instruction up to a maximum of 10 rigs.

Necessary instructions will usually include:

- the order in which parts are removed
- methods for recording each of the parts
- the tools required
- the fastening devices (screws, nuts and bolts)
- safety warnings
- storage requirements

RIGOR TASK #4: GAMING

Produce a set of instructions so that a group of children aged between 7 and 10 years old can play a game within one hour using either a deck of 52 playing cards, tennis balls or plastic drinking straws.

The game will be scored according to the completeness of the instructions. Score 2 rigs for each of the following points:

- the game requirements are specified, e.g., 3 tennis balls
- the number that can play the game
- how the game starts, e.g., the youngest shuffles the pack of cards
- how each person gets a turn
- how each person can score
- how the game finishes
- how to determine the winners and losers

RIGOR TASK #5: A TO B

Find the answer to the following puzzle:

I drive from A to B at an average speed of 40 miles per hour. WITHOUT STOP-PING OR CHANGING MY ROUTE IN ANY WAY, I return to B. At what speed would I have to drive the return trip in order to AVERAGE a speed of 80 miles per hour for the total journey?

You will be awarded 10 rigs for the right answer. The presenter's decision is final.

PRAGMA

The tasks in PRAGMA are concerned with realistic matters, such as the coordination of effort and the management of time. It is important that you understand these objectives and seek to achieve them. You need to consider the feasibility of each task.

Will your plan of action work? Then do it!

PRAGMA TASK #1: GRAVITY

According to theory, the Earth's gravity will have the same pull on 1 kilo of feathers as it will on 1 kilo of lead. Outline an experiment to prove this theory.

This task will be scored as follows:

Explain stages in detail: 10 pragms

Explain later stages: 5 pragms

Explain stages but does not totally convince: 3 pragms

Does not convince: 0 pragms

PRAGMA TASK #2: GETTING BETTER

Refer back to your analysis of group strengths and weaknesses developed by your team on the 'Group Reflection' task in MIRA. Produce an action plan for using your strengths and avoiding your weaknesses in future tasks.

If you have not yet visited MIRA, you will have to return to PRAGMA later to complete this task.

Method of scoring: Your action plan will need to be seen as practical and effective.

A practical action plan that is effectively linked to previous task: 10 pragms

An action plan that could be practical and is linked to previous task: 5 pragms

An action plan which is not practical and not linked to previous task: 0 pragms

PRAGMA TASK #3: PROJECT MANAGER

This project involves the completion of activities A to I.

You have been given the following information on how the tasks should be managed:

- you can start work immediately on activities B, C, D, F and G
- activity A must follow D and I
- activity E must follow G and H
- activity H must follow A and C
- activity I must follow B and F.

Produce a diagram to represent how the activities should be completed.

Method of scoring:

All relations correctly shown:10 pragms

Most relations correctly shown: 5 pragms

Most relationships not shown or incorrect: 0 pragms

PRAGMA TASK #4: RETROSPECT

You should plan a repeat of any previous task that you completed in TEMPORA. Show a brief plan to the presenter to indicate how you will improve on your previous result.

Method of scoring: The plan should be accepted as feasible and include ideas for improvement.

5 or more ideas for improvement: 10 pragms

3 or 4 ideas for improvement: 5 pragms

0 pragms otherwise

PRAGMA TASK #5: A DAY OUT

You are required to plan a day out for children at a local orphanage.

You have 15 minutes to produce a coherent logical plan to present to local businesses in order to get funding for the event. Produce a written outline of the plan and be prepared to give a verbal presentation if required.

Method of scoring: 2 pragms are awarded for each stage (part) of the plan successfully completed.

2 pragms – clear objectives

2 pragms – key activities

2 pragms – target dates

2 pragms – resources needed

2 pragms – criteria for success

Further reading

Books

Bloom, B.S. 1984. *Taxonomy of Educational Objectives*. New York: Allyn & Bacon.

Davis, B.G. 1993. *Tools for Teaching*. San Francisco: Jossey-Bass.

Gudykunst, W.B. and Ting-Toomey, S. 1988. *Culture and Interpersonal Communication*. Beverley Hills, CA: Sage.

Gudykunst, W.B. and Young, K.Y. 1984. *Communicating with Strangers; An Approach to Intercultural Communication*. New York: McGraw-Hill.

Hall, E.T. 1976. *Beyond Culture*. New York: Doubleday.

Harris, P.R. and Moran, R.T. 2004. *Managing Cultural Differences*. Oxford: Elsevier Butterworth-Heinemann.

Hofstede, G. 1980. *Culture's Consequences: International Differences in Work-Related Values*. Beverley Hills, CA: Sage.

—— 1991. *Cultures and Organizations: Software of the Mind*. New York: McGraw-Hill.

—— 2001. *Culture's Consequences: Comparing Values, Behaviors, Institutions, and Organizations across Nations*. Thousand Oaks, CA: Sage.

Lewin, K. 1948. *Resolving Social Conflicts: Selected Papers on Group Dynamics*, ed., K/ Lewin and W. Gertrude. New York: Harper & Row.

Salili, F., Chiu, C.-y. and Hong, Y.-y. 2001. *Student Motivation: the Culture and Context of Learning*; http://www.wkap.com [12 May 2012].

Senge, P. 1990. *The Fifth Discipline: The Art and Practice of the Learning Organization*. New York: McGraw-Hill.

—— 1994. *The Fifth Discipline Fieldbook: Strategies and Tools for Building a Learning Organization*. New York: McGraw-Hill.

Triandis, H.C. 1994. *Culture and Social Behavior*. New York: McGraw-Hill.

Trompenaars, F. and Hampden-Turner, C. 1998. *Riding the Waves of Culture: Understanding Diversity in Global Business*. New York: McGraw-Hill.

Journals

Academy of Management Learning and Education
International Journal of Lifelong Education
Journal of Multilingual and Multicultural Development
McGill Reporter
Organizational Dynamics
TQM Magazine

References

Badre, A.N. 2000. *The Effects of Cross Cultural Interface Design Orientation on World Wide Web User Performance*; ftp://ftp.cc.gatech.edu/pub/gvu/tr/2001/01-03.pdf [accessed 9 November 2010].

Barber, W. and Badre, A.N. 1998. 'Culturability: The merging of culture and usability', *The 4th Conference on Human Factors and the Web* (Basking Ridge, NJ: AT&T Labs)); http://research.microsoft.com/en-us/um/people/marycz/hfweb98/barber/ [accessed 9 November 2010].

Beckman, M. 1990. 'Collaborative learning: Preparation for the workplace and democracy'. *College Teaching*, 38 (4), pp. 128–33.

Bentley, J.P.H., Tinney, M.V. and and Chia, B.H. 2005. 'Intercultural Internet-based learning: Know your audience and what it values'. *Educational Technology Research & Development*, 53 (2), pp. 117–27.

Biggs, J.B. 1996. 'Western misperceptions of the Confucian-heritage learning culture'. In D.A. Watkins and J.B. Biggs, (eds), *The Chinese Learner: Cultural, Psychological and Contextual Influences*. Hong Kong: Comparative Education Research Centre, pp. 45–67.

Catterick, D. 2007. 'Do the philosophical foundations of online learning disadvantage non-Western students?' In A. Edmundson (ed.), *Globalized E-Learning: Cultural Challenges*. Hershey, PA: Idea Group Inc., pp. 116–29.

Chan, S. 1999. 'The Chinese learner – a question of style'. *Education + Training*, 41 (6/7), pp. 294–305.

Chen, S.J. and Ford, N. 1998. 'Modeling user navigation behaviors in a hypermedia-based learning system: An individual differences approach', *International Journal of Knowledge Organization*, 25 (3), pp. 67–78.

Chickering, A.W. and Gamson, Z. F. (eds) 1991. *Applying the Seven Principles for Good Practice in Undergraduate Education*. San Francisco: Jossey-Bass.

Confucius 1992. *Analects (Lun yu)*, translated by D.C. Lau. Seoul: Eun Kwang.

Cooper, M. 1999.'Postmodern pedagogy in electronic conversations'. In G.E. Hawisher and C.L. Selfe (eds), *Passions, Pedagogies and 21st Century Technologies*. Logan, UT: Utah State University Press, pp. 140–60.

Curtin, J.S. 2004. 'Suicide also rises in land of rising sun', *Asia Times*, 28 July; http://www.atimes.com/atimes/Japan/FG28Dh01.html.

Cyr, D. and Trevor-Smith, H. 2004. 'Localization of web design: An empirical comparison of German, Japanese, and United States website characteristics', *Journal of the American Society for Information Science and Technology*, 55 (13), pp. 1199–208.

Dahlgaard-Park, S.M. 2006. 'Learning from East to West and West to East', *TQM Magazine*, 18 (3), pp. 216–37.

Davis, B.G 1993. *Tools for Teaching*. San Francisco: Jossey-Bass.

Del Galdo, E. and Neilson, J. 1996. *International User Interfaces*. New York: Wiley.

Dewey, J. 2003. *Experience and Nature*. Kessinger Publishing, p. 246

Dong, Y. and Lee, K. 2008. 'A cross-cultural comparative study of users' perceptions of a webpage: With a focus on the cognitive styles of Chinese, Koreans and Americans'. *International Journal of Design*, 2 (2), pp. 19–30.

Faigley, L. 1999. 'Beyond imagination: The internet and global digital literacy'. In G.E. Hawisher, and C.L. Selfe, (eds), *Passions, Pedagogies and 21st Century Technologies*. Logan, UT: Utah State University Press, pp. 129–39.

Fox News 2010. 'Confucius in the classroom controversy?', 2 June; http://video.foxnews.com/v/4223162/confucius-in-the-classroom-controversy?playlist_id=86912.

Gay, G. 2000. *Culturally Responsive Teaching: Theory, Research and Practice* (New York: Teacher's College Press).

Gupta, A. 2007. *Early Childhood Education, Postcolonial Theory and Teaching Practices in India: Balancing Vygotsky and the Veda*. Basingstoke: Palgrave Macmillan.

Ho, I.T. 2001. 'Are Chinese teachers authoritarian?' In D.A. Watkins and J.B. Biggs (eds), *Teaching the Chinese Learner: Psychological and Pedagogical Perspectives*. Hong Kong: Comparative Education Research Centre, pp. 99–114.

Hofstede, G. 1986. 'Cultural differences in teaching and learning'. *International Journal of Intercultural Relations*, 10, pp. 301–20.

—— 2001. *Culture's Consequences: Comparing Values, Behaviors, Institutions, and Organizations across Nations*. Thousand Oaks, CA: Sage.

Hofstede, G. and Hofstede, J. 2005. *Cultures and Organizations: Software of the Mind*, 2nd edn. New York: McGraw-Hill.

Karababa, G. 2006. 'Culturally appropriate pedagogy: The case of group learning in a Confucian heritage culture (CHC)'. *Intercultural Education*, 17 (1), pp. 1–9.

Kennedy, P. 2002. 'Learning cultures and learning styles: Myth-understandings about adult (Hong Kong) Chinese learners'. *International Journal of Lifelong Education*, 21 (5), pp. 430–45.

Kolb, D.A. 1984. *Experiential Learning: Experience as the Source of Learning and Development*. Englewood Cliffs, NJ: Prentice-Hall.

—— 2007. *Kolb Learning Style Inventory Workbook*. Boston, MA: Hay Learning Transformations.

Littlewood, W. 1999. 'Defining and developing autonomy in East Asian contexts'. *Applied Linguistics*, 20 (1), pp. 71–94.

Marcus, A. and Gould, E.W. 2000. 'Cultural dimensions and global web user-interface design'. *Interactions*, 7 (4), pp. 33–46.

Marton, F., Dall'Alba, G. and Tse, L.K. 1996. 'Memorizing and understanding: The keys to the paradox?' In D.A Watkins and J.B. Biggs (eds), *The Chinese Learner: Cultural, Psychological and Contextual Influences*. Hong Kong: Comparative Education Research Centre, pp. 69–83.

Masuda, T. and Nisbett, R.E. 2001. 'Attending holistically versus analytically: Comparing the context sensitivity of Japanese and Americans'. *Journal of Personality and Social Psychology*, 81, pp. 922–34.

Mei, Y. 2010. 'Confucius classroom draws controversy for embedding communism ideology'. *Epoch Times*, n.d.; http://www.theepochtimes.com/n2/content/view/36300/.

Nisbett, R.E. and Norenzayan, A. 2002. 'Culture and cognition'. In D. Medin and H. Pashler (eds), *Stevens' Handbook of Experimental Psychology*, 3rd edn. New York: Wiley; http://www-personal.umich.edu/~nisbett/cultcog2.pdf [accessed 9 November 2010].

Nisbett, R.E., Peng, K., Choi, I. and Norenzayan, A. 2001. 'Culture and systems of thought: Holistic versus analytic cognition'. *Psychological Review*, 108 (2), pp. 291–310.

Ostler, N. 2008. 'English's bleak future', *Forbes*, 21 February; http://www.forbes.com/2008/02/21/future-english-chinese-tech-cx_no_language_sp08_0221lingua.html.

Palloff, R.M. and Pratt, K. 1999. *Building Learning Communities in Cyberspace*. San Francisco: Jossey-Bass.

Park, M.Y. 2002. 'Debate over bilingual education rages', Fox News, 6 March; http://www.foxnews.com/story/0,2933,47223,00.html.

Peterson, B. 2004. *Cultural Intelligence: A Guide to Working with People from Other Cultures*. Boston, MA: Intercultural Press.

Riding, R. and Rayner, S.G. 1998. *Cognitive Styles and Learning Strategies*. London: David Fulton.

Riding, R.J. and Sadler-Smith, E. 1997. 'Cognitive style: Some implications for training design', *International Journal of Training and Development*, 1 (3), pp. 199–208.

Ryan, R.M. 1991. 'The nature of the self in autonomy and relatedness'. In J. Strauss and G.R. Goethals (eds), *Multidisciplinary Perspectives on the Self*. New York: Springer-Verlag, pp. 208–38.

Salili, F. 2001. 'Teacher–student interaction: Attribution implications and effectiveness of teacher's evaluative feedback'. In D.A. Watkins and J.B. Biggs (eds), *Teaching the Chinese Learner: Psychological and Pedagogical Perspectives*. Hong Kong: Comparative Education Research Centre, pp. 77–98.

Salili, F. and Hau, K.T. 1994. 'The effects of teachers' evaluative feedback on Chinese students perceptions of ability: A cultural and situational analysis', *Educational Studies*, 20 (2), pp. 223–36.

Saphiere, H.D., Kappler Mikk, B. and Devries, B.I. 2005. *Communication Highwire: Leveraging the Power of Diverse Communication Styles*. Yarmouth, ME: Intercultural Press.

Smith, D.G. 2008. '"The farthest west is but the farthest east": The long way of Oriental/Occidental engagement'. In C. Eppert and H. Wang (eds), *Cross-Cultural Studies in Curriculum: Eastern Thought, Educational Insights*. Mahweh, NJ: Lawrence Erlbaum Associates, pp. 1–34.

Song, B. 1995. 'What does reading mean for East Asian students?', *College ESL*, 5 (2), pp. 35–48.

Storti, C. 1999. *Figuring Foreigners Out: A Practical Guide*. Yarmouth, ME: Intercultural Press.

Sun, H. 2001. 'Building a culturally-competent corporate website: An explanatory study of cultural markers in multilingual web design'. In M.J. Northrop and S. Tilley (eds), *Proceedings of the Nineteenth Annual ACM SIGDOC Conference on Computer Documentation* (New York: ACM Press), pp. 95–102.

Ting-Toomey, S. 1999. *Communicating across Cultures*. New York: Guilford Press.

Ting-Toomey, S. and Chung, L. 2005. *Understanding Intercultural Communication*. Los Angeles: Roxbury.

Vygotsky, L.S. 1978. *Mind in Society: The Development of Higher Psychological Processes*. Cambridge, MA: Harvard University Press.

Watkins, D.A. and Biggs, J.B. 2001. 'The paradox of the Chinese learner and beyond'. In D.A. Watkins and J.B. Biggs (eds), *Teaching the Chinese Learner: Psychological and Pedagogical Perspectives*. Hong Kong: Comparative Education Research Centre, pp. 69–83.

Watts, J. 2005. 'Suicide blights China's young adults: Survey reveals main cause of death of people under 35', *Guardian*, 26 July; http://www.guardian.co.uk/world/2005/jul/26/china.jonathanwatts.

Wu, A. 1999. *The Japanese Education System: A Case Study Summary and Analysis*. A report from the National Institute on Student Achievement, Curriculum, and Assessment, US Department of Education; http://www2.ed.gov/pubs/ResearchToday/98-3038.html.

Zhengdong, G. 2009. '"Asian learners" re-examined: An empirical study of language learning attitudes, strategies and motivation among Mainland Chinese and Hong Kong students'. *Journal of Multilingual and Multicultural Development*, 30 (1), pp. 41–58.

PART THREE

The Third Dimension: Going Global

CHAPTER 7

Command and Control: International Negotiations and Alliances

Elizabeth Christopher; Philip R. Harris; Meena Chavan

Objectives of the chapter

- To recognise why firms seek to form international alliances;
- To identify and rank staffing priorities for these alliances;
- To distinguish between ethnocentric, polycentric/regio-centric and geocentric controls and monitors for international alliances;
- To view designs for country-specific policies and procedures;
- To consider some socio-political aspects of internationalisation;
- To list the major reasons why negotiations break down over mergers and acquisitions;
- To acknowledge major culture-based differences in negotiation styles.

Chapter contents

- Outline of chapter
- Philip R. Harris: China's African partnership
- Discussion and questions
- Case study: Benefits of foreign investment: Amazon in Scotland
- Discussion
- Meena Chavan: Global alliances among multinational corporations
- Discussion
- Classroom exercises
- Conclusion
- Key points
- Experiential exercises
- References

- Recommended reading
- References

Outline of chapter

The first dimension of communication across cultures was argued to be that of 'different voices' in leadership, communication styles, verbal and non-verbal languages. Thus the first three chapters of the book led upwards to the second dimension: that of the international management contexts in which these different voices are heard. This has now expanded into a third dimension of global negotiations, alliances and networks.

Chapter 7 begins with descriptions of various kinds of alliance. The first contribution is by Philip Harris. His account of the China–Africa alliance raises larger issues of why corporations and governments form alliances, who benefits most from them and in what ways. He draws attention also to some of the results of post-colonial independence for African countries, and this leads to contemplation of another aspect of cross-cultural communication, that of anti-colonial activism. Harris refers also to Chinese expatriate management as highly ethnocentric, thus opening the topic of staffing policies for international alliances; these are discussed in the commentary that follows.

After that there is an account of Amazon's recent investment in Scotland, including infrastructure and job creation: another example of the benefits of international alliances.

Meena Chavan writes about mergers and acquisitions as outcomes of corporate strategy. She offers AOL Time Warner as an example of vertical integration – by which production and distribution are controlled by a single company to increase its power in the marketplace; and Exxon–Mobil as a horizontal merger of firms at the same stage of production in the same industry. She cites Cemex as an example of growth through international acquisition; and HIH and FIA for acquisition mismanagement. Chavan argues further that failure from mergers and acquisitions occurs through lack of planning and accurate assessment of both companies in the proposed acquisition; from over-optimism; from failure to anticipate accurately the results of the alliance; and from neglect of differences in national cultures and business systems.

In the commentary that follows it is suggested that Chavan's arguments support the notion that negotiations in general run through five major stages: planning; building a relationship with the other parties; exchanging relevant information, bargaining; and reaching agreement or compromise. Neglect of any one of these steps is likely to lead to the failure of the entire project. Quaker Oats and Snapple Beverages, and Sprint and Nextel Communications are offered as examples.

After this discussion there are a number of examples of alliances over a wide range, from the wine industry to international arrangements for the detention of asylum seekers, to deep-sea exploration; and creating successful agent–bank alliances. The objective is to identify common characteristics of the communication tactics these respective allies employ in their very different settings.

The chapter ends as usual with a summary of key points and conclusion; some experiential exercises to reinforce the main arguments of the chapter; a list of internet resources and recommendations for further reading, and chapter references.

CHINA'S AFRICAN PARTNERSHIP   Philip R. Harris

Reprinted with permission of Philip R. Harris, Ph.D. from his book, Managing Cultural Differences, 8th ed., 2011, published by Routledge/Taylor and Francis Group (www.routledge.com).

China takes a long view of its relationship to the continent of Africa and its people. It began in 1414 when Emperor Ming sent Admiral Zing He to East Africa. Zing He took his vast fleet of 62 galleons for seven voyages there to engage in trade and establish diplomatic relations (Dowden, 2008: Ch. 17).

After 1431, the Chinese did not return until the 1960s when Chairman Mao Zedong supported African liberation movements and newly independent states. This time, the Chinese built roads, bridges, stadiums, water systems and even the Tanzum railway from Tanganyika to Zambia, using thousands of Chinese labourers (Bailey, 1975).

They also established farms and factories, provided materials and loans – all with a view of obtaining political support from Africa's fifty-four nations for China in the United Nations, World Trade Organisation and other international fora. They also send doctors, nurses and medical aid. It is no wonder that, in 2000, governments in both China and Africa formed the China–Africa Conference (POCAC).

By the China–Africa Summit in 2003, China was writing off billions in African debts. Their managers in Africa live at the level of their workers, buying local products and selling their own wares made in China. Even traditional African fabrics are now made in Guangdong for export to Africa and elsewhere.

The Centre for Chinese Studies at Stellenbosch, South Africa monitors considerable Chinese activities on the continent. China treats Africa as an equal, so their leaders appreciate that China presents itself as neutral, non-imperialist, value-free outsider wanting a friendly trade relationship.

Chinese there emphasise the best in Africa, avoiding references to its failures. Further the Chinese keep their promises, building infrastructure on time and often under budget. But the Chinese employ their own labour, providing little training or limited jobs for the locals. In their African projects, the Chinese do not show much regard for environmental damage, human rights, combating poverty, nor for the Charter of the African Union. The African governments have yet to successfully manage their business relationships with China, which views them as business opportunities.

But it is the new professional middle class in Pan Africa that are taking control of the continent's development and transformation.

Commentary

Harris's account of this China–Africa alliance includes a number of issues that can be generalised to the whole topic of communicating across cultures. Perhaps the most important questions are why entities seek to form alliances and who are likely to be the biggest beneficiaries.

As Harris suggests, China's expansion into Africa has been the subject of many reports. One commentator, Princeton N. Lyman, Director of Africa Policy Studies, Council on Foreign Relations, suggests (2005) the current level and intent of China's involvement is different from past alliances in Africa. He noted that in earlier days China's presence was marked by lavish infrastructure projects, often with little connection to economic development; and during the following several decades provided technical expertise, doctors, scholarships and various forms of aid. Lyman reported that in 2005 more than 900 Chinese doctors were working in African countries.

What has changed in recent years is China's emergence as a significant world player on the economic scene and its own need for oil and other natural resources, with the money to pay for them. Ian Taylor (who lectures in international relations at the University of St Andrews) wrote in 2007 of environmental damage by resource-hungry Chinese companies, facilitated – according to Taylor – by corrupt government agencies. He offered evidence of Chinese companies flouting conservation laws and collaborating with 'criminals' in the exploitation of Africa's natural assets.

Cheryl Igiri and Princeton N. Lyman (2004: 15–17) point to the Sudan as a good example of how China comes to Africa with a 'complete package': money, technical expertise and influence in such bodies as the UN Security Council to protect the host country from international sanctions. Igiri and Lyman argue that China, with its partner Malaysia, replaced Western companies and enabled Sudan to become a net exporter of crude. Meanwhile, China has successfully prevented the UN Security Council from serious sanctions or similar measures in face of the alleged genocide and crimes against humanity perpetrated in the Darfur region.

On the other hand, in many ways the economic growth in Asia, and the subsequent growth in demand, is good for Africa (Lyman, 2005). Mineral prices have been high for some years (Kaswende, 2005), reversing a decades-long decline for many of Africa's major exports; and in 2005 Nigeria negotiated a favourable debt relief programme from the Paris Club because of its oil windfalls (Africa Focus, 2005). China is also investing in areas of the African economy that Western aid agencies and private investors have long neglected: physical infrastructure, industry and agriculture.

Joseph E. Stiglitz (2002) is one of a number of commentators to suggest that China's alliances in Africa have stimulated international discussion and overview of the International Monetary Fund (IMF) loan conditions in general. Stiglitz is not sure that such enquires will be successful in promoting change, but notes that at least they are being made. It is interesting to record in this connection that Oxfam International, on 10 January 2011 (http://www.oxfam.org/en/getinvolved/jobs/senior-policy-adviser-international-financial-institutions-110110), advertised the vacant position of Senior Policy Adviser, International Financial Institutions, in the following terms:

> ... *the impact you make in this high-profile role could last a lifetime. You will develop, lead and implement advocacy strategies which influence the policies and strategies of the IMF and World Bank, particularly around issues to do with the global economic crisis and development finance. The lobbying you undertake, relationships you forge and intelligence you gather will all be crucial in making certain these policies constitute a positive, pro-poor response.*

To return to China's role in Africa, Lyman (2005) for one admits it is important not to identify China as the sole exploiter of Africa, or of being unique in its disregard for Africa's environment. The history of Western involvement in the continent is not a proud one. Chinese exploitation of Africa's resources pales into insignificance when compared to Western colonist activities both past and present. In his contribution to this chapter Professor Harris writes of an emerging professional middle class in Pan-Africa; but economic prosperity of this kind in the region may not have been possible without another aspect of cross-cultural communication, namely anti-colonial activism, for example, by George Padmore (Baptiste and Lewis, 2009).

Padmore was a Trinidadian Pan-Africanist (1902–59). Though he is almost forgotten now, he stands as a towering figure of the twentieth-century 'black Atlantic'. George Padmore was the pseudonym of Malcolm Nurse, born in 1902 in Trinidad, then a British crown colony. He was a journalist but left the Caribbean to study law in the United States in 1924. He became a student radical and joined the Communist Party of the USA, becoming George Padmore in the process.

He was appointed head of the Communist International's 'Negro Bureau' and from 1929 to 1933 agitated for black liberation and colonial revolution, undertaking daring underground work in colonial Africa. In 1935 he moved to London, the 'dark heart' of the British Empire, and for the next twenty years devoted all his energies to the struggle to liberate Africa and the Caribbean from colonial rule. His greatest triumph undoubtedly came when one of his African disciples, Kwame Nkrumah, led the Gold Coast to independence as Ghana in 1957. Padmore ended his life working as an adviser to Nkrumah in Ghana.

There has been much criticism of the failings of Nkrumah's Pan-Africanism (Whiteman, 2010), but it animated the Organisation of African Unity (OAU) and was a driving force for its successor, the African Union, and the new momentum to continental union. Padmore's extraordinary life as an activist of anti-colonial movements in Africa and the Caribbean remains in many ways inspiring for anti-imperialists today.

Another comment by Harris concerns Chinese foreign investment in infrastructure in Africa. He states that Chinese expatriate management is highly ethnocentric and provides little training and limited jobs for the locals. Thus he draws attention to staffing policies as an integral part of strategy for international alliances.

Staffing deals specifically with the acquisition, training and allocation of the organisation's employees, to keep it supplied with the right people in the right positions at the right time. Basically international managers take one of three approaches to staffing for overseas alliances, known respectively in the literature as ethnocentric, polycentric/regiocentric or geocentric, i.e., worldwide (Deresky and Christopher, 2011: Ch. 9). Underlying a policy of ethnocentrism is the belief that parent-country nationals are better qualified and more trustworthy than host-country nationals. Polycentrism and regiocentrism result from a belief that local people know the local environment better than outsiders; and that staffing policies should be varied to suit particular geographic areas. Geocentrism is the result of believing the best people should be employed regardless of their nationality.

Ames Gross (2001) is one writer on the topic of international staffing, who reports on the situation in South Korea, implicitly offering lessons for all international staffing managers. Gross describes South Korea's workforce as well trained and well educated, and that recent layoffs and increased unemployment have made hiring easier for foreign firms. In addition he argues that creating a 'local presence' is often essential to ensure a comfortable working relationship that can withstand occasional bouts of anti-foreigner sentiment. Many foreign firms do this successfully by including some Koreans in management, designing country-specific policies and procedures, and working to improve the company's long-term image.

Discussion and questions

Why do firms seek to form international alliances? According to the literature (e.g., Deresky and Christopher, 2011: Ch. 6), the main reasons are:

- to gain better access to attractive country markets;
- to take advantage of local market knowledge and working relationships with key government officials in the host country;
- to achieve economies of scale in production and/or marketing;
- to share technical knowledge, distribution facilities and dealer networks, to put together technical and financial resources.

The above report by Harris and the commentary that follows suggest two more reasons:

- Shortage of needed resources at home;
- To strengthen relationships in the area where alliances are sought.

Can you think of others?

Who are likely to be the biggest beneficiaries, the foreign investors or the host country? What do you see as the net profit and loss to the nations of Pan Africa as a result of Chinese investment? What suggestions can you make for international staffing policies other than those above?

Case study: Benefits of foreign investment: Amazon in Scotland

There is a saying that the arrival of one swallow doesn't make a summer, and maybe the same has to be said about one Amazon. But the fact that the massive online sales company announced plans in January 2011 to set up a major Scottish base in Edinburgh offered hope to people who found themselves out of work or their careers halted in recent poor economic times.

Established in 1998, Amazon offers a wide variety of products over the internet, including books, movies, music, PC and video games, software and electronics. Now this online retail giant will to create 950 new jobs in Scotland, the majority (750) to be at a newly built plant distribution centre in Dunfermline, Fife, replacing a smaller plant at Glenrothes, also in Fife. All permanent staff will transfer to the new site, and another 200 jobs will be added at the firm's warehouse in Gourock, Inverclyde, with possibly up to a 1,500 temporary jobs at times of peak demand. The new one million sq ft distribution centre in Dunfermline – about the size of 14 football pitches – will be Amazon's biggest in the UK.

Allan Lyall, vice president of European operations at Amazon, said:

Our decision to base this major expansion in Scotland, against stiff international competition, is due not only to the excellent local workforce but to the impressive professionalism of Scottish Development International.

The investment was welcomed by local politicians and by Alex Salmond, the Scottish First Minister, as a much-needed boost to the Scottish economy, which had been hit by a series of factory closures, including in call centres and distribution centres. Michael Moore, Secretary of State for Scotland, said it was:

a great boost for these areas and for the Scottish economy as a whole. Amazon is the latest company to realise that, whether you are a foreign or domestic company, Scotland is a good place to invest. The UK government is committed to growing the economy to take advantage of future investment opportunities.

Amazon, which made worldwide profits of $384 million (£242 million) in 2010, up by 71 per cent on the previous year, was given a regional assistance grant of £2 million and a training grant of £500,000 by Scottish Enterprise, supported by its inward investment arm, Scottish Development International.

There is also a wider picture. The arrival of Amazon in the Scottish capital will send out a message that this is a city in which big corporations want to work. The presence of such big bodies affects other investors, who see the attraction of a well-educated and resourceful workforce. Amazon will rub shoulders with fellow tenants Microsoft, while H&M, NHS Lothian and Creative Scotland have all taken space.

Sources

BBC News 2011. 'Amazon to create 950 jobs at Scottish centres', 13 January; http://www.bbc.co.uk.

Carrell, S. 2011. 'Amazon boosts Scottish economy with new distribution centre', *Guardian*, 13 January; http://www.guardian.co.uk/.

Scotsman 2011. 'Amazon's arrival – "The omens do seem to be getting better"', 13 January; http://news.scotsman.com.

Discussion

The above account seems to suggest a win/win outcome for Amazon's alliance with Scottish Enterprise and Scottish Development International to invest in jobs and infrastructure in Edinburgh. A useful exercise for students would be to go online and find other examples of such apparently mutually profitable alliances. Meanwhile Meena Chavan offers her own examples of the good, the bad and the ugly alliance.

GLOBAL ALLIANCES AMONG MULTINATIONAL CORPORATIONS | Meena Chavan

Mergers and acquisitions are outcomes of corporate strategy, corporate finance and management dealings. They involve the buying, selling and combining of different companies (Hill, 2009), and are two of the most effective strategies to expand a business.

For example, an alliance such as a merger can help a growing company to develop rapidly in its industry because it represents a combination of two companies into one larger company for stronger competitive advantage. Normally such mergers are voluntary and the new company combines the original names.

An acquisition (also termed a takeover) consists of the purchase of one company by another. Thus Firm A buys Firm B and there is no Firm B any more. Acquisitions may be friendly or hostile. If friendly, the companies negotiate cooperatively; if hostile, the takeover target is unwilling to be bought or the target's board has no prior knowledge of the offer. An example of a fairly recent friendly takeover was when Microsoft bought Fast Search and Transfer in 2008 (http://www.microsoft.com/enterprisesearch/en/us/fast-customer.aspx). The CEO of the acquired company (FAST) revealed that he had been working with Microsoft for more than six months to get the deal, which was announced in January 2008.

Although mergers and acquisitions are often thought of as synonymous, the terms mean slightly different things. When one company takes over another and clearly establishes itself as the new owner, the purchase is called an acquisition (SG Legal Solutions, 2009). From a legal point of view, the target company ceases to exist, the buyer 'swallows' the business and the buyer's stock continues to be traded. A merger occurs when two firms, often of about the same size, agree to go forward as a single new company rather than remain separately owned and operated. Both companies' stocks are surrendered and new company stock is issued in its place. For example, both Daimler-Benz and Chrysler ceased to exist when the two firms merged, and a new company, DaimlerChrysler, was created (Hill, 2009).

A purchase deal will also be called a merger when both CEOs agree that joining together is in the best interest of both of their companies. But when the deal is unfriendly – when the target company does not wish to be purchased – it is always regarded as an acquisition (Harwood, 2006). In effect, whether a purchase is considered a merger or an acquisition really depends on whether the purchase is friendly or hostile, and how it is announced. In other words, the real difference lies in how the purchase is communicated to and received by the target company's board of directors, employees and shareholders. It should be noted that many such communications take place in a so-called 'confidentiality bubble' whereby information flows are restricted owing to confidentiality agreements.

Mergers and acquisitions have become an attractive strategy for companies' international development and expansion, partly owing to pressures from key stakeholders to increase shareholder value. With competition from globalisation of markets, companies seek to combine core competencies and expertise through external alliances to become more competitive. For example, Boeing and McDonnell Douglas are both commercial jet manufacturers with considerable overlap in management, information technology, marketing and research and development. Their merger was to provide operating synergies by eliminating duplicate functions, costs and excess capacity (Jovanovic and Rousseau, 2002).

Obtaining a global presence is also acknowledged as a motive for mergers or acquisitions (Schraeder and Self, 2003). Another is to improve a target management that has systematically underperformed in a particular industry. Historically poor performance could be a matter of bad luck, but also from the firm's managers making poor investment and operating decisions, or deliberately pursuing goals that increase their personal power but at the cost of shareholders. Acquisition would enable head management to work more efficiently under a new management style.

Corporations invest billions of dollars annually in pursuit of such strategies but the success rate is relatively low. Acquisitions are often poorly understood and managed, and they often result in divestiture or poor performance. They bring companies together that have very distinct products, services, marketing, history, leadership and culture; and despite the popularity of the strategy, research indicates that three out of four alliances fail to achieve their financial and strategic objectives (Marks, 2005).

Many factors account for the failure of mergers and acquisitions, including buying the wrong company, paying the wrong price and making the deal at the wrong time (Marks and Mirvis, 2001). In addition, the new management of the acquired firm is often too optimistic about the value that can be created from the acquisition (Hill, 2009). This is known as the 'hubris hypothesis' – from the Greek word *hubris*, meaning overbearing pride or presumption, excessive pride or self-confidence, and doomed to invoke the wrath of the gods. For example,

Daimler's acquisition of Chrysler involved paying a premium of 40 per cent over the market value of Chrysler before the takeover bid because Daimler thought it could use Chrysler to help it grow market share in the United States.

Another reason for failure can be attributed to inadequate screening before executing a merger or acquisition. Many firms undertake the strategy without analysing the potential benefits and costs. Also they may move in undue haste for fear that their competitors may pre-empt them. As a result, after the merger or acquisition, they may run into numerous problems. These will be exacerbated in cross-border alliances because the acquiring firm may not fully understand the target firm's national culture and business systems. In such circumstances, it is recommended that firms thoroughly investigate the respective national culture, economic, legal and political systems, and include this in their pre-planning and integration stages. Additionally, the appointment of local managers may help firms to reduce the risk of cross-border clashes and reduce the risks of failure.

There is need to plan well in advance and have a systematic set of procedures and policies because these will affect outcomes. The first priority is to develop a baseline assessment of both companies and a projected profile of the acquired/ merged company. Aspects of the target company that should be analysed include its business plan, assets required, technological, financials, projects and processes. In addition due diligence – which involves an analysis of the strengths, weaknesses, opportunities and threats (SWOT) of both companies – is part of a successful international strategy.

Yet another reason for failure is a clash between the cultures of the involved firms. Organisational culture is one factor. According to Cartwright and Cooper (1993), financial benefits are often unrealised because of incompatible cultures. Organisational culture can be defined as something 'unique to a particular organisation, composed of an objective and subjective dimension, and concerned with tradition and the nature of shared beliefs and expectations about organisational life' (Schrader and Self, 2003: 512, citing Bruono et al., 1985). Since there is often more than one culture in a single organisation, managing an acquisition can be quite challenging, especially in relation to the amalgamation of two cultures.

Many ventures fail because problems may arise when firms try to integrate the operations of the involved firms. Differences in management philosophy and company culture can slow the process and exacerbate the problems. National or organisational cultural differences can be source of hostility and distrust between organisational members and become major obstacles to success (Stahl and Voigt, 2004). The 'cultural distance' hypothesis suggests that difficulties, costs and risks associated with cross-cultural contact increase with growing cultural differences between two individuals, groups or organisations. The cultures of merging firms have to be compatible in order to integrate successfully (ibid.).

Culture clash is intensified when firms from different countries combine. Differences in business orientations include distinctions in social values and norms, a major cause of high failure rate (Marks, 1990). Moreover, Cartwright and Cooper (1993) posit that cultural fit is just as important as structural fit. Poor cultural fit is a major pitfall for many acquisitions despite the parties being strategically compatible.

For example, the failed merger between Monsanto and American Home Products has been attributed to difficulties in trying to integrate the two disparate cultures (Schraeder and Self, 2003). The CEOs of the respective companies demonstrated polar differences in their management styles and disagreed on a variety of issues, including employee layoffs. It has been suggested that the cultural differences between the two firms should have been recognised prior to the merger, and might have led to them considering other strategic partners with more compatible cultures.

Thus, it is important to maintain an analysis of cultural compatibility when thinking of merging two organisations as well as identifying, evaluating, assessing and selecting potential partners. Additionally, companies engaging in a international mergers and acquisitions strategy can minimise the risk of cultural clash by employing local managers, which will provide knowledge of the local culture, legal, market and economic systems in that country.

After executing a cross-border merger or acquisition, it is recommended that firms develop a flexible and comprehensive integration plan. The characteristics of the integration phase have been linked to the success/failure of an acquisition, as the degree of integration influences the way employee expectations are formed (Nikandrou and Papalexandris, 2007).

Managers must move rapidly after a merger or acquisition to implement and execute an integration plan. Employees may try to slow or stop it, particularly when loss of management or union power is involved and there are likely to be employment layoffs. Managers should have a plan for dealing with such issues before they arise. A successful integration plan should create mutual understanding, increase the speed of change and lower both human and capital costs. It enables a realistic timeline for change based on the current organisational situation, which is essential in gaining acceptance (Anderson, 2007). Leaders and managers need to understand the human dynamics of change, what triggers and motivates people to change and what creates the foundation for resistance.

AOL Time Warner: Vertical integration

AOL's purchase of Time Warner for $165 billion in 2001 was the largest merger in history at the time (Adams, 2002). It immediately became the largest media, entertainment and service conglomerate in the world but since 2002 it has been widely deemed unsuccessful (Shleifer and Vishny, 2003). Analysts agree that the primary causes were the excessive premium AOL paid to buy Time Warner; and the crash of inflated internet company valuations (Faulhaber, 2002).

The merger was seen as a combination of the strengths of the new media through AOL's strong internet base, and the old media through Time Warner, with its presence in television, newsprint and cinema. Individually both were performing strongly prior to the takeover and the potential to vertically integrate was the logical next step. AOL sought to merge with a firm that would provide it with real content, and Time Warner wanted new opportunities through a developed market base. Despite this the assumed synergies between the two firms failed to materialise. The company's market capitalisation decreased by $223 billion in the first two years following the merger, and Time Warner shareholders engaged in a legal battle against management because of the 70 per cent fall in the value of their shares.

Directly following the merger, AOL managers largely dominated because of the reputation of their past successes. Consequently they were unwilling to recognise emerging problems, stressing instead an upbeat future. Overall AOL Time Warner prepared well for the merger by quickly integrating new staff teams, and trying to establish combined cultural standards. Within the first year the signs of the merger were positive, with key members knowing their role and what was expected of them, and employee motivation remaining high. However, by 2004 AOL's performance had declined so badly that the new CEO, Richard Parson, considered spinning off AOL as an independent business to protect Time Warner.

At the time of the merger neither AOL nor Time Warner were seen as functioning poorly, and together there was minimal cultural resistance or conflict. This case can be seen as a strong example of one firm paying too much for an acquired unit and of the power of external economic forces to make or break. In particular the stock market made a price correction for internet-based stocks, forcing the newly merged firm to take a large step backwards almost concurrently with the merger. This led an otherwise potentially strong merger to ultimately fail.

Exxon–Mobil: An archetype for horizontal mergers

Repeated oil price shocks within the industry over the last three decades have caused oil firms to engage in a wide variety of responses (Weston, 2008). Substantial merger activity took place between 1980 and 1985, and major mergers took place between 1998 and 2001. Most notably the BP–Amoco merger, announced in 1998, projected $2 billion in savings, thus stimulating other companies to seek improvements in their operations. Similarly the Exxon–Mobil combination was announced in late 1998, along with nine other high-profile mergers and acquisitions.

This activity can be viewed as a response to price instability. The overriding objective for the mergers beginning in 1998 was to increase efficiencies to lower breakeven levels. The major motivations behind the Exxon–Mobil merger, completed in November 1999, were both cost- and market-based. By combining complementary assets, Exxon–Mobil sought a stronger presence in the regions of the world with a high potential for future oil and gas discoveries. Complementary exploration and production operations existed in West Africa, the Caspian region, Kazakhstan, South America, Russia and Eastern Canada. Because of the increased size of the company it would also be in a stronger position to invest in programmes involving large outlays and high prospective risks and returns.

At the time of the merger operating synergies of $2.8 billion were predicted. Two-thirds of the benefits would come from eliminating duplicate facilities and excess capacity. Additional synergy benefits would come from combined general and administrative costs, and by applying each company's best business practices throughout the world. By 2000 Exxon–Mobil reported that synergies had reached $4.6 billion.

Despite mergers often being associated with failures, particularly when the purchase price of the firm greatly exceeds its market value, such as AOL Time Warner, the Exxon–Mobil merger should be deemed a success. Since the merger the enlarged company has tripled its overall market value and, more importantly, the substantial premium that was paid to Mobil to enter the merger ($15.5 billion) has been recovered and profited upon. Weston (2008) attributes this success to increase in demand for oil across the industry, and the behaviour of the value drivers in the financial analysis of the merger.

Cemex: Growth through international acquisition

In just over a decade Cemex, Mexico's largest cement manufacturer, has transformed itself into the third largest cement company in the world. In 2008 it was operating within four continents with 66 cement plants (Sirkin et al., 2008). It has achieved this success primarily through smart investment and strategies.

Cemex's international expansion focused on four main factors. Firstly, the company wished to reduce its reliance on the domestic market, Mexico. Secondly, Cemex understood that the opportunity and need for cement in developing countries was growing. Thirdly, Cemex, with its Mexican background, understood the developing nation market better than many of its Western-based competitors. Fourthly, Cemex had confidence that it could transfer its core competencies and create competitive advantages in other inefficient cement firms in foreign markets.

Cemex's initial strategy focused on similar developing nations. This led to the acquisition of cement makers in Venezuela, Colombia, Indonesia, the Philippines and Egypt, as well as Costa Rica and Spain. This policy was largely successful because Cemex sought the efficient transfer of its technological, management and marketing know-how to acquired units, thereby improving their performance. Cemex then adapted its strategy by investing in developed nations such as the USA, the UK and many other European nations. In 2008 only about 15 per cent of the company's sales were generated from Mexico. Cemex aimed to implement further acquisitions in China and India where the opportunities for growth were seen to be vast. This suggested that their strategy of entering foreign markets through acquisitions was paying dividends for investors overall, and that this strategy for growth was likely to continue into new markets.

However, since 2007 the sub-prime crisis in the USA and Europe, and the subsequent impact on global financial markets, have had a major impact on such activities worldwide (Wall Street Journal, 2008). In August 2010 Cemex SAB, the largest cement maker in the Americas, reported the largest market decline in seven months of Mexico City trading, after plunging sales of existing US homes signalled that the demand for cement might miss expectations (Levin, 2010).

HIH and FIA: Acquisition mismanagement

Within Australia the acquisition of FAI General Insurance Company by HIH Insurance in 1998 has become synonymous with HIH directors Rodney Adler and Ray Williams and their role in the former firm's subsequent collapse. The collapse of the HIH group resulted in a deficiency of up to $5.3 billion, making it Australia's largest corporate failure. The reasons for this collapse are attributed largely to poor decision-making and the influence of senior management.

The decision by HIH to purchase FAI without due diligence by senior management is one accusation. Firstly, the board meeting that convened to discuss the acquisition of FAI was not called until earlier on the very day of the meeting. Secondly, of the twelve directors of HIH, five failed to be present at the meeting and of the seven who were present, four participated by videoconferencing. It was at this board meeting that the decision to take over FAI was approved.

Furthermore, Rodney Adler, the CEO of FAI, refused to allow due diligence to be undertaken by HIH in its takeover preparations. This resulted in HIH not having a general knowledge about FAI and its financial position. At the board meeting when the takeover was given the 'green light' the directors of HIH did not have the correct board papers, nor did they have access to HIH's financial advisers' report concerning the takeover. Instead, HIH relied on publicly available information, which did not disclose the considerable under-reserving of FAI's insurance business. The takeover therefore proceeded even though it was not possible to make a considered assessment of FAI's worth.

The decision to proceed with the takeover can be seen as grave mismanagement. The decision itself was hastily taken after scant consideration and with insufficient preparatory and investigative work. The proposed threat of a third party interested in FAI only sped up the decision and forced directors of HIH to avoid considering the potential risks. Despite these factors, the $300 million HIH takeover bid for FAI at the end of 1998 went through. This resulted in estimated losses of $590 to $650 million arising from the FAI takeover.

Because of the nature of the collapse and the suspicious circumstances surrounding it, businessmen Rodney Adler and Ray William faced charges over a thousand possible breaches of laws and corporate practices. They blamed the collapse on the principal players in FAI and HIH, as well as failure by advisers to the insurers to adhere to basic corporate disclosure and governance. Ultimately the root cause of the HIH collapse was chronic under-reserving and under-pricing combined with unsustainable growth, the reasons for which are a direct result of senior-level mismanagement.

Discussion

Chavan writes about negotiations that break down between corporate leaders when mergers and acquisitions are under consideration. She suggests the main reasons may be:

■ Lack of planning, of devising a set of policies and procedures for the new company;

■ Lack of a baseline assessment of both companies and a projected profile of the acquired/merged company (a SWOT analysis);

■ Attitudes of over-optimism about the future of the amalgamation, leading to overpayment;

■ Failure to analyse accurately the potential benefits and costs of the proposed acquisition;

■ Neglect of differences in national cultures and business systems.

Deresky and Christopher (2011: Ch. 6) state there are major differences in the behaviour people exhibit in negotiation that involves an organisational cultural dimension as well as being particular to individuals. These differences reveal themselves in five identifiable stages before and during negotiation (though there may be some overlap between them): planning and preparation; forming relationships with the other parties; exchanging relevant information; bargaining; and reaching settlement or compromise.

Stage 1: Preparation

In the preparation stage (before the actual negotiations begin), the time, extent and kind of preparation will vary, as will the number of people to be involved and their relative status.

Chavan points out the foolhardiness in failing to make proper preparations for such major organisational change. Wainhouse Research (2004) suggest corporate leaders should begin their preparation by asking themselves several broad strategic questions. However, these need to be considered in the context that strategy is ultimately about making choices and trading off between possible courses of action. Organisational vision and mission provide a good sense of direction, but they are not meant to serve as, or take the place of, the actual strategy.

Therefore managers should ask each other:

■ If they had to, could our resources and market sustain us as a stand-alone company and if so, for how long? If not, how should we proceed?

■ What are our unique assets – what is it that we do or possess that is truly different?

■ Based on our assets, our target customers and our competition, what is our product

■ strategy?

■ Are our product and markets strategies integrated? How?

■ What are our capabilities – do we have 'what it takes' to form mergers and make acquisitions? If not, what advice do we need to supplement our internal capabilities?

Since the mid-1980s, three of the most widely read books on competitive analysis probably have been Michael Porter's *Competitive Strategy*, *Competitive Advantage* and *Competitive Advantage of Nations*. Porter developed three generic strategies to be used singly or in combination to create a defendable position and to outperform competitors, whether they are within an industry or across nations. The strategies are cost-leadership (lowest unit cost), differentiation (best total solution) and focus (addressing a distinct, well-defined customer target not well served by competitors). They can be called trade-off strategies because Porter argues that a firm must choose to embrace one or risk not having a strategy at all (Porter, 1980, 1985, 1989, 2001; also Academy of Management Executive, 2002).

Cost-leadership is a strategy by which firms try to gain competitive advantage by reducing costs below those of competing firms and developing, manufacturing and distributing products more efficiently. Differentiation strategy is based on confidence in superior products or services rather than low cost, such as customer service, product quality or unique style.

To put these strategies into context Wainhouse Research offer the example of Wal-Mart as pursuing a cost-leadership strategy and Harley Davidson as pursuing a differentiation strategy.

Stages 2 and 3: Building relationships and exchanging relevant information

According to Deresky and Christopher (2011), the next two stages of negotiation, whether to acquire another company or for any other motive, are getting to know the other parties and exchanging relevant information. That is, there will be relative emphasis on interpersonal relationships rather than task. This supports Dr Chavan's premise that a major factor in negotiation failure is neglect of differences in national cultures and business systems.

Wainhouse Research (2004) refer to the case of a services company, privately held Magen Biosciences, a Massachusetts-based company focused on novel dermatology treatments. In spite of showing little or no profit, it was acquired by the contract research firm PPD in December 2010 for $14.5 million (Hub Tech Insider, 2010). Analysts suggest that Magen's success could be ascribed to a clever combination of planning, forming relationships with prospective buyers and responding effectively to task-related information.

Magen was founded in 2006 by a well-known group of biotech entrepreneurs and investors. In 2008 the firm obtained licences for a number of dermatology compounds that showed positive anti-inflammatory and anti-proliferative results in preclinical studies. These were the primary reason for PPD's interest in the biotech, and the buy-out offered PPD an entrée into the specialist field of dermatology.

Some of Magen's success was related to the market space it occupied; however, much was owed to its ability to position itself as a leader in that specific market and squarely in the sights of strategic buyers. In its planning Magen 'looked in the mirror' and concluded that an exit via merger or acquisition would be a much more likely outcome than trying to build a larger company on its own. It undertook a broad strategic review of its business model, including partnerships, products and services. This assessment of its product and technology core competencies led Magen to make operational changes, adjust its positioning and redefine its product mix.

Finally, when Magen's principals approached prospective partners, they did so with an eye toward the end game. In a conscious planning process they thought about their core business and competencies, and then how to enhance these to attract buyers. In their case, this meant consciously forging certain partnerships, building brand around certain types of activities, and positioning services to dovetail with those from companies who were potential acquirers.

Stages 4 and 5: Bargaining, concessions and agreements

Differences in emphasis on task or relationship will appear again when the negotiators begin to bargain, to persuade or reason, bully or cajole; and again in the fifth and final stage when agreements are made, concessions are granted and compromises achieved.

Chavan identifies two attitudes that contribute to failure in negotiations at these two stages: over-optimism about the future of the amalgamation, leading to overpayment; and failure to analyse accurately the potential benefits and costs of the proposed acquisition. Two more examples of unsuccessful acquisitions in support of her comments are Quaker Oats and Snapple Beverages; and Sprint and Nextel Communications (see Bloomberg Business Week, 2004; Deighton, 2002; Dumon, 2008; Pressler, 1994; Reuters, 2008; Weekly Corporate Growth Report, 1997; Witowski, 2008).

Quaker Oats and Snapple Beverages

Quaker Oats successfully managed the widely popular Gatorade drink and its managers over-optimistically thought they could do the same with Snapple; but they failed to identify critical factors during the negotiations. In 1994, despite warnings from Wall Street that the company was paying $1 billion too much, the company acquired Snapple for a purchase price of $1.7 billion. In addition to overpaying, management broke fundamental negotiation principles in mergers and acquisitions: make sure you know how to run the company before your acquire it; and bring specific value-added skills sets and expertise to the operation.

In 1997, Quaker sold Snapple to Triarc Beverages for $300 million – a tremendous loss, but in the circumstances the sum could be considered generous. The financial disaster cost both the chairman and president of Quaker their jobs and hastened the end of Quaker's independent existence (it is now a unit of PepsiCo). In October 2000, Triarc sold Snapple to Cadbury Schweppes for about $1 billion. The turnaround would be astonishing in any industry, but especially in the beverage-marketing business, where short-lived brands are depressingly common. Why did Snapple lose $1.4 billion in value under Quaker's stewardship in just four years, only to have Triarc restore most of that value in less than three years?

Quaker Oats' management thought it could leverage its relationships with supermarkets and large retailers. However, about half of Snapple's sales came from smaller channels such as convenience stores, gas stations and related independent distributors. The acquiring management also fumbled on Snapple's advertising campaign, and the differing cultures translated into a disastrous marketing campaign for Snapple by managers not attuned to its branding sensitivities. Snapple's previously popular advertisements became diluted with inappropriate marketing signals to customers. While these challenges defeated Quaker Oats, gargantuan rivals Coca-Cola and PepsiCo launched a barrage of competing new products that ate away at Snapple's positioning in the beverage market.

Thus overpayment as a result of over-optimism, plus failure to 'do the homework', particularly in preparation for cross-cultural problems, were major factors in communication breakdowns in the negotiation stages; and the same factors seem to have been critical factors in the Sprint–Nextel case.

Sprint and Nextel Communications

In August 2005, Sprint acquired a majority stake in Nextel Communications in a $35 billion stock purchase. The two companies combined to become the third largest telecommunications provider, behind AT&T and Verizon.

Prior to the merger, Sprint catered to the traditional consumer market, providing long-distance and local phone connections and wireless offerings. Nextel had a strong following from businesses, infrastructure employees and the transportation and logistics markets, primarily owing to the press-and-talk features of its phones. By gaining access to each other's customer bases, both companies hoped to grow by cross-selling their product and service offerings.

Unfortunately over-optimism about solutions to cultural problems arising from the venture and failure to analyse beforehand the potential benefits and costs of the proposed acquisition led to its downfall. Soon after the merger large numbers of Nextel executives and mid-level managers left the company, citing cultural differences and incompatibility. Sprint was bureaucratic, Nextel was more entrepreneurial. Nextel was attuned to customer concerns, Sprint was not. In such a commoditised business, the company did not deliver on this critical success factor and lost market share. Further, a macroeconomic downturn led customers to expect more from their dollars.

Cultural concerns exacerbated integration problems between the various business functions. Nextel employees often had to seek approval from Sprint's higher-ups in implementing corrective actions, and the lack of trust and rapport meant many such measures were not approved or executed properly. Early in the merger, the two companies maintained separate headquarters, making coordination more difficult between executives at both camps.

Sprint Nextel's managers and employees diverted attention and resources towards attempts at making the combination work at a time of operational and competitive challenges. Technological dynamics of the wireless and internet connections required smooth integration between the two businesses and excellent execution amid fast change. Nextel was simply too big and too different for a successful combination with Sprint.

Sprint saw stiff competitive pressures from AT&T (who acquired Cingular), Verizon and Apple's wildly popular iPhone. With the decline of cash from operations and with high capital expenditure requirements, the company undertook cost-cutting measures and laid off employees. In 2008, the company wrote off an astonishing $30 billion in one-time charges owing to impairment to goodwill, and its stock was given a junk status rating. Thus with its $35 billion price tag, the merger clearly did not pay off.

Classroom exercises

The above commentary on Dr Chavan's article is based partly on the assumption that negotiation, particularly in contexts of cross-cultural communication, proceeds in steps or stages, each one distinct though connected to the others. An interesting classroom exercise would be for each student to research an example of an international alliance between entities of any kind that seems to support or refute the argument that planning, developing relationships, exchanging needed information, bargaining and reaching some form of conclusion are all essential steps for successful completion. Students should compare notes on their respective findings. The following are examples.

1. The African Equity Fund (AEF)

African Equity (http://www.africanequity.org/ [accessed 20 January 2011]) is another example of how successful enterprises form alliances to achieve their strategic objectives – whatever these might be. Alliances between foreign investors and host governments have been discussed, and alliances in the forms of mergers and acquisitions. Another form of alliance is between non-government agencies, their sponsors and business connections. The following account of the operations of African Equity Fund is another illustration of the stages of negotiation to find and maintain these connections.

Based in Queensland, Australia, the African Equity Fund (AEF) is a non-profit organisation dedicated to improving lives and communities in Africa. Through a broad network of supporters in government, financial markets and non-profit organisations, AEF plans and executes sustainable solutions to poverty.

Planning

While development is AEF's long-term vision, its business strategy (http://www. africanequity.org/principles-and-strategy [accessed 21 January 2011] is to generate a return on each donation by using volunteers, making sound investments and focusing on sustainability. The strategy of its managers is to:

- Pool resources, experience and ingenuity to start successful and profitable micro-enterprises in African communities.
- Focus on educating, training and developing employees into competent and confident managers and business owners.
- Gradually transfer the business by helping employees understand their ability to pay off debt or return dividends on borrowed capital.
- Sell, franchise or further grow the business with the help of now-ready employees and third-party financing.

■ Reinvest all profits and proceeds of the business into the education, development and care of employees, or into more micro-enterprises.

In 2007, AEF built a dormitory for 80 girls, and four school classrooms. In 2008 it paid for the construction of a senior boy's dormitory; installed a power supply; and bought four acres of adjoining land for a market garden; started a dairy herd; bored a hole for a water pump; contributed $20,000 towards a radio station building and bought a transmitter.

In 2009, AEF constructed eight classrooms, two laboratories, administration rooms and a computer room; purchased 2.5 acres for staff housing; launched a community newspaper; started a garage business; expanded an existing poultry farm; provided $80,000 for operating costs, emergency food and medical support; and $10,000 to fit out a dining hall. AEF also that year provided two ambulances and two ultrasound machines; and procured ten containers (200 tonnes) of clothing, household, medical and educational equipment. It funded cultural exchange visits to Australia for training seven people; and $100,000 in general support for development of existing facilities.

In 2010, AEF provided sanitation blocks (flushing toilets to the entire campus); scholarships for 20 homeless children to attend the Heroes of the Nation orphanage; and $20,000 in general support.

Plans for 2010 and beyond included provision of a dental team; constructing staff housing for ten families; building a guest house, to be paid for out of the revenue stream; upgrading the access road to be navigable in all weathers; developing a crèche and preschool; improving water storage and amenities on the site; continuing shipments of goods from Australia; funding scholarships for the 2009 high school graduates to attend university; building a library, resource and recreational facility; developing and financing micro businesses in the surrounding community; and procuring more land for expansion of the campus and for agricultural purposes. In November 2010 the Fund brought a performance group of children to Australia.

Developing relationships

One of the ways in which AEF finds sponsors is by publishing its news stories online (http://www.african-equity.com/ [accessed 21 January 2011]) in order to promote interest in and support for the Fund. An example is the story of John Ndungu (Ngungu, 2010).

At the time of the story John was 36 years old and worked as a houseboy at the Thompson's Falls Lodge, Nyahururu, Kenya. He lights fires for visiting tourists and does odd jobs to survive. John works 16 hours a day, seven days a week – often sleeping at his workplace and not seeing his own wife and children for many days at a time. He earns the equivalent of $60 a month, and in conjunction with a small amount of crop growing is able to keep his family (including his mother) housed and fed.

John's family was abandoned by his father at a young age, and his mother was left to raise John and his four siblings. The family struggled for many years to find food and gain a basic education in the poverty-stricken slum where they lived.

John has long had a dream (like many Kenyans) of being a runner. He is trying to live that dream, training vigorously in the few hours each day that he is not working, covering up to 30 km most days. The altitude is 7,300 feet above sea level and is used as the training ground for many of the world's top runners. John's childhood friend and inspiration, Sam Wanjiru, is the current world record holder for the half marathon and won the Gold Medal at the 2008 Beijing Olympics Marathon.

In 2008 a visiting team from AEG (Australia) met John in Nyahururu, Kenya. John's pursuit of his dream, his character and faith inspired one of the visitors to sponsor John and fufil his dream of running in an international event. In conjunction with the *Sunday Mail* newspaper, John (who has never seen the ocean) arrived in Australia on 15 August to compete in both the Bridge to Brisbane and Sydney Half Marathon events.

While organising his visit it became apparent that John's dream was closer than anybody realised. In a time trial John ran only 4 minutes outside the current world record time for the half marathon – not bad for a part-time jogger running in a pair of cross-trainers three sizes too big, left behind by an overseas visitor (Dalla, 2010). A diverse field of entrants took part in the run, with participants hailing from as far as Melbourne, Chicago and Africa. John was the 10 km winner, completing the course in just over 32 minutes.

If you would like to sponsor John or even offer encouragement, please call/ email or deposit funds to the African Equity account.

Another example (Atkinson, 2010) is the story of developer Chris Anderson and his wife Virginia, who helped build one of Africa's biggest orphanages in the Great Rift Valley in Kenya. They are said to be reshaping the nation's economic landscape with a business incubator system based on the sale of second-hand goods.

'The whole of civilisation marched out of the Rift Valley more than 40,000 years ago,' Chris Anderson was reported as saying from African Equity headquarters in Cleveland. 'I was there as a backpacker more than twenty years ago and have been overwhelmed by the lives they lead.'

Exchanging information

By the end of 2010 AEG had collected more than 20,000 pairs of shoes, televisions, computers and clothes, bound for Africa to be sold in a lucrative second-hand market. It was reported that the money raised would reach thousands of impoverished locals through a self-sustaining trickle-down effect.

Bargaining and agreement

Anderson agreed with AEG that he should pay for the first few containers to be sent to Africa. 'Now,' he said: 'the business is paying its own way.'

A New Zealander from the Bay of Plenty, he landed in Australia with a $1,400 loan from his family in 1991 and started building the Australian dream, hitting Australia's rich list early in his thirties. 'I come from a tough environment', he recalled, pointing to a photo of a an African labourer hoisting cement up a makeshift scaffold. 'I relate to that because it used to be my job. A few years back I had the Ferrari, a motor yacht, a super-charged Hummer, and we just started to realise this is not what's important in our lives. We've got rid of it all now.' After cruising through the global financial crisis, Anderson says the challenge of building his business empire remains a key motivator. 'But I can help a lot of other people at the same time, and this is really what's important to us', he said.

The Kenya orphanage he and his wife support, The Heroes of the Nation orphanage, held its first graduation class early in 2011, attended from Australia by high-profile supporters like Brisbane Lions' captain Jonathan Brown,. The orphanage plans to house more than 1,000 students, starting from preschool to postgraduate levels, in the next couple of years.

2. Australia and Afghanistan sign asylum repatriation deal

The following is an example of an alliance between two national governments as part of negotiations to seek solutions to a specific problem (Jerusalem Post Australia, 2011).

Planning

Asylum seekers arriving in Australia are subject to mandatory detention. Australia has signed a deal with the Afghan Government allowing for the involuntary repatriation of failed asylum seekers. It is the first time such a mechanism has been put in place between the two nations.

Forming relationships

As part of the deal, Australia will help Afghanistan upgrade its passport system. In 2010 over 2,700 Afghans arrived in Australia by boat – more than double the number from any other nation.

Exchanging relevant information

The agreement was signed in Sydney by Immigration Minister, Chris Bowen, and the Afghan Minister for Refugees and Repatriation, Dr Jamaher Anwary. Bowen told ABC radio that the move was aimed at dissuading Afghans from undertaking a perilous journey to Australia. He said no one would be sent back to face persecution.

Bargaining with the intention to reach agreement or compromise

Ian Rintoul from the Refugee Action Coalition said he was concerned by the deal. Asylum – and in particular those seeking asylum who arrive by boat – continues to be a hot political issue in Australia, with both parties talking tough on border issues.

Asylum seekers are subject to mandatory detention while their cases are decided. Those arriving by boat – a figure that increased sharply in 2010 – are sent to Christmas Island for offshore processing. Late in 2010, at least 30 asylum seekers were killed when their boat went down just off the island.

Both on- and offshore centres have seen protests by detainees angry at conditions and the length of time it takes for their cases to be assessed.

3. Climate secrets of the Marianas Trench

This is an example of scientific collaboration, another form of alliance.

Planning

The climate secrets of the deepest part of the ocean, the Marianas Trench in the western Pacific Ocean, have been probed by scientists (Morelle, 2011).

Forming relationships

The international team used a submersible, designed to withstand immense pressures, to study the bottom of the 10.9 km-deep underwater canyon.

Exchanging relevant information

The team's early findings reveal that ocean trenches are acting as carbon sinks. This suggests that they play a larger role in regulating the Earth's chemistry and climate than was thought.

Although two explorers, Jacques Piccard and Don Walsh, reached the deepest part of the Marianas Trench – a point called the Challenger Deep – in 1960, no humans have been back since. And the handful of scientific missions, including this recent visit to this deepest spot, have been carried out using unmanned underwater vehicles.

Bargaining to reach agreement or compromise

Lead researcher Professor Ronnie Glud, from the University of Southern Denmark and the Scottish Association for Marine Science (SAMS), said that working at more than 1,000 atmospheres of pressure was challenging, but advances in technology had made it possible. He told BBC News: 'This is the first time we have been able to set down sophisticated instruments at these depths to measure how much carbon is buried there.'

Professor Glud, working with scientists from the Japan Agency for Marine Earth Science and Technology (JAMSTEC) and from the UK and Germany, used a lander equipped with special sensors packed in a titanium cylinder that was able to resist the remarkable pressures. The lander was launched from a ship and took three hours to free-fall to the sea bottom, where it carried out pre-programmed experiments before releasing its ballast and returning to the surface. The tests helped the scientists to assess the abundance of carbon at those murky depths.

Dr Alan Jamieson, from Oceanlab, said the new study was helping researchers to build up a better idea of what happens in the very depths of the ocean.

4. Creating successful agent–bank alliances

The generalisations to be drawn from the following account include the need for mutual interests in prospective alliances, mutual understanding of each other's business, mutual expectations of benefits and mutual trust (National Underwriter Life & Health, 2003).

Planning

It's a long and complicated process for banks to learn how to sell insurance, and this is where many opportunities for agents come in. Short of buying an agency outright or setting up their own agency, banks often seek to partner with established producers who know life and health insurance, annuities, employee benefits and related products that can add to the bank's fee-based income.

Building relationships

Many of these alliances have failed because they got off to a bad start or ultimately because of failure to understand each other's business.

Exchanging relevant information

Even an informal alliance must start off with thorough discussions between agency and bank. Moreover banks are often fearful that outside agents might erode customer's trust. Agencies view banks as lead-generation sources, but only as one source among others, whereas bank employees have only the bank's interests at heart. For these major reasons, joint ventures and other formal alliances with banks have not generally worked, and many are dissolved after a relatively short life.

Bargaining to reach agreement or compromise

A new approach for bank–agency alliances is being discussed by one or two banks and local agencies. The proposed alliances would take the form of a limited partnership established jointly by a bank and an agency that offers commercial lines, but also employee benefits, as well as some life and health insurance and annuities. The bank would provide most of the money but the partnership would be owned 50–50 by bank and agency. The agency would commit a few employees and a great deal of know-how to the venture. Ultimately, the partnership should expand through acquiring other agencies.

It would be a separate business that the bank and the agency together would build and manage: an arrangement that offers some promise and potential. In a typical insurance marketing alliance, the agency winds up essentially creating two classes of business: policies sold internally and those sold through the bank. Because business sold through the bank requires the agency to split commissions, that business can be given short shrift. Under the proposed format, the partnership would pay compensation expenses rather than the original agency. In addition to most of the capital, the bank would bring cross-selling opportunities to the partnership and facilitate meetings between agents and commercial customers.

Another approach currently growing in use in Connecticut and Virginia is for the state bankers' association to create an agency, which then places agents directly in local banks. The agents act as third-party marketers; and this works well for smaller banks. Existing agencies can also partner successfully with banks on a less formal basis to cross-sell a variety of insurance products, but this would be a more difficult arrangement because decisions would have to be made about how the bank would be compensated, for instance, by a percentage of the premium.

Most banks that enter into alliances do so because they are not completely ready to make a long-term commitment to the insurance business. Alliances can be a way of testing the waters; but a cross-referral programme seldom works unless the bank CEO supports it by insisting that customers will be referred to the agency. Even then, to be successful with referral programmes, the bank must first become familiar with the agency's special expertise. If the bank starts referring business that the agency can't write, then the partnership won't work.

5. Cheers again to Oneworld, as best alliance for in-flight wine

The final example in this section illustrates the endless tug-of-war between competition and collaboration in any given industry (etravelblackboard.com, 2010).

Planning

Judges at a leading wine-tasting competition have raised their glasses to the Oneworld® alliance and many of its member airlines.

Forming relationships

Oneworld was named the best alliance for wine in the 2010 Wines on the Wing survey by US magazine *Global Traveler*, which confirms the findings of the Cellars in the Sky awards presented by the UK's *Business Traveller* in February 2010.

Bargaining to reach agreement

Besides winning the 'best alliance' title, Oneworld's member airlines also flew high in the *Global Traveler* Wines on the Wing awards, just as they did in *Business Traveller*'s Cellars in the Sky.

American Airlines took the toast as best North American airline for wines, as well as Best North American Red Wine and Best North American Sparking Wine. American, British Airways, LAN and Mexicana were named among the top ten for Champagne and Sparkling Wine. American, BA and LAN were also in the top ten for white wines, while Iberia, American, LAN and Mexicana were in the top ten for reds.

Twenty-six airlines submitted 46 white wines, 49 red wines and 23 champagne or sparkling wines currently on their international Business Class and North American premium class wine lists for a blind taste test in the Wines on the Wing awards. The tasting was organised by *Global Traveler*'s wine columnist and noted wine expert, Eunice Fried, using 30 independent judges who are noted wine-industry experts.

Oneworld was named the World's Best Alliance in the 2010 World Airline Awards and has been voted the World's Leading Airline Alliance for the past seven years in the World Travel Awards. It is the only winner of this award since it was introduced in 2003.

Conclusion

Communication across cultures includes various forms of international alliances, for profit or otherwise, between corporations and between corporations and governments. The partners benefit in different ways and to greater or lesser degrees. Post-colonial nation states, whose freedom often was won through anti-colonial activism, tend to trade natural resources with developed and emerging economies in exchange for help with infrastructure development. African nations' trade with China is a good example. Foreign investment in local alliances – at any rate to start with – is usually managed by an ethnocentric policy in which the home country partner makes the rules. When the partnership is more balanced, as illustrated by the example of Amazon in Scotland, job creation is another benefit of international alliances.

Many fail, however, through lack of planning, inaccurate and overly optimistic assessment of the situation; and neglect of differences in national cultures and business systems.

Alliances may be vertically integrated – in which case production and distribution will be controlled by one company – or a horizontal merger of firms at the same stage of production in the same industry.

Negotiation over alliances, as in other issues, seems to run through five stages: of planning; building a relationship with the other parties; exchanging relevant information, bargaining; and reaching agreement or compromise. Neglect of any one of these steps is likely to lead to failure of the entire project.

Key points

1. The main reasons why firms seek to form international alliances are to gain better access to attractive country markets; to take advantage of local market knowledge and working relationships with key government officials in the host country; to achieve economies of scale in production and/or marketing; to share technical knowledge, distribution facilities and dealer networks, to put together technical and financial resources; to overcome shortages of needed resources at home; and to strengthen relationships in the area where alliances are sought.

2. Staffing deals specifically with the acquisition, training and allocation of the organisation's employees, to keep it supplied with the right people in the right positions at the right time.

3. Foreign investors tend to take one of three major approaches to managing operations in the host country: ethnocentric (the home office knows best); polycentric/regio-centric (the host country people know best; and in any case staffing policies should suit the location); and geocentric (the best people should be employed no matter where they come from).

4. Creating a 'local presence' by foreign businesses tends to result in a comfortable working relationship with the local people, including them in management, designing country-specific policies and procedures, and working to improve the company's long-term image.

5. In many developing nations, as in Africa, a relatively prosperous professional and middle- class society is emerging; but economic prosperity of this kind is the indirect result of freedom from colonial rule.

6. The major reasons why negotiations break down over mergers and acquisitions are lack of planning; lack of a SWOT analysis; over-optimism about the future of the amalgamation; failure to assess accurately the potential benefits and costs of the proposed acquisition; and neglect of differences in national cultures and business systems.

7. There seem to be major culture-based differences in negotiation styles, revealed in five identifiable stages: planning; forming relationships with the other parties; exchanging relevant information; bargaining; and reaching settlement or compromise.

Looking ahead

'Going global' is not merely the formation of self-contained alliances between international partners; it involves the intricate and delicate formation of communication webs and organisational networks. Chapter 8 explores various forms of networks in the management of communication across cultures.

Experiential exercises

1. Negotiation role-plays

Situation 1

A You have just arrived in London from Tokyo. You are alone. It is late and there is only one bus that will take you to your hotel tonight. You realise that you don't have any pounds to pay for the bus fare. The exchange counters have already closed and the ATM cash machine won't accept your bank cards. You are very tired and worried that you can't get to the hotel. You need 20 pounds. If anyone would give you the money, you would send it back to them tomorrow after you have exchanged your money. You see a man and decide to ask him.

B You are a man living in London. You have just returned from a trip abroad. A girl comes to you and asks for some money. She says she will return it, but where you come from, you don't trust anybody. There is no reason to trust

Table 7.1   When you negotiate, do you...

	Yes	Not always	No
Feel open to many possibilities?	—	—	—
Seek to find common ground?	—	—	—
Focus on the long term?	—	—	—
Deal with each issue independently?	—	—	—
Try to avoid irritating the other party?	—	—	—
Help the other party express their ideas?	—	—	—
Explore ideas without taking sides?	—	—	—
Express support for the other party's ideas?	—	—	—
Disagree without being negative?	—	—	—
Assess the value of your own and others' ideas?	—	—	—
Give and receive information calmly?	—	—	—
Make others think?	—	—	—
Give the impression of answering queries without actually doing so?	—	—	—
Bring negotiation to conclusion?	—	—	—
Leave the other party with something to think about?	—	—	—
Separate the people from the problem?	—	—	—
Focus on interests, not positions?	—	—	—
Think of options for mutual gain?	—	—	—
Invite comments and suggestions?	—	—	—
Avoid attack and counter-attack?	—	—	—
Recognise the other party's position?	—	—	—
Get issues out into the open?	—	—	—
Reduce the gap between parties' positions?	—	—	—
Pinpoint areas of agreement and disagreement?	—	—	—
Compromise?	—	—	—

anybody in an airport. Your girlfriend thinks you should give the girl some money, but you don't agree at all. She can't be trusted and you don't want your girlfriend to give her anything either.

Situation 2

A You are a third-year high school student and will be taking entrance examinations this year. You have always wanted to live alone in Tokyo. The university you desperately want to go to is luckily in Tokyo, but it is a private university. You can't study what you want to in public universities. Your parents don't like your idea, but you want to live your own life. You have to persuade your parents.

B You are the parent of a third-year high school students. Your son/daughter insists on going to a university in Tokyo and renting an apartment to live alone. You and your husband/wife are completely against the idea because you have heard of many dangerous cases of university students (especially girls) who live alone. You can't afford to pay for a private university. You have taken it for granted that your daughter should go to Utsunomiya University (a public university).

2. Negotiation skills quiz

What are your major strengths? How can you build on them?
Where do you have difficulty? Why? What can you do about it?
What kind of a negotiator would you like to be? How can you become it?

References

Bellenger, L. 1978., *Les techniques d'argumentation et de négotiation.* Paris: EME.
Casse, P. and Deol, S.P.S. 1985. *Managing Intercultural Negotiation.* Washington, DC: SIETAR.
Fisher, R. and Ury, W. 1984. *Getting to Yes.* Harmondsworth: Penguin.
Nierenberg, G.I. 1971. *Creative Business Negotiation.* New York: Hawthorne Books.

Recommended reading

Books

Deresky, H. and Christopher, E. 2011. *International Management: Managing across Borders and Cultures*, 2nd edn. Frenchs Forest, NSW: Pearson Education Australia.
Dowden, R. 2008. *Africa: Altered States and Ordinary Miracles.* London: Portobello.
Hill, C.W.L. 2009. *International Business: Competing in the Global Marketplace*, 7th edn (Chicago: McGraw-Hill).
Porter, M. 1980. *Competitive Strategy: Techniques for Analyzing Industries and Companies* (New York: Free Press).
—— 1985. *Competitive Advantage: Creating and Sustaining Superior Performance.* New York: Free Press.
—— 1989. *Competitive Advantage of Nations.* New York: Free Press.
Stiglitz, J.E. 2002. *Globalization and its Discontents.* New York: W.W. Norton.

Online

China Dialogue; http://www.chinadialogue.net

Journals

Academy of Management Executive; www.aomonline.org/
American Economic Review; www.aeaweb.org/aer/
Bloomberg Business Week; www.Businessweek.com
British Journal of Management; www.blackwellpublishing.com/BJOM/
Harvard Business School Working Knowledge; hbswk.hbs.edu/
HR Magazine; www.humanresourcesmagazine.com.au
Human Resource Management Journal; www.wiley.com/bw/journal.asp?ref=0954-5395
Journal of Financial Economics; jfe.rochester.edu/

Leadership Excellence; www.leaderexcel.com/
Management Decision; http://www.emeraldinsight.com/products/journals/journals.htm?
id=md
Telecommunications Policy; www.elsevier.com/locate/issn/03085961
The Wall Street Journal; www.wsj.com

References

Academy of Management Executive 2002. 'Retrospective on Michael Porter's *Competitive Strategy*'. *Academy of Management Executive*, 16 (2), pp. 40–65.

Adams, M. 2002. 'Making a merger work: Culture, business and talent are key issues for HR in the AOL Time Warner merger'. *HR Magazine*, 47, pp. 52–60.

AfricaFocus Bulletin 2005. 'Nigeria: Debt deal views', 27 October; http://www.africafocus.org/docs05/nig0510.php.

Anderson, D. 2007. 'Change leadership: Minimize the chaos of transformation'. *Leadership Excellence*, November, p. 19.

Atkinson, G. 2010. 'African Equity building brighter futures in Kenya'. 17 November; http://wynnum-herald.whereilive.com.au/news/story/african-equity-building-brighter-futures-in-kenya/.

Bailey, M. 1975. 'Tanzania and China: A friendship between most unequal equals'. *African Affairs*, 74 (294), pp. 39–50.

Baptiste, F. and Lewis, R. (eds) (2009) *George Padmore: Pan-African revolutionary.* Kingston, Jamaica: Ian Randle.

Bloomberg Business Week 2004. 'Why Sprint and Nextel got hitched'. *Bloomberg Business Week*, 27 December; http://www.businessweek.com/magazine/content/04_52/b3914031_mz011.htm.

Cartwright, S. and Cooper, C.L. 1993. 'The role of culture compatibility in successful organisation'. *Academy of Management Executive*, 7 (2), pp. 57–69.

Dalla, H. 2010. 'Sea FM Sunshine Coast Half Marathon', 14 September; http://www.g3photography.com.au/content.cfm?ContentType=Module&ContentID=18176&NewsID=7134.

Deighton, J. 2002. 'How a juicy brand came back to life', *Harvard Business School Working Knowledge*, 4 February; http://hbswk.hbs.edu/item/2752.html [John Deighton is the Harold M. Brierley Professor of Business Administration at Harvard Business School].

Deresky, H. and Christopher, E. 2011. *International Management: Managing across Borders and Cultures*, 2nd edn. Frenchs Forest, NSW: Pearson Education Australia.

Dowden, R. 2008. *Africa: Altered States and Ordinary Miracles.* London: Portobello.

Dumon, M. 2008. 'Biggest merger and acquisition disasters'. *Investopedia*; http://www.investopedia.com/articles/financial-theory/08/merger-acquisition-disasters.asp [accessed 16 January 2011].

etravelblackboard.com 2010. 'Cheers again to Oneworld, as best alliance for in-flight wine', 6 August; http://www.etravelblackboard.com/article/107331/cheers-again-to-oneworld-as-best-alliance-for-in-flight-wine.

Faulhaber, G. 2002. 'Network effects and merger analysis: Instant messaging and the AOL–Time Warner case'. *Telecommunications Policy*, 26, pp. 311–33.

Gross, A. 2001 'Recruiting in Korea for foreign firms: An overview'. July; http://www.pacificbridge.com/publication.asp?id=17.

Harwood, I.A. 2006. 'Confidentiality constraints within mergers and acquisitions: Gaining insights through a "bubble" metaphor'. *British Journal of Management*, 17 (4), pp. 347–59.

Hill, C.W.L. 2009. *International Business: Competing in the Global Marketplace*, 7th edn. Chicago: McGraw-Hill.

Høgsbjerg, C. 2009.'A forgotten fighter' [review of Fitzroy and Lewis, *George Padmore*]. *International Socialism: A Quarterly Journal of Socialist Theory*, 124; http://www.isj.org.uk [posted 1 October 2009].

Hub Tech Insider 2010. 'Magen Biosciences, a Waltham, MA-based company focused on novel dermatology treatments, is acquired by the contract research firm PPD for $14.5 million'. 18 December; http://hubtechinsider.wordpress.com/.

Igiri, C.O. and Lyman, P.N. 2004. *Giving Meaning to 'Never Again': Seeking an effective response to the Darfur crisis and beyond*, Council on Foreign Relations Special Report, No. 5, September.

Jerusalem Post Australia 2011. 'Afghanistan signs deal on refugees', 17 January.

Jovanovic, B. and Rousseau, P.L. 2002. 'The Q theory of mergers'. *American Economic Review*, 92 (2), pp. 198–204.

Kaswende, K. 2005. 'Copper prices continue to rise', *The Post (Lusaka)*, 8 June; http://allafrica.com/stories/printable/200506080487.html.

Levin, J.J. 2010. 'Mexico's Cemex tumbles most in seven months on U.S. home sales', 25 August; http://www.bloomberg.com.

Lyman, P.N. 2005. 'China's rising role in Africa', presentation to the US–China Commission, 21 July; http://www.cfr.org/publication/8436/chinas_rising_role_in_africa.html.

Marks, M.L. 1990. 'Consultations for facilitating international mergers and acquisitions'. *Academy of Management Proceedings*, pp. C144–8.

—— 2005. 'Making mergers work'. *Associations Now*, November 2005; http://www.asaecenter.org/Resources/anowdetail.cfm?ItemNumber=14025

Marks, M.L and Mirvis, P.H. 2001. 'Making mergers and acquisitions work: Strategic and psychological preparation'. *Academy of Management Executive*, 15 (2), pp. 80–92.

Morelle, R. 2011. 'Climate secrets of Marianas Trench probed', BBC News, 17 January; http://www.bbc.co.uk/news/science-environment-12183244.

National Underwriter Life & Health 2003. 'Creating successful agent–bank alliances' [cover story], 10 March, Financial Services Edition; http://goliath.ecnext.com/coms2/gi_0199-2578030/Creating-successful-agent-bank-alliances.html.

Ndungu, J. 2010. 'Dreams come true: Bridge to Brisbane', 29 August; http://www.africanequity.org/, www.johnndungu.com.

NEWS.com.au 2011. 'Australia funds homes for returned refugees', 17 January.

Nikandrou, I. and Papalexandris, N. 2007. 'The impact of M&A experience on strategic HRM practices and organisational effectiveness: Evidence from Greek firms', *Human Resource Management Journal*, 17 (2), pp. 155–77.

Porter, M. 1980. *Competitive Strategy: Techniques for Analyzing Industries and Companies*. New York: Free Press.

—— 1985. *Competitive Advantage: Creating and Sustaining Superior Performance*. New York: Free Press.

—— 1989. *Competitive Advantage of Nations*. New York: Free Press.

—— 2001. 'Strategy and the Internet'. *Harvard Business Review*, March, pp. 63–78.

Pressler, M.W. 1994. 'Quaker Oats agrees to buy Snapple; $1.7 billion purchase is part of refocusing', *Washington Post*, 3 November; http://www.highbeam.com/doc/1P2-917343.html.

Reuters 2008. 'Moody's cuts Sprint debt to junk status', 10 December; http://www.reuters.com/article/idINN1034736720081210.

Schraeder, M. and Self, D.R. 2003. 'Enhancing the success of mergers and acquisitions: An organizational culture perspective'. *Management Decision*, 41 (5), pp. 511–22.

SG Legal Solutions 2009. http://sglegalsolutions.com/Mergers%20-%20revised.pdf [accessed 20 May 2009].

Shleifer, A. and Vishny, R.W. 2003. 'Stock market driven acquisitions'. *Journal of Financial Economics*, 70, pp. 295–311.

Sirkin, H.L., Hemerling, J.W. and Bhattacharya, A.K. 2008. 'Globality: Challenger companies are radically redefining the competitive landscape'. *Journal of Applied Finance Strategy & Leadership*, 36 (6), pp. 36.

Stahl, G.K. and Voigt, A. 2004. 'Meta-analyses of the performance implications of cultural differences in mergers and acquisitions', *Academy of Management Best Paper Proceedings*, pp. 1–16.

Stiglitz, J.E. 2002. *Globalization and its Discontents*. New York: W.W. Norton.

Taylor, I. 2007. 'China's environmental footprint in Africa'. *China Dialogue*, 2 February; http://www.chinadialogue.net.

Wainhouse Research 2004. 'Preparing for the merger/acquisition decision: How to position your company in a consolidating collaboration & conferencing marketplace'. April; http://www.cityis.com/assets/downloads/preparingforthemerger.pdf.

Wall Street Journal 2008. 'M&A burnout', n.d.; http://online.wsj.com/public/resources/documents/info-Deals_MA_Q108-04.html [accessed 15 May 2009].

Weekly Corporate Growth Report 1997. 'Quaker's sale of Snapple ends one of the worst merger flops in history', *BNET*, Australian edition, 21 April; http://findarticles.com/p/articles/mi_qa3755/is_199704/ai_n8776577/.

Weston, M. 2008. *Prophets and Princes: Saudi Arabia from Muhammad to the Present*. Wiley, ISBN: 978-0-470-18257-4 http://www.wiley.com/.

Whiteman, K. 2010. 'Osagyefo Dr. Kwame Nkrumah: liberator and Pan-Africanist', 17 June, Voice of Africa Radio; http://www.voiceofafricaradio.com/news/385-liberator-and-pan-africanist.html.

Witkowski, W. 2008. 'S&P cuts Sprint Nextel ratings to junk status'. *Wall Street Journal*, Market Watch, 1 May; http://www.marketwatch.com/story/sp-cuts-sprint-nextel-ratings-to-junk-status.

CHAPTER 8

Communication Webs: Organisational Networks

Elizabeth Christopher; Ron Goodenow

Objective of the chapter

To explore various forms of networks in the management of communication across cultures.

Chapter contents

- Outline of chapter
- Elizabeth Christopher: The nature of service relationship networks: cross-cultural view
- Discussion
- Questions
- Case study: Electronic networking
- Discussion
- Ron Goodenow: Paradigms and practice: personal perspectives on ever-shifting 'telework' sands
- Questions
- Case study: Working from home
- Questions
- Conclusion
- Key points
- Experiential exercise
- Recommendations for further reading
- References

Outline of chapter

This chapter deals with aspects of global networks, business and social. It illuminates the previous chapter by shedding light on reasons – some of them cultural – why three-quarters of all joint ventures fail. Elizabeth Christopher begins by exploring the nature of service relationship networks. The discussion that follows is of free trade agreements as international networks.

Electronic linkages are opening new ways of communicating, and creating new patterns that support joint work and collaboration. A case of electronic network studies the enormous worldwide popularity – and the exploitation – of online social forums such as Facebook, LinkedIn and Twitter. Criticisms of these media are mainly that they serve to isolate, rather than connect, their visitors and insulate them from 'reality'.

Ron Goodenow writes a personal memoir of decades of experience in electronic networking and asks a number of pertinent questions about the future of collaborative technologies across cultures. Are societies moving towards a global community, linked electronically, whose citizens work from home in cross-cultural collaborative networks to provide better services, and improve cultural understanding? Or are these networks effectively helping the rich to get richer while leaving the poor poorer?

The final case study is of the growing demand for, and provision of, teleworking – by which employees work for much of their time in their own homes rather than in a designated common workplace. Advantages and disadvantages are discussed, for employers, for workers and for society at large.

As usual, the chapter ends with a conclusion and summary of key points, then suggestions for experiential exercises, a recommended reading list and chapter references.

THE NATURE OF SERVICE RELATIONSHIP NETWORKS: CROSS-CULTURAL VIEW	Elizabeth Christopher

Introduction

In trade networks there is no sale of goods that does not include some aspects of service. Services may be interpersonal, as between customer and sales assistant; they may be impersonal and after the sale, as in honouring a warranty; or informational as in assembly manuals. They may be before or after the goods have been bought, or bear no direct connection with the goods at all – like an insurance policy or delivery instructions: but in whatever guises they appear, services will be there, linked with goods or standing alone.

Moreover as William Murphy (1999) observed, service networks are critical to economic growth all over the world, in the less as in the more developed countries; and service providers need more and more to operate across national and cultural boundaries for increasingly diverse consumers. Market decisions should be made on the assumption that these relationships will be long-term, will adapt to and grow stronger with change.

D.K. Rigby et al. (2002) point out that executives have spent ten years analysing why as many as 55 per cent of customer relationship management (CRM) systems fail. They suggest one reason for these failures is that many executives do not understand that CRM is designed to 'align business

processes with customer strategies to build customer loyalty and increase profits over time' (ibid.: 101).

They do not mention another reason for the failure of so many customer
relationship tactics: a lack of acceptance that firms should create internal networks of loyalty to clients as well as vice versa. De Chernatony et al. (2003)
have constructed a model of factors involved in building a services brand from
scratch; and they compare it with a goods model. They argue that when building services brands, the organisational culture will be of critical importance.
They recommend that firms should develop networks of cross-functional teams
with a strong internal culture of support for the brand; and strong customer
orientation.

Providers and consumers

In general the literature and practice of services marketing seems to be based on
two questionable assumptions about the nature of the relationship between sellers and buyers. The first is that 'they', the customers, are somehow a completely
different breed from 'us', the marketers. The second assumption is that company
success is more important than customer satisfaction. Yet neither can stand up
to examination because they take no account of the vital importance of service
networks.

'Us' and 'them'

It appears from the literature that marketers study service relationships only to
learn more effective methods by which they can manipulate customers. The
result is an entirely artificial – and therefore ultimately unhelpful – division of
the population of the global marketplace into 'we' who sell and 'they' who buy.
Under this assumption, marketing authors tend to write about customers as if
they were non-human. They are Pavlovian dogs; collateral damage in wars of
competition; pawns on the chessboards of organisational strategy; aliens from
outer space: anything, in fact, except people like themselves. This is the point
that many writers on buyer behaviour overlook: that the nature of the assumptions made by marketers about consumers is the critical sales factor in any given
instance. If marketing managers assume their customers are less than human,
they will behave in less than humane ways themselves.

Customers as 'manager's best friend'

Authors of textbooks with titles such as Henry Assael's *Consumer Behavior and
Marketing Action* (1998) and David Loudon and Albert J. Della Bitta's *Consumer Behavior: Concepts and Applications* (1993) summarise the principles of
classical conditioning, by which Pavlov trained dogs to behave as he wished
(Coon and Mitterer, 2008).

For instance, Assael – highly regarded and respected for his managerial approach to consumer behaviour – writes statements such as:

> *As consumers gain experience in purchasing and consuming products, they learn what brands they like and do not like (and) adjust future behavior based on past experience.*

(Assael, 1998: 66)

So might a dog owner speak about training her dog by giving it a biscuit when it fetches the morning paper from the front step; and hitting it when it doesn't. This works fine within a relationship where dogs are dependent on, and love and trust their owners. However, consumers are humans, not dogs; nor are they dependent on one supplier; and they are not prepared to give brand loyalty unless there is an established network of trust.

Loudon and Della Bitta (1993: 68) are typical of marketing writers who discuss the concept of relationship marketing as a form of 'loyalty segmentation'; but they refer to a one-way loyalty, that of customers towards products. They do not even touch on the notion of networks of trust: that managers might owe loyalty to their customers as well as vice versa. Thus they define consumer behavior (ibid.) as:

> *... the decision process and physical activity individuals engage in when evaluating, acquiring, using or disposing of goods and services.*

They write:

> *Efforts to establish stronger bonds with buyers, known as relationship marketing, have great potential. By using database programs to identify and reach customers with relevant rewards, companies can cement the buyer-seller relationship.*

(ibid.)

This seems an odd use of the world 'relationship' to describe an essentially one-way process.

Customers as war victims

'Targeting prospects for a new product' (Kotler et al., 2001): consider the assumptions behind such language. The word 'target' suggests training for battle rather than business; and the word 'prospects' dehumanises people into victims, into inanimate targets for the kill. It is the cultural sign of a greedily materialistic society when providers of goods and services forget their common humanity with the people they serve.

Customers as chess pieces

Many firms are now switching from product-based to customer-based structures. Ryals and Knox (2001), for example, argue that a key driver for this change is the advent of customer relationship management to improve the implementation of relationship marketing principles. But they go on to suggest that three main factors in the development of customer relationship management are the organisational issues of culture and communication; management metrics; and cross-functional integration.

In other words, Ryals and Knox, like most of their colleagues, are looking internally, within the organisation, to find answers to customer relationships through operational improvements. In this scenario customers are pawns on the organisational chess board, to be moved around and sacrificed at will for larger goals; and the only reason for keeping customers happy is economic. Withers (2003) comments on a Genesys-commissioned study, which indicated that 84 per cent of contact centre managers believe their revenue would be impacted if they did not meet their customer satisfaction levels. Desk and call centre executives measure customer satisfaction – and try to 'improve their business metrics' – with customer relationship management software. Managers who adopt this kind of strategy should also look outwards, to the wider environment in which these relationships will flourish or fall by the wayside, depending on how they are nurtured.

Customers as aliens

Almost without exception, studies of services marketing are from the viewpoint of organisational managers and mostly from Western (i.e., US, British and European) perspectives. To give just one example, Matzler, Sauerwein and Heischmidt (2003) reflect that measurement and management of customer satisfaction have become key issues over the previous decade. Writing of the banking industry, they agree that banks should understand customers' needs and design products and services to meet and even exceed their expectations. They go on to suggest such understanding can be reached by improving the design of the IPA ('importance–performance analysis', a widely used two-dimensional grid for management of customer satisfaction). They argue that the traditional IPA can be misleading because it does not take account of three satisfaction factors: basic, performance, and excitement factors. These have been identified as relevant for customers in cultures of deregulation and competition. The topic of banking services for developing countries becomes irrelevant in this context; yet it is an important growth area.

Even when other cultural norms are referred to, the implication is that 'we' (i.e., Westerners who set behavioural norms) are studying 'them' (e.g., people from Asia, Latin America or the Middle East). We study them as foreigners or aliens as unlike us as creatures from outer space; their habits must be studied as anthropologists study remote tribes. Even if the assumption is that they are friendly aliens, the attitude is ethnocentric and hegemonic, and has serious ethical and social implications for services marketing.

Providers of goods and services are also their consumers, and vice versa. An analogy may be made with car drivers and pedestrians. When driving, we tend to regard all pedestrians as mentally deficient. When we are on foot, we are likely to regard all drivers as dangerous lunatics. If this kind of perceived and artificial divide is created between 'buyers' and 'providers', how can any empathy exist between them? Yet empathetic networks are essential in the service industry and in service provision.

R. Bruce Money (2010) refers to advertising and word of mouth as the two dominant factors in people's decision to buy. Word of mouth, as with any form of communication grapevine, can only exist in a shared cultural context. It assumes a relationship – a network – between consumers, and between consumers and providers: it is dynamic behaviour, generated by perceived roles, expectations and common interests. Mark Farrell (2000) is one of many market researchers who conclude that:

> *a learning orientation has a stronger significant positive effect on business performance than does a market orientation.*

Profiting without pleasing

The second major assumption in the literature of services marketing is apparently that more emphasis should be placed on profits for shareholders and rewards for corporate executives than on employee and customer satisfaction (Capon and Hulbert, 2007). This assumption can only be counter-productive, especially in the long run, if service provision is seen to be a one-sided relationship in which the providers take as much as they can get and offer as little as possible in return. Commitment must be mutual, in terms of international networks of service relations.

Commitment and culture

It is inevitable that perceptions, by consumers of service providers, and vice versa, will shift and alter, depending largely on the viewers' cultural backgrounds, their respective ethical values, social and individual perspectives. This being so, can there be such a thing as an 'ideal' service relationship between people of different regions, nations and communities? Or is it the case that the returns should each receive in exchange for mutual commitment will vary, depending on the total environment in which each network of relationship develops?

The need for role models

Furthermore, any discussion of ethical behaviour and corporate social responsibility should include the need for role models and the provision of good examples from the top.

Unfortunately, they are hard to find among corporate leaders. For example, bank failures, near failures and crises are common throughout the world, and particularly in the major G-10 trading countries. Already in 1998 Benton Gup had cast doubts on the effectiveness of bank regulation and emerging technologies and argued that change in regulatory methods was needed.

Educators should be good role models but education is another service provision that has come under attack. For example, Kent den Heyer's collection of work in education (2011) follows French philosopher Alain Badiou in grappling with what he might mean for the enterprise of schooling. It challenges contemporary and conventional Anglo–US theories, and has particular relevance to the export of education through networks of providers to international students at undergraduate and graduate levels who study at foreign universities and pay high fees to do so.

Characteristics of an ideal services network

What, then, should be the 'ideal' relationship between international service providers and their clients? Pei Xu (2007) acknowledges the value of networks when he writes on the effectiveness of business-to-business word-of-mouth marketing strategies; but these are subject to cultural differences. Jan H. Schumann (2009) writes on the impact of culture on relationship marketing in international services, and Jerrold Winter (2007) studies cultural dimensions in international services vendor selection criteria. These examples suggest that we should look for a definition of an ideal service relationship within a cultural framework.

Richard Lewis writes (2005: 2):

By focusing on the cultural roots of national behaviour, both in society and business, we can foresee and calculate with a surprising degree of accuracy how others will react to our plans for them, and we can make certain assumptions as to how they will approach us.

The first characteristic

According to this suggestion, an essential feature of service relations is that of *mutual recognition, based on a set of common assumptions.* This implies networks of two-way relationships in which the return that each party expects is mutual benefit in exchange for mutual commitment. But this does not mean all service relationships will be the same. The nature of the relationship is that it will vary, and so will the bonds created during the process.

The second characteristic

It follows that a second characteristic of service relations should be *intercultural sensitivity in its broadest meaning*: being attentive to differences between people not only of race, nationality, colour and creed but also of age and gender, class and caste, educational background and life experience. In other words, a whole range of networks between people who are consumers and people who provide the goods and services they consume.

The World Trade Organisation (WTO) as an international network

In 1994 the General Agreement on Trade in Services (GATS) was signed as part of the agreements that set up the WTO. The provisions of this international agreement cover basic services such as healthcare, education, water supply and infrastructures for mass communication; public transport; cultural services, including films and television, museums and libraries, and so on. There are 160 sectors included under the GATS, and they account for most of the world's economy. The GATS includes a commercial presence in services and has been described by the World Trade Organisation (WTO) as 'the world's first international investment agreement' (Friends of the Earth, 2002).

Kern Alexander and Mads Tønnesson Andenæs (2008) write that though traditionally international trade laws and regulations have been analysed primarily from the trade-in-goods perspective, the growing importance of services trade to the global economy makes application of the GATS an important concern. The Agreement is making a growing impact on the regulatory practices of WTO member states. The role of the WTO in promoting liberalised trade and economic development has come under serious strain because of the breakdown of the Doha Development Round negotiations, and there is need for a more durable GATS framework.

It is true that governments open up their service industries under commitments that are theoretically voluntary. In practice, however, the poorer countries increasingly face complex agreements that are difficult to understand, with tiny budgets, few government advisers and no assessment on the likely impacts of interventions under the GATS. Thus it is becoming more and more important that the relationship between service providers and the people they serve be created and maintained to the benefit of both parties.

The GATS applies if services are supplied commercially or in competition with the private sector. And in practice there are few service sectors in most countries that do not include some element of service provision by companies such as in broadcasting, private medicine and education. There is an ongoing debate regarding the potential impact of the GATS on the provision of public services, like healthcare and education (Education International/Public Services International). It will intensify as the potential reach of the Agreement expands over public services, both through the inclusion of more specific commitments in WTO Member schedules, and through the development of new disciplines on domestic regulation.

There is ongoing pressure to increase the scope of liberalisation, and commitments are subject to a ratchet principle in that they can be made but not reversed.

Under the GATS, the intention is that supplies of all services should be competitive (Information for Action, n.d.). All work involving a service – including control of health, education, libraries, water, electricity, sewage, waste disposal, communications, transport, environmental protection and other public works provided by governments – should be put out to tender, and the lowest tender from anywhere in the world ought to be accepted. From this perspective environmental laws, immigration laws, labour laws and state management of publicly owned services are restraints on trade.

Thus the GATS is a free trade agreement because it proposes to open markets to competition between companies if countries are signatories to the agreement. It opposes protectionism even when protectionism has positive social and environmental benefits, and is designed on principles of economic rationalism.

The number, type and level of public services differ widely between countries; and some privatised services such as health and education have proved to be highly profitable. In the US public services are mostly run by private operators licensed by the various State governments – also in developing countries where governments cannot afford to provide services and rely on private contractors. Public services are the most developed in Europe, whereas in Canada, Australia and New Zealand there is a mix between public and private (ibid.).

If the networks created by the GATS are to benefit both providers and recipients of services they should extend over both public and private sectors – as they do for the most part in the developed countries. Marketing assumptions, however, seem to be based on profit rather than customer satisfaction. If so, and if essential services are to be increasingly under the control of private enterprise, networks of relationships need to develop between business, governments and consumers to ensure that everybody benefits from provision of healthcare, education, museums, art galleries, libraries, safe drinking water, gas and electricity, sewage, waste disposal, communication media, transport facilities and environmental protection

Summary

This discussion has raised the argument – using a number of metaphors – that too many marketing strategies in the private sector are adversarial in that firms 'target' their 'prospects' rather than attempting to serve the public. Also that they tend to structure their organisations as chess boards on which consumers as pawns can be moved around in response to strategic planning. A third metaphor is of consumers as dogs, salivating to a Pavlovian manipulation. The observation has been made that all such approaches to marketing become even more highly debatable in the context of the GATS, whereby more and more essential services are being privatised. Two suggestions are offered: that international service marketing networks should be broadened to include consumers as equal participants rather than victims; and that awareness of cultural and economic differences between nations and regions should lead to a greater range of such networks.

Discussion

Mariya Tetervatnikova (2008) argues that trade agreements between countries are modelled on networks. She writes that nodes represent countries; and links between nodes indicate the existence of a trade agreement. In this framework, multilateral agreements are represented by a complete network, while the overlap of regional agreements is represented by the hub-and-spoke trade system (Alba et al., 2010; De Benedictis et al., 2005) (for example, most passenger airlines use a hub-and-spoke network to route their plane traffic; the hub is a central airport through which flights are routed and the spokes are the routes).

Globally there is an expanding network of free trade agreements (FTAs) that play an important role in supporting global trade liberalisation and are explicitly allowed for under the WTO rules. FTAs can cover entire regions with multiple participants, or link just two economies. Under these agreements, parties enter into legally binding commitments to liberalise access to each other's markets for goods and services, and investment. FTAs also typically address a range of other issues such as intellectual property rights, government procurement and competition policy.

To cite just one example, Australia (see http://www.dfat.gov.au [accessed 16 November 2011]) has six FTAs currently in force with New Zealand, Singapore, Thailand, the US, Chile and (with New Zealand) the Association of South East Asian Nations (ASEAN). The countries covered by these FTAs account for 28 per cent of Australia's total trade. Nine more FTAs are under negotiation, including with China, Japan and the Republic of Korea. The countries covered by these negotiations account for a further 44 per cent of Australia's trade.

In general, FTAs help national exporters to gain access to new markets and to expand trade in existing markets.

Questions

Can you think of 'networks' in your own life that can be generalised to organisational networking? What purposes do these networks serve for you? Are they essentially the same services that aid organisational performance? What aspects of your personal network do you most value and why?

Case study: Electronic networking

Researchers report that social-networking websites, including LinkedIn, Facebook, Twitter and CarerBuilder.com, are becoming increasingly popular with job seekers, particularly in recent difficult economic times.

The general consensus is that job seekers who want to use social networking need to upload their profile to sites such as LinkedIn. They need to include key words describing their expertise so that their profiles show up on searches. They need to display a professional photograph and to include connections and recommendations from colleagues and peers. The word 'social' implies that people can use groups to communicate with members who share an industry or interests inside and outside their own connections.

LinkedIn seems to be an important medium for keeping in touch with colleagues, for people who already have a job; but some companies also use Twitter to draw attention to job vacancies in their organisations. There is a dramatic growth in the availability of online profiles; and professional information on the web is changing the nature of recruiting.

Moreover, in response to demand, a number of companies offer social media marketing and management. Wispa and Digital Niche are Australian firms. Wispa advises those 'not sure how to get started in social media' that it creates 'powerful' social media marketing campaigns. Digital Niche is the largest independent technology advertising network in Australia; and Deepend is one of the most highly regarded social media experts in the country.

In the US, Jobvite, a company that develops software to help employers use social networks for recruiting, was founded by Jesper Schultz 'to solve problems that growing businesses confront in attracting and hiring the best people'. Anne Murguia, vice president of marketing at Jobvite, says the firm can take that kind of activity online and get more of it done than individual recruitment managers are able to do. According to a Jobvite survey in 2010, 92 percent of those hiring said they would use or plan to use social networking in their recruiting efforts. One in two companies planned to invest more in social recruiting. Another such firm is Foxtrot Media, owned by Deborah Smith. She says that though it is still important for job seekers to go to networking events, to call up friends and former co-workers and to scour job advertisements and boards, it is not enough.

Nancy Anderson, owner of Blackbird Learning Associates in New Jersey, and the author of 'Job Search for Moms', opened her business 18 months ago after being laid off. Blackbird Learning Associates now provides job-search training, primarily through the Somerset County Library System. She finds that many companies no longer use recruiters, print advertisements and job boards because of the expense. Instead they rely on social media to multiply their job search efforts.

In the UK in September 2010 Matt Tran reported that a social media application (app) has been added to the BBC's new iPlayer. The function that allows users to catch up on TV and radio programme shows after they have been broadcast now includes the ability to personalise an iPlayer by making a user account that interacts with Facebook or Twitter. As a result members can share favourite shows over their Twitter or Facebook accounts.

It is likely the BBC has upgraded its service to get one step ahead of rivals such as Channel 4's 4 On Demand (4OD) and ITV's ITV player. All of these services operate in a similar fashion, but the BBC's is the first to include social media integration. The BBC announced that 'personalisation' is the main theme behind the project and that it wants to bring a social dimension to watching and listening.

In January 2011, also in the UK, Charlotte McEleny reported in *Marketing Week* that Asos.com was launching a fully transactional Facebook shop, allowing people to buy its entire range from within the social network. Launched at the end of January, it was one of the first to allow people to buy directly from a brand without leaving Facebook. Previously brands had used third-party social commerce providers or used Facebook as a shopfront, directing shoppers to their site to complete the transaction.

Asos will have its entire stock on the Facebook store, adding 1,300 products each week. The Facebook application (app) will also have increased social media functions including 'like' buttons and comments, which Asos said it would later consider adding to its main site. The Asos Facebook app is powered by Usablenet, which also powers the fashion retailer's mobile site.

Also in January 2011 there was a spate of articles on OnlineSocialMedia by various reporters, all writing on the general topic of social media marketing. For instance, Maddy Rowe reported that some UK businesses have been slow to use social media.

This is somewhat surprising in view of how much the internet is used nowadays and particularly that of social networking sites such as Facebook and Twitter. In theory social networking should be an ideal ways of marketing their brands.

Ms Rowe asked why networking sites were not being more used. She speculated that maybe some companies simply have not yet explored these avenues; but another explanation could be the increase in cyber crime such as spams and viruses. Companies might be afraid of the consequences should information be delivered to the wrong hands. If this is the case, then the solution might be training programmes for employers as well as employees in how to avoid this.

Debbie Turner wrote that in spite of hesitation in some quarters, marketing through these social networks is increasing rapidly. Apparently the most popular social media site used by retailers to push their brands online is Facebook. Amazingly, one brand, Topshop, now has over 1 million customers following its news on Facebook.

It seems that fashion retailers are still predominant across social media sites, over other retail categories. On Facebook the top five spots for retailers are Topshop, River Island, New Look, Next and Amazon, in that order, with only Amazon not being a fashion retailer.

However, in October the previous year Lauren Indvik, an assistant editor of Mashable (social media news blog), wrote for CTV (Canada) that, for a sector as forward-thinking as the fashion industry, the reluctance with which it has ventured into e-commerce and other digital platforms was more than a little perplexing. She reported that an affinity for traditional commerce and marketing channels is still strong among many purveyors of luxury goods, both in the fashion sector and elsewhere. She quoted Federico Marchetti, founder and chief executive of Italian retailer Yoox, that he estimates only half of luxury brands sell directly online, though several others suggest that the percentage is higher, due largely to recession pressures. Many brands, particularly European manufacturers of high-end wristwatches and other luxury goods, refuse to set up shop online.

Ms Indvik also quoted Jean-Claude Biver, chief executive of Hublot. Apparently at the Reuters Global Luxury Summit in the summer of 2010 Biver said:

We have an exclusive network of over 400 retailers but that cannot work online. When you are online, you are not exclusive anymore.

He is not alone in believing that e-commerce is not an option because the shopping experience their brands provide cannot be successfully translated for the web. When consumers walk into a luxury store they will be paying for more than just the goods. If they are going to spend US$1,000 on a pair of shoes they want an experience as well as a purchase. From store design to employee training, luxury firms have invested heavily in offering these for customers, making retail locations feel less like sales rooms and more like intimate boutiques. It is difficult to recreate that environment on the web.

Some brands, like Burberry and Christian Louboutin, offer close-up video footage of their products, allowing shoppers to examine the texture and drape of a python trench coat or glitter of a jewelled strap as if they were holding the product in the store. Online retailer Net-a-Porter represents virtually the high-calibre service of a real store by offering same-day shipping to customers in New York and London, and handling returns for its premier customers. Oscar de la Renta extends its in-store services, such as styling advice and garment alterations, to online shoppers by phone and e-mail.

Ms Indvik notes that the web has also become an important marketing channel for many high-end brands. Even those adverse to e-commerce are producing brand-enriching media content to display on their websites and, for those willing to sacrifice a little design control for better distribution, platforms like Facebook, Twitter and YouTube. Chanel, which does not sell directly online, released a series of artistic short films directed by designer Karl Lagerfeld and Martin Scorsese in the summer of 2010. Dozens of high-end fashion, jewellery and travel firms have released image and video-rich apps for Apple's iPhone and iPad devices in recent years as well.

During London Fashion Week, Burberry chief creative officer Christopher Bailey wrote on Twitter that Burberry is 'now as much a media-content company as [it is] a design company because it's all part of the overall experience'. Like many other fashion houses, Burberry released a heavy amount of video and photographic footage of its catwalk show, giving fans the ability to peek backstage and watch the show live online.

However, luxury brands are less enthusiastic about social media marketing. Many managers are not comfortable with the lack of control that a Facebook page allows. They see it as the differences between attending a party given by somebody else instead of inviting carefully chosen guests to one's own fashion runway. While large consumer brands like Pepsi and Dunkin' Donuts are launching major interactive campaigns across many social networks – engaging sometimes millions of fans in the process – few such campaigns are coming from luxury brands. Most use it social media as another channel to distribute news and imagery to enhance the brand; some use it as a direct attempt to drive sales on their websites, for instance, by posting a link to purchase alongside an image of a new product.

There are exceptions among brands whose managers market to aspirational shoppers. In social campaigns on Facebook in 2010 both BMW and Marc Jacobs publicised the launch of products aimed at a younger demographic – an SUV and a men's fragrance, respectively. Jimmy Choo attracted considerable attention in mainstream and online press with a Catch-a-Choo campaign on location-based social gaming network Foursquare. The campaign had women running around London in order to grab a pair of the company's new line of sneakers at various venues the brand broadcasted over the network. Oscar de la Renta was even able to promote the purchase of a bridal gown after tweeting about a bridal trunk show taking place at Bergdorf Goodman.

These instances, however, are rare, according to Ms Indvik; and they do not provide opportunities to engage affluent – rather than aspirational – shoppers. In a market where brands are constantly making products more innovative to stay ahead of the competition, it seems odd that so few resources are invested in reinventing how that product is marketed and delivered on the web. Leaders are beginning to emerge in the luxury sector; it will remain to the rest to decide whether to innovate and thrive, or be left behind.

The number of people using social media is staggering, and its growth is astronomical. In 2009, for example, the population of Facebook – more than 500 million – surpassed that of the USA. LinkedIn had more than 85 million and Twitter more than 145 million registered users at that time.

Whatever the arguments for and against, there is no doubting the power of social networks, and businesses have been quick to take advantage of it with social media management strategies. For example, Pepsi Cola pulled out of the Super Bowl for the first time in 23 years and put their advertising dollars into social media marketing. Word-of-mouth marketing has always been popular, and social media networks are like word-of-mouth marketing multiplied astronomically. Firms can gain invaluable feedback on the reputation of their company and brand, and about their competitors. An essential part of online network strategy seems to be not only participating in and engaging with audiences, but also monitoring public conversations on social media platforms like Facebook and Twitter.

Monitoring social networks is maybe one of the best, quickest and cheapest ways of taking the pulse of an industry. Moreover if false information is being spread that can potentially damage a firm, it can quickly be corrected and replace with a more credible and positive image.

The phenomenon of social media is not without its critics. A rising number of academics argues that sites such as Twitter and Facebook don't connect people, rather they isolate them from reality. A leading US sociologist, MIT Professor Sherry Turkle, suggests that the way people frantically communicate online via Twitter, Facebook and instant messaging can be seen as a form of modern madness. She leads an attack on the information age with her book, *Alone Together* (2011), published in the UK and creating a sensation in the US. Her thesis is simple: technology is threatening to dominate our lives and make us less human. Under the illusion of allowing us to communicate better, it is actually isolating us from real human interactions in a cyber-reality that is a poor imitation of the real world.

Professor Turkle's book represents an intellectual backlash against some of the values and methods of modern communications. A recent bestseller in the US, *The Shallows* by Nicholas Carr (2010), suggests that use of the internet is altering the way we think, to make us less capable of digesting large and complex amounts of information, such as books and magazine articles. The book was based on an essay that Carr wrote *in The Atlantic* magazine in 2008, 'Is Google making us stupid?'

Another kind of cyber-scepticism is expressed by Evgeny Morozov in *The Net Delusion* (2011). He argues that social media have bred a generation of what he calls 'slacktivists'. Social media have made people lazy and have enshrined the illusion that clicking a mouse is a form of activism equal to real-world donations of money and time. Other books on similar themes include *The Dumbest Generation* by Emory University Professor Mark Bauerlein (2008) – in which he maintains 'the intellectual future of the US looks dim'– and *We Have Met the Enemy* by Daniel Akst (2011), who claims the proliferation of communication tools is a key component in an increasing and dangerous lack of individual self-control in the modern world.

The backlash has crossed the Atlantic. In *Cyburbia*, published in Britain in 2010, James Harkin surveyed the modern technological world and found many reasons to be worried as well as pleased about the new technological era. Elsewhere, the hit film *The Social Network* (2010) has been seen as a thinly veiled attack on the social media generation, suggesting that Facebook was created by people who failed to fit in with the real world.

On the other hand, many writers leap to the defence of social media, pointing out that emails, Twitter and Facebook have led to more communication, not less – especially for people who may have trouble meeting in the real world because of great distance or social difference. Defenders say theirs is just a different form of communication, but it is still communication. Some experts believe the debate is so fierce because social networking is a new field that has yet to develop its own rules and etiquette.

Also there is an argument that many social media critics hark back to a world that never really existed; and that before everyone travelled on the bus or train with their heads buried in an iPad or a smart phone, they didn't talk to each other, they just travelled in silence.

Sources

Akst, D. 2011. *We Have Met the Enemy; Self-Control in an Age of Excess.* New York: Penguin Press.

Baurerlein, M. 2008. *The Dumbest Generation: How the Digital Age Stupefies Young Americans and Jeopardizes Our Future, or Don't Trust Anyone Under 30.* New York: Tarcher/Penguin.

Blackbird: Blackbirdlearningassociates.com [accessed 23 January 2011].

Bugeja, M. 2005. *Interpersonal Divide: The Search for Community in a Technological Age.* New York: Oxford University Press.

Carlgerber n.d. 'Do you have a social media management and marketing strategy?'; http://carlgerber.hubpages.com/hub/Social-Media-Management-Now [accessed 23 January 2011].

Carr, N. 2008. 'Is Google making us stupid? What the Internet is doing to our brains'. *The Atlantic Magazine*, 301, July/August.

—— 2010. *The Shallows: What the Internet is Doing to Our Brains.* New York: W.W. Norton.

Deepend Sydney: http://deepend.com.au [accessed 23 January 2011].

Digital Niche: http://www.digitalniche.com.au [accessed 23 January 2011].

Foxtrot Media: http://www.foxtrotmedia.com [accessed 23 January 2011].

Harkin, J. 2010. *Cyburbia: The Dangerous Idea That's Changing How We Live and Who We Are.* New York: Hill & Wang.

Harris, P. 2011. 'Social networking under fresh attack as tide of cyber-scepticism sweeps US'. 22 January; guardian.co.uk.

Indvik, L. 2010. 'Luxury brands still tread lightly with social media'. Forbes.com, Mashable, 23 October; http://www.ctv.ca/CTVNews/SciTech/20101022/forbes-luxury-101023/.

Jobvite: http://recruiting.jobvite.com/company/management.php [accessed 23 January 2011].

McEleny, Charlotte (2011) 'Asos unveils Facebook store'. 18 January; http://www.marketingweek.co.uk.

Morozov, E. 2011. *The Net Delusion: How Not to Liberate the World.* London: Allen Lane.

OSM Online Social Media: http://www.onlinesocialmedia.net.

Social Media; http://social-media.co.uk/ [accessed 24 January 2011].

Smith, D.L.: http://deborahlsmith.com [accessed 23 January 2011].

Turner, D. 2011. 'Retailing & social media: Facebook still most popular'. 22 January; debbieturner.com.

Turkle, S. 2011. *Alone Together: Why We Expect More from Technology and Less from Each Other.* New York: Basic Books.

Willis, D.P. 2011. 'Social-networking websites helping job seekers find new work', 21 January; http://www.azcentral.com/business/articles/2011/01/21/20110212job-seekers-social-networking.html.

Wispa: http://www.wispa.com.au/social/.

Discussion

Class leaders might like to initiate discussion of the pros and cons of social networks. One suggestion is to form small groups of three or four people, preferably consisting of at least one person who does, and one who does not, use these networks. Age is likely to be a factor in this selection – assuming there is a fairly wide age range in the class – because overwhelmingly it is young people who are the most frequent and enthusiastic of users.

PARADIGMS AND PRACTICE: PERSONAL PERSPECTIVES ON EVER-SHIFTING 'TELEWORK' SANDS	Ron Goodenow

Introduction: Nomenclature and culture

Use of the internet to support workplace collaboration has both fascinated and supported me for many years. After several years as an academic historian with international interests, I was bitten by a technology bug that has enabled me to make a good living and have a very independent life since the late 1980s, working out of my home near Boston, Massachusetts, for and with some of the largest corporations, health systems, universities and government agencies in America.

This perspective shares my observations on a rapidly shifting world of work and technology, focusing on my work in healthcare and concluding with some observations on the global context.

In the early days the buzzword was usually 'telecommuting', a term which referred to workers who spent time in a home office rather than in a corporate building, keeping in touch with their corporate group via email. Recognising that this was not comprehensive enough to cover a range of collaborative, technical, training and other issues, my colleagues and I shifted to 'telework', a much more comprehensive, and in many ways challenging, paradigm that included telecommuting, but also collaborative document authoring and more.

Changes in collaborative work have been accompanied by, and enabled, changes in the culture of work, enhanced communication 'across cultures', and, I believe, gaps between 'haves' and 'have not' populations and organisations – some of which can be closed if technology is applied with care and social conscience.

In the early days of my experience one generally ran a pre-Windows personal desktop or laptop capable primarily of authoring messages and documents, which were sent either to primitive archive (such as the Digital Equipment Corporation's Notes system) or exchanged with colleagues via email. There were few if any operative conceptions of distributed work, telework or even telecommuting. There was no 'work at home' culture and, indeed, the idea of working for oneself as an independent contributor or consultant was a foreign one, more so in the UK than the USA in my experience.

Today my co-workers, virtually all of whom work from home and hotel rooms, and I, plan and implement research and instructional programmes, edit and exchange documents on line, build libraries for mutual access, put together and deliver webinars, share graphics and provide content to hundreds of end users at a time. We are recognised as a class of workers, whether independent contractors or employees, and in many organisations, the blending of workers from around the world is common, the main barriers very often being time zones.

Thanks to increased bandwidth, new communications technologies and acceptance of remote workers, I not only continue to do my work from a home office, but on speeding trains and remote pubs in the UK, airports, planes and even resorts in some pretty exotic places. If I'm not a 'teleworker' nobody is. I can not only 'cross cultures' in my daily work, but literally do so with ease. And, as a former academic interested in the interplay of theory, practice, barriers and logistics, I am fascinated by how my experience may parallel important shifts in how telework has changed with the nature of work itself. Surely a new nomenclature will come along.

A pilgrim's journey: University experiences

Back in the 1980s I became fascinated by the potential of the early university dial-in capabilities and, eventually, email ones. It all started when I directed a teacher training and research programme in the UK for Boston University, largely from my home in Connecticut. I supervised students and completed a book (Goodenow and Marsden, 2003) on urban education with a British colleague, dialling into his university's computer system and passing on messages to and from him and students in our somewhat experimental teachers' training programme.

We were helped by an individual 'point person' in Liverpool, who checked his mail several times a day and often printed out messages and put them in old-fashioned mail boxes. A handful of colleagues and I were both well in advance of most support staff, many of whom were just adjusting to electric typewriters – and more than a few academics mired in a yellow pencil habit born of years of secretarial assistance, habit and, yes, Luddism – opposition to technological change!

I concluded early on that this was a whole new world that had the potential to change not only how we work collaboratively, but how we might better serve 'customers', whether they be students or sick people in remote areas; for me it was an extension of personal values that included living a highly independent life and serving others.

This was before hotels had phone jacks, let alone wi-fi! My travelling tool kit included lists of hotels in New York City and Washington, DC, for example, from which I could send and receive email on academic trips. I always carried headphones for my computer modem to hold over a telephone headset, and clips to attach to phone lines, as well as a screwdriver to remove plates from phone jack areas, quite often with the help of a hotel employee.

In those days we were plagued by computer modems that were glacially slow (I once sent and received international messages at 150 baud), and so one could only send crude text messages via early email service providers (prone to crashing) or corporate systems that permitted dial-in. Indeed, the computers themselves, like my Radio Shack Model 100 (which provided backup via cassette recording that made very funny noises) and the first laptop Toshiba made, had limited memory and text-only ability.

I can still remember the day it became possible to dial into the *New York Times* and struggle through the day's news in plain text on a paragraph-by-paragraph basis at 1200 baud. Heaven that was!

One thing led to another, and I was attracted rather inevitably to the corporate world, where I was one of the first employees of the Digital Equipment Corporation, a huge computer company, to be given a laptop so I could collaborate with colleagues and customers (who had email) while travelling.

I was now a pioneer corporate telecommuter, in the nomenclature of the day. I also found that with the power of a large corporation behind me, I could not only realise my personal goal of independence, but begin to realise my objectives to provide new services to those who needed them. It took a long time for universities to marshall the power of technology I saw up close.

Early lessons learned: Intimacy, status, technical barriers

This capacity to take my work with me, and to keep in close contact with customers and the office, opened up a whole perspective. I persuaded Digital to let me set up a home office and then convinced Clark University, with the help of DEC, to let me develop courses on the social and organisational uses of the new technologies. This led to a course on the new internet and international relations and, using the university's VAX capabilities to store files and make them available to anyone with a password, build some of the first distance learning courses in the Northeast US, directing student research on my now favourite subjects thanks to the university's dial-in and email capabilities.

Right away I learned some good lessons. In terms of teaching I found that the ability to use new distance learning processes led to more intimacy than I would expect to get during office hours or standing in the back of the room after class.

I learned about student worries, fears, concerns about their skills. Questions which revealed weaknesses seemed more easily asked. And, of course, it made it easier to complain about some aspect of the class! In terms of student research, it opened the door to much better collaboration than I would expect using traditional methods. I remember answering research methodology questions from a student team while sitting at a terminal in a digital facility in the UK.

Our early research on manufacturing and healthcare environments showed that the introduction of computers and new communications capabilities shifted the balance of power in the office. The 'man in charge' worried that his secretary would have more control over the business, everyone recognising in a crude way that information is power and status relationships can be impacted by it. This was as true in a medical office as it was in a small manufacturing company.

At a faculty level I witnessed a lot of opposition to distance learning and, indeed, the use of new technologies such as overhead slide projectors; I remember worries about the influence of Xerox machines on teaching. Fears such as these were deadly problems, especially when compounded by a basic lack of knowledge about computers, quirky equipment and the failure of vendors to understand their customers and train them effectively. Such problems exist to this day. In the early days one was often either a 'non-believer' or a 'true believer', and was as true in medical schools as it was in small manufacturing companies.

This all said, there were many other barriers. The simple fact of the matter is that then, as now, there were huge pockets of resistance born of habit, lack of exposure to communications technology and, of course, poor communications infrastructure. These were important components of the cultural mix.

Campuses, medical schools and many companies were not wired, and before the World Wide Web and robust Windows and Mac programs, interfaces were unfriendly and slow – or often not interoperable or based on open standards – again a problem that persists today. High school and college 'computer' classes focused on programming, and not the use of technology for developing and communicating content and fostering interaction. In many educational and even corporate settings workers – professors, teachers, company officials – preferred to work unto themselves, eschewing 'teamwork' and the modes of collaboration much more common today.

With all this spinning through my mind I persuaded the Digital Equipment Corporation, which I had left as it downsized, to support a short-lived Telework Initiative for the University of New Hampshire, where I was able to work with Dr Elizabeth Christopher (www.ElizabethChristopher.net), who was visiting the university from Australia, and Professor Dennis Meadows (http://en.wikipedia.org/wiki/Dennis_Meadows#Biography), who directed its Institute for Policy and Social Science Research, which I had helped fund when I worked for DEC. These visionaries were experts on game theory, team training and other skills absolutely essential to pulling together a research and training agenda. We set our sights high, hoping to establish the first multidisciplinary research and training programme in the country.

Digital was moving into telecommuting, along with Xerox and some other major US companies, and the US General Services Administration was exploring it on a large scale for the ever-expanding federal workforce. The vision was to provide employees, many of who had to commute every day on increasingly clogged highways, a day or two working at home every week. Motives were, of course, mixed. Corporations were generally looking to cut down on facilities costs. The government's motives were related to facilities planning and utilisation little more complex. Some were related to getting cars off the road, creating more 'family friendly' work environments and looking at alternative ways to increase morale and productivity.

Our effort was disappointingly short-lived because Digital's funding dried up as the company headed for being bought out, and because in a small state like New Hampshire at a university just beginning to develop major research initiatives, capturing funds was so difficult – particularly on a subject as new as this odd thing called 'telework.' There were also pockets of suspicion, based in part on a fear that telework might lead to distance learning programmes that could threaten existing continuing and other education programmes.

We learned the important lesson that there can be enormous lags between where technology can take the workplace, and how well people understand both the technology and the road ahead.

Lessons from healthcare

My work in healthcare began when I was a Digital manager, coordinating a manufacturing technology programme at the University of South Carolina.

Thanks to some very exciting conversations with a medical school associate dean responsible for new programmes, I helped develop one of the first telemedicine programmes in the country, the technology for which permitted workplace collaboration between the university's medical school, urban hospital and remote rural clinic and its physicians. Digital images of fractured limbs and severe dermatological problems, the results of heart monitoring and other tests, could be sent immediately via T1 lines to a large hospital in Columbia, where physicians and medical professionals, such as radiologists, could consult with medical school faculty and offer televideo services to the small clinic, home of two general practitioners and a group of medical students being trained to work in rural areas.

This led to advising the US Government on the importance of research on the interactions, barriers and economics involved, and establishing requirements to include it in federal grant programmes. Like many 'tele' fields, telemedicine grew initially with promise based primarily on anecdotal evidence on the use of telephones, the development of prototype imaging equipment – all without a solid base of empirical research beyond some cost-savings research.

Shortly after I left Digital and the University of New Hampshire, I spent a year at the Centre for Operations Research at the Crummer Graduate School of Business at Rollins College, near Orlando. With the support of the telecommunications company Sprint we did a study demonstrating effective business models for a hospital system interested in providing remote diagnostic and other services to patients living in small towns. The kind of empirical lapses about which I worried were beginning to be addressed.

As in telecommuting, early telemedical pioneers were anxious to know about cost savings, and we learned that focused studies could demonstrate savings thanks to reduced nurse visits, drive time for patients and many other factors, which could also increase the quality of care.

I have provided healthcare IT research and training services since that time, funded by Compaq, IBM, Sun, Dell, Hewlett Packard and many other companies, and offer short-term consulting to several medical centres. In the United States it is fair to say that the provision of healthcare in the fifty states is driven more by market factors than national policy, which is playing 'catch-up' in terms of access, technology and standards. Anything that reduces costs while improving access and quality is attractive to providers, insurance companies and many professionals. It's where I put my stake.

The telemedical experience was quite interesting as a collaborative exercise. As a medical one it was plagued in part by legal, licensure and reimbursement issues that constrained investment and use. Installing T1 lines and other technologies was expensive, and there were few early studies on telemedicine's value. But more than this it was plagued by the overall suspicions of physicians who were, to put it bluntly, information technology-adverse, a problem that remains to this day as the US moves to electronic medical records and complex Health Information Exchange and other networks that will require tight online collaboration.

Some of this is age- and even gender-related. Much of it is because until very recently few medical schools introduced students to medical informatics and its value. Terms like 'workflow' were virtually unknown.

Telework, like many endeavours so influenced by technology, relies on gaps between organisational development, technological capabilities and individual attitudes to be closed. Nowhere is there clearer than in healthcare where status reigns supreme, doctors exercise great power and organisational culture is a myriad of interests influenced increasingly by contentious issues of healthcare reform and applied technology.

Of course, the 'virtual' world of collaborative work these days includes not only tools for working together, but social networks like Facebook, an endless variety of blogs, highly portable wireless devices, iPads, iPhones and much more. The use of all of these is exploding in healthcare and many other industries at a rate utterly unexpected five years ago. Today, in the US, and in other countries, pressures for uniform standards, paperless environments and paperless records are not only being driven by the need to cut costs and improve care, but by policies driven at federal and state levels made realisable by radical changes in technology.

Telework today includes human–machine interactions never possible, or dreamed of, in my early telecommuting days. The web, the cloud, incredible storage capabilities, new imaging technologies, interoperable hardware and software systems, and highly trained information officers are driving huge investments in infrastructure and enterprise growth. 'Workflow' is now a term with profound implication for the workplace.

My own observations lead me to the conclusion that regardless of how it is paid for, the new communications-rich environments in many countries are the same, particularly in healthcare.

Some conclusions: Globalisation and beyond

In his recent book, *Ghost Train to the Eastern Star* (2008), Paul Theroux describes a visit to a company in India that provides outsourced call centre customer services to American companies. Thousands of men and women are housed in huge rooms, the likes of which could be seen in the film *Slumdog Millionaire* (2008: http://www.imdb.com/title/tt1010048/). They are paid dirt-cheap wages in these post-industrial sweat shops, and as often as not they leave customers less than happy – because of poor phone connections, cultural differences that impact language usage or menus of items to be run through before any kind of diagnostic help can be provided. India is now under threat from Vietnam, the Philippines, China and other countries that can provide even cheaper labour.

There is resistance. Business customers of Dell Computer told the company to stop this outsourcing, and much of it has been cut back. Accepting a paradigm that these endeavours include close collaboration between workers and customers in many countries, what are the trends we need to watch? Are they truly 'collaborative' or do they simply take advantage of new communications technologies? Are long sessions in which call centre workers and customers work together to fix a problem 'collaborative'?

We are not just talking about providing services to people who have purchased computers and technology gadgets. The call centre for my bank is in the Philippines. Perhaps more to the point, large healthcare providers, under constant stress to save money, are sending medical images abroad to be studied. In turn, American hospital systems are making money by providing diagnostic and other services in cooperation with professionals on the ground in the Middle East, Africa, South America and, of course, Europe. Collaborative work of this nature not only pays bills, but it cuts down on travel and keeps US health systems from having to absorb actual bodies from abroad.

Questions

Goodenow concludes his personal account of teleworking with the following questions:

- What do we know about the actual transfer of collaborative technologies across cultures, and how do we look at this issue in comparative perspective? Who is copying whom? What new scholarship is needed, and how is it transferred to systems that are moving to new collaborative programmes?
- Are these technologies leading to improved services for the poor and underserved, or are they building new elites and concentrating services for the well-off?
- By looking at these issues comparatively, what are we learning about interpersonal relationships, the home lives of teleworkers, and the overall physical and mental health of these people? What is the impact of the new '24/7' work culture in various countries?
- Are we moving to a 'globalised' definition of telework? How does it take shape in different countries? Is a 'home work' culture, such as in the US, rising elsewhere, and what are its permutations?
- Do cross-cultural collaborative relationships build better networks, provide better services and improve cultural understanding?

Case study: Working from home

The Western Regional Office of The Guardian Life Insurance Company of America (Guardian) in Spokane, WA, with 635 employees, ran out of office space some years ago, yet continues to expand its workforce and increase productivity. Fifty top-notch claims approvers and customer service representatives – who are happy working full time from their homes – play leading roles in Guardian's success story. Despite an investment in hardware and telecommunication services, and the five months it took to plan a detailed telework programme from scratch, the response is the same from people at all levels within the company: 'It was worth it.'

The case of the Guardian illustrates that though in the past working from home has never quite lived up to the hype associated with it, things may be starting to change. One of the chief complaints that teleworkers make – that they miss all the chatter at the water cooler – is becoming redundant as enlightened firms allow employees to use social networks such as Facebook. Social networks enable remote workers to keep up with some of the office gossip and to link up with other people in their industry.

The Guardian's reasons for embracing telework were many – from space efficiency to increased productivity, to employee satisfaction and retention of top-performing employees. The first need was to assess the feasibility and cost of the required technology; then to determine selection, monitoring and workflow processes. Finally, the legal department had to approve the plan and develop an official teleworker agreement.

For the first two or three years, teleworkers were grouped together under one supervisor. Today, they are divided evenly between supervisors and attend weekly group meetings with in-office staff. They are required to visit the office two or three times a week to pick up work. They call 24 hours ahead to have their mail prepared, but may vary the time of the visit. Turnaround for processing claims averages four days, but of the total claims taken home, 95 per cent have a one-day turn around.

Guardian discovered that offering telework to top performers is motivational. Staff stay with the company longer, and employees from other departments sometimes request a transfer and step down in pay for the flexibility of telework. Guardian teleworkers are more willing and able to work overtime during peak periods, since they have more flexible hours and no regular commute. Another benefit is lower absenteeism. Outstanding results and satisfaction with telework voiced by all levels of employees within the organisation have encouraged Guardian to begin implementing similar programmes within select departments at other regional offices in the country.

In the UK there is also enough evidence that many people want to work from home. Phil Daoust, writing in the *Guardian* in August 2010, reported that banks, call centres, councils, management consultancies, software companies, law firms and PR agencies are among firms increasingly allowing their staff to work at home at least part-time. BT, the pioneer in Britain in the 1980s, employed 65,000 flexible workers in the summer of 2010, of whom 10,000 did not come in to the office.

According to the official Labour Force Survey, in the spring of 2009 there were 691,000 British home workers (working mainly in their own homes, using both a phone and a computer), up from 582,000 three years before. But those figures may be an underestimate. Even in 2008, a survey for the Confederation of British Business found 46 per cent of businesses allowing their staff to work from home, up from just 11 per cent in 2004. Melanie Pinola, who writes about home working for About.com, says the jobs that can be done remotely range from accountancy to telemarketing, via financial analysis, translation, data entry, graphic design, illustration, insurance, media buying, speech-writing, research, sales, travel agency, stockbroking, website design, writing and editing. Virtually any office job that requires computers and telecoms can be done remotely for at least part of the week. For example, nurses in a hospital have to be physically present when they're caring for patients, but they also do a lot of paperwork, which can be done anywhere.

In the UK, how does one join the home-working force? Parents with a child under 16, or 18 if disabled, have a head start. Employers are legally obliged at least to consider a request to work flexibly, which could include working from home for at least part of the week. They must also consider applications from employees who are caring for a friend or a family member. But even with nobody to look after, there are still forceful arguments to be made for teleworking.

Not only do home workers reduce the need for expensive premises, they are often vastly more productive. BT claims it gets an average of 20 per cent more work out of its 10,000. When the Automobile Association (AA) based some of its call-centre staff at home their productivity rose by more than a third. This may be due at least partly to cessation of the daily commute. Most of the time saved seems to go back into work. Teleworkers value their new way of working, and to protect it they do more work. Companies that offer flexible working find it easier to attract staff, and easier to hang on to them. At BT at least 97 per cent of women who take maternity leave come back to work afterwards, against a national average of about half that. Also there are bonuses for society. Home working encourages a more diverse labour force, bringing in not just carers but those who have difficulty travelling because they are disabled or live in remote locations.

Teleworking has also been promoted, particularly in the UK, as helping to reduce CO_2 emissions. According to the IT industry, teleworking has the potential to reduce global CO_2 emissions by as much as 260 million tonnes by 2020. BT claims that, in 2005, internal use of videoconferencing allowed it to save more than 54,000 tonnes of CO_2 by reducing the need for travel and face-to-face meetings. Similarly in 2010 Cisco reckoned it saved more than 47,000 tonnes of CO_2.

At first glance this seems to make sense. Moving electrons across the world is always going to require less energy than moving molecules, and for this reason countless governments have endorsed teleworking as a laudable environmental solution. The trouble is there's very little concrete evidence to back this up. Existing studies tend to be carried out internally by the companies promoting the technology, with little transparency about how the figures were derived. What's more, they often make rather bold assumptions. For example, they tend to focus on scenarios where employees telework full-time or spend only one day in the office. Many of the energy savings claimed come from businesses significantly reducing the size of their premises; and rail operators scaling back their services to reflect this absentee workforce.

These environmental savings evaporate if employees only work at home half the time or less, as do the arguments for smaller buildings and fewer trains. And in countries that operate efficient transport networks the potential benefits are reduced further. In fact even with pervasive adoption of teleworking, taking the optimistic scenario of 50 per cent of information employees working from home four days a week, countries like the US and Japan are predicted to make national energy savings of just 1 per cent. Currently, teleworking in the US is saving just 0.01 to 0.4 per cent, according to one study. With computers now already responsible for 2 per cent of global CO_2 emissions, videoconferencing software is likely to help drive up the existing 60 per cent annual increase in internet traffic.

This brings the argument to the rebound effects, where energy-saving strategies or technologies inadvertently lead to behaviour that increases energy usage. Not only has teleworking been found actually to increase travel for some workers – usually those who travel the most – but also there is a case that the availability of videoconferencing software has increased the number of meetings now held. Of the 120,000 videoconference meetings held by Cisco in 2005, only 20,000 actually replaced a physical journey, implying that the other 83 per cent wouldn't have taken place if the technology hadn't been there.

Other reasons for negative views of teleworking may be more human than technological. For example, it only suits certain types of occupation, so it can be seen by blue-collar workers as another perk for middle-class professionals. Unions have to be vigilant that taking work home does not become part of mainstream organisational culture: it is not easy to argue that people are being overworked if extra, non-contracted time is done at home. Another human problem is that since the industrial revolution a work environment is where people get together in the same place to work, and a manager stands there and watches what they do. If managers are now to be told they can't see what their workers are doing any more but you have to trust them to get on with the job, this can come as a culture shock. On the other hand, it may be something of a myth that managers have control over what their people do just because they sit in the same location: most managers sit in their offices and rarely interact with the rank and file.

Moreover in an office some people have the ability to look really busy when they are not. At home there is no point in pretending: people who work from home are judged by what they do. However, the logical accompaniment to home working is a more relaxed attitude to working hours.

Nevertheless for some people the office is important. It provides clear lines between work from home, a break from the family, colleagues to talk to and a creative environment. It probably is not for parents with a very young family and nowhere separate to work. It usually doesn't suit people who are in their early 20s and still living with their parents. Young people also want to get a social life out of their work life. And the over-55s whose children have left home or whose partner has died might well be happier back in the office. Thus though it has been technically possible for years for people to sit at home with a phone and a computer and work co-operatively with distant colleagues, comparatively few actually choose to do so.

The scheme is more appealing to employers, especially if they have high office rents. Camden Council in London has moved some workers to remote working. The borough covers not only increasingly fashionable Camden Town, but stretches through the West End almost to Covent Garden. Its town hall is in King's Cross, an area being targeted by developers. All this is very nice for the business rates but very expensive to expand into, so getting bodies out of buildings is an attractive proposition.

For some years Surrey County Council has been decentralising its workforce, setting up small regional offices into which any council employee can drop in and work. This has a number of advantages. Employees who don't want to commute across the county can work closer to home. And council taxpayers who have to arrange a meeting with an official can set it up at the nearest office and the official will come to them.

When the London borough of Enfield advertised posts with a teleworking option, it received 1,000 replies. One council that has taken the concept further than others is Sefton Metropolitan Borough Council, which won a commendation in BT's eWell-Being Awards for its teleworking pilot in 2002. Sefton, just north of Liverpool, set up 19 of its 3,000 office-based employees at home with laptops and workstations. The volunteers – from education, social services, housing, personnel, technical services and finance – were given training in time management, planning and priority setting, workflow management and health and safety. The European-funded project came out of a 'green initiative' to reduce traffic congestion.

Six of the 19 Sefton volunteers said it would be difficult to continue to work at home because of demands back at the office. On the other hand, the remaining 13 have continued to telework, describing it as a positive experience.

Where could this all end? An imaginary scenario would be to turn up at the office one day, only to be asked: 'What are you doing here, sitting around chatting and drinking coffee? You should be at home, working!'

Sources

Coles, M. 2002. 'Battle to survive on home front', *Guardian*, 14 September; http://www.guardian.co.uk/money/2002/sep/14/workandcareers.jobsandmoney2.

Daoust, P. 2010. 'The rise of home working', *Guardian*, 3 August; http://www.guardian.co.uk/money/2010/aug/03/rise-working-from-home.

Economic and Social Data Service 2009. SN 6200, *Quarterly Labour Force Survey, January–March 2009*: Special Licence Access; http://www.esds.ac.uk/findingData/snDescription.asp?sn=6200.

Graham-Rowe, D. 2009. 'Does teleworking really cut emissions?', *Guardian*, 12 June; http://www.guardian.co.uk/environment/blog/2009/jun/23/teleworking-carbon-emissions.

Guardian 2007. 'In praise of ... teleworking', 7 September; http://www.guardian.co.uk/commentisfree/2007/sep/07/money.workandcareers.

Guardian Life Assurance Company of America n.d. 'The Guardian Life Insurance Company of America: Telework'; http://www.commuterchallenge.org/cc/casestudies/cs_guardian.html.

Pinola, M. n.d. *About.com Guide*; http://mobileoffice.about.com/bio/Melanie-Pinola-74202.htm [accessed 24 January 2011].

Saunders, B. 2001. 'The inside track: teleworking', *Guardian*, 30 July; http://www.guardian.co.uk/money/2001/jul/30/careers.jobsadvice4.

To balance the case for working at home via media networks, the chapter should not end without reference to family networks in the workplace.

Mcjobs for all the family

In 2006 McDonald's began a trial of a 'family contract', which now allows husbands, wives, grandparents and children over 16 to job-share and swap shifts without notifying management.

McDonald's argument is that diversity not only values and respects individuals, but recognises that everyone has different needs. Under the contract, the first of its kind in Britain, each worker clocks on and is paid separately through their own bank account. It was tried first in six cities around Britain; it included cohabiting partners and same-sex partners and was later expanded to include friends and extended family such as cousins.

McDonald's Restaurants Limited has operated in the UK since 1974 and now has over 1,200 restaurants, employing some 67,000 people, half of whom are aged under 21. Managers say flexible working reduce the number of sick days; and that the scheme is supported by the Department of Trade and Industry.

In 2006 the first family to sign up for a Family Contract were Rita Cross, 42, and her two daughters Laura, 18, and Natalie, 16, in Cardiff. Laura said the main advantage of the arrangement was its flexibility. 'We get up in the morning and decide which of us really wants to go to work,' she said. 'We get a better work and life balance. I'd love my husband to join up too, so that we can all plan our work and family life as one unit.'

Sources

Diversityatwork.net (2005): http://www.diversityatwork.net/EN/en_case_005.htm; 05-02-2005.
Thomas, Dan (2006) 'McDonald's agrees shift-swapping contract', *Personnel Today*, 25 January; http://www.personneltoday.com/articles/2006/01/25/33606/mcdonalds-agrees-shift-swapping-contract.html.
Trembath, Brendan (2006) 'McDonald's introduces family contracts' ABC News, 27 January; http://www.abc.net.au/am/content/2006/s1556505.htm.

Questions

Would you prefer to work from home or in the social environment of a work-place? What reasons have you for your answer?

Conclusion

For the purposes of this chapter, professional, political and business networks have been defined as informal or formal linkages between groups to serve common interests, to exchanges ideas and resources, knowledge and expertise. The general conclusion from the material presented above is that when formal networks, such as joint ventures, fail (as most of them do), they do so for several major reasons. One is when irreconcilable differences arise between the respective organisations, their technological capabilities and individual attitudes towards these. Another is that international alliances have become 'immensely complex and chaotic' but also require cohesion and coherence; and often these prove impossible to impose.

Other reasons are failure to decentralise – to make organisational structures less hierarchical – in order to take advantage of the 'wisdom, experience, and expertise' of local people in partner countries; too much focus on the process of change rather than its outcomes; and failure to develop trusting relationships.

Electronic networks include social-networking websites such as LinkedIn, Facebook, Twitter and CarerBuilder.com. They are becoming increasingly popular as advertising sites and with job seekers. Their advantages and disadvantages have been discussed; and the main conclusion seems to be that because of the ubiquity of modern communication media there is a real danger in subscribing to all their values – implicit and explicit. In particular, the internet may be altering the way users think, making them less capable of digesting large and complex amounts of information; and that, effectively, social media isolate, rather than connect, their visitors. Moreover it remains debatable whether these new technologies do in fact lead to improved services for the poor and underprivileged or only for 'new elites'.

The final issues discussed in the chapter are the extent and implications of the change in work culture across the world, propelled electronically, by which more and more employees and private individuals can work from home rather than within institutional walls. Does this change herald a 'home work culture' in which less value is placed on individual privacy and right to leisure?

Key points

1. Business, political and organisational networks are relatively informal linkages between loosely connected groups to serve common interests or more formal arrangements such as partnerships, coalitions and joint ventures based on contractual agreements.

2. Networks are formed to exchange ideas and resources, including knowledge and expertise; and to provide linkages to potential collaborators and other stakeholders. Networks help organisations to keep up with advances in their fields, and give access to up-to-date information, especially through electronic linkages.

3. New organisational patterns are emerging worldwide that support collaboration, including networks of non-hierarchical relationships. The high rate of failure of joint ventures can be lowered if the parties are prepared to share personal and organisational power; to share resources, to work together across cultural divides and to develop trusting relationships.

4. Professional information is increasing on social-networking websites such as LinkedIn, Facebook and Twitter. The population of Facebook is well over 500 million, surpassing that of the USA. In view of this potential market, many firms now offer social-media marketing and management advice and software to job seekers, employment recruitment officers and advertising executives.

5. Social media applications (apps) include functions that allow users to access a wide range of information and media (social media integration); also the ability to create external user accounts that interact with Facebook or Twitter.

6. Fully transactional shopping is now possible through social networks, for example, Facebook (social-media marketing). This is designed primarily to appeal to young, aspiring consumers.

7. Some firms hesitate to use networking sites for fear of cyber crime such as spams and viruses; and many luxury brands still prefer traditional commerce and marketing channels for relative exclusivity and provision to offer customers an experience as well as goods. Video and photographic footage is sometimes used to provide a virtual experience.

8. Social media have been criticised by academics who argue that technology threatens real human interactions in a cyber-reality that is a poor imitation of the real world: that it undermines self-control, creates antisocial feelings and 'dumbs down' people's ability to understand large and complex amounts of

information. Defenders say online forums are just a different form of communication, but still communication.

9. Social networking is a new field that has yet to develop its own rules and etiquette.

10. There are many reasons why more firms are now arranging for some employees to work at home, full time or part time, including space efficiency need to increase productivity, to improve employee satisfaction and to retain top-performing employees. Not only do home workers reduce the need for expensive premises, they are often more productive. Enlightened firms allow home-based employees to use social networks such as Facebook to keep up with some of the office gossip and to link up with other people in their industry.

11. There is strong evidence that many people want to work from home at least part time. Virtually any office job that requires computers and telecoms can be done remotely for at least part of the week. Parents with small children, carers, people with disabilities and people who live in remote locations are particularly likely to prefer work at home. On the other hand, the sociability of a formal workplace is more attractive to many employees.

12. Teleworking only suits certain types of occupation, therefore it can be seen negatively by blue-collar workers as another perk for middle-class professionals; and unions are suspicious that taking work home might become part of the mainstream organisational culture. Managers may be unwilling to trust employees to work if not watched.

13. Teleworking has been promoted as helping to reduce CO_2 emissions, but so far there is little evidence that this is the case.

Looking ahead

Finally, the fourth dimension of communication across cultures: the dimension of space. The contributors to Chapter 9 listen to voices in cyberspace and read messages via mass media.

Experiential exercise

ALLIANCES: A game of negotiation

Players: Played in multiples of four groups, maximum 3 people in any group. Observers may be appointed to monitor the negotiations.

Time: 20–30 minutes, followed by discussion.

Materials: 10 counters or play-money for each group to represent financial capital; Group A: 3 cans of beans; Group B: 3 can openers; Group C: 3 bowls; Group D: 3 spoons.

Setting: All groups are free trade businesses. All groups want raw materials (beans), technology (to process the food), equipment (to eat it) and financial capital (to stay in business). All groups have only one of these resources.

Objectives

The objective of all players is to end the game with all four resources. Those who do, and with the most financial capital, win the game and get the prize.

Recommendations for further reading

Books

Cummings, T.G. and Worley, C.G. 2008. *Organization Development & Change.* Andover: Cengage Learning.

Haebeck, M.H., Kroger, F. and Trum, M.R. 2000. *After the Mergers: Seven Rules for Successful Post-Merger Integration.* New York: Prentice Hall.

Kessler, E.H. and Bailey, J.R. (eds) 2007. *Handbook of Organizational and Managerial Wisdom.* Thousand Oaks, CA: Sage.

Morgan, G. 1998. *Images of Organization, The Executive Edition.* San Francisco: Berrett-Koehler.

Scherer, A.G. 2008. *Handbook of Research on Global Corporate Citizenship.* Cheltenham: Edward Elgar Publishing.

Journals

California Management Review
Financial Times
Harvard Business Review

References

Alba, J., Hur, J. and Park, D. 2010 *Do Hub-and-Spoke Free Trade Agreements Increase Trade? A Panel Data Analysis*, ADB Working Paper Series on Regional Economic Integration No. 46, April: http://aric.adb.org.

Alexander, K. and Andenæs, M.T. 2008. *The World Trade Organization and Trade in Services.* Leiden: Brill.

Assael, H. 1998. *Consumer Behavior and Marketing Action.* Cincinnati, OH: South-Western College Publishers.

Capon, N. and Hulbert, J.M. 2007. *Managing Marketing in the Twenty-first Century.* Gillingham: Wessex Publishing.

Coon, D. and Mitterer, J.O. 2008. *Introduction to Psychology: Gateways to Mind and Behavior.* Andover: Cengage Learning.

De Benedictis, L., De Santis, R. and Vicarelli, C. 2005. 'Hub-and-spoke or else? Free trade agreements in the "enlarged" European Union'. *European Journal of Comparative Economics*, 2 (2), pp. 245–60; http://eaces.liuc.it.

De Chernatony, L., Druty, S. and Segal-Horn, S. 2003. 'Building a services brand: Stages, people and orientations'. *The Service Industries Journal*, 23, pp. 1–21.

Den Heyer, K. 2011. *Thinking Education through Alain Badiou.* Wiley/Google eBook.

Education International/Public Services International 2008. 'Session 5: The GATS and public services: Trading into or trading away the future?' 24 September, www.ei-ie.org.

Farrell, M.A. 2000. 'Developing a market-oriented learning organisation', *Australian Journal of Management*, 25 (2), pp. 201–23.

Friends of the Earth 2002. *GATS Primer: Understanding the WTO General Agreement on Trade in Services*, November; http://www.foe.co.uk/.

Goodenow, R.K. and Marsden, W. 2003. *The City and Education in Four Nations.* Cambridge: Cambridge University Press.

Gup, B.E. 1998 *Bank Failures in the Major Trading Countries of the World: Causes and Remedies.* Westport, CT: Greenwood.

Information for Action n.d. 'Globalisation: General Agreement on Trades in Services (GATS)'; http://www.informaction.org [accessed 16 November 2011].

Kotler, P., Cunningham, M.H. and Turner, R.E. 2001. *Marketing Management.* Toronto: Pearson Education Canada.

Lewis, R.D. 2005. *When Cultures Collide: Leading across Cultures: A Major New Edition of the Global Guide.* London: Nicholas Brealey.

Loudon, D.L. and Della Bitta, A.J. 1993. *Consumer Behavior: Concepts and Applications.* New York: McGraw-Hill.

Matzler, K., Sauerwein, E. and Heischmidt, K.A. 2003. 'Importance–performance analysis revisited: The role of the factor structure of customer satisfaction', *The Services Industries Journal*, 23 (2), pp. 112–29.

Money, R.B. 2010. 'The service hand-off: Effects of multivendor service performance on customer satisfaction. An experimental study'. *Journal of Services Marketing*, edition 3, 24 (3), pp. 184–95.

Murphy, W.H. 1999. 'Hofstede's national culture as a guide for sales practices across countries: The case of a MNC's sales practices in Australia and New Zealand'. *Australian Journal of Management*, 24 (1), pp. 37–58.

Rigby, D.K. et al. 2002. 'Avoid the four perils of CRM'. *Harvard Business Review*, 80 (2), pp. 101–9.

Ryals, L. and Knox, S. 2001. 'Cross-functional issues in the implementation of relationship marketing through CRM'. *European Management Journal*, 19 (5), pp. 534–42.

Schumann, J.H. 2009. *The Impact of Culture on Relationship Marketing in International Services: A Target Group-Specific Analysis in the Context of Banking Services.* Weisbaden: Gabler Verlag.

Teteryatnikova, M. 2008. 'Recent empirical evidence has shown that trade liberalization promotes innovation and productivity growth in individual firms', World Trade Organization, November, No: ERSD-2009-03; http://www.wto.org.

Theroux, P. 2008. *Ghost Train to the Eastern Star.* New York: Houghton Miffli).

Van Winter, J.A. 2007. 'The impact of selected cultural dimensions on international services vendor selection criteria: An exploratory investigation'. PhD thesis, George Washington University, ProQuest 3291992.

Xu, P. 2007. 'The effectiveness of business-to-business word-of-mouth marketing strategies'. PhD thesis, Purdue University, ProQuest, 33707385.

The Fourth Dimension: The Planet and Cyberspace

PART FOUR
The Fourth Dimension: The
Planet and Cyberspace

CHAPTER 9

Voices in Cyberspace: Messages by Mass Media

Elizabeth Christopher; Thomas Tufte; Anne Jerslev;
Thorbjörn Broddason; Kjartan Ólafsson

Objective of the chapter

To help students become more skilful and effective international communicators via digital media.

Chapter contents

- Outline of chapter
- Elizabeth Christopher: Flaming emails and sexy typefaces
- Questions
- Case study: Web power
- Discussion
- Questions
- Thomas Tufte: Citizenship, communication and *glocal* development in the digital era
- Discussion
- Questions
- Anne Jerslev: *X-Factor* audiences on the internet – affective performances
- Questions
- Case study: In response to *The X-Factor*: The sound of silence
- Questions
- Elizabeth Christopher: International conflict online and off
- Discussion and questions
- Thorbjörn Broddason and Kjartan Ólafsson: Youth and new media in Iceland
- Discussion and questions
- Case study: The Internet's cyber radicals: Young heroes of the web changing the world
- Discussion and questions
- Conclusion
- Key points
- Experiential exercises

■ Recommended reading
■ References

Outline of chapter

This final section of the book is concerned with the fourth dimension of communication across cultures – that of space. Thus the content of the book has grown and expanded from its origins in communication styles and contexts, through international alliances and networks, and now finally into messages by mass media.

Chapter 9 focuses on aspects of social change associated with the ever-increasing range of digital media communication. The people with whom corporate managers communicate include young and old; East and West, North and South; by cellular telephone, email, blog sites, social networks, online chat, teleconferences and videoconferences as well as good old-fashioned 'snail mail', landline phone calls and faxes.

All forms of organisational communication involve the transfer of information from one party to others. If recipients don't understand the meaning of the information conveyed by the senders, communication has not taken place. Hence corporate managers need a wide understanding of modern communication media if their messages are to be understood as they intend and need.

Therefore the chapter begins with brief introductory comments on the role of email in business transactions, on 'email etiquette' and the concept of 'flaming' in email correspondence. This section is followed appropriately by Thomas Tufte, writing on citizenship, communication and 'glocal' development in the digital era. His central theme is that ordinary citizens today have become leaders in communication-based strategies for change, yet have to battle a climate of fear that may be to a large extent illusory.

Then comes Anne Jerslev's report on the relationship between viewers and the television talent shows *The X-Factor* and *Dancing with the Stars* through a study of postings by viewers on a related Internet debate forum. She concludes that the content of internet postings is affected not only by writers' opinions of the show but also by the technological context of the online debate. This section of the chapter raises further questions on how interpretation of messages is affected by the medium through which they are transmitted. Jerslev's essay is followed by a report of a backlash against the ubiquity of *The X-Factor* in the form of a silent protest. There are lessons here for international managers on how to set up and control social networks within their organisations.

Thorbjörn Broddason and Kjartan Ólafsson argue that the introduction of digital media has already had a lasting impact on society and will continue to do so. Key factors in understanding modern society are the new ways in which people – particularly young people – engage with communication media and use them to interact with others. The findings of these researchers offer insights into the ways in which young people in particular use digital media, to the management of telecommunications in general and of education media.

The case study that follows continues the theme of young people's use of media with examples of young cyber rebels. Then Elizabeth Christopher discusses cultural factors in international conflicts as 'wars of words'.

Further discussion points, questions and case studies illustrate and expand all this material; and after a summary of the key points of the chapter some experiential exercises are suggested for the classroom; also Internet resources, a list of recommended reading for further study and chapter references.

FLAMING EMAILS AND SEXY TYPEFACES	Elizabeth Christopher

Emails

The advantages of electronic communication in business can be seen in small and large organisations alike. Sproull and Kiesler (1986) are two writers who studied the role of email in business as early as the mid-1980s, and the topic has been in debate ever since. Emails, conference calling, videoconferences and teleconferences all help to increase productivity and decrease costs. Small businesses use free online email services, their only costs being for computers and their Internet connection. There are savings also in postage, telephone bills and even travel expenses.

The speed of email allows businesses to work at a faster pace and communicate more easily. Almost real-time status updates help managers make more informed decisions. Information and ideas can be shared simultaneously between huge numbers of people up and down the organisational hierarchy over large geographic regions. Thus email plays a positive role by flattening organisational structures, allowing for greater information exchange between more people and enhancing socialisation. Businesses can answer customer questions quickly, which increases customer loyalty. Marketing and advertisements can be sent to selected customer lists or widespread groups of potential clients.

Email allows for more teamwork in problem-solving and business processes. Representatives from various departments and functional areas can collaborate without face-to-face meetings. Data transfer is rapid and more secure than by letters or faxes. Emails can create records in a safe environment and be easily backed up for future use.

However, email is not without its hazards, as the story, in Chapter 2 illustrates, of the accountant in New Zealand who emailed an instruction in upper case to all employees; and was sacked three months later, on the grounds that her email caused 'disharmony in the workplace'.

It is argued also that this form of communication invites conflict through depersonalisation that can lead to exchanges of hostile emails. Friedman & Currall (2003) and Landry (2000) are only two of many researchers who have studied this phenomenon in detail. Sending aggressive messages is often referred to as 'flaming', for example by Baruch (2005) and O'Sullivan and Flanagin (2003). The term first appeared in print in 1983 in Steele's *The Hackers Dictionary*, when it was defined as: 'to speak rapidly or incessantly on an uninteresting topic or with a patently ridiculous attitude' (1983: 63).

Since then a general agreement seems to have been reached that emails are 'flaming' if they are negative in tone. Examples include deliberate postings on Internet bulletin boards and to online groups with the intention of insulting the recipients or creating dissent. Internet flames are usually full of coarse language, personal insult and negative criticism, sarcasm, profanity and over-use of upper case or punctuation marks (excessive exclamation points or question marks). 'Emoticons' may be forms of 'flaming' such as smiley faces [:)], sad faces [:(] and acronyms such as LOL! [laughing out loud] and J/K [just kidding]. Extejt (1988: 63), for instance, warns against using all capital letters in any context, noting that it is 'the equivalent of screaming'.

One explanation for flaming is anonymity in Internet posting: those afraid to insult people in person are offered a degree of protection not afforded face to face. Researchers theorise also that email encourages uninhibited and aggressive communications because social norms exercise less influence in this medium. Landry (2000) is one scholar who believes that depersonalisation and lack of social cues create misunderstandings that can lead to flaming. Also, because emails are by nature less social than other forms of communication, people staring at computer screens in isolation can forget that other human beings are on the receiving end and send messages without thinking about the consequences.

The Internet has accorded enormous power to individuals to express themselves freely. Some researchers, Andersson and Pearson (1999), for example claim that as organisational cultures have become less formal, they have also become less civil, creating a situation where flaming may be more prevalent. Gonthier (2002) suggests that work alienation and environmental conditions lead to workplace incivility. The issue of flaming is therefore an important topic in organisational conflict, particularly since email has become a preferred medium for communication (Baruch, 2005; Hal Berghel's Digital Village, 1996; Friedman and Currall, 2003).

Turnage (2007) is one researcher who has studied emails as sources of organisational conflict. She wanted to find out whether flaming as described in the literature is in fact recognised as such by actual email users. She examined users' responses to a set of messages in relation to eight characteristics: hostility, aggression, intimidation, insults, offensive language or tone, uninhibited behaviour, sarcasm, and unfriendly tone. She chose those items because they are most consistently used to describe flaming in relevant literature.

The messages that the majority of the surveyed email users reported as 'flaming' included the following:

- 'Here's the deal with this stupid fucking thing. We want the bottom half to be white instead of gray and reduce the background words some. I will be so glad when this shit is over and done with!'
- 'I don't care. I just don't have time for this @&#$%! right now!'
- 'Now how in the hell would I know that if nobody tells me??? GEEZ! :0.'
- 'CAN YOU PLEASE GIVE ME THE FINAL ON THIS AND DO YOU KNOW WHO WAS TO SEND THIS OUT?????????????????????'

- 'Do these guys actually know what the curriculum is or are they making it up as we go along?'

In contrast, the messages that scored the lowest for flaming included the following:

- 'Hi, everyone. I need to get an update from you on each of your funded projects ASAP. What I'm looking for is any progress you can report on the projects. We're working on the annual report and we want to be able to include this information. Thanks!'
- 'Jan and I want to have a meeting on Friday morning at 10:30. Please plan on being there. And let me know ASAP if you can't make it. We want to do this on a weekly basis and this meeting is very important. Thanks.'
- 'Hi, folks. What happened to the news release for the department name change?'
- 'As it is now, it works well and it's really not necessary. Tell "them" that I said no.:)'
- "Sally … There is no posting of the RUL 01.25.1 – So the question is still moot.'
- 'Man! That's cheap for those awareness bracelets! And they don't have to pay for the deboss charge? Damn!'

The remaining messages scored in the middle of the scale:

- 'Damn! You're not a lot of help today, are you? JUST KIDDING. LOL!'
- 'WE NEED YOUR INPUT BY TOMORROW! PLEASE!'
- 'Shit! We need those umbrellas before that!'

Thus not all of the emails using profanity scored as flames; and the addition of softening words or phrases such as 'please' detracted from the aggression in capitalisation and exclamation points. Thus 'tone' seems to be important in determining whether an email is a flame.

Turnage's research indicated also that age and work experience could be a factor in how people perceive message and whether they consider a particular message to be a flame; there seemed to be no significant difference between men and women on whether they considered the items to be flames.

Turnage concludes that misunderstandings will always occur in email correspondence, regardless of how carefully the message is written. Most business messages are understood within the organisational framework, and if an email is misunderstood, it could be that cultural problems contribute to misunderstanding. In other words, the technology cannot take all the blame for angry email exchanges; it is merely the channel for this form of communication, with the potential for exacerbating aggressive behaviour by its characteristics of speed, synchronicity, reach and anonymity. Abuse of technology is not prevented by more technology but by more responsible use of the technology already in place.

Turnage advises that the best way to prevent flaming is to be as polite as possible over email or to speak to the other person face to face or via telephone to avoid any misunderstandings. Moreover lack of 'netiquette' (net etiquette) may cause people to misinterpret messages. Furthermore, Friedman and Currall (2003) claim that email can exacerbate conflict. They note that email becomes a much more dangerous tool once conflict has been created. For this reason, the medium should not be used to settle disputes or engage in arguments with another party. Those matters are better handled face to face.

Perhaps the best approach organisations can take is to create email training programmes for management and staff to establish rules of netiquette, such as never send messages that contain profanity; do not use all capital letters or excessive punctuation. If misunderstanding arises over meaning or intent of an email, the parties should not allow the debate to spiral out of control by meeting (perceived) insult with insult.

Writers should read over their emails before they click the 'send' or 'reply' command to ensure the message is politely neutral in tone. Cleary and Freeman (2005) advise emailers to avoid writing something in the heat of the moment that will be regretted when it is too late to retrieve it. Whether or not an email is considered to be a 'flame' the critical factor is whether it reads as hostile, aggressive, insulting or as in any way offensive.

Questions

1. What are the stylistic cues that suggest the following message is an example of 'flaming'?
   'Now how in the hell would I know that if nobody tells me??? GEEZ! :0.'

2. How might you rewrite the above to 'douse the flame'?

3. What 'flames' have you lit in the past?

4. What has the above suggested to you about 'email etiquette'?
   Imagine you are a departmental manager. Compose the wording of an email to be sent to all members of your department on 'email etiquette'. Compare your text with those of your fellow students.

Case study: Web power

On 12 July 2010 the *Guardian* newspaper reported that Justine Roberts' name had been included in MediaGuardian 100. For nearly ten years MediaGuardian 100 list has been the *Guardian*'s annual guide to the most powerful people in television, radio, newspapers, magazines, digital media, media business, advertising, marketing and public relations. Candidates are judged on three criteria: their cultural, economic and political influence in the UK. The objective is to 'snapshot' individuals who run or influence the UK media during the year.

As founding partner and chief executive of Mumsnet ('by parents for parents'), Justin Roberts was acclaimed for giving a voice to a section of the population that had previously struggled to be heard.

Ms Roberts is a former sports journalist. She created Mumsnet in early 2000 after a disastrous holiday with her one-year-old twins at a very non-child-friendly resort. Resentful that she hadn't known she was going to pay good money for being miserable, it occurred to her that the Internet would be a good place to swap this kind of information with other parents. She asked Carrie Longton, a TV producer and friend from antenatal classes, to help her set up a website.

In 2004 they produced a 15-part series for the Discovery Health channel called 'Mum's the Word'; and in 2008 the small firm Mumsnet Towers relocated from Ms Roberts' back bedroom to offices in London's Kentish Town. In 2009 it launched a series of parenting and lifestyle books, published by Bloomsbury. In March 2010 the firm celebrated its first ten years with a party at Google HQ. The site now has more than a million visitors each month. Its discussion forum, Mumsnet Talk, attracts around 25,000 posts every day.

Mumsnet Towers is staffed mostly by women working flexible hours, motivated by enthusiasm to make parents' lives easier. The firm is something of a social as well as a business enterprise. Its aim are to serve the community as much as its shareholders and to conduct business in an ethical manner. It supports the WHO/UNICEF International Code on the Marketing of Breast-milk Substitutes and doesn't accept advertising from a number of companies including Nestlé and McDonald's, or for products such as formula milk and cosmetic surgery that offend the firm's corporate philosophy.

Mumsnet describes itself as a community, not a lobby group. It is independently funded and has no particular political axe to grind – though members can be very active when roused. In July 2007 they caused the Madeleine McCann ad to be pulled from British cinemas, and after a much-publicised legal battle with Gina Ford they lobbied hard for a change to the Internet libel law. In April 2008 the firm began a campaign for improved health care for pregnant women who lost their babies through miscarriage; and drew up a Miscarriage Standard Code of Practice with 11 recommendations for improving standards of National Health Service care for women in this unhappy situation.

In January 2010 after an outcry and mass letter-writing campaign on Mumsnet the Outdoor Advertising Association pulled posters for a £1.25 million campaign that unwisely declared 'Career women make bad mothers'. In April 2010 the firm launched a 'Let Girls Be Girls' campaign, challenging retailers and manufacturers to pledge only to offer products that don't play upon, exploit, or emphasise children's sexuality.

Mumsnet's membership has been consulted by government on policy issues. Ms Roberts talked with Gordon Brown when he was prime minister on ways the government might best spread parenting advice. He cited Mumsnet as a 'great Internet organisation'.

During the 2010 general election campaign the Mumsnet website was courted by politicians from all three political parties eager to attract swinging voters from the upmarket, educated demographic that makes up a large proportion of Mumsnet's more than 1 million monthly users. Government officials were told to watch Mumsnet – not for nothing was it dubbed the 'Mumsnet election'.

Sources

MediaGuardian 100 2010. http://www.guardian.co.uk/media/2010/jul/12/justine-roberts-mediaguardian-100-2010.
http://www.mumsnet.com/.

Discussion

Information found on the Internet can come from any source and may not necessarily be assessed or reviewed before publishing. Also it may be heavily biased. One checklist for evaluation of any Internet document is known as AAOCC:

Authority
Accuracy
Objectivity
Currency
Coverage.

Expanding the keywords, the following questions can be asked:

Authority

- Does a statement of ownership appear on the document?
- Does the site provide contact details – at least a name and email address?
- Is it the official site of a company or organisation?
- Is there a copyright statement for the owner?
- What type of organisation does the URL domain name indicate for the site?
- What country does the site come from?

Accuracy

- Is there some way you can check the information provided? For instance, are sources given?
- Are there links or at least references to other sources given to verify its claims?

Objectivity

- What seems to be the motivation for publishing the information?
- Are both sides of any argument presented or is bias evident?
- Is advertising clearly differentiated from information?

Currency (how up to date is it?)

- Are there dates on the page to indicate when the page was written and last updated?
- Are there any other indications that the material is kept current?
- Is past material archived and easy to access?

Coverage

- Is the page completed, or is it still under construction?
- Is adequate detail given?
- How different is the web coverage from coverage in other media?

Questions

1. Do you use the Internet to exchange professional or academic information with friends, colleagues and others, or is your use of the Internet purely social?

2. When you research information from the Internet, how critical are you of the sources you find?

3. Do you have your own website? If so, what were your reasons for setting it up? If not, under what circumstances would you consider creating your own website? What do your answers suggest in general about the purpose of such sites?

4. Do you post messages on one or more online discussion forums? If so, what are your motivations for doing so?

5. Would you say you are a member of an online 'community'? If so, what do you feel you get out of it? If not, why do you think people might want to join these virtual communities?

CITIZENSHIP, COMMUNICATION AND *GLOCAL* DEVELOPMENT IN THE DIGITAL ERA	Thomas Tufte

The following is a revised version of a keynote address, given in Spanish, at the conference 'Comunicación y Desarrollo en la Era Digital' in Malaga, 3–5 February 2010.

Media development is both an extension of established practices *and* a new challenge to established social order by citizens who are not only receivers but participants and activists in communication-based strategies for change.

Manuel Castells (2009: 302) has stated that:

> ... *in a world marked by the rise of mass self-communication, social movements and insurgent politics have the chance to enter the public space from multiple sources. By using both horizontal communication networks and mainstream media to convey their images and messages, they increase their chances of enacting social and political change – even if they start from a subordinate position in institutional power, financial resources, or symbolic legitimacy.*

Civil society, social movements and non-government organisations (NGOs) in many countries have gained tremendous influence and space in recent years.

James Holston (2008) calls this movement 'insurgent citizenship'. Civil society organisations (CSOs) include NGOs, trade unions, faith-based organisations, indigenous peoples' movements, foundations and many others; examples include Action Aid; Friends of the Earth; Human Rights Watch; the International Trade Union Confederation (ITUC-CSI); the Institute of Harzrat Mohammad (SAW); Oxfam International; Save the Children; Transparency International; and World Vision.

Governments and decision-makers are the most common targets for CSO mobilisation. Members of CSOs orchestrate campaigns at all levels in transnational networks and with all forms of media. Increasingly they are playing decisive roles in enhancing social and political change. Social movements, individuals and civil society in all its diversity are making use of media platforms to articulate cyber protests and network activists, reclaim space in the public sphere and drive mediated political action.

This is happening not only in the developed countries but also, for example, in the African continent, in moves away from one-party to multi-party systems, emerging civil societies, and the gradually developing, increasingly free and independent media sector. In Tanzania, for instance, though only about 3 per cent of Tanzanians have access to the Internet at home, approximately 50 per cent today have mobile phones – an exponential growth in the last two to three years. Many African countries have furthermore experienced strong economic growth – it has been around 6 per cent per year in Tanzania for the last decade (World Bank, 2007).

A major constraint for poor people and citizens of low-income regions or countries like Tanzania is the lack of an effective voice in public life, and particularly in regard to decisions on policies and laws that directly affect the livelihood of young people. They have been – and are – severely affected by the HIV/AIDS pandemic and by high unemployment, leaving them marginalised. However, in recent years, youth have for good reasons become the new focus of development policies of states and inter-national donor agencies as well as among CSOs. Not only are youth perceived as key to economic, democratic and socio-cultural development but also as decisive agents in peace processes and political stability on a local and global scale.

In media use, the young are the innovators; they are the generation of actors and (future) citizens who are increasingly exposed to and make use of media/ICT, both for entertainment and informational purposes, for social networking and mobilisation, and for knowledge sharing. The recent years' mobile phone boom underlines the eagerness with which young Tanzanians, and Africans more broadly, seek to appropriate the new digital media, even under the constrained socio-economic conditions the majority of them face.

In this Tanzanian context one NGO has had particular success in developing a strong and influential media platform from which to preach empowerment and social change. It is the Femina Health Information Project (http://www.comminit.com/en/node/127975/304 [accessed 15 February 2011]), or Femina HIP, founded in 1999 as a health information project, servicing secondary school youth with a glossy magazine telling stories and providing information about sexual and reproductive health. The magazine, called FEMA today, is distinctive in the sense that it is very embedded in youth culture, in the topics it takes up, in the colloquial language used, in publishing primarily in Swahili and not English, and thus in many ways putting a strong effort into connecting with the life-world of the young.

While Femina HIP began as a health communication NGO, today it is engaged in many types of communication. A recent national survey showed that through its magazines, radio drama, 500 youth clubs in secondary schools, inter-active website, TV talk show, active use of mobile phones, and their community outreach programme it altogether exposes almost 25 per cent of Tanzania's 44 million citizens to its products. It is developing a Femina Facebook group and exploring other ways of incorporating the Internet, along with the booming mobile phone access, with their other and most important media and communi-cation vehicles: print, radio and TV.

Femina's media platforms constitute one of the strongest civil society-driven communication initiatives in the country. Its aims are ambitious: to stimulate open talk, critical thinking and social change that will foster healthy lifestyles and positive, responsible attitudes toward sexuality, HIV/AIDS and democratic culture. Many things point towards Femina achieving this, not the least of which is the interconnection between global, national and local discourses in its opera-tions. The director and other core staff of Femina HIP participate many times a year in international meetings abroad, interacting with other experts from bilateral donor organisations, UN agencies and NGOs.

Globalisation creates the conditions for localisation (Eriksen, 2005: 28). This interrelationship between the global and the local, given the name 'glocaliza-tion' by Roland Robertson (1995) offers a perspective from which to understand processes of change. James Holston, in his book *Insurgent Citizenship* (2008) refers to 'disjunctions of citizenship', reflecting critically upon the way democ-racy, conceived narrowly as electoral democracies, has swept the globe as a uni-versal norm for the organisation of decision-making in nation states.

However, Holston argues this kind of political focus fails to account ade-quately, if at all, for precisely the sort of disjunctions of citizenship prevalent in most emerging democracies: the coincidence of democratic politics with wide-spread violence and injustice against citizens.

This disjunction has become just as global a condition of contemporary democratisation as free elections (Holston, 2008: 311).

Development is no longer a process reserved for 'developing countries': all societies are developing as part of a global process, making the dichotomy of 'first' and 'third' worlds obsolete – at least in the geopolitical sense. The entire world is in transition, and development must therefore be rethought as a regional, tran-snational, global project. The *glocal* perspective and the notion of world develop-ment provide a relevant conceptual entry point.

Recognising the interdependency of peoples and nations, Bauman (2010) argues for the creation of a global equivalent of the 'social state', but not to rein-forcement of the UN or similar international governmental bodies. Rather, he argues that non-governmental bodies will take the lead in these processes. The problem, avers Bauman (2010: 65), is that 'the state is today unable, and/or unwilling, to promise its subjects existential security ("freedom from fear", as

Franklin D. Roosevelt famously phrased it)'. This leaves individuals, for example, the marginalised youth in Tanzania, the *favelados* in Brazilian mega-cities or the immigrants in the suburbs of Paris, to pursue life based on skills and resources of each individual on their own in situations of 'enormous risks, and suffering the harrowing uncertainty which such tasks inevitably include'.

In response to the failure of the state in many places, many non-governmental organisations have taken action, resulting in exponential growth in the number of NGOs and social movements in the world. This has become most manifest in the parallel NGO events at the large UN summits and G8 summits, but most significantly the large World Social Fora, starting in Porto Alegre in Brazil in 1999, assembling many thousands of civil society activists.

The World Social Fora have been gigantic encounters of NGOs and other civil society organisations to deal with lack of government response to glocal development challenges. They have established space for hundreds and thousands of small NGOs to meet, learn, speak out and bring new ideas back home to the local struggle for social and political change. The global network of civil society has evolved into large transnational advocacy networks, e-networking being an instrument alongside face-to-face encounters. They correspond to the rise of what the late British media sociologist Roger Silverstone called 'the rise of the mediapolis' (2007): a mediated public sphere where civic action and participation can grow.

Silverstone draws on the political philosopher Hannah Arendt (1958: 198) in determining the character of this space:

> *The polis, properly speaking, is not the city-state in its physical location: it is the organisation of the people as it arises out of acting and speaking together, and its true space lies between people living together for this purpose, no matter where they happen to be...*

Silverstone moves on to unfold some of the criteria of media hospitality, media justice and media ethics as morally based reference points, which can contribute to achieve a fully effective communication in the mediapolis. He regards this mediated public sphere as a dialogic space, which 'is both an encompassing global possibility and an expression of the world's empirical diversity'. He views people in the mediapolis as participants; and any form of participation involves agency.

Silverstone's concept of a 'mediapolis' illuminates the mediated public sphere in which citizens' everyday practices are both influenced and conditioned; but a fundamental human need for security explains the subjective position from which they speak and act, living in a risk society with prevalent cultures of fear and insecurity. Any theory of communication for social change is challenged to establish the bases for trust and emphatic communication.

The late British professor of global politics, Caroline Thomas (2007: 108–9), defines human security as:

> *... a condition of existence in which human dignity is realized, embracing not only physical safety but going beyond that to include meaningful participation in the life of the community, control over one's life ...*

This definition is broad. It connects both the material and non-material dimensions that help establish conditions of human security; to be free from domination and exploitation. Frank Füredi argues (2002) that many people currently are experiencing unprecedented levels of personal security; and the Spanish social scientist Jaume Curbet (2006: 8) suggests that 'more than deciphering the reality of insecurity, we (should) dedicate our energies to the search for security'.

His point relates well, for example, to HIV and AIDS communication and prevention. Many media initiatives have focused on delivering rather simple messages of hope that the HIV virus will not spread if people abstain from sexual encounters, remain faithful to one partner or use condoms. However, as research in Southern Africa has shown, there is a tremendous degree of insecurity expressed by young people in their ability to cope with HIV and AIDS in their own lives (Tufte et al., 2009). While the problem can be defined narrowly as a health issue, it is also so much more. HIV and AIDS is so entangled with poverty, culture, gender roles, power and spirituality that the epidemic cannot be prevented from spreading merely by providing solutions to the immediate physical mode of transmission of the virus.

Other examples of insecurity can be found in the sites where the majority of the world population today lives: the cities. Many have developed into 'non-places', as the French sociologist Marc Augé (1995) describes them: urban spaces filled with many people but with limited or no social interaction. A growing body of literature (Reguillo, 1996) – not least on the Latin American cities – explores cities where fear is prevalent owing to crime, violence or narco-traffic (Martinez et al., 2003), and where people struggle with deteriorating living conditions in increasingly segregated ghettoes. Jesus Martin-Barbero (2002) has also explored urban modernisation and what he calls 'a change in sensibility' in the Latin American cities. An intensified process of urbanisation, seen more recently in Africa than in Latin America, is producing some of the 'conditions of existence' Caroline Thomas speaks about (2007), where human *in*security is prevalent.

Social realities such as these provide an important context when exploring the rise, and proliferation, and social and political uses of new social media in times of human insecurity.

Curbet (2006) further distinguishes between *objective insecurity* and *citizen insecurity*. The first deals with material facts that generate insecurity, such as the likelihood of being infected with HIV, or fear owing to the prevalence of crime or violence in particular areas. The second concept, citizen insecurity, applies the insecurity of not knowing how to cope with intangible causes of fear – for example, with the existence of HIV in your community. It cannot be seen but it is there. Other examples of citizen insecurity include fear of unemployment, natural disasters or of not being able to afford healthcare. These feelings are not less real than fear of tangible danger, but are usually more difficult to explain and resolve. Again, exploring the relation between social uses of new social media and the articulation of citizen insecurity constitutes an interesting emerging research agenda in developing countries.

Awareness of human need for security raises questions on how global, national and local structures and forces interrelate and what will be their cumulative impact on individuals and communities. Therefore research from a human security approach should be a strong call to understand in depth the conditions of existence of civil society-driven media and communication initiatives. Such research also would place new social media in particular contexts where focus is on need for deep social change and, not least, for governance to address the identified insecurities.

Human security, in addition to framing a policy agenda for communication research, also reveals the difficulty and complexity of the task of communicating for social change. Attention is drawn to the lived experience of globalisation, especially the lived experience of the most marginalised – those who are excluded, as Caroline Thomas argues, from 'international production'.

In summary, three conceptual clusters seems to emerge as central in the exploration of communication and development in the digital era. These are:

Human security and how it relates to both material and immaterial conditions of existence, and thereby is deeply connected to questions of identity, community and subjectivity.

Mediapolis, conceived as a mediated public sphere, a space that hosts both possibilities and limitations for the cultivation of civic action and participation. It includes the flows of media and communication practices.

Citizenship, which means not just a set of rights and responsibilities bestowed by the state, but is rather (drawing on ideas by political sociologist, educator and civil society practitioner John Gaventa (www.ids.ac.uk/idsperson/john-gaventa)) a multi-dimensional concept, which includes the agencies, identities and actions of people themselves (Tufte et al., 2009: 14–15); hence James Holston's concept of insurgent citizenships as way to conceptualise people's actions.

From these three entry points, a series of other questions emerge. First, whether the digital era is qualitatively different from former times. There is argument for the co-evolution of old and new media, but at the same time there is need to recognise the unique potential of the network society – as Castells (2009: 303) puts it: 'the potential synergy between the rise of mass self-communication and the autonomous capacity of civil societies around the world'.

Zygmunt Bauman (2010: 166) states that

Paradoxically, the widening of ... opportunities (for)... ready-made 'like minds' ... narrows and impoverishes, instead of augmenting and enriching, the social skills of the seekers after the 'virtual community of minds'.

In other words, while some new social and political dynamics have arisen with the coming of the new social media, they don't necessarily represent a communication practice that Roger Silverstone advocates for a mediapolis: that of recognising cultural (and social) differences. By Bauman's argument the new social media are not articulating new social relations, rather just reinforcing the old.

In times of a networked society, with interconnected world development processes and global human security issues, the first and the third world distinctions are rendered obsolete, as are many other conceptual dichotomies. Rather, there may be a three-dimensional dynamic interrelationship between human security, the mediapolis and citizenship to explore how communication for social change – both offline and online – is enacted in the real world.

Discussion

The 'risk society' is a term that emerged during the 1990s to describe how people respond to, experience and think about risk as part of their everyday lives and how modern societies are organised in response to perceptions of risk.

Anthony Giddens and Ulrich Beck are two key writers in the field. According to sociologist Giddens (1990a and b), a risk society is one that is increasingly pre-occupied with the future, and this generates the notion of risk. German sociologist Ulrich Beck (1992) defines it as a systematic way of dealing with hazards and insecurities induced and introduced by modernisation itself. These authors argue that while humans have always been subjected to a level of risk – such as natural disasters – these have usually been perceived as produced by non-human forces. Modern societies, however, are exposed to risks such as pollution, newly discovered illnesses, crime, that are the result of the modernisation process itself.

Frank Füredi (2002) agrees that fear has become an ever-expanding part of life in the twenty-first century: fear of disease, abuse, stranger danger, environmental devastation and terrorist onslaught. However, compared to the past, or to the developing world, people in contemporary Western societies enjoy an unprecedented level of personal safety. He suggests, for example, that what happened on September 11, 2001 with the destruction of the World Trade Centre in many ways represented the destructive side of human passions, whereas the tendency in modern developed societies is to panic about the side effects of constructive progress such as genetically engineered food, genetic research and the health dangers of mobile phones.

He argues that facts often fail to support these scare stories. Rather it is an obsession with theoretical risks that is in danger of distracting people from old-fashioned dangers that have always threatened their lives.

Adam Curtis argued, in a 2004 BBC documentary film series, *The Power of Nightmares* (subtitled *The rise of the politics of fear*), that politicians have used people's fears to increase their power and control over society. He looked at the US neo-conservative movement and its depiction of the threat first from the Soviet Union and then from radical Islamists; and insisted there has been a largely illusory fear of terrorism in the West since the September 11 attacks, and that politicians such as George W. Bush and Tony Blair had stumbled on a new force to restore their power and authority: using the fear of an organised 'web of evil' from which they could protect their people. Curtis's film castigated the media, security forces and the Bush administration for expanding their power in this way.

Thus there are a number of examples in the literature to illustrate Tufte's dual theme of citizens as the new leaders of social change, yet constrained and handi-capped by a larger social climate of fear that may be to a large extent illusory, created by political propaganda for purposes of control.

Sources

Beck, U. 1992. *Risk Society: Towards a New Modernity.* London: Sage.

Curtis, A. 2005. [writer, producer and narrator], *The Power of Nightmares*; http://news.bbc.co.uk/2/hi/programmes/4202741.stm.

Farrell, J.M. and Hoon, A. 2009. 'What's your company's risk culture?', *Business Week*, 12 May; http://www.businessweek.com/managing/content/may2009/ca20090512_720476.htm.

Frey, R.S., McCormick, S. and Rosa, E.A. 2007. 'The sociology of risk'. In C.D. Bryant and D. Peck (eds), *The Handbook of 21st Century Sociology.* Thousand Oaks, CA: Sage.

Füredi, F. 2002. *Culture of Fear: Risk-Taking and the Morality of Low Expectation.* London: Continuum.

Giddens, A. 1999a. 'Risk and responsibility'. *Modern Law Review*, 62 (1), pp. 1–10.

—— 1999b. *Runaway World: How Globalization is Reshaping Our Lives.* London: Profile.

Tulloch, J. and Lupton, D. 2003. *Risk and Everyday Life.* London: Sage.

Questions

1. What is your response to the suggestion that inflated terror threats may be fabricated and used by politicians for their own ends?

2. Do you believe the modern world is filled with more fear than in times past? Can you give some examples to support your answer?

3. Do you feel empowered by your ability to broadcast your ideas, beliefs and opinions worldwide via social networks? Again, can you provide some examples?

X-FACTOR AUDIENCES ON THE INTERNET – AFFECTIVE PERFORMANCES	ANNE JERSLEV

Based on a report to the 'Transforming Audiences 2' conference, University of Westminster, London, 3–4 September 2009, the study was part of a collaborative project on TV entertainment, funded by the Danish Council for the Humanities. It deals with the relationship between viewers and the television talent shows *The X-Factor* and *Dancing with the Stars*. Analysis suggests that data from Internet debate forums cannot be compared altogether with those collected in interviews because it appears that watching a 'live' television show consists of more than understanding its content: the content of Internet postings is affected not only by the writers' opinions of the show but also by the technological context of the online debate.

The X Factor is a television talent show franchise, a singing competition, origi-nating in the UK and now held in various countries. Contestants are aspiring pop singers drawn from public auditions. The prize is usually a recording contract (in addition to the publicity that the show generates not only for the winner but also for other highly ranked contestants).

Dancing with the Stars is the name of several international television series based on the format of the British TV series *Strictly Come Dancing*, distributed by BBC Worldwide, the commercial arm of the BBC. Currently the format has been licensed to more than thirty countries, with Australia the first country to adapt it.

Exchanges of opinion about *The X-Factor*, on a related Internet debate forum, were studied (though *debate* is hardly the term for a mixture of discussion and quarrel). Overall it was observed that postings continually questioned and discussed the relationship between viewers, judges, and participants, mostly within a framework of moral conduct.

Analysis was based on postings on two evenings, during and immediately after the second audition and live shows respectively (altogether around 1,000 postings and 350 threads). On these occasions debate was particularly intense. On the first of the chosen dates postings can be divided into three topics:

1. The judges: in particular Judge Thomas Blachman's behaviour towards contestants (he was the Danish 'bad guy' judge);
2. Whether contestants should be assumed to know the rules of the game they had voluntarily entered;
3. The judges' evaluations of contestants.

It is interesting to note that the two first topics were of such interest that they continued to be as eagerly discussed five programmes later.

In addition, writers declared their preferred acts and whom they wanted to win; and debated the judges' reliability. Overall, debates were whether Blachman should be regarded as a hero because of his honesty or a villain because of his rude behaviour; whether participants are manipulated and ridiculed victims, or responsible agents who had voluntarily chosen to appear on the show; and who should win and who should be voted out.

Thus audience debate was about behaviour; primarily of judges and participants in the programme but also about the proper tone of voice and how to – or whether to – communicate decently. Debate was also about the rules of the game: whether the voting procedure is just, whether or not the week's elimination was justified by the quality of the acts, and whether or not the programme's invitation to viewer participation was, in effect, a swindle.

After the second audition show – and because the judges' final decision seemed extremely unjust to a large number of viewers – there was heated debate about power relations between the programme and the viewers: for example, how much power does a talent show have the right to exert? Are viewers real participants? Does voting matter at all?

Online contributors *to The X-Factor* debate forum voice their opinions not only on the social conduct of the show's participants but also on the conduct of media institutions in general. Postings demonstrate clearly that, to the discussants, relations between media institutions, media programmes and viewers are not simple givens. The forum constitutes an affective environment where the contributors' relatedness to the programme (Zillmann and Vorderer, 2000) is through three media:

■ Opinions expressed directly by the show's judges (primarily by the 'bad guy' judge);

- Opinions expressed by members of the Internet debate community in general ('us');
- Responses to opinions expressed in prior postings.

In Internet debate forums of this kind, which resemble newsgroups, comments are often emotionally tense and committed. Hence part of the debate/discussion might more precisely be called quarrelling. Capital letters and exclamation marks emphasise strong moral opinions and create a sense of presence and simultaneity. These markers constitute also a process of taking turns in discussion. Visitors cannot enter the forum and say nothing; posting an opinion is an action, an intimation that they are there and ready to participate.

It can be argued that Internet debate – where comments are posted almost simultaneously with the broadcasting of the programme – does not only *present* audience's meanings (i.e., record them faithfully) but also *represents* them (i.e., interprets them via audiences' use of the medium). Internet debate forum discussions are a particular kind of 'talk' formed by context, medium, technology and the genre to which *The X-Factor* belongs.

For example, a recurrent opinion voiced *on The X-Factor* forum is that diversity of opinions is 'a good thing'. The effect of these repetitions is to evoke individualistic responses in Internet postings. It supports opinion as a form of rhetorical strategy in newsgroups in general (Hine, 2000) by which 'agreeing with a posting is not enough to justify posting a message saying that you agree' (ibid.: 125).

This strategy results in frequent quarrels. According to philosopher and rhetorician Douglas Walton (Walton et al., 2008), this kind of adversarial and non-collaborative debate is defined rhetorically by a high degree of irrelevant argument (often jumping from one incident to another, apparently unrelated), attacks on others' characters and competence, insults, maledictions and ridicule. These quarrels may not only be regarded as affective outbursts over whatever the debate is about; but also as formal rhetorical claims of the right of the writers to contribute to the debate. According to Christine Hine (2000: 125):

> *agreeing with a posting is not enough to justify posting a message saying that you agree (on the contrary) disagreeing with a message is seen as a justification for the author to post.*

Disagreement is often easier than agreeing with the previous post, and is adding something further to the discussion. It shows how this particular communication technology shapes the way audiences discuss and thus make meaning of the programme.

The data from *The X-Factor* Internet forum in this study may challenge both the idea of 'meaning' and 'the real world'. There is an implied difference between 'the real world' (where viewing actually takes place) and interviews about what happened there. There is no information in the forum about the actual viewing of the show by the contributors, just their opinions about it; but there are some contributions that indicate the act of posting an opinion might be embedded in the reception process (i.e., how posters perceived the show). The postings have immediacy and a sense of nearness to the programme and its participants. Most of the writers entered the forum either right after the programme finished or even during it.

This observation justifies the assertion that the data are something other than reports of a viewing. They can be conceptualised as a part or extension of the actual viewing; or at least as a means of extending the affective output from watching the programme. If so, there is no 'real world' different from the meaning-making world – watching and debating are part of the same process.

Thus the Internet debate shows how members do more than make meaning out of the actual TV shows. No matter the constraints of the Internet genre the debates show that *The X-Factor* triggers important discussions about conduct and thus contribute to the viewers' negotiations and coming to terms with everyday moralities. This is probably a large part of the show's entertainment value: the programme (one of the genre of talent shows) invites subjective and moral reactions that do not oblige or call for rational factual arguments as justification and may thus boost pleasant feelings of autonomy in the viewer (Zillmann and Vorderer, 2000).

Consequently even though the postings, on the whole, voice moral opinions and thus are concerned with making meaning of the show, and even though many postings are extremely heated, as a collection they may be regarded as something more. These Internet dialogues may be seen as actions intended to prolong or repeat an affective experience, namely the pleasurable experience of being entertained.

Cognitive psychologists Bryant and Miron (2002) regard entertainment as a media effect and argue that it is:

> *The primary effect that is sought and pursued for the benefits that it entails – benefits such as being distracted from acute grievances, having boredom removed, being cheered up, being given great excitement, being helped to calm down, or being fed pacifying messages.*

Therefore perhaps posting messages on the Internet after watching *The X-Factor* is not only about making meaning but also about voicing opinions for the mere joy of being permitted to do so without someone demanding an ensuing argument. Watching *The X-Factor* and debating it on the Onternet are about mood and affective states, about entertainment as a sought-after effect: and this is exactly what the debate forum allows as an Internet genre.

In conclusion: as empirical evidence of audience reception, data from the Internet debate forum may not answer some questions research interviews can ask; but it can indicate that watching a 'live' television show consists of much more than understanding its content.

Questions

Online discussion postings demonstrate clearly that, to the discussants, relations between media institutions, media programmes and viewers are not simple givens.

Do you watch 'reality TV'? If so, do you take part in related online discussion forums? If you do not, then maybe others in the class do so and you can listen to their debate, and comment on it. The question for discussion is whether or not you/they agree that 'watching a "live" television show consists of much more than understanding its content'.

In what ways do viewers 'engage' with shows of this kind? Do they identify with the contestants? With the judges? In what ways?

The objective of the enquiry is to 'listen to voices in cyberspace'; to learn why viewers post messages on the Internet after watching shows such as *The X-Factor*.

Do you agree that 'visitors cannot enter the forum and say nothing; posting an opinion is an action, an intimation that they are there and ready to participate'?

Do viewers write objectively to discuss the show, or subjectively to express their opinions and feelings, or both? Does cyberspace evoke individualistic responses in Internet postings and thereby offer a particular kind of freedom in crossing communication boundaries?

What does this study suggest for managing communication across cultures? (Hint: think in terms of organisational communication: for example, internal discussion forums to gauge or reduce employee resistance to change.)

Case study: In response to *The X-Factor*: The sound of silence

On a *Guardian* (UK) blogsite on 13 December 2010 Luke Bainbridge posted a message headlined 'Why I'm backing Cage Against the Machine for Christmas No 1', claiming that

You can hate The X-Factor's *chart dominance without hating pop, which is why I'm backing these Cage fighters to bring some silence to the festive top spot.*

His posting provides an entertaining example of silence as communication. He described how a group of musicians had recorded a charity single to compete against *X-Factor* winner Matt Cardle in the charts for Christmas No. 1. The musicians, including the Kooks, Orbital, Enter Shikari, Dan Le Sac, Scroobius Pip, Suggs from Madness, and (by phone) Billy Bragg and Imogen Heap, 'recorded' a cover of John Cage's '4'33', consisting of 4 minutes and 33 seconds of silence. They called it 'Cage Against the Machine', after the success in 2009 of 'Rage Against the Machine', and theirs was a silent protest against Simon Cowell's monopoly of the singles chart. Bainbridge wrote that given the 'suffocating near omnipresence of *The X-Factor*' this silent protest seems a fitting response.

He went on to defend his dislike of *The X Factor* as not being distaste for pop music in general but of 'Cowell's creation'. He wrote that *The X-Factor*'s stranglehold extends 'from the tabloids to the *Guardian*, from Twitter to Facebook'; and that avoiding being 'sucked into Cowell's world' is becoming increasingly difficult: hence his wish for 'a silent night this Christmas'.

His reference to 'Cowell's world' was in conjunction with other media stories of Simon Cowell's success as creator of *The X-Factor*. Jo Adetunji, for instance, writing in the *Guardian* on Sunday 12 December 2010, commented that the four *X-Factor* finalists – Cher Lloyd, One Direction, Rebecca Ferguson and Matt Cardle – were fierce rivals for the 2010 title but the victor and the three runners-up could all score lucrative deals.

Cardle emerged as the winner of the contest but, as Adetunji pointed out, the real winner was Cowell himself, since the personal stock held by the music mogul and show creator had risen by £40 million to £165 million since 2009. While Cardle's £1 million contract might sound large, by contrast Cowell has seen his coffers overflow, with plans for a US version of the show imminent and a nationwide *X-Factor* live UK tour kicking off in February 2011. The winners and runners-up of the previous two series were both snapped up by Sony Music, which also owns Cowell's own label, Syco Music.

However, while Cowell's *X-Factor* earnings keep growing, so does the backlash. One winner, Joe McElderry, failed to top the 2009 Christmas singles chart after hundreds of thousands of fans, driven by an anti-Cowell Facebook campaign, bought the expletive-heavy 'Killing in the Name' by Rage Against the Machine instead. In 2010 *The X-Factor*'s chart dominance is challenged by a number of comedy spin-off campaigns. Cowell may have the Midas touch of gold; but maybe silence is even more golden.

Questions

The case offers two linked examples of the power of silence as a mass communication medium to effect change: the recording of a silent music single; and a Facebook-driven boycott of an *X-Factor* single – both in protest against the commercialisation of popular music. Can you see any implications here for organisational communication? For example, how might the tactics of silence and silent protest be used to effect organisational change?

INTERNATIONAL CONFLICT ONLINE AND OFF	Elizabeth Christopher

BBC News reported on 28 November 2010 that the 'whistle-blower' website Wikileaks feared a hacking attack prior to its release of secret US documents; but the founder of the website, Julian Assange, boasted that that a number of newspapers – including Spain's *El Pais*, France's *Le Monde*, Germany's *Spiegel*, the UK's *Guardian* and the *New York Times* – would publish details of the US embassy cables even if the website were to go down.

The conflict was over Wikileaks' proposal to release classified messages sent by US embassies, accompanied by a warning that this next release of documents would be nearly seven times larger than the nearly 400,000 Pentagon documents relating to the Iraq war it had published in October. Wikileaks argued the messages shed light on the wars in Afghanistan and Iraq, in particular allegations of torture by Iraqi forces and reports that suggested 15,000 additional civilian deaths in Iraq to those officially reported.

This latest leak was understood to include US dealings with, and diplomats' confidential views on, Australia, Britain (apparently including an unflattering US assessment of UK Prime Minister David Cameron), Canada, Israel, Russia and Turkey, among others. Assange told reporters that the material covered 'essentially every major issue in every country in the world'.

In their war of words the US State Department threatened Assange, urging him not to release the documents because to do so would be against US law and would put 'countless' lives at risk – from journalists to human rights activists and bloggers – and imperil US military operations. Assange apparently asked in return for details of individuals who would be in danger as a result of the leak and offered to negotiate over some limits to the releases. However, the US State Department's legal adviser Harold Koh insisted that Wikileaks return official documents to the US Government before any such negotiations could begin.

The language of conflict

The intransigent attitude of the US Government, as reported in this news item above, is a reminder of another of its 'war of words' in which the same non-negotiable approach led to a great deal of international turmoil. The case concerned a quarrel between China and the US in 2001 over the fate of a US spy plane grounded by the Chinese. China demanded a US government apology while the Americans insisted on immediate release of the aircraft and its crew (Phatak et al., 2005).

The Chinese claimed that the US had clearly broken international law, and wanted the US Government to admit responsibility for intrusion into their airspace by US surveillance flights. Such flights are relatively normal in international relations. During the Cold War it was very common for the Russians to fly surveillance flights along the coast of the UK, and the RAF would intercept them. Today in the Middle East surveillance planes from the US, Iraq and Iran regularly patrol the skies over the Gulf. In January 2010 Australian Prime Minister Julia Gillard criticised the Japanese Government for hiring Australian aircraft to track the activities of anti-whaling protesters after light planes went out from Western Australia and Tasmania to locate 'Sea Shepherd' protest vessels on the high seas (AAP, 2010).

But what appears, at least on the surface, to have happened in 2001 was that interception (by the Chinese of a US spy plane) went wrong. A pilot on one side or the other made a serious mistake, the two planes collided and the accident caused an international crisis. China's argument was that its plane was carrying out routine monitoring, shadowing the US aircraft, when the American pilot veered into the path of the Chinese plane, causing the death of the Chinese pilot, loss of the Chinese plane and an emergency landing of the US plane. The US Government representatives said it was the other way round.

The Chinese expressed genuine anger and concern over the event in which they saw themselves as victims. A Chinese airman was missing, presumed dead – a man with a wife and 6-year-old child. These were emotive issues, and if it had been the other way round and a US airman had been killed, no doubt people in the US would be very upset over it. The Chinese wanted an apology while the US Government insisted no wrong had been done; but cultural differences were crucial to the way the stand-off grew into something bigger. The disaster seemed on the surface to be nothing to fight over: it was an accident; but the Chinese leaders were furious at the way that the then new Bush administration in Washington dealt with its aftermath.

On the Sunday after it happened and on the Monday, the second day, US Government statements were strongly worded: you must release our crew – this is an accident, we are not going to admit fault; we are not wrong. In China that was perceived as arrogant, unsympathetic and completely undiplomatic: the US Government should show some sympathy and some regret. Peace-making efforts could have – should have – been made quietly behind the scenes; perhaps a phone call from President Bush or even somebody not quite so senior, but at least quietly contacting the Chinese and saying, look, how should we deal with this? We don't want this to get out of control.

Instead the US Government made very strong demands of China: and that may be one reason why China decided to dig in its heels and say; no, we are not going to release this crew until we get a proper apology and an admission of responsibility for a provocative act. However the US Pacific Command insisted their plane was on a routine mission.

This Washington–Beijing standoff over the downed US spy plane involved differences in interpretation of the words 'regret', 'sorrow' and 'apology' – and provides an illustration of the complications of cross-cultural communication. Language is perhaps the biggest problem. Even the best translations can fail when trying to interpret phrases and concepts that have little cultural equivalent. Americans may be particularly at risk of making mistakes because, for many of them, getting to the point is more important than choosing words carefully. The culture is one of 'low-context', to quote Edward T. Hall (1959), in which what people say is more important than how they say it.

In some cases cultural gaffes by US nationals can be dismissed as the funny mistakes of foreigners, but at other times they can be infuriating – particularly when those who offend blame those who are offended. One classic example was the US explanation for why the Chevy Nova automobile sales campaign flopped in Latin America. The word was put out that the locals wouldn't buy the car because 'no va' means 'it doesn't go' in Spanish. In fact Spanish-speaking people are not likely to read 'nova' (which means 'star' in Spanish) as 'no va', any more than native English speakers are likely to read 'therapist' as 'the rapist'. The truth is more likely to have been it wasn't a very good car.

A similar comment can be made about a popular 'Got milk?' campaign that apparently was reworded for Spanish-speaking markets after advertisers learned that Latinos interpreted the query as applying to nursing mothers. The fault here appears to be simply one of poor translation by the US marketers; yet again the impression is left that the Spanish speakers were somehow being foolish.

US confectioner Mars Inc is supposed to have confused Russians with billboard advertising that the sweets M&Ms 'melt in your mouth, not in your hands'. The marketers argued that the ad campaign backfired because the cold climate in Russia keeps anything from melting in anyone's hands. However, a less ethnocentrically US view suggests that probably it was simply a poorly designed campaign.

Drinks companies Coca-Cola and Pepsi both faced marketing challenges in China, but again the reasons may not be as stated by the US marketing managers. They suggested that 'Coca-Cola', when originally translated into Chinese, could mean 'bite the wax tadpole' or 'mare stuffed with wax', depending on the dialect. However, this has never been confirmed by Chinese, and a more probably explanation is poor translation. In fact eventually Coke did switch its name to a phonetic Chinese equivalent that translates as 'happiness in the mouth'. Pepsi translated its slogan 'It brings you back to life' into Chinese so insensitively that it was interpreted as bringing somebody back from the grave; but once again this is reported in marketing literature as being a comic misunderstanding by the Chinese rather than incompetence by US sales and advertising managers.

Language misunderstandings can be funny, expensive, even embarrassing for advertisers, tourists or business travellers. But when it comes to international incidents, such as an 11-day dispute over a spy plane, the stakes are greater. And often such conflicts reveal deeper communication problems between countries. Many Chinese were baffled when US legislators decided to air their opinions publicly by speaking out on television. Elected officials in China are considered government representatives, not professional politicians with individual agendas. Another culturally important issue was the Chinese Government's insistence that the US Government should apologise in writing. In US culture a letter is just a letter, but in Chinese culture sending a letter symbolises a show of respect that translates as an apology, even if the words don't exactly spell it out – and such a letter from the US Government, grudging as it was, was finally accepted as an end to the dispute.

There are also major differences in the way US Americans and Chinese perceive the concept of group responsibility. Because the former are far more individualistic than the latter (see, e.g., Binder, 2007), they tend to reject the notion that an entire country can or should be held responsible for a military action. This suggestion brings the discussion back to the controversy over Wikileaks. Julian Assange is an individualistic Australian in a head-to-head confrontation with the US Government that represents people very accustomed to having things all their own way. Assange owes no allegiance except to his own values; and it seems unlikely that the US would accept any corporate liability for the sins of their diplomats.

Discussion and questions

1. What are some arguments for the importance of a formal apology in negotiating conflict?

A possible answer might be that if Hofstede's cultural dimensions are taken as a guide, then collectivist cultures value harmony, and acceptable behaviour would be to apologise for any disruption even if it wasn't the fault of the individual. On the other hand, individualists would be more likely to argue their case. Another view is that formal apologies are rituals that validate and maintain power hierarchies; and another that members of 'masculine' cultures 'never apologise, never explain' (a saying attributed to the Greek historian Herodotus (484 to 425 BC), see www.age-of-the-sage.org).

However if members of a masculine culture demand apology from others, they are more likely to insist on formalities than members of more feminine cultures – where informal, mutual apologies are more common. Members of cultures low in the need for uncertainty avoidance seem also to have less need for formalities. As for time orientation, those who live in the present are more inclined to avoid formalities because they may have to be changed if circumstances change.

2. What is a summary of some major characteristics of US negotiation style, based on the above?

Reasonable answers:

(1) Accepts compromise only in deadlock.
(2) Takes firm initial and final stands.
(3) Sets up principles, leaves details to subordinates.
(4) Leaves many options open.
(5) Lacks trust.
(6) Is well briefed.
(7) Keeps position hidden as long as possible.

3. Why might this style be inappropriate in some international negotiations?

Reasonable answer: this style would be inappropriate if:

(1) Compromise would avoid escalation of conflict.
(2) The situation is ambiguous; thus taking a firm stand from the beginning could lead to everybody getting off on the wrong foot (e.g., US soldiers being killed by 'friendly fire' from their own side because an officer decided arbitrarily that they must be the enemy).
(3) The details are important ('The devil is in the fine print') and should not be left to subordinates.
(4) An ethical principle is involved and many options are not morally acceptable (e.g., retention of the death penalty in some states of the US).
(5) Trust is essential (e.g., for effective teamwork).
(6) The negotiators have to go beyond their brief because of unforeseen events.
(7) The negotiators' position needs to be made clear to all concerned (e.g., in response to a terrorist threat).

4. What are the strengths of this style?

Appropriate answer: this style may be the most effective if:

(1) Comprise is likely to be seen as weakness and exploited.
(2) A firm stand is likely to intimidate the opposition.

(3) The 'big picture' is the really important issue (e.g., are we going to invade Iraq?).

(4) Flexibility is essential to the negotiation (e.g., between a doctor and patient if they don't share a language. The doctor has to negotiate meaning with a sick person).

(5) Trust has not been established (e.g., before a relationship has developed).

(6) Knowledge is power, and to be well briefed is essential.

(7) The negotiators need to keep resources in reserve.

YOUTH AND NEW MEDIA IN ICELAND	THORBJÖRN BRODDASON AND KJARTAN ÓLAFSSON

Communications research is an increasingly central aspect of the scientific and scholarly study of society. James W Carey's definition of communication (1989) runs as follows:

> *Communication is a symbolic process whereby reality is produced, maintained, repaired, and transformed.*

The increased emphasis on communication research goes hand in hand with the growing sophistication at all levels of technical communication, ranging from interpersonal mobile communication to global mass communications networks. In the mid-1990s a communications scholar could note that:

> *we now take television entirely for granted ... in a way similar to how we take everyday life for granted. ... Our experience of television is of a piece with our experience of the world: we do not expect it to be, nor can we imagine it to be, significantly otherwise*
>
> Silverstone, 1994: iii

We are now obliged to add more recent communication tools, in particular the Internet and the mobile telephone. We are witnessing the evolution of a universal, interconnected network of audio, video and electronic text communications that will blur the distinction between interpersonal and mass communications and between public and private communications (Neuman, 1991). Indeed, few seem to have really understood the nature of the revolution that took place between September 1993 and March 1994 when a network that had been dedicated to academic research became a network of networks open to all (Briggs and Burke, 2005).

Young people and new media

The assumption that young people are more future-oriented, more apt and more technologically aware and interested than adults is not new (Rushkoff, 1996).

But what do we know about this age group and their online behaviour? What does current research tell us about how children use online media? And does children's use of the Internet tell us anything about how changes in the media environment might change society in the future?

The first decade of the new millennium saw a rapid growth in research on children's use of the Internet and online media (Donoso et al., 2009). In many EU countries children and young people were leading in the use of Internet, with 75 per cent of 6 to 17 year olds across the EU27 using it in 2008, rising to more than 90 per cent in the UK, Sweden, the Netherlands, Denmark and Finland.

This implies rapid saturation of Internet access in the homes of ordinary people of the more affluent parts of the world (Livingstone and Bovill, 2001; Livingstone and Haddon, 2009). If 'community' is defined socially and not spatially, it is clear that contemporary communities are rarely limited to neighbourhoods (Wellman, 2001). Especially the role of the mobile phone

affords liberation from both place and group, and – rather than being embedded in one social network – person-to-person interactors continuously switch between networks.

ibid.

Although there are substantial cross-national differences in youth access to the Internet (Hasebrink et al., 2008), in many countries such access has become integral to all aspects of adolescent life. The Internet should not be considered a separate kind of medium but rather as a medium of integration, reuniting different kinds of media, school, home, leisure and work in a process of communication (Johnson-Smagardi et al., 1998). This includes maintaining and extending friendship networks (Blais et al., 2008), harassment and bullying (Slonje and Smith, 2008), scoring drugs (Schepis et al., 2008), completing homework (Madden et al., 2007), sexual exploration (Cameron et al., 2005), plagiarising (Stephens et al., 2007), health information (Borzekowski et al., 2006) and self-harm (Adler and Adler, 2008). In a very real sense, adolescents in many Western societies are not only permanently online, but their adolescent communities have literally become embedded in the Internet.

Although the Internet has an immense potential as an amazingly accessible and efficient provider of knowledge, information, news and entertainment it also makes certain demands on its users.

First, they have to be literate. It is almost a commonplace to point out that, contrary to reading, television viewing requires no special skills. Yet young people who wish to participate in early twenty-first-century communications (mass or otherwise) and benefit from the Internet's horn of plenty will not get very far unless they have reached a tolerable level of reading and writing skills (and acquired a second language if born of non-English-speaking parents).

Research project

Some key findings of the ongoing research project 'Children and Television in Iceland' include a persistent decline in newspaper reading; fundamental changes in the uses of television; the rapid penetration of the Internet and the explosive introduction of mobile phones. The trend of a steady erosion of book reading now may have come to a halt.

The study is conducted in Iceland, an independent island nation in the North Atlantic where over 90 per cent of the roughly 300,000 inhabitants use the Internet regularly and 76 per cent of all households are connected to the Internet via broadband. As in most Northern European countries, Internet use is near-universal among children 12 years and older in Iceland (Hasebrink et al, 2008). The geographical boundaries of the island and linguistic boundaries of the Icelandic language provide an ideal case to study the new processes of communication that are transforming adolescent communities around the globe and may provide the infrastructure for a truly adolescent society.

Various tools of communication

The aim of the first study in 1968 was to collect data on the introduction of television in Icelandic society. Some 92 percent of respondents where television signals could be picked up had a TV set at home. A pattern that was to emerge in later surveys was that the mere presence of a boy in the household seems to contribute to the household acquiring a TV set.

In the 1979 survey, a question was added regarding the respondent's personal ownership or possession of certain communication tools, .namely, a radio, a record player and a cassette player. By 2009, the list had grown to 18 items. Between 1997 and 2003 mobile phones went from being almost non-existent to being owned by nearly all respondents. The general pattern for all new introductions to the media market seems to be that there is a time when that particular medium changes from being new and exotic to being an everyday phenomenon. For television in homes, this time was at the introduction of Icelandic television services in the late 1960s. For television sets in the bedrooms of adolescents, it was the mid-1990s. For mobile phones, it was the beginning of the millennium. For computers it was the first decade of the new millennium, and these computers were increasingly being connected to the Internet (in 2009, some 9 per cent of our respondents possessed both kinds of computers, hence the net percentage for ownership of either or both kinds of computers was 58 per cent).

Personal ownership of television among respondents, which increased by leaps and bounds between 1991 and 2003, seems to have levelled off entirely by 2009, but (and this is of importance) at different saturation levels for boys and girls. The well-known truth that boys acquire gadgets faster than girls do is handsomely demonstrated.

Apparently the personal computer, in particular the laptop, is to some extent replacing ordinary television receivers in the communications arsenal of Icelandic youths. The most conspicuous change is related to the ownership of mobile phones. Practically a non-existent phenomenon among adolescents in 1997, only six years later it had become nearly pervasive among the older respondents, and in 2009 the situation was even closer to saturation.

Clear gender differences, which were apparent already in 2003, persisted in 2009. A mobile phone constitutes the exception to the above-mentioned rule that boys acquire new gadgets ahead of the girls. Not unexpectedly, mobile ownership increases with age, even though the extremely high ownership percentage within all age groups is perhaps more noteworthy.

Although Marshall McLuhan's description of the media as the 'extensions of man' (McLuhan, 2001) was coined several decades before cell phones were nearly omnipresent, as they are today, it aptly reflects the uses of the mobile phone, as reported by our respondents. Not only is mobile phone ownership more widespread among girls than the boys, it is also of considerably more importance to them. It is not an exaggeration to claim that in mid-adolescence, the mobile phone has become a social lifeline for a large proportion of girls, but less so among boys. It is also noteworthy that the traditional use of the phone as a speech medium is important both to keep contact with parents and friends, whereas the texting function is primarily reserved for contacts with friends.

Newspaper reading: An alarming decline continues

We can offer two explanations. The first has to do with the inherently weak position of traditional printed newspapers compared with the increasingly sophisticated electronic news media (including of course the newspapers' own websites). In terms of immediacy, depth, background and flexibility, the comparison is increasingly to the newspapers' disadvantage. The end of the old-fashioned newspaper seems to be in sight. Ordinary printed books, for example, fiction, perhaps several hundred pages in length, on the other hand, have not met with equally serious electronic competition thus far. Consuming tens or hundreds of pages of leisure reading on the screen simply has not caught on. Most likely, however, this is only the lull before the storm. At the time of writing, there are already on the market electronic alternatives to the printed book, whatever its length or content, that appear to have such huge advantages and may have such wide-ranging consequences for the reading public that not only the newspaper part of the next questionnaire, but also the book reading questions, will have to be completely rewritten.

Concluding remarks

Researchers agree that a fundamental change has occurred in the communication environment and the communication behaviour of young people in the industrialised world during recent years and decades. The material gathered in the research project 'Children and Television in Iceland' throws some of these changes into sharp relief. From one point of view, the Golden Age of television is approaching its end more rapidly than many of us would have anticipated, but at the same time television is becoming an integral part of the new electronic media environment and will survive in a recognisable shape, if not in name. Nothing, it seems, will stop the rapid decline of printed newspapers, whereas books in the traditional sense of the word, although handsomely defending their position for the time being, will probably undergo a monumental transformation in the near future.

Discussion and questions

Increasing workforce diversity includes younger and better-educated employees, younger managers with more academic qualifications, and older people who have opted to continue working after official retirement age. Moreover, and especially in developing and emergent economies, youth culture holds very different values from those of mature members of society; and organisational management includes the need to understand and work with them.

A major factor is the increasing use by young people of electronic media communication rather than newsprint, and this has implications for inter- and intra-organisational communication methods. For example, the findings in the above report imply the days of the in-house journal as hard copy seem to be numbered.

What other advice can you suggest to managers for more effective communication with younger employees?

Case study: The Internet's cyber radicals: Young heroes of the web changing the world

Aleks Krotoski, writing in the UK newspaper *The Observer* on 28 November 2010, reported on what he described as the transformation of political activism since 2003 with the setting up of new publishing platforms, blogs and social networks. They have given cyber-revolutionaries virtual access to printing presses, radio stations and cable TV channels, and are developing technologies that create grassroots communities. According to Jody McIntyre, a 20-year-old British activist and freelance journalist, whose blog gives a concise alternative to mainstream media, the power is with the people.

In particular, there has been an explosion of technologies to circumvent censorship. For example, Walid al-Saqaf developed an encryption technology called 'alkasir' when the Yemeni Government closed down his news aggregation site, YemenPortal. net. 'Information freedom is essential if you're really going to live a dignified life,' he argued.

The Chinese Government is an indefatigable web censor but even its Great Firewall has loopholes. The country's most popular blogger is Han Han, a 28-year-old who is openly critical of the government. Because he speaks in the youth vernacular and enjoys such a tremendous following, his personal politics are generally overlooked by the powers that be. He says: 'Although the Internet is controlled, when compared with traditional media, it better reflects reality.'

Kenyan-born Ory Okolloh helped create the website Ushahidi in the aftermath of her country's disputed presidential election in 2007. It collected eyewitness reports of violence sent in by email and text message, and placed them on a Google map, and the open-source software has since been released freely and used elsewhere for similar projects.

Tom Steinberg is the founder and director of mySociety (http://www.mysociety. org/), a company that builds digital tools to provide a direct pipeline between individuals, local communities and local government. He has great respect, shared by other modern cyber-radicals, for the scale of attention that newspapers and TV can bring. He says if he were running an election campaign he would spend his money on TV ads, leaflets and posters because the Internet, though powerful, is not particularly good at 'shoving your message down the throats of people who don't care'. On the other hand, on the web 'you can make things that say, "Go on, just have a go."'

Christopher Poole is the US creator of 4chan. *Time Magazine* reported on Monday 27 April 2009 that 'in a stunning result' the winner of the third annual TIME 100 poll and new owner of the title World's Most Influential Person was the bulletin board moot. The 21-year-old college student and founder of the online community 4chan.org, whose real name is Christopher Poole, received 16,794,368 votes and an average influence rating of 90 (out of a possible 100) to handily beat such contenders as Barack Obama, Vladimir Putin and Oprah Winfrey. Since moot launched 4chan.org in 2003, the site has given birth to Internet memes as diverse as Lolcats and Rickrolling. 4chan averages 13 million page views a day and 5.6 million visitors a month; by some estimates it is the second largest bulletin board in the world.

By contrast, Peter Sunde is the co-founder of the Pirate Bay, a site that allows for the peer-to-peer sharing of computer files of any kind, but one that was set up with an explicitly political purpose. Josh Halliday reported in the *MediaGuardian* of 26 November 2010 that a Stockholm court of appeal had ruled that Fredrik Neij, Peter Sunde and Carl Lundstrom were guilty of helping Pirate Bay users illicitly share copyrighted music and film content via their website. P2P-blog.com commented on 24 November 2009 that for years the Pirate Bay was the place to go to share movies, music or other digital goods. Peter Sunde, who resigned from his job as the site's spokesperson earlier in 2009, is one of the founders of the Swedish start-up Kvittar, which promises to keep track of all of users' purchases and offers a kind of online locker for receipts.

Aleks Krotoski wound up his report by arguing that what today's crop of cyber-radicals demonstrate is that power does reside in the hands of the people, thanks to the foundations laid by Tim Berners-Lee some twenty years ago when he opened the Internet to the world and allowed a new generation of social activists to exploit the technological tools available to them for their own agendas.

Sources

Walid al-Saqaf, http://www.websitedescription.com/yemenportal.net
Han, H. 'Finding happiness by being different' (www.chinaview.cn 2009-09-23 09:49:40)
McIntyre, J. (http://jodymcintyre.wordpress.com/)
Okolloh, H. (http://www.kenyanpundit.com/)
Poole, C. (4chan.org/)
Steinberg, T. (http://www.mysociety.org/)
Time Magazine (http://www.time.com/)

Discussion and questions

Corporate managers have been aware for many years of the power of the Internet as a mass communication medium and have set up their websites accordingly: but can they learn anything from these young cyber-radicals on how to mobilise public opinion? Catchphrases are common, such as Sony's 'make believe'. What other examples can you find of visionary rhetoric in corporate websites?

Conclusion

Exchange of information, in organisations as elsewhere, is the prelude to action. If it is to be positive there must be not only understanding (which can lead to war) but mutual agreement that cooperation is preferable to conflict. Since the creation of the Internet by Tim Berners-Lee more than two decades ago and subsequent development of electronic spyware – not to mention 'pilot error' in pressing the wrong key when sending an email – private messages have become almost things of the past, as extinct as the dinosaurs.

The range of digital media communication is virtually infinite. Managing it across cultures requires intimate understanding of its different styles including emails, websites, blog sites and social networks. Understanding is needed also of the different media preferred by young people and seniors, men and women, petitioners and activists. Persuasive power is acquired through appropriate use of medium as much as by the actual wording of the message.

Key points

1. The importance of electronic 'etiquette' in sending and replying to messages by email or via online discussion forums and social networks.
2. The Internet gives individuals a powerful voice, loud enough to be heard around the world and to be a force for change.
3. The content of Internet postings is affected not only by writers' uploads but also by the technological context that promotes individualism and supports the concept that everybody has a right to their personal opinion.
4. As a corollary of this, the Internet is a sympathetic medium for voicing discontent.
5. Silence is also a communication tool, for example, in mass refusal to respond to a mass medium.
6. Young people have colonised many electronic spheres almost as their personal domains. Since the age range of employees worldwide is widening (getting younger and older) young managers will be citizens of these brave new worlds while older managers may struggle to gain entry.
7. Lack of understanding of cultural content can create dangerous levels of misunderstanding in long-distance communication between governments and organisations.
8. Correspondence in cyberspace can go a long way, literally and metaphorically, towards good communication, but the non-verbal as well as verbal

cues in face-to-face meetings may have to complete the journey. Paradoxically, the expansion of communication media may narrow and impoverish as well as widen opportunities for social skills.

9. Ordinary citizens today – particularly young people – are becoming leaders of change worldwide via Internet communication and mobilisation.

10. The notion of a 'mediapolis' is that of a mediated global public sphere where civic action and participation can grow and whose citizens are participating agents for change.

11. Organisational and political leaders are sometimes accused of creating a global 'climate of fear' in order to increase their power and influence.

12. One of the important challenges for world leaders is to create a climate of confidence rather than fear; to understand civil society-driven media and communication initiatives for deep social change and address identified insecurities.

Looking ahead

Point 12 above summarises one of the topics of this chapter: the need for social change driven by initiatives within an international climate of confidence. Such a climate cannot be sustained without social responsibility by governments, agencies and corporations.

Last, but definitely not least, the final chapter in the book pursues this theme with discussion of ways of communicating ethical values and environmental sustainability across cultures.

Experiential exercises

1. An exercise to demonstrate the importance of interpersonal as well as electronic communication is as follows:

Face a partner and hold both your hands outward and horizontal, with palms upward, in a gesture of giving, while saying 'No'. Then place both hands down flat in front of you on the table, close together and say 'No' again, in the same tone. Your partner will very likely say the second 'No' was more convincing than the first because the accompanying body language was more appropriate.

2. Lecturers might organise for half the class to give a short PowerPoint or other digital presentation on some aspect of their cross-cultural experience; and the other half use analogue communication on the same topic, such as telling or reading a story or singing a song, showing photographs, etc. In discussion afterwards, students should compare and contrast their reactions to the two communication media.

3. Lecturers who have experience of teaching both in classrooms and online might give a talk on the two experiences – the similarities and differences. Those who do not have this dual experience might like to invite a guest lecturer with the experience to speak to the class.

Recommended reading

Donoso, V., Olafsson, K. and Broddason, T. 2009. 'What we know, what we do not know'. In S. Livingstone and L. Haddon (eds), *Kids Online: Opportunities and Risks for Children.* Bristol: Policy Press.
Gonthier, G. 2002. *Rude Awakenings: Overcoming the Civility Crisis in the Workplace.* Chicago: Dearborn.
Hall, E.T. 1959. *The Silent Language.* New York: Doubleday.
Phatak, A.V., Bhagat, R.S. and Kashlak, R.J. 2005. *International Management: Managing in a Diverse and Dynamic Global Environment.* New York: McGraw-Hill Irwin.
Steele, G.L. 1983. *The Hacker's Dictionary.* New York: Harper & Row.
Zillmann, D. and Vorderer, P. 2000. *Media Entertainment: The Psychology of its Appeal.* London: Routledge.

References

AAP 2006. 'Julia Gillard slams Japanese whaling protest surveillance flights from Western Australia'. 6 January; http://www.perthnow.com.au/news/julia-gillard-slams-japanese-whaling-protest-surveillance-flights-from-wa/story-e6frg12c-1225816711464.
Adler, P.A. and Adler, P. 2008. 'The cyber worlds of self-injurers: Deviant communities, relationships, and selves'. *Symbolic Interaction,* 31 (1), pp. 33–56.
Andersson, L.M. and Pearson, C.M. 1999.'Tit for tat? The spiraling effect of incivility in the workplace'. *Academy of Management Review,* 24 (3), pp. 452–71.
Arendt, H. 1958. *The Human Condition.* London: University of Chicago Press.
Augé, M. 1995. *Non-Places: Introduction to an Anthropology of Supermodernity.* London: Verso.
Bainbridge, L. 2010. 'Why I'm backing Cage Against the Machine for Christmas No. 1'. 13 December; guardian.co.uk.
Baruch, Y. 2005. 'Bullying on the net: Adverse behavior on e-mail and its impact'. *Information & Management,* 42, pp. 361–71.
Bauman, Z. 2010. *Living on Borrowed Time.* Cambridge: Polity.
BBC News 2010. http://www.bbc.co.uk/news/world-us-canada-11858637, 28 November.
Binder, J. 2007. 'Tompenaars' dimensions'. 7 July; http://www.globalprojectmanagement.org. Blais, J.J., Craig, W.M., Pepler, D. and Connolly, J. 2008. 'Adolescents online: The importance of internet activity choices to salient relationships'. *Journal of Youth and Adolescence,* 37 (5), pp. 522–36.
Borzekowski, D.L.G., Fobil, J.N. and Asante, K.O. 2006. 'Online access by adolescents in Accra: Ghanaian teens' use of the internet for health information'. *Developmental Psychology,* 42 (3), pp. 450–8.
Briggs, A. and Burke, P. 2005. *A Social History of the Media.* Cambridge: Polity.
Bryant, J. and Miron, D. 2002. 'Entertainment as media effect'. In J. Bryant and D. Zillmann (Eds), *Media Effects: Advances in Tand Research.* USA: Sage, pp. 549–82.
Bryant, J. and Zillmann, D. 2002. *Media Effects: Advances in Theory and Research.* London: Routledge.
Cameron, K.A., Salazar, L.F., Bernhardt, J.M., Burgess-Whitman, N., Wingood, G.M. and DiClemente, R.J. 2005. 'Adolescents' experience with sex on the web: Results from online focus groups'. *Journal of Adolescence,* 28 (4), pp. 535–40.
Carey, J.W. 1989. *Communication as Culture: Essays on Media and Society.* New York: Routledge.
Castells, M. 2009. *Communication Power.* Oxford: Oxford University Press.
Cleary, M. and Freeman, A. 2005. 'Email etiquette: Guidelines for mental health nurses'. *International Journal of Mental Health Nursing,* 14 (1), pp. 62–5.
Curbet, Jaume (2006) *La glocalización de la (in)seguridad* (La Paz: Plural Editores).
Donoso, V., Olafsson, K. and Broddason, T. 2009. 'What we know, what we do not know'. In S. Livingstone and L. Haddon (eds), *Kids Online: Opportunities and Risks for Children.* Bristol: Policy Press.

Extejt, M.M. 1998. 'Teaching students to correspond effectively electronically'. *Business Communication Quarterly*, 61 (2), pp. 57–67.

Featherstone, M., Lash, S. and Robertson, R. 1995. *Global Modernities.* London: Sage.

Friedman, R.A. and Currall, S.C. 2003. 'Conflict escalation: Dispute exacerbating elements of e-mail communication conflict'. *Human Relations*, 56 (11), pp. 1325–47.

Füredi, F. 2002. *Culture of Fear: Risk-Taking and the Morality of Low Expectation.* London: Continuum.

Garfield, S. 2010. *Just My Type: A Book about Fonts.* London: Profile.

Gonthier, G. 2002. *Rude Awakenings: Overcoming the Civility Crisis in the Workplace.* Chicago: Dearborn.

Hal Berghel's Digital Village 1997. 'Email: the good, the bad and the ugly'; http://www.berghel.net/col-edit/digital_village/apr-97/dv_4-97.php.

Hall, E.T. 1959. *The Silent Language.* New York: Doubleday.

Hasebrink, U., Livingstone, S. and Haddon, L. 2008. *Comparing Children's Online Opportunities and Risks across Europe: Cross-National Comparisons for EU Kids Online.* London: EU Kids Online.

Hine, C. 2000. *Virtual Ethnography.* London: Sage.

Holston, J. 2008. *Insurgent Citizenship: Disjunctions of Democracy and Modernity in Brazil.* Princeton, NJ: Princeton University Press.

Hylland Eriksen, T. 2005. 'How can the glocal be local? Islam, the West and the globalisation of identity politics'. In O. Hemer and T. Tufte (eds), *Media and Glocal Change: Rethinking Communication for Development.* Göteborg & Buenos Aires: Nordicom & CLACSO.

Johnson-Smaragdi, U., d'Haenens, L., Krotz, F. and Hasebrink, U. 1998. 'Patterns of old and new media use among young people in Flanders, Germany and Sweden'. *European Journal of Communication*, 13 (4), pp. 479–501.

Landry, E.M. 2000. 'Scrolling around the new organization: The potential for conflict in the on-line environment'. *Negotiation Journal*, 16 (2), pp. 133–42.

Livingstone, S. and Bovill, M. 2001. *Families and the Internet: An Observational Study of Children and Young People's Internet Use* (http://www.lse.ac.uk/collections/media@lse/pdf/btreport_familiesinternet.pdf).

Livingstone S. and Haddon, L. (eds) 2009. *Kids Online: Opportunities and Risks for Children.* Bristol: Policy Press.

Madden, A.D., Ford, N.J. and Miller, D. 2007. 'Information resources used by children at an English secondary school: Perceived and actual levels of usefulness'. *Journal of Documentation*, 63 (3), pp. 340–58.

Martín-Barbero, J. 2002. *Oficio de Cartógrafo: Travesías latinoamericanos de la comunicación en la cultura.* Santiago de Chile: Fondo de Cultura Económica.

Martinez, M.I.V. et al. 2003. *El Rostro del Miedo: Una investigación sobre los miedos sociales urbanos.* Medellín: Corporación Región.

McLuhan, M. 2001. *Understanding Media: The Extensions of Man.* USA: Routledge.

Neuman, W.R. 1991. *The Future of the Mass Audience.* Cambridge: Cambridge University Press.

O'Sullivan, P.B. and Flanagin, A.J. 2003. 'Reconceptualizing "flaming" and other problematic messages'. *New Media & Society*, 5 (1), pp. 69–94.

Phatak, A.V., Bhagat, R.S. and Kashlak, R.J. 2005. *International Management: Managing in a Diverse and Dynamic Global Environment.* New York: McGraw-Hill Irwin.

Reguillo, R. 1996. *La construcción simbólica: Sociedad, desastre y comunicación.* Guadalajara: ITESO.

Rushkoff, D. 1996. *Media Virus! Hidden Agendas in Popular Culture.* New York: Ballantine.

Schepis, T.S., Marlowe, D.B. and Forman, R.F. 2008. 'The availability and portrayal of stimulants over the internet'. *Journal of Adolescent Health*, 42 (5), pp. 458–65.

Silverstone, R. 1994. *Television and Everyday Life.* London: Routledge.

—— 2007. *Media and Morality: On the Rise of the Mediapolis.* Cambridge: Polity.

Slonje, R. and Smith, P.K. 2008. 'Cyberbullying: Another main type of bullying?', *Scandinavian Journal of Psychology*, 49 (2), pp. 147–54.

Sproull, L.J. and Kiesler, S. 1986. 'Reducing social context cues: Electronic mail in organizational communication'. *Management Science*, 32 (11), pp. 1492–1512.

Steele, G.L. 1983. *The Hacker's Dictionary.* New York: Harper & Row.

Stephens, J.M., Young, M.F. and Calabrese, T. 2007. 'Does moral judgment go offline when students are online? A comparative analysis of undergraduates' beliefs and behaviors related to conventional and digital cheating'. *Ethics and Behavior*, 17 (3), pp. 233–54.

Thomas, C. 2007. 'Globalization and human security'. In A. McGrew, and N. K. Poku (eds), *Globalization, Development and Human Security.* Cambridge: Polity.

Tufte, T. et al. 2009. 'From voice to participation? Analysing youth agency in letter writing in Tanzania'. In T. Tufte and F. Enghel (eds), *Youth Engaging with the World: Media, Communication and Social Change.* The International Clearinghouse on Children, Youth and Media (University of Gothenburg: NORDICOM and UNESCO).

Turnage, A.K. 2007. 'Email flaming behaviors and organizational conflict'. *Journal of Computer-Mediated Communication*, 13 (1): article 3; http://jcmc.indiana.edu/vol13/issue1/turnage.html.

Walton, D., Reed, C. and Macagno, F. 2008. *Argumentation Schemes.* Cambridge: Cambridge University Press.

Wellman, B. 2001. 'Physical place and cyberplace: The rise of personalized networking'. *International Journal of Urban and Regional Research*, 25 (2), pp. 228–52.

World Bank 2007. *World Bank Development Report.* Washington, DC: World Bank.

Zillmann, D. and Vorderer, P. 2000 *Media Entertainment: The Psychology of its Appeal.* London: Routledge.

CHAPTER 10

Actions Speak Louder than Words: Ethical Behaviour, Social Responsibility and Protecting the Environment

Elizabeth Christopher; Josh Brahinsky; Diana J. Wong-MingJi

Objectives of the chapter

To study interpretations of the concept of corporate social responsibility; and ways of communicating ethical values and environmental sustainability across cultures.

Chapter contents

- Outline of chapter
- CSR Asia Corporate social responsibility in Asia: Who is getting it done? The role of CSR professionals in Asia
- Discussion
- Questions
- Case study: Hungarian toxic mud disaster
- Discussion
- Josh Brahinsky: Evangelism and culture: A history of missiology as intercultural communication
- Discussion
- Questions
- Case study: Missionaries deported from Morocco
- Diana J. Wong-MingJi Indigenous knowledge for international management of environmental resources
- Case studies
- Discussion and questions
- Case study: Intellectual Property Rights: Who benefits?

- Discussion
- Conclusion
- Key points
- Experiential exercises
- Recommended reading
- References

Outline of chapter

This chapter follows the thesis developed in Chapter 9: that social change involves social responsibility to communicate ethical values and environmental sustainability across cultures.

It opens with a report by CSR Asia on corporate social responsibility initiatives by Asian firms. A survey revealed that in general these companies are conservative in their efforts to promote such policies, and very often relevant activities are left to junior managers without decisional powers. Moreover most programmes are philanthropic (charitable) works outside the main focus and operations of the firm and have no impact on corporate strategies.

Discussion of this report refers to the argument that 'the business of business is business' and that social responsibility programmes are no part of competitive capitalism. The discussion includes some general comments on the concept of corporate social responsibility, based on Ebert and Griffiths' identification of four socially responsible levels of corporate behaviour, with examples. It is followed by a news account of a case of corporate irresponsibility, the Hungarian toxic mud disaster.

Since religion is at the root of so much sectarian and other violence in society, a chapter on ethics would not be complete without some comment on religious ethics. Therefore the next section includes an essay by Josh Brahinsky on the ethics of Christian missionary work and modern concepts of missionaries as cross-cultural communication specialists – albeit with a specific agenda.

The discussion that follows comments on some mutually contradictory aspects of missionary engagement with native cultures; and refers to Berger and Huntington's claim that Evangelical Protestantism has become a globalising force representing a 'global culture' (along with the global cultures of business and non-government organisations and popular culture) (Berger, 1997).

The illustrative case is from a recent news report that Evangelical Christians have been deported from Morocco on the grounds of undermining public order by trying to convert Muslims to Christianity under the guise of charitable work.

After that Diana Wong discusses the importance of including indigenous (local) knowledge of environmental protection in conservations plans using Western technologies. She describes how native peoples' traditional wisdom has for too long been ignored, dismissed or denigrated as superstition. Now there is growing recognition that their perspectives and management approaches to environmental issues, accumulated over hundreds of years and possibly millennia, can benefit international managers. Agricultural lands may also include places of value to the community such as indigenous sites of cultural importance and natural heritage areas. These places are not only irreplaceable but contribute to a sense of regional identity. They may have potential for activities such as tourism or education. Managing agricultural activities to avoid negative impacts will help ensure they survive for the future.

The case study to complement Dr Wong's report is based partly on an article in www.tradewatch.org.au. It discusses trade-related aspects of the Intellectual Property Agreement as part of the World Trade Organisation's General Agreement on Tariffs and Trade; and offers a more cynical view of international managers' appropriation of indigenous knowledge.

As usual the chapter ends with a conclusion and summary of key points; experiential exercises to link practice to theory; a list of internet resources, recommended further reading and chapter references.

CSR Asia Corporate social responsibility in Asia: Who is getting it done? The role of CSR professionals in Asia

Playing it Safe!

This survey was created by CSR Asia and is supported by the Asian Institute of Management's Ramon V. del Rosario, Sr; the Center for Corporate Social Responsibility; and the Singapore Compact for CSR (http://www.csr-asia.com [accessed 6 February 2011]).

The data was collected using an online data collection tool. The survey was announced at the CSR Asia Summit in Bangkok on 2 November 2008, the Asian Forum on CSR in Singapore on 21 and 22 November and was available online at www.csr-asia.com. The deadline for data collection was 10 December 2008.

This was deliberately a short survey for 2008, and asked ten basic questions. This survey was to be repeated, expanded and updated for 2009 to include what salary CSR managers are receiving, how they benchmark the work they do and how they measure the value of their position, the size of CSR teams, the type of company that employs a CSR manager (listed/private), the background of the CSR manager and who their key external and internal stakeholders are.

In this report, 'CSR manager' is used as a generic term to describe any person employed to manage corporate social responsibility within their organisation. This may include employees with a range of job titles, including but not limited to CSR, CR, sustainability, corporate relations and community relations among others.

The survey was designed to determine the status of corporate social responsibility (CSR) professionals in Asia. Companies are increasingly recognising the strategic importance of building business practices that create sustainable bottom lines, sustainable global economies, environments and societies: but how are they building capacity within their organisations to meet these challenges? The issues of priority in the research are the degree of development of CSR strategy, community investment, health and safety, and internal awareness and training in Asian organisations.

The survey returns were completed by 80 CSR managers from 14 countries in Asia. This report allows those working in CSR roles within companies in Asia to understand how their role compares to others. It should enable supporting organisations to understand what is needed to build capacity and to review developments.

Seventy per cent of the respondents referred to their activities as corporate social responsibility (CSR), the remainder being evenly split between describing their activities as sustainability, corporate responsibility (CR) and corporate citizenship. No matter how they describe themselves, there are clearly a number of CSR managers who are tackling global challenges and are responsible for creating value for their employing companies; but it is obvious that a large number are managing projects – mainly philanthropic – that are separated from the core focus of the business.

Overwhelmingly the current cohort of CSR managers are working in high-risk industries rather than across a range of industries. However, the survey is subtitled 'Playing it Safe' because the results show that the majority of companies seem to be somewhat conservative in the take-up and implementation of CSR as indicated by the status of their respective CSR managers. Less than a third of CSR managers are looking at broader issues, integral to the long-term performance of a business, including the development of CSR policy, climate change, poverty alleviation, water and broader community health issues. Even fewer managers are addressing issues related to supply chain, product responsibility, responsible marketing, diversity and biodiversity.

It is encouraging to note there are companies where the CSR manager reports directly to the board or CEO, though this is the case only for 19 per cent of respondents. Twenty-nine per cent reported that the operational level of the CSR manager is only that of an administrator or junior manager.

Given that CSR should be directly linked to corporate strategy and the ways in which a company enacts its business, it seems unlikely that CSR managers within these companies are making an impact on the company's activities. CSR managers must have a clear job specification, which identifies the area that they are responsible for and what the company expects as value for the position. If the activities of the CSR manager are not aligned with the core activities of the business then the ability of the CSR manager to deliver value is compromised.

CSR managers must deliver value to the organisations that employ them. In order to be able to do this the employer must ensure that the CSR manager has access to the board in order for company strategy to address long-term issues that will create sustainability. It is not feasible to expect a junior member of staff, an administrative assistant or a volunteer to drive sustainability throughout an organisation. CSR managers must be empowered to work with others in the business to assess key priority areas based on assessment of need and stakeholder expectations. Moreover they should engage with material social and environmental issues for the company. Their role is to manage risks and identify business opportunities inherent in a move towards sustainable development.

An increasing number of companies are employing CSR managers. CSR Asia will track this development through an annual survey to determine what issues they are working on, how CSR is managed within the organisation, what challenges exist and the status of CSR managers within the organisation over time. As the number of CSR managers increases in the Asia Pacific region year on year this body of professionals need internal and external support and ongoing guidance and clarity as to what is excellence in this profession.

The survey questions

Question 1: In which country are you currently located?

The survey results show that there are a number of CSR managers operating throughout the region and that the data therefore captures a variety of country concerns. There are clearly some countries that are better represented than others. The survey does not show a high response level from Japan, which is surprising, given the high level of CSR disclosure among Japanese companies.

Conversely, it is also surprising that there is a high level of CSR managers responding from Singapore despite a very low number of Singaporean companies who currently disclose their CSR activities.

It is noted that a high number of multinational companies headquartered outside of Asia also employ local CSR managers with regional responsibilities, which could account for the fact that, overall, given the number of businesses operating in the region, the total response of 80 CSR managers is low. However, it would be reasonable to conclude that this is a reflection of the current level of implementation of CSR in Asia. It is still unusual to find a business that has a CSR function. We would argue that the respondents to this survey are among the leading companies in this regard in Asia.

Question 2: In which industry does your company operate?

The energy sector has the highest number of CSR manager. This is unsurprising given the high environmental, social and governance risks associated with this industry. The remainder of the respondents are spread across different sectors, with the highest representation after energy being in healthcare, manufacturing, hospitality, telecommunications and transportation. Those in the 'other' category were representatives of government, media, services and insurance.

Question 3: What term is most commonly used in your company to mean corporate social responsibility?

Question 4: What department does the CSR function belong to in your company?

CSR is often confused with philanthropy in Asia, with many companies reporting only their philanthropic activities under the banner of CSR. Sixty-nine per cent of respondents reported that the term CSR is used within their company, corporate responsibility (CR) and sustainability being the second most commonly used terms. A number of other terms were also reported, including: community relations, philanthropy and citizen engagement. Thirty-eight per cent of companies responding to the survey have CSR departments within their company.

Apart from charity, CSR managers report mostly (25 per cent) to communications, marketing and public relations departments. Other departments that oversee CSR include human resources and the legal function. It is interesting to note that collectively a healthy 19 per cent of CSR managers report directly to the board or CEO, but worryingly 6 per cent report that CSR is run from a company foundation, a legal body separate from the operations of the company itself. One company reported that CSR was run on a voluntary basis.

Question 5: Is the CSR role at your company part time, full time or part of another role?

Question 6: What is the operational level of the CSR manager at your company?

Nearly a quarter of all respondents are not full-time CSR managers but undertake the CSR function as part of wider responsibilities within their firm. Only 15 per cent of all respondents are at board level. Most concerning is the number of CSR managers who responded that they are either at operational level of administrative staff or junior management. It is hard to imagine a company creating a sustainable business strategy with an administrative or junior manager being responsible for strategy development and implementation.

Question 7: What areas of CSR is the CSR manager responsible for?

It is apparent that CSR managers are responsible for a diverse portfolio. Given current trends it is not surprising that reporting and the environment are the areas that share the most common responsibility. The response also reflects that very few CSR managers (21 per cent) are responsible for managing human rights. Perhaps the most surprising result was the small number of CSR managers (21 per cent) who reported that they have responsibility for CSR issues in the company supply chain.

Understandably CSR managers seem to be involved mostly with tangible data (for example, the environment). Only a few CSR managers seem to be managing those areas where it is harder to set targets, monitor or understand the impact of the area on the overall business (for example, diversity).

Question 8: What are the biggest challenges faced by the CSR manager?

In line with expectations, the highest response to this question was the issue of budget. Forty-six per cent of CSR managers feel that their biggest challenge is lack of available funding; 44 per cent feel that the biggest challenge is lack of internal capacity to manage CSR with very small teams. As reported in Question 7 above, CSR managers report that they have a wide variety of responsibilities. This in itself was felt by 40 per cent to be the biggest challenge of all, and in this regard it is not surprising that the results of Question 7 also demonstrated that not all areas of CSR are being managed adequately.

Conversely 11 per cent reported their scope of responsibilities is too narrow, potentially leading to an incomplete approach to CSR. Twenty per cent reported they receive no leadership support or support from their fellow employees. This response will inevitably lead to large question marks about the quality and sincerity of CSR within organisations whose employees behave in this way.

A number of respondents reported that CSR was still only a recent undertaking within their organisation, and they were therefore working to create buy-in and understanding.

Question 9: What support from external parties would assist the CSR manager?

Sixty-three per cent reported they would welcome both more networking opportunities and training and seminars. This response seems quite surprising given the very high number of public events in this area, specifically in Asia, in 2008. Perhaps this reflects that CSR professionals wish to look for benchmarking opportunities and external support to build their knowledge given some of the challenges they face with some stakeholders.

Just under half (44 per cent) of all respondents expressed a wish that there be government legislation in the area of corporate social responsibility, and 40 per cent require more relevant research for their industry. It is very interesting to note that approximately a quarter of all respondents (26 per cent) responded that they would like to see more Asia-specific voluntary requirements with regard to CSR. However, law set by government is still seen as preferable to these voluntary soft laws. Twenty-six per cent would like a relevant professional qualification.

Respondents noted that one of the challenges is the overwhelming number of codes of conduct that are to be complied with, and stated that a universal code or expectation would assist them in their work.

Question 10: What are the key strategic focus areas for CSR within your organisation over the coming five years?

The key strategic focus areas for the next five years are arguably the most interesting set of data given their fundamental importance in driving the business approach to the current global big issues. Over half of the respondents (51 per cent) felt that a strategy itself was the key issue.

Companies in Asia clearly feel that community investment also has to be the priority for the coming five years, with over half (51 per cent) of respondents reporting that this is a key focus area. (A number in addition noted that education was the key focus area, although it is unclear whether this is in relation to community investment or more generic internal education on CSR.)

The survey found health and safety (49 per cent), internal awareness (43 per cent) and governance (35 per cent) as the next key focus areas, ranked above climate change (34 per cent) and poverty alleviation (34 per cent). Health (31 per cent), water (30 per cent) and policy development (30 per cent) are also reported as focus areas.

In view of recent corporate scandals it is surprising – given the make-up of industry respondents – that only 23 per cent reported supply chain management and product responsibility are key focus areas, and only a very few report that responsible marketing (15 per cent), diversity (14 per cent) and biodiversity (10 per cent) are key focus areas for the next five years.

It would seem that the philosophy reported here is very much that of a 'play it safe and tangible'. It could be argued that a very cautious approach to CSR is being advocated in these responses, and only time will tell whether or not these strategic areas are enough to sustain business through the next five years.

Discussion

Friedman and Friedman (2002) argue that competitive capitalism serves as both a device for achieving economic freedom and a necessary condition for political freedom. By this argument, businesses should focus on generating profits, and any collateral damage to the environment may be regrettable but is irrelevant to the main purpose of the firm.

However, in an era of internationalisation neither multinationals nor local businesses can conduct destructive and unethical practices, such as polluting the environment, without at least attracting negative media publicity worldwide. Together with increasing media attention there is pressure from non-governmental organisations, demands from consumers, governments and society at large to persuade corporations to conduct sustainable business practices. Moreover there is a growing tendency in Western business thinking towards longer-term planning, including development of strategies to preserve natural resources. In addition, in order to attract and retain employees and customers, companies are beginning to realise the importance of ethical corporate behaviour.

Corporate response since around the 1970s seems to indicate a gradually awakening collective conscience, commonly known as corporate social responsibility. The phrase is often abbreviated to CSR, which is a pity, since it reduces the concept mentally to a meaningless initialisation.

Social responsibility by corporations should represent 'the integrity with which a company governs itself, fulfils its mission, lives by its values, engages with its stakeholders, measures its impact and reports on its activities' (UK Department of Trade and Industry). Although there has been an increase in most firms' public commitment to responsible policies, in at least some cases this may be due mostly to enlightened self-interest. Multinational corporate leaders may insist on their people acting ethically in highly regulated areas – in Europe, the UK and the US, for example – while allowing them to behave differently elsewhere, such as by exploiting cheap or child labour.

Unfortunately, while corporations now need to maintain their reputations by promising responsibility, they are also expected, as always, to maximise profits. Therefore there is great temptation to allocate insufficient resources to keep their word to support non-financial areas such as human rights, business ethics, environmental policies, corporate contributions, community development, corporate governance, safe working conditions for employees, environmental stewardship, and contributions to community groups and charities.

The result is that many companies claiming to be socially responsible fail to live up to their self-imposed standards. They promote an image of responsible behaviour whether or not they have a true strategy in place and results to show for it. This is the background to the survey on the status of corporate social responsibility professionals in Asia, conducted by the agency CSR In Asia. The survey reveals that in many cases charitable projects, separate from the core business of the firm, take the place of an organisation-wide policy on corporate social responsibility. Moreover the surveyed firms appear to be generally 'conservative' in devising and implementing such policies. Nearly a third of the respondents reported that the operational level of the corporate social responsibility manager in their firms is only that of an administrator or junior manager and therefore unlikely to play any part in senior management decisions.

Corporate social responsibility is also the concern of primary industries. They are involved in growing, harvesting, extracting and sometimes processing of natural resources. They represent the first step in the chain of production. For these industries sustainability requires adaptive management and use of the latest scientific knowledge to maintain the environment and natural resources, communities and economies.

One example is that commercial and recreational fishing place direct pressure on fish stocks because of increasing competition for limited fisheries resources in estuarine and coastal waters: so conservation and management is now based on the principle of sustainable harvesting. This means that the fish and other organisms harvested are replaced by natural breeding or restocking, with no long-term effect on the diversity of species and size of populations. The non-fishing community also has an impact on fish stocks by placing environmental pressure on aquatic habitats. This occurs through processes such as urban and rural runoff, which carries pollutants into waterways; sewage and industrial discharges; littering and habitat degradation: also other people using the marine environment, like scuba divers and recreational boaters, can also have indirect impacts on fish stocks.

The relationship between the agricultural sector and rural and regional communities also is one of interdependence. Agriculture provides the economic base of many towns and rural communities in countries all over the world. Conversely, agriculture often depends on many services provided by rural and regional centres. These can include effective communication, transport, financial services, networks for the supply of water and energy, and other agricultural products and services. Towns also provide a social focus for people involved in their surrounding agricultural industries, and are also the source of goods and services for the maintenance of general community welfare. For agriculture to operate in an environmentally sustainable manner, mechanisms are needed to facilitate cooperation between industry, government, local authorities and community groups – for instance, urban encroachment and community concern over dust, odour and noise are placing increasing pressures on agricultural activities. State government agencies, local government, the agricultural sector and the wider community need to understand the issues and manage them through appropriate planning strategies and agricultural practices.

Some traditional agricultural practices are now recognised as unsustainable; and technology and research are finding innovative primary industries practices, for example, by farmers to maintain and even enhance the quality of soil and water, to minimise the amount of water they use and reduce the use of fertilisers. However, action by farmers to protect natural resources largely depends on profitable production. Therefore development of best management practices, incentives, guidelines and training in farm business and risk management are necessary, including the care of animals and plants in a diverse and healthy farming system.

Alternative farming systems are emerging in response to consumer demand for organically grown 'clean' food. The growth of markets for organic produce and the resulting techniques trialled successfully on organic farms can be transferred to conventional farms.

Management of pests and weeds is vital to agricultural productivity. To take an Australian example (http://landlearnnsw.org.au), farming is threatened by pests including rabbits, feral pigs, foxes, wild dogs and weeds. All these can and do lower the productive capacity of the land, threaten or displace native species, and affect human and animal health. Pest and weed control are therefore crucial for sustainable agriculture, not only in Australia but everywhere. However, concern remains about the toxic effects of over-use of chemicals and also, in relation to pesticides, about the loss of effectiveness. Other concerns include the potential of chemical products to alter predator–prey relationships. Biological controls and integrated pest management strategies are being developed and implemented. With careful use of fertilisers, productivity will be enhanced while residues in products and in the environment generally are minimised.

Levels of socially responsible corporate behaviour

All these issues are matters for socially responsible corporate as well as civil behaviour. Ebert and Griffin (2007) propose four levels of socially responsible corporate behaviour: obstructionist, defensive, accommodative and proactive.

Obstructionist stance to corporate social responsibility

This implies do as little as possible; deny or avoid responsibility. An example: pharmaceutical firm Merck & Co. paid the Australian branch of Elsevier, a company that publishes a wide range of scholarly journals, to put together a bogus journal for them (MacDonald, 2010). Elsevier initially said that the company 'does not today consider a compilation of reprinted articles a "journal"'. Elsevier later retreated and apologised.

Defensive stance

The firm complies with legal requirements but does nothing more. Example: an attorney for reality TV shows such as Survivor and America's Next Top Model was quoted (Weinstein, 2007) as saying:

> *Television producers are not policemen. On a moral level, you get to the point where stepping in seems like it would be something you'd want to do. But from a legal standpoint, third parties causing injuries to other third parties is not something a television program is really responsible for.*

The comment related to the case of a TV crew encouraging a woman to drive a car on a public road, while drunk.

Accommodative stance

The firm exceeds minimum requirements only by special request; agrees to participate in social programmes if requested; matches contributions by employees;

responds to requests from non-profit organisations – but engages in no active behaviour to seek such opportunities. Example: it was reported by Fortune 500 News in September 2005 (http://money.cnn.com) that corporations were contributing millions of dollars in relief aid to help cope with the destruction left by Hurricane Katrina. Alcoa donated $220,000 to the Red Cross and agreed to match employee donations. In view of the wealth of Alcoa, this response may be described as accommodative rather than proactive.

Proactive stance

This is argued to be highest degree of social responsibility a firm can show, in which its managers act as citizens in society, actively seek opportunities to contribute. Example: the Ronald McDonald House programme (see http://www.rhmc.org.au/whatwedo/learning [accessed 8 February 2011]).

Excessive bonuses for CEOs

Finally, it is interesting, in the light of the CSR in Asia report, to reflect on accusations of excessive bonuses for CEOs in business areas that have nothing directly to do with corporate social responsibility, such as the banking industry.

Back in 2007 journalists such as Francesca Rheannon (writing for www.social-funds.com) were already reporting on excessive executive compensation in the US. Ms Rheannon claimed this was taking a staggering economic and social toll on US society, threatening leadership in business, government and non-profit sectors, and creating instability in the economy. She gave the statistic that in 2006 the average US employee had to work for a year to make what the majority of Fortune 500 CEOs made in one day, and noted that the gap between lowest- and highest-paid employees was widening.

She quoted from 'Executive Excess 2007', the fourteenth annual survey of executive compensation from the Institute of Policy Studies, a liberal think tank, and 'United for a Fair Economy', a non-partisan organisation focused on income/wealth distribution issues. These groups argued that this pay disparity was threatening the foundations of US democracy, endangering leadership development, and creating the conditions for economic and social instability. Subsequent history has proved the prophecy to be accurate.

However, any discussion of ethical behaviour and corporate social responsibility should include the need for role models and the provision of good examples from the top. Unfortunately, they are hard to find among corporate leaders. Aman Dhall and Ravi Teja Sharma (2010) are two writers who suggest that maybe the latest global recession has literally been a man-made disaster, 'a testosterone-fuelled meltdown caused by men with high-risk appetite'; and that the world economy might be on a sounder base today if the banking and finance sectors were governed by women. They argue that having more women on the boards of companies helps stability because women tend to moderate risk and to be more balanced.

They suggest one reason why Indian banks have so far scraped though the economic slowdown unscathed is because they have better gender equality on their boards than their Western counterparts. Banking in the West has traditionally been a male bastion and continues to be so; but though the Indian banking sector did have its male domination till the 1980s, the gender equilibrium became better balanced over the last three decades.

Dhall and Sharma quote a study by Standard Chartered Bank about women on corporate boards in India. Apparently it found the financial sector performs best in terms of gender diversity: nine of the eleven banks listed on the Bombay Stock Exchange (BSE-100) have a woman on their board, and two of these banks have a female CEO. In fact, through the recent recession, the central Reserve Bank of India had two women deputy governors on its board, Usha Thorat and Shyamala Gopinath.

ICICI Bank, India's second largest bank after the State Bank of India, is headed by a woman, Chanda Kochhar. So is the third largest in the private sector, Axis Bank, with Shikha Sharma at its helm. HDFC Ltd, India's largest housing finance group, has Renu Sud Karnad as its managing director; Kalpana Morparia heads the Indian arm of global financial leviathan JPMorgan Chase & Co; Meera Sanyal is the country executive for Royal Bank of Scotland; and Manisha Girotra is the managing director of Union Bank of Switzerland's India operations.

In defence of Western men as financial sector role models, reference can be made to Adam Schwab's online account of US banker Vernon Hill (2010). Schwab wrote of Australia's 'banking oligopoly' and claimed it has tended to treat depositors with disdain, regularly losing money on loans made to 'flamboyant' businessmen during boom periods, being only too willing to lend to borrowers on residential property and charging substantial fees to depositors. In contrast, Schwab cited 65-year-old Vernon Hill, one of the US's most successful retail bankers, as a very different kind of banker 'from those who run Australia's financial institutions'.

Schwab suggested that 'instead of treating depositors like cost centres', Hill realised in 1973 when he founded Commerce Bank that low-cost deposits are a key element to running a successful bank. Most banks compete for deposits almost purely on price; that is, they give depositors a higher interest rate when trying to increase their funding levels. Hill, however, took an entirely different approach, investing large amounts of money in training staff to look after their customers on a personal basis. Commerce was among the first banks in the US to stay open in the evenings and on Saturdays. Hill introduced free coin-counting machines. 'Those machines cost $40,000 each, and they're free to non-customers!' Schwab reported Hill as boasting: 'Just try to get a committee at a big bank to approve that expense.'

Apparently Hill considers himself first and foremost as a retailer; and though the banking business has earned him a fortune (apparently he lives in one of America's largest homes) he insists that 'the worst thing that could happen is that we turn into bankers!'

Questions

1. Do you agree that managers whose responsibility is supposed to be for the moral and ethical well-being of their firms should have clear job specifications that identify the area and duties they are responsible for?

2. Do you agree that their activities should be tailored to the core activities of the business? Or do you agree with Friedman and his supporters that such a policy 'increasingly taxes work and subsidizes nonwork'? How do you respond to the following, one of his most famous quotations?

> *So the question is, do corporate executives, provided they stay within the law, have responsibilities in their business activities other than to make as much money for their stockholders as possible? And my answer to that is, no they do not.*
> (Interview 'Milton Friedman Responds' in *Chemtech* (February 1974) p. 72.)

3. What do you think about the large scale of executive compensation? Is there an ethical dimension in failing to link pay to performance for chief executives, yet insisting on it for the lesser ranks of employees?

4. How much accountability is society entitled to from international companies who wield such global influence as do, say, Monsanto or BP – or the MAL Hungarian Aluminium Production and Trade Company in the following case study?

5. Who are your corporate role-models? A useful exercise would be to carry out some research to find at least one such model, and compare your findings with others in the class.

Case study: Hungarian toxic mud disaster

International news media reported in October 2010 the failure of a reservoir at an alumina plant in western Hungary. It caused a torrent of red sludge, about 800,000 cubic metres, to pour through local villages, when a corner wall of the reservoir collapsed. At least seven people were killed and around 150 injured or missing as the deluge destroyed housing, cars, livestock and the entire fish stock of the Marcal River – a comparatively small waterway near the plant.

Viktor Orban, Hungary's Prime Minister, said that parts of Kolontar, the village worst hit by the spill, would never be lived in again. 'It is difficult to find words,' he said. 'Had this happened at night, everybody would be dead.' He called the disaster an ecological tragedy unprecedented in Hungary's history and said there would be 'very severe' consequences for anyone found responsible.

Volunteers joined engineers and crews who operated cranes and bulldozers in a frantic race to build an emergency dam up to five metres in height to prevent further toxic spill, acting on fear that part of the reservoir could collapse for a second time and release another tide of red sludge. Rescue teams warned that the reservoir – which lies in Ajka, 100 miles south-west of the capital Budapest – might soon give way as recently discovered cracks began to widen. It was estimated that at least another 500,000 cubic metres of sludge could spill if the dam failed again About

1,000 residents from the nearby village of Kolontar were evacuated and others in the area put on alert.

The toxic sludge from the spill reached the Danube, one of Europe's most vital waterways, evoking huge efforts to neutralise contaminated waterways and limit ecological damage. Hungarian authorities tried to stem the pollution by pouring gypsum into tributary rivers, opening sluice gates to boost water levels and using weak acid to offset the impact of alkaline deposits. Their efforts were successful to the extent that when the spill reached a branch of the Danube, its pH level had fallen from 13 to less than 10 (normal pH levels are between 7 and 8). Moreover it was hoped that the huge volume of water in the main stretch of the Danube would dilute the alkaline material almost completely, thus limiting damage to flora and fauna.

The risk of lasting environmental damage remained at the site of the spill. Tests by Greenpeace showed high concentrations of heavy metals in the sludge. MAL Hungarian Aluminium Production and Trade Company, which owns the Ajkai Timfoldgyar plant where the spill occurred, rejected claims that it should have taken more precautions. The company pledged funds to aid the clean-up but claimed it could not have diagnosed or averted the disaster. Mr Orban's comment was: 'the wall did not disintegrate in a minute. This should have been detected.' He added: 'Human errors and mistakes must exist ... and the [legal] consequences will be very serious.'

Hungarian police confiscated documents from the company, while the government suspended production at the plant and launched a full investigation. The managing director, Zoltan Bakonyi, was taken into custody for questioning. Environment State Secretary Zoltan Illes reckoned MAL could face having to pay up to 73 million euros ($102 million). Prime Minister Orban told parliament in Budapest that MAL should be called to account for the disaster and the company placed under state control. 'Since it was not a natural disaster, but man-made, it won't be the taxpayer who foots the bill, but those who caused the damage,' he said.

In Brussels, officials said the European Union was to re-examine laws covering industrial waste in light of Hungary's ecological disaster. MAL secured authorisation for storage of toxic waste in 2006 under an EU law that stipulates companies must use best practice techniques. The factory underwent an inspection by national supervisors before the accident, according to an EU Commission spokesman; 'so we have to assess what went wrong'. He said it was unclear whether MAL 'overloaded the reservoirs or not. But if that is the case, it's illegal storage of waste and that constitutes a crime.'

MAL meanwhile denied suggestions that it might have overfilled the reservoirs, insisting the company observed technical regulations strictly. A statement posted on its website claimed the firm had spent 30.3 billion forints (€110 million euros, $150 million) on maintenance and renovation. The company's three owners are among Hungary's 100 richest people, with personal fortunes of between €61 million and €85 million. MAL, set up in 1995, posted annual revenues of €157 million euros and a profit of €715,000 in 2008.

Sources

Batty, D. and agencies 2010. 'Hungary evacuates village threatened by toxic sludge', 9 October; Guardian.co.uk.

BBC News 2010. 'Protective ring built to beat new toxic sludge spill'. 11 October. 2010.

Bryant, C. 2010a. 'Hungary toxic sludge spill reaches Danube'. *Financial Times*, 7 October.

―――― 2010b. 'Hungary fears further toxic spill'. *Financial Times*, 10 October.

Doward, J. 2010. 'Toxic sludge reservoir damage could lead to repeat of Hungarian flood', *Observer*, 10 October.

Gorondi, P. and Szandelszky, B. 2010. 'Company MD arrested over Hungary sludge', *The Age*, 12 October.

Molnar, G. 2010. 'First arrest in Hungarian toxic mud disaster as toll rises', Agence France-Presse, 12 October.

Discussion

This news item calls to mind the occasions when employees or other interested parties have 'blown the whistle' on what they see as illegal or even unethical corporate behaviour. Whistle-blowing means speaking out in the public interest, typically to expose corruption or dangers to the public or the environment. An example was given in Chapter 1 of the Tailhook scandal after Paula Coughlin blew the whistle on the debauchery at the US Navy's 1991 Tailhook Association convention of naval aviators in Las Vegas. Two more examples here (Haines, 2011) are taken from the UK in 2003 and Canada in 2004.

In March 2003 there was a scandal in the UK after a civil servant declared to a journalist that the Prime Minister's Office had 'glamorised' information in a dossier later to be used as a reason to go to war with Iraq. Dr David Christopher Kelly was a British scientist and expert on biological warfare, employed by the British Ministry of Defence, and formerly a United Nations weapons inspector in Iraq. He admitted anonymously to a BBC journalist, Andrew Gilligan, to doubts about the government's dossier on weapons of mass destruction in Iraq. He said he felt that Prime Minister Tony Blair's advisers had exaggerated the threat Iraq posed to the Western world in this dossier by the security services; and that it had been 'doctored' to serve the government's political ends.

When the story broke, it caused great controversy, and the government carried out an investigation of who was behind the allegations. At first Dr Kelly was identified only as 'Gilligan's source', but his name was leaked to the press, and once he was found to be the source of the comments, certain elements from the civil service set out to destroy his professional reputation. He was called to appear on 15 July before the parliamentary Foreign Affairs Select Committee, which was investigating the issues Gilligan had reported, and questioned aggressively about his actions. Apparently being in the eye of the political storm was too much pressure for the doctor, and a couple of weeks after the story first broke, he committed suicide. The after-shock of the affair was felt severely in the UK and the government was heavily criticised, not only over its presentation of the war (although this was exonerated by an independent enquiry) but also for having a hand in a whistle-blower taking his own life.

In Canada in January 2004, the Royal Canadian Mounted Police launched a full criminal investigation into the spending habits of former Privacy Commissioner George Radwanski and a number of his subordinates. Radwanski had resigned in June 2003 following a storm of allegations, including claims that he and his communications director, Dona Vallieres, racked up almost $500,000 in hospitality and travel expenses during a two-year period. Other concerns were over two improper advances of $15,000 and claims that Radwanski's staff cashed out $100,000 worth of vacation leave that they had already taken. It was widely reported at the time that Radwanski threatened to end the career of the 'rat who squealed to MPs' if he ever found out who it was.

On 15 March 2006 he was charged with fraud and breach of trust following a 26-month-long Royal Canadian Mounted Police investigation into his expense claims while a public servant. He was acquitted on 13 February 2009, although his former chief of staff Art Lamarche was convicted for breach of trust by an Ontario Court judge.

This case and the threats made to the whistle-blower increased pressure on the government to do more to protect those who disclose information for the public good. A study of whistle-blowers in the US found that 100 per cent of them were fired – most were unable to find new jobs; 17 per cent lost their homes; 54 per cent were harassed by peers at work; 15 per cent were subsequently divorced; 80 per cent suffered physical deterioration; 90 per cent reported emotional stress, depression and anxiety; 10 per cent attempted suicide.

| EVANGELISM AND CULTURE: A HISTORY OF MISSIOLOGY AS INTERCULTURAL COMMUNICATION | Josh Brahinsky |

The following account is of Christian proselytism as a form of communication across cultures. It raises the topic of religious ethics within the general context of communication agendas. These were mentioned in Chapter 4 as a list of priorities in negotiation. Negotiation was referred to in more detail in Chapter 6 as an iterative process of planning: building a relationship with the other parties; exchanging relevant information, bargaining and reaching agreement or compromise.

It is interesting to read the following account by Brahinsky of negotiations undertaken by Evangelical Christians that seem to follow the same pattern, beginning with the plan to move away from a religious view of evangelism towards a more anthropological perspective. According to this plan, relationship-building and exchange of information in attempts to convert non-Christians include respect for local cultures and communities; but 'in the last resort', as Brahinsky puts it, all compromise is an attempt to achieve the final aim of conversion. Thus there is always an element of persuasion to try to move potential converts away from their existing beliefs, however integral these may be to their native cultures.

Introduction

Missiology is the area of practical theology that investigates the mandate, message and work of Evangelical missionaries. Often the terms 'Evangelical' and 'Christian' are conflated, that is, assumed to be synonymous; but the following discussion specifically refers to Evangelical missionaries.

Over the past forty years, in teaching and in texts and journals such as *Evangelical Missions Quarterly* (http://www.emisdirect.com) there has been a movement away from a religious view of evangelism towards a more anthropological perspective. As an example, the Fuller Theological Seminary, Pasadena, California (http://www.fuller.edu), is the largest multi-denominational Christian seminary in the world. Its School of World Mission, founded in 1965, has now been renamed the School of Intercultural Studies with the aim of equipping students to serve in ministries and organisations with a cross-cultural focus.

More than 3,500 graduates serve in over 150 countries in a wide range of cross-cultural contexts and areas of work including missions and non-profit organisations, church planting and pastoral ministry, education and international development. The following report traces this change of emphasis in the study of missiology through the argument for 'hybridity' (Kraidy, 2005) as part of a central strategy for cross-cultural conversion efforts. Hybridity basically means mixture. The term originated from biology and is used now across many academic disciplines, particularly those concerned with of popular culture, multiculturalism and globalisation.

Finding the balance

Evangelicals comprise a group of Protestant Christians that has been, at least for the past ninety years, closely wedded to understanding the Bible as infallible. Such a reading makes cultural fluidity difficult, if not impossible; but it is exactly what these missionaries have been attempting. The result has been the emergence of this peculiarly Evangelical model for cross-cultural communication. It is a response to the pressures of post-colonial converts who bring concern for local culture and communities into their faith, thus challenging previous Evangelical rigidity with the pragmatic complexity of real-life missions.

Religion, Christianity and especially Christian missions, pose particular problems for intercultural communication. As some of the first consciously to explore cross-cultural interactions, early missionaries are the forebears of modern-day anthropology, linguistics and communications studies; and yet the very nature of their project makes communication especially challenging. As outsiders, missionaries bring with them their home culture, often – but not always – one they value far and above that of their recipients. At times they have even served directly as the emissaries of foreign powers, providing conversion at the point of a sword or gun. Yet they also try to disentangle the religious from the cultural, posing Christianity as a universal faith in a different sphere from local tradition or community. This religion–culture divide, however, is difficult to maintain, especially in the face of religions like Hinduism (http://www.religionfacts.com/hinduism/ beliefs.htm), which are not imagined as a set of beliefs separate from culture, but much more as a way of being in the world, something done as part of a community.

In the last resort conversion is at the core of Christian missionary projects, no matter how service-oriented they might be. This means that there is always an element of persuasion, which makes it hard to initiate a reciprocal dialogue, one in which both parties can learn from each other. Even so, and perhaps because of these challenges, missionaries have been inspired to dig deeply into the potential for fruitful intercultural encounters.

The ugly missionary

The image of missionary as cultural imperialist is powerful; and it has been well earned (Porter, 1997). It is easy to picture missionary schools with young boys and girls torn from their parents, cloistered and having Christianity thrust upon them: these are real stories.

Other difficulties developed when missions become entangled with cultural, economic and political projects – which they almost always did, to some degree. For instance, when David Livingstone brought the 'three Cs' ('commerce', 'civilisation' and 'Christianity') to Africa in the nineteenth century (Brockman, 1994), he imagined he was channelling the benefits of the West to a people in need. That this might also include slavery, economic and political exploitation and the rapid refiguration of indigenous culture was oftentimes a reality only recognised much later.

One solution to the difficulty in blending Christian and secular projects was to eliminate culture, economics and politics from the mix and only preach the (ostensibly non-cultural) gospel. However, a second challenge emerged simply from this encounter between separate religious views. For instance, missionaries who assumed their targets had never heard of God, were nonplussed when not only did they know a God, but heartily agreed that the Christian God was real. The struggle came with the claim that the Christian God was the only God, not simply the most effective, or Western one.

Some seventeenth-century missionaries found this native tolerance made solid conversions difficult to achieve. Native belief was too open-minded, too non-dogmatic. This question of toleration versus exclusivity haunted Christian missions that preached the love and kindness of a very singular and singularly jealous God.

A self-conscious psychology of conquest and displacement was certainly the dominant ethos of many missionary ventures. As one nineteenth-century missionary explained, the attitude of Christianity 'is not one of compromise, but of conflict and of conquest', an effort to displace all other religions. But at the same time, there was a discernible thread of practice and thought resting on a different sensibility, a spirit of love, not of antagonism.

The sensitive missionary

The earliest visible proponents of cross-cultural sensitivity among missionaries were Jesuits. For example, the Jesuit missions established in New France (now Canada) during the seventeenth century were an integral part of French colonisation efforts in North America (Long, 2010); and advocated 'inculturation' or adapting to the culture they served. This meant learning local languages, modifying their clothes (not insisting on Western dress), and even advocating the ordination of native priests (Robert, 2009).

One Jesuit, Matteo Ricci, lived in China as a Confucian scholar and translated Chinese classics (H2O News, 2010). Others, in Spanish America, helped Guarani Indians escape from and defend themselves against exploitative settlers. Jesuit cultural awareness followed the Pope's proclamation of 1622 calling for sensitivity to local 'manners, customs and uses', except where such usages were 'evidently contrary to religion and sound morals'. (It was unclear, of course, what was 'evidently contrary'.) Even with this initial Papal mandate, Jesuit intercultural awareness was too radical for later church leaders, and the Catholic Church suppressed the Jesuits in 1773 (Robert, 2009).

Protestants also had their share of culturally conscious missionaries, although some of the missions with the greatest orientation to social justice were also the most culturally incautious. In what was generally considered the heyday of foreign missions (1880–1930) (House, 1999) socially oriented Protestant missionaries struggled against alcoholism, opium, gambling, infanticide, adultery, polygamy, slavery, human sacrifice and for frugality, industry, agriculture; and a particularly Victorian sense of respect for women. Yet, no matter how well intentioned, this long list of dos and don'ts made for a mighty cultural clash.

At the same time, however, some advocated 'self-government, self-support and self-propagation', conversion as product of relationships instead of abstract propositions and a stripped-down Christianity suitable for export, something that might run into fewer cultural obstacles. Some even recognised the centrality of native cultures and taught the gospel through local mediums, songs, poetry and traditional metaphors. Further, a Protestant emphasis on individual choice – choosing to be born again – and the priesthood of all believers offered useful foundations for missionaries arguing that the receivers of missions ought to also feel free to choose both Christianity and culture.

As the twentieth century evolved some missionaries even suggested working together with other religions to offer a spiritual counter to growing materialism. By the 1960s full-blown theories of partnership developed among Protestants while Catholics responded with the vernacular movement promoted by Vatican II.

But the twentieth century also saw a shift from a missions field dominated by a broad array of Protestant theologies to one led by a new form of Evangelicalism – known best for strict adherence to the Bible, a belief that conversion to Christianity entailed a massive rupture from previous cultures, and a robust sense of their own righteousness.

Emerging Evangelicals

Throughout the twentieth century, the numbers and kinds of missions changed dramatically. Although the statistics vary pretty drastically depending on who you ask, it is clear that the century involved an overall increase in the number of missionaries, a shift from a mainline dominance to a conservative Evangelical one, and missions that now came nearly all from the US. US missionary numbers went from roughly 14,000 in the 1920s, dipping to 11,000 in the mid-1930s, to 35,000 in the 1980s and 42,787 by 2001, with another 65,000 foreign nationals under US sponsorship plus up to 350,000 short-term American missionaries, giving between two weeks and a year annually.

In the 1930s mainline missions had dominated ten to one. Currently some claim that as many as nine of ten are Evangelicals. Spending by US churches on overseas missions has also increased rapidly. By 2001 it reached $4 billion annually, up over 50 per cent from 1991. The results have been mixed. Of course, the project is a big one. With roughly 2.6 billion of the world's 7.8 billion people estimated to be Christian, there are certainly lots to convert. Christians have remained roughly 32–34 per cent of the world's population, but just keeping up with population growth has meant a huge increase in adherents, more in the global South and an increasing Evangelical influence in global Christianity.

At first, Evangelicals resisted the authority of Southern converts, as it seemed tinged by cultural compromise and an emphasis on social concerns rather than evangelism. In fact, early in the century, Evangelicals fought increasing native influence, complaining that native leaders were shaky in their theology and arguing that only highly trained advocates could responsibly teach an inerrant Bible and, further, that a focus on social justice and service undermined efforts at genuine conversion.

Yet, following World War II and decolonisation, it became apparent that most Christians in the world were not in the West, and the centre of Christian authority and culture was shifting South. This forced a reconsideration of the role of culture in missions. Even so, the initial reaction to these pressures was resistance. In fact, a substantial portion, perhaps nearly half, of the shift to Evangelical missions boards likely came from reaffiliation, in which missionaries switched their allegiance to escape pressure to accommodate native church structures.

But, at the same time, the fact that church leadership now included voices other than those of white Westerners resulted in changes in priorities. These new leaders suggested that true Christianity ought to include a concern for the social welfare of all of its adherents, and the whole globe for that matter. The poverty of the South made economics as central a concern as conversion. Further, as members of emerging post-colonial nations and newly powerful ethnicities, they were not interested in full-fledged conversion to Western culture, although modernisation, at least at first, certainly offered many seemingly positive possibilities. These protest voices gained prominence as millions converted along with tremendous population growth in Africa, Asia and Latin America.

Contextualisation became the Evangelical counterpart to inculturation, and the question, 'which first, the rice bowl or the book?' increasingly resolved in favour of temporal, not spiritual, sustenance – food. In other words, late in the twentieth century, Evangelicals, considered especially rigid at home, became missionaries and were forced into far more flexible postures by the realities of emerging mission priorities.

Intercultural Evangelicals

A tale characteristic of recent Evangelical mission texts describes the monkey who 'saved' the fish. A monkey, as it is told, was hanging in a tree branch above a roaring river and saw a horrible sight. There was a fish crossing the stream, struggling in the burbling waters. The monkey felt concern and love. He moved into action. Diving into the cold waters, he dragged the fish to the shore, saving him from the dangerous waters, and then gallantly clambering off into the woods, letting the fish recover and settle in for a nice rest on the beach. In case you missed it – the fish died.

The point, of course, is that it is easy to misunderstand another's context and do more damage than good, even with the best of intentions. Evangelical missions theory increasingly rests on the idea that by translating the Bible into the vernacular, missionaries not only do not destroy indigenous cultures, but actually contribute to their survival and authority. Translation, in this understanding, is a fundamentally destabilising and unpredictable process, one that inevitably invigorates local language culture. This thesis is far from generally accepted, but it has played a tremendous role in shaping the missionary ethos of contemporary Evangelicals.

By contrast there is a different kind of translation, something closer to appropriation. It occurs during attempts at conversion to Christianity when local pantheons are co-opted by missionaries but refigured as demons instead of benign spirits. These remain powerful and active in daily life, only as enemies rather than supporters, traditional rather than modern. But in each case, translation preserves local cultures in ways that promote their continuance.

Evangelicals struggle to reconcile the ambiguity that arises within a missions ethos that includes both a sense of concern over cultural appropriation and imperialism, as well as aspiration to convert its recipients to a new sensibility. In *Anthropology for Christian Witness* (1996), Charles Kraft suggests that missionaries are often paternalistic and insensitive: 'the enemy is often us'. But at the same time there is a clear distinction between 'REALITY' and 'reality', the former being the kind of understanding posed by the Bible, the latter a relativism engendered by anthropology.

Paul Hiebert in *Anthropological Reflections on Missiological Issues* (1994) takes a softer line, on the surface at least, by carefully balancing what he calls systematic theology and anthropological theology. Even so, after promoting contextualisation and cultural sensitivity, he goes a step farther, or backwards, to what he calls a 'Supra-Cultural Theology', in which theology trumps any concerns over culture.

Daniel Shaw and Charles Van Engen (2003) expand this logic. They suggest that awareness of the cultural context of the audience makes it impossible to ignore the cultural context of the Bible – what did it mean to Jesus in his time?

But, in contextualising both, they work in 'ever-changing, context-specific circumstances' to proclaim an 'eternal, unchanging truth, applicable to everyone'.

These shifts in Evangelical thinking – towards cultural fluidity and social concerns – are highly contested. Within Evangelicalism many express continued anxiety over syncretism and universalism, and over the new dialogic, less prescriptive modes of engagement. Others argue that even the softer side of missions such as vernacularisation entails the 'colonisation of consciousness', the kind of process that led to things like Apartheid in South Africa.

Still others see more hopeful cultural formation via even the dark side of missions:

> *Despite its superficiality and cruelty, this forceful evangelization of Indians and African slaves produced a syncretic religion, one of Latin America's few genuinely indigenous creations.*
>
> (Gema ORTEGA, 2011)

Such a claim obviously misses much of indigenous creativity while downplaying the pain of colonialism.

However, it also strikingly asserts the ambiguity of the missionary engagement with culture. Missions include real encounters with real people, and these are not linear or predictable. When Evangelicals took control over missions, they expected to win converts to a deculturised Biblical literalism, not reassess their own approach to local culture and social concerns – but that is exactly what happened.

Discussion

The article begins by describing how the largest multi denominational Christian seminary in the world has renamed its School of World Mission as the School of Intercultural Studies.

Apparently this reflects an acceptance by some Christian missionaries that Biblical authority needs to be balanced by cultural sensitivity and that 'compromise has to surpass ethical rigidity'. Since traditionally Evangelicals understand the Bible as infallible, this is a difficult undertaking. Moreover missionaries in the past have descended as outsiders on native communities, imposing their own culture 'at the point of a sword or gun', and even serving the political interests of their home governments as colonising powers. Slavery, economic and political exploitation and the destruction of indigenous cultures followed in the wake of the Christian missionaries. And conversion ('conflict and conquest') is still at the core of Christian missionary projects 'no matter how service-oriented they might be'. This suggests questions about the ethics of all missionary intercultural encounters.

Brahinsky argues that seventeenth century Jesuits were the first proponents of cross-cultural sensitivity: though learning local languages, wearing local dress and ordaining native priests hardly suggests a great degree of integration with local cultures. Brahinsky reports that some missionaries recognised the centrality of native cultures only to respond by teaching the Christian gospel through local media of songs, poetry, stories and traditional metaphors. In any case, by the twentieth century apparently a self-righteous and conservative Christianity prevailed among Evangelical missionaries and an enormous increase in their numbers, heavily funded by Churches in the US and resulting in an increasing Evangelical influence in global Christianity.

Brahisnksy suggests there are now new leaders in the Church who actually believe that true Christianity should include a concern for the social welfare of all of its adherents and indeed the whole globe. However, this concern seems to be met only by translating Christian texts into local languages and demonising the spirit beings venerated by indigenous people. Brahinsky's account brilliantly captures what he calls the 'ambiguity' of the missionary engagement with native cultures.

Berger and Huntington (2002) discuss Evangelical Protestantism as a globalising force that is best seen by comparing it with the other modern dynamic religious phenomenon, the resurgence of Islam. While the latter has been limited to countries that have always been Muslim and to Muslim communities, Evangelical Protestantism has been exploding in parts of the world to which this religious tradition has always been alien, indeed mostly unknown. The most dramatic explosion has occurred in Latin America, but also in East Asia (with the notable exception of Japan), in all the Chinese societies, in the Philippines, the South Pacific and throughout sub-Saharan Africa. And while the origins of this religion are in the United States it has become thoroughly indigenised.

Evangelical Protestantism brings about a cultural revolution in its new territories: radical changes in the relations between men and women, in the upbringing and education of children, in the attitudes toward traditional hierarchies. This new international culture has vast social, economic and political ramifications. While the new Protestantism should not be misunderstood as a movement of social protest or reform (its motives are overwhelmingly personal and religious), it has large and unintended consequences. These are decidedly favourable to pluralism, to the market economy and to democracy. It should be observed here that there may be other globalising popular movements, but Evangelicalism is clearly the most dynamic.

Questions

1. Are you a Protestant Christian yet come from a non-Christian heritage? If so, you are part of what Berger and Huntington call the 'global culture' of Evangelical Protestantism. What do you think about this?

2. What do you think they mean by writing that conversion to this Christian sect has 'large and unintended consequences' of cultural change towards 'pluralism, the market economy and democracy'?

3. What do Berger and Huntington mean by Evangelical Protestantism bringing about a cultural revolution in its 'new territories': of radical changes in the relations between men and women, in the upbringing and education of children, in attitudes toward traditional hierarchies?

Case study: Missionaries deported from Morocco

Evangelical Christians in the developing world are rarely accused of undermining public order, but in 2010 about a hundred missionaries were deported from Morocco on those grounds. The missionaries, mostly from the United States and Europe, were accused of trying to convert Muslims to Christianity, a crime punishable by imprisonment under Moroccan law, which protects the freedom to practise one's faith but forbids any attempt to convert others.

Rules against proselytising are quite common in Muslim countries, but Morocco for many years has been renowned for religious tolerance in the region. Almost all the country's 32 million citizens are Sunni Muslims but churches and synagogues exist, alongside mosques, to cater for the 1 per cent of the people who are Christian or Jewish.

This broadmindedness presumably appealed to the Christian missionaries who ran the Village of Hope home for children 80 km (50 miles) south of Fez, a former capital known for religion and scholarship. The 16 aid-workers had cared for abandoned children for over a decade when, in March 2010, the Moroccan authorities sent inspectors to the orphanage, and gave the workers a few days' notice to leave the country. Witnesses reported distraught farewells between the Moroccan children and the foreigners who had acted as foster parents.

Morocco's communications minister, Khaled Naciri, said the missionaries 'took advantage of the poverty of some families and targeted their young children'. The aid-workers denied force-feeding Christianity to the children, but sympathisers said that even if they did, a few hours of preaching was a small price to pay for education and pastoral care. There have been further expulsions since then, most recently of an evangelical Spanish teacher.

Local residents were quick to point out that it is not only Christians who have been targets: a similar campaign was waged recently against Morocco's even smaller population of Shia Muslims. But the motivation for the crackdowns is probably political more than religious. Morocco's constitution is based on the hereditary position of the king, Muhammad VI, as 'commander of the faithful'. Any religious movement away from the dominant stream of moderate Sunni Islam might seem to diminish his authority.

The US branch of an Evangelical organisation, Open Doors, which speaks up for persecuted Christians across the world, is backing a campaign by a Republican congressman, Frank Wolf, to press the Moroccans to be kinder to the Evangelicals. But though Morocco is one of America's closest Arab allies, the US administration has been notably silent.

Sources

Economist 2010. 'Stop preaching or get out: The king is unamused by Christians who proselytise', 29 July; http://www.economist.com/node/16705501.

Islamiclife.com 2006/. 'Hispanic missionaries used to target Muslim countries', 9 April; http://www.islamic-life.com/forums/fiqh-dawah-tips/hispanic-missionaries-target-muslim-countries-852.

Sikand, Y. 2005. 'The Evangelical challenge: A new face of Western imperialism', 15 March; http://www.christianaggression.org/item_display.php?id=1110917956&type=articles.

INDIGENOUS KNOWLEDGE FOR INTERNATIONAL MANAGEMENT OF ENVIRONMENTAL RESOURCES	Diana J. Wong-MingJi

The following account by Wong continues the theme of communicating across indigenous cultures. She recognises – as does Brahinsky – the need for respect by members of developed economies for local cultures and communities, but – also with Brahinsky – she acknowledges the imbalance of power between indigenous communities and Western contacts.

Introduction

Managing organisations in an era of globalisation requires increasing attention to environmental issues related to sustainable development. Mounting evidence of climate change, depletion of natural resources, environmental degradation, desertification and many other dangers challenge international managers – especially leaders responsible for operations of multinational corporations – to change business practices fundamentally.

Any deep transformational change requires shifting from a short-term focus on achieving economic profit almost by any means to long-term views that account for holistic complexities, stakeholder dynamics and the needs of future generations. Sustainability means going beyond achieving and maintaining a competitive advantage in the global marketplace.

Based on the Brundtland Commission (1987) definition, sustainability is:

... development that meets the needs of the present without compromising the ability of future generations to meet their own needs.

This time horizon is of maybe 25 to 50 years to as much as seven generations, and is in sharp contrast to a view restricted to the next quarterly earnings, as seen by the managers of many publicly traded US corporations.

Many businesses and organisations attempt to address environmental sustainability by 'going green' with initiatives such as recycling, reusing and reducing waste. Some go further with the mandate of government regulations. New entrepreneurial businesses are also emerging with advanced technologies that help to address the challenges of environmental sustainability, but they are often still in early stages and many are fledging operations.

On the other hand, indigenous (local) knowledge for engaging with the environment in a sustainable manner has existed for many generations. Under Western industrialisation and contemporary market economies, this has all too often been ignored, dismissed or denigrated as superstition. Now, however, as international managers and political leaders seek solutions to a growing range of global environmental problems, many are looking to the stores of knowledge from indigenous peoples for possible directions and solutions. Indigenous peoples have different perspectives and management approaches to environmental issues that have accumulated over hundreds of years and possibly over millennia. International managers can benefit from the many different voices of indigenous peoples around the world.

Indigenous peoples and indigenous knowledge

In the twenty-first century, over 370 million indigenous peoples live in approximately 5,000 different local communities in over 90 countries (UN Declaration on the Rights of Indigenous Peoples, 2007). This means there are great variations between different groups of indigenous peoples who speak about 4,000 of the 7,000 spoken languages in the world.

The term indigenous refers to people who are 'the original origins' in a specific geographical location. More commonly they are known as natives, aboriginals, people of the Fourth World or (in Canada) as the First Nation. The term 'indigenous' replaced earlier anthropological terms such as primitive, tribal and savage, all of which carried pejorative sentiments of condescension and denigration.

José Martínez Cobo (1986/7) developed a working definition of indigenous peoples in his work with the United Nations:

> *Indigenous communities, peoples and nations are those which, having a historical continuity with pre-invasion and pre-colonial societies that developed on their territories, consider themselves distinct from other sectors of the societies now prevailing on those territories, or parts of them. They form at present non-dominant sectors of society and are determined to preserve, develop and transmit to future generations their ancestral territories, and their ethnic identity, as the basis of their continued existence as peoples, in accordance with their own cultural patterns, social institutions and legal system.*

In addition to the United Nation's definition, many researchers have identified what is meant by indigenous peoples. For example, after reviewing a range of definitions and research studies, Purcell (1998) defined indigenous people as the:

> *existing descendants of non-Western peoples who, in general, continue to occupy their ancestral lands even after conquest by Westerners, or who have been relocated forcibly in the process of colonization.*

Many definitions refer to three important elements:

1. extensive and intimate engagement with a local environment over time;
2. adaptation and accumulation of knowledge that is passed down through the generations;
3. knowledge and wisdom that is often challenged by disruptions and conflicts from colonising newcomers who construct asymmetrical power relationships.

Extensive work on determining who is and who is not an indigene has often carried high stakes in terms of legitimating political, social and economic rights in many different countries.

Indigenous peoples accumulate a vast store of knowledge based on historical experiences of close interactions with their environment (Barnhardt and Kawagley, 2005). This enables long-term viability for these communities over hundreds, if not thousands, of years through highly developed and sustainable social practices (Menzies and Butler, 2006: 1–17). But from an empirical scientific perspective, much of what is known in indigenous communities tends to be dismissed as superstitious beliefs or legends irrelevant to industrial progress, especially when it does not lead directly to profitable corporate outcomes.

Indigenous knowledge is described by Boyce (1973) as:

a body of information about the interconnected elements of the natural environment which traditional indigenous people have been taught, from generation to generation, to respect and give thanks for...

Traditional ecological knowledge is:

the knowledge and beliefs that indigenous peoples hold of their environments that is handed down through the generations.

Menzies and Butler, 2006: 6

Berkes et al. (2000: 1252) defined it as:

a cumulative body of knowledge, practice, and belief, evolving by adaptive processes and handed down through generations by cultural transmission, about the relationship of living beings (including humans) with one another and with their environment.

Many innovations that led to industrial progress are increasingly being recognised also to contribute to environmental degradation, with serious consequences for the collective existence of many societies unless radical changes alter current trajectories. Traditional ecological knowledge may provide directions for initiating various environmental reforms.

However, a warning note is that not all indigenous knowledge itself is impervious to change. Many established generations of indigenous societies have met their demise when environmental disruptions overwhelm a community's adaptive capacity. Many societies have failed to survive when they were not able to adapt to their ecosystem or when sudden environmental shifts occurred (Diamond, 2005).

Traditional approaches differ from much of Western industrial orientation to the environment. Menzies and Butler (2006) summarise important characteristics of these that include

■ Long-term accumulation of knowledge over many generations and historical understanding based on cumulative experiences;

- Dynamic revisions of practices to integrate contemporary information and technology;
- Locally specific resource use;
- Holistic connections between living beings and their environment as a way of understanding the world;
- Moral and spiritual grounding where the environment is often infused with spirits;
- Defined moral codes for proper relationship with the environment.

There is a growing awareness in industrialised societies about indigenous knowledge systems as alternative bodies of knowledge, arising from at least four interrelated major motivations. Depending on the environmental issue and location, the importance of the different drivers will likely differ; but many of the issues are shared to some extent across different environments and societies.

First, there is increasing need in developed economies to acknowledge the struggles of indigenous peoples to assert their rights to co-exist with colonising arrivals; and of the need to compensate these native inhabitants for constant encroachments on their land. For example, the Maori people of New Zealand faced significant cultural decline until about the 1960s, through erosion of their rights and in spite of negotiation for redress for breaches of the Treaty of Waitangi in 1840. The United Nations Declaration on the Rights of Indigenous Peoples took over twenty years before being adopted in 2007.

Second, it is now plain that indigenous communities are fragmenting and dwindling, owing to Westernised industrial societies' search for and extraction of resources. Whole knowledge systems are disappearing, and the loss of diversity has global implications for the future sustainability of the human ecosystem.

Third, the environmental impacts from industrialisation lead to search for solutions beyond the boundaries of Western science. Three examples in the US offer possible alternatives: the Hohokam's canal and hydraulic system in the water-scarce region of Phoenix, Arizona (Wilcox et al., 2008), the Menominee's achievement of sustainable development with forestry in Wisconsin (Davis, 2000; Tromper, 2007), and the formation of the Intertribal Council on Utility Policy in 1994, composed of tribes of the northern plains, to create renewable energy from wind power.

Fourth, the recent resurgence of interest in indigenous peoples arises from a growing recognition about the potential economic market value of their knowledge for global businesses. Pharmaceutical companies and healthcare businesses are expanding their research into many 'alternative' systems – sometimes exploitatively. One major global case study of intellectual property rights over indigenous knowledge involves Monsanto's attempt to patent products extracted from the neem tree. In another example Phytopharm licensed the Hoodia plant drug to Pfizer for $21 million after extracting and patenting the herbal medicine from the Bushmen of South Africa (Kihwelo, 2005).

Increasing encounters between indigenous communities and international businesses will continue to raise the importance of these four issues as well as raise many others. Hence international managers need to find ways of developing mutually viable relationships with indigenous peoples and to protect environmental resources of common concern.

One motivation may likely hold the key to the other. International managers have barely started to learn how to collaborate with various indigenous communities. Prior approaches of colonisation, domination and manipulation have benefited the former but not the latter. Imbalance in power relationships has led to dire consequences for indigenous peoples. Their environmental knowledge has been treated with contempt as witchcraft, heathen and barbaric (Kihwelo, 2005). Foreign investors' desire for economic profit has prevailed over native sacred places, precious time, human dignity, collective rights and mutual obligations (Lauderdale, 2009).

Collaborative environmental learning between international managers and indigenous peoples requires 'unlearning' by the former of previously held socialised perceptions of indigenous knowledge systems; and recognition of multiple orientations to the environment. Briggs (2005), however, warns of the danger of going too far in the other direction. Too favourable a perspective on indigenous knowledge can lead to a romanticised and static view of it as an untainted and pristine source of unquestionable wisdom. Nevertheless there are examples from different parts of the world, of different environmental issues, that illustrate how international managers are learning to develop viable relationships with indigenous communities that are mutually respectful and less exploitative for only economic profits.

Case studies

1. The Arctic Climate Impact Assessment

In 2004 Susan Joy Hassol published a summary of the Arctic Climate Impact Assessment (ACIA), a comprehensive examination of climatic changes in the Arctic Region and what they may portend globally. The ACIA is based on five climate models, the results of findings from hundreds of Arctic researchers worldwide and perspectives of Arctic Indigenous Peoples.

The Arctic is now experiencing some of the most rapid and severe climate change on Earth. Over the next hundred years, climate change is expected to accelerate, contributing to major physical, ecological, social and economic changes, many of which have already begun. Changes in Arctic climate will also affect the rest of the world through increased global warming and rising sea levels. Arctic Climate Impact Assessment was prepared by an international team of over 300 scientists, experts and knowledgeable members of indigenous communities. The report has been thoroughly researched, is fully referenced and provides the first comprehensive evaluation of Arctic climate change, changes in ultraviolet radiation and their impacts for the region and for the world. The results provided the scientific foundations for the ACIA synthesis report – *Impacts of a Warming Arctic* – published by Cambridge University Press in 2004.

2. The Chisasibi Cree elders

Berkes (1999: Ch. 6) reports that according to narratives by Chisasibi Cree elders in the 1980s, a disaster occurred in 1910 at Limestone Falls, near the centre of the Quebec-Ungava peninsula. Equipped with repeating rifles that had just become available, hunters abandoned their hunting restraints and conventional ethics of respect for the animals, and slaughtered large numbers of caribou at the river crossing point.

The caribou had already been in decline along the Hudson Bay coast. Following the event at Limestone Falls, the herd disappeared altogether from the lands hunted by the Cree and did not reappear until the 1980s. The Cree believe that all changes occur in cycles, and the elders at that time had predicted that the caribou would return 'one day'.

Over the next seventy years, the story was retold of the arrogance of the hunters in 1910, so when the caribou reappeared in the 1980s, it was easy for the elders to convince people to be respectful, and not kill the animals wastefully.

The story illustrates that after some kind of disaster, a society can self-organise, learn and adapt (Berkes and Turner, 2006). The process of knowledge development and learning has the potential to increase the resilience of resource use systems. Hence, conservation knowledge can develop through a combination of long-term ecological understanding and learning from crises and mistakes. This learning has survival value, as it increases the resilience of integrated social–ecological systems to deal with change in ways that continue to sustain both peoples and their environments.

3. Adaptation of forestry management in Michoacán, Mexico

This case study of indigenous communities in highland Michoacán, Mexico (Klooser, 2009), examines data on forest change, woodcutting practices, social history and a recent forest inventory and management plan prepared by a professional forester. It assesses the social and environmental fit of both local knowledge and scientific forestry, and considers their abilities to contribute to sustainable forest management.

Both bodies of knowledge are limited in their ability to inform the social practice of environmental management. The local forest knowledge system is particularly hampered by a limited ability to monitor the forest's response to woodcutting, while scientific forestry lacks the institutional flexibility to ensure the just and effective implementation of restrictions and prescriptions.

The author of the study, Daniel James Klooser, recommends cross-learning between scientific resource managers and woodcutters, participatory environmental monitoring to assess the results of different cutting techniques, and the promotion of institutional learning at the community level. He argues that this kind of adaptive management of sustainable natural resources can be applied also to scientific resource managers, and points to the Maori in New Zealand and the Dusun in Brunei Darussalam, where scientific management relating to spatial and seasonal distribution of natural resources has benefited from local knowledge of the plants and animals living in their territory, leading to sustainable harvesting and habitat management.

4. Contributions to disaster risk reduction in volcanic eruption in Papua New Guinea

Indigenous communities in Small Island Developing States (SIDS) are increasingly vulnerable to environmental hazards (Mercer, 2006). While scientific developments in the form of early warning systems, for example, have provided significant positive benefits to the field of disaster risk reduction, there has been a tendency to focus upon the physical components of risk rather than the human, societal and cultural factors that surround the risk.

In many cases, as with indigenous communities in SIDS, vulnerability to environmental hazards is increasing. This has resulted in an increased call within disaster risk reduction for the benefits of indigenous knowledge to be identified and utilised to reduce vulnerability to environmental hazards. However, while the benefits of indigenous knowledge are gradually being acknowledged there continues to be a gap in reaching the right people with the correct strategies for disaster risk reduction.

In 2006 Jessica Mercer undertook a research project, funded by a grant from Macquarie University, Sydney, to fill a current gap in disaster risk reduction literature. She developed a Process Framework for identifying how indigenous knowledge might be incorporated with scientific knowledge in a culturally compatible manner to reduce vulnerability of indigenous communities in SIDS to environmental hazards. She argues that this Process Framework can be applied by disaster risk reduction practitioners, in partnership with indigenous communities, to implement sustainable and effective disaster risk reduction strategies.

5. The Adi, Monpa and Khasi tribes of northern India

Ranjay Singh et al. in 2010 reported on grassroots activities to promote learning and conservation of traditional knowledge and related biocultural resources among Adi, Monpa and Khasi tribes of north-east India. The results indicated that these activities enhance the promotion of traditional practices, learning of knowledge and conservation of related resources.

The researchers wrote that knowledge-holders of varying age groups and social systems have many notable traditional practices that provide promising solutions to current challenges. They promote conservation of resources and the subsistence survival of people. The authors conclude that strong multi-level networks between all stakeholders are needed to ensure the sustainability of traditional knowledge and conservation of biocultural resources of communities of north-east India.

6. Darjeeling tea and basmati rice

Jena and Grote reported in 2010 how methods have evolved in recent years to protect indigenous knowledge in the agrifood sector without hampering the ethics of free trade. These include measures to protect national property rights while offering new export opportunities – though there are opponents who still consider them as barriers to trade. Jena and Grote justify them, basing their arguments on insights from the New

Institutional Economics – an economic perspective that focuses on the social and legal norms and rules that underlie economic activity. They cite Darjeeling tea and Basmati rice as Indian examples, highlighting some of their dynamic institutional aspects.

Other cases of learning from indigenous peoples can be found; but in many there is evidence that exploitation of indigenous knowledge has resulted in a significant imbalance of economic and political power, under which indigenous communities have become more impoverished than before Western industrial contact. It is to be hoped that collaborative environmental learning with indigenous peoples will grow with increasing pressures for sustainable environmental management in international management.

Discussion and questions

Traditional indigenous knowledge has developed from intimate long-term interactions with the environment. Local knowledge can benefit contemporary concerns for sustainable management of natural resources but international managers – trained in Western scientific methods – need to be willing to learn about environmental management from indigenous people.

Many examples do exist for collaborative learning between international managers and indigenous communities, but much more work remains. Indigenous intellectual property rights are a major international ethical business concern, as also are ways in which resources should be distributed between investors and local people. These issues are critical for the future of sustainable environmental management. Some important questions require further investigation as the relationship between international managers and indigenous peoples continues to unfold. The following are a couple of suggestions for further consideration:

1. If foreign investors claim intellectual property rights over knowledge gained from native people, how can those people be compensated?
2. In small groups, identify an important environmental issue and research answers to the question: what are two different ways in which investors collaborate with local people for sustainable development of resources?

Case study: Intellectual Property Rights: Who benefits?

Intellectual Property Rights (IPRs) is a relatively new concept, first put on the global trade agenda as part of the 1984 Uruguay Round of the GATT; in 1995 the 'Trade Related aspects of Intellectual Property' (TRIPs) Agreement became international law.

IPRs are not a traditional part of 'free trade', and even many free-trade economists oppose their inclusion on the agenda of the World Trade Organisation (WTO). They are there thanks to the lobbying of a committee of thirteen major companies. In the negotiations that followed, 96 out of the 111 members of the US delegation working on intellectual property rights were from the private sector.

Corporations in the rich world are the world's biggest owners of intellectual property. Industrialised countries hold over 97 per cent of patents worldwide, and almost 90 per cent of these are held by large corporations. The WTO's TRIPs Agreement is essentially about extending their rights over the world's foods, medicines and even human genes. Under TRIPs, a patent owner has the exclusive right to prevent anyone from making, using, selling, offering for sale or importing a patented product.

The benefits of TRIPs have flowed almost totally to multinational corporations. Corporations have abused their power by increasing the prices of medicines to even the poorest people. They have used TRIPs to secure patents, and thus 'ownership' over indigenous and traditional knowledge, and even living organisms. The TRIPs Agreement extends Western patent laws into the furthest reaches of rural areas in developing countries. TRIPs grants corporations the right to patent life-forms from micro-organisms to plants, animals and non-biological processes for producing plants and animals. TRIPs also allows biotechnology companies to engage in 'biopiracy': patenting indigenous knowledge, which in many cases has been used for thousands of years, and ignoring millions of years of evolution that preceded the company's 'invention'. These patents allow a company to 'own' the traditional knowledge of indigenous communities for use in developing new products such as medicines:

> Patents and intellectual property rights are supposed to be granted for novel inventions. But patents are being claimed for rice varieties such as the Basmati for which my Valley – where I was born – is famous, or pesticides derived from the Neem which our mothers and grandmothers have been using. Rice Tec, a U.S. based company, has been granted Patent no. 5,663,484 for Basmati rice lines and grains. Basmati, Neem, pepper, bitter gourd, turmeric … every aspect of the innovation embodied in our indigenous food and medicinal systems is now being pirated and patented. The knowledge of the poor is being converted into the property of global corporations, creating a situation where the poor will have to pay for the seeds and medicines they have evolved and have used to meet their own needs for nutrition and health care.
>
> Vandana Shiva (2000), 'Poverty & Globalisation', BBC Reith Lecture, 14 May; http://news.bbc.co.uk/hi/english/static/events/reith_2000/lecture5.stm.

> I served on the Clinton administration's Council of Economic Advisors at the time [of developing the TRIPS Agreement], and it was clear that there was more interest in pleasing the pharmaceutical and entertainment industries than in ensuring an intellectual-property regime that was good for science, let alone for developing countries.
>
> Joseph Stiglitz [former Chief Economist, World Bank] (2005) 'Intellectual-Property Rights and Wrongs', Project Syndicate, August; http://www.project-syndicate.org/commentary/stiglitz61.

Other sources

CAFOD (Catholic Agency for Overseas Development) 2003. 'Rough Guide to the World Trade Organisation', June; http://www.cafod.org.uk/policy_and_analysis/policy_papers/rough_guides/wto.

CBC News 2004. 'Percy Schmeiser's battle', CBC News Online, 21 May; http://www.cbc.ca/news/background/genetics_modification/percyschmeiser.html.

Oxfam UK 2001. 'Formula for fairness: Patient rights before patent rights', July; http://www.africafocus.org/docs05/ind0503.php.

Tripathi, Ruchi 2000. 'Implications of TRIPs on livelihoods of poor farmers in developing countries', ActionAid, 13 October; http://www.actionaid.org.uk/content_document.asp?doc_id=240.

WTO 2006. *The World Trade Organisation: An Australian Guide*, 2006 edition; http://www.tradewatch.org.au/guide/intellectual_property.html [accessed 30 January 2011].

Discussion

The GATT (General Agreement on Tariffs and Trade) should not be confused with the GATS (General Agreement on Trade in Services). Yet the concept of intellectual property rights is relevant to trade in services as well as goods (e.g., the media, the arts, education, health provisions, and so on). The GATS gives multinational corporations many rights that should go hand in hand with relevant responsibilities; but they are unlikely to do so unless the culture of profit becomes more in alignment with a culture of service.

In 1994 GATS was signed as part of the agreements that set up the World Trade Organisation (WTO). The provisions of this international agreement cover basic services such as healthcare, education, water supply, infrastructures for mass communication, public transport, cultural services including films and television, museums and libraries, and so on. There are 160 sectors included under the GATS, and they account for most of the world's economy. The GATS includes a commercial presence in services, and has been described by the WTO as 'the world's first international investment agreement'.

Edgar Hibbert (2003) is one writer who defends the global commercialisation of services, and specifically the positive impact of the GATS regulatory framework. He discusses the organisation and protocols of GATS and their likely impact on global trade in services. He argues that the Agreement will foster the global expansion in services under a fair, transparent set of rules, with procedures for recourse by those governments and enterprises that claim to have been unfairly discriminated against in one or other service sector.

Critics include Mehta and Madsen (2005), who argue that under the GATS international trade is expanding over a wide range of services from tourism to telecommunications and education. They claim that in recent years the Agreement has come under attack worldwide from civil society organisations for having a detrimental impact on poor people's right to basic services. Using the example of water services, the writers focus on the impact of the GATS on poor people's right to water. They argue that effectively the liberalisation of water-related services under the GATS undermines the ability of governments to introduce legislative measures to protect poor people's right to water. Their arguments are that exercise of policy autonomy is often limited by inherent ambiguities in treaty interpretation, by the politics of power inequalities and lack of transparency in processes of negotiation as well as institutional and other deficiencies in the domestic politics of WTO member states.

The GATS applies if services are supplied commercially or in competition with the private sector. And in practice there are few service sectors in most countries that do not include some element of service provision by companies such as in broadcasting, private medicine and education. It is true that governments open up their service industries to privatisation under commitments that are theoretically voluntary. In practice, however, the poorer countries increasingly face complex agreements that are difficult to understand, with tiny budgets, few government advisers and no assessment on the likely impacts of interventions under the GATS.

Thus it is becoming more and more important that the relationship between service providers and the people they serve be created and maintained to the benefit of both parties. Unfortunately, the ethics of what is often called 'customer service relationship management' often seem to include an unethical dimension in which management projects focus on the mechanics rather than the ultimate goal of increasing the value of the customer relationship; and that many customer initiatives are to manipulate rather than to benefit customers.

Conclusion

The objective of the chapter was to examine some ethical dimensions to behaviour in various corporate settings. These include responsibility management policies and practices in Asian firms; environmental protection and disaster prevention and management; missionary work by Evangelical church organisations; the ethics of intellectual property rights under the General Agreement on Tariffs and Trade; and of services provisions under the General Agreement on Trade in Services.

Thus the chapter began with the concept of corporate social responsibility, and related it first to a survey of Asian views of corporate responsibility management; then to a discussion of various forms and levels of social responsibility by corporations. The illustrative case study was a European example of what seems to be a case of corporate irresponsibility.

Unfortunately, other examples are not hard to find, witness a February 2011 report (Mason, 2011) that according to Mississippi's attorney general, BP's oil spill compensation fund is underpaying relatives of the victims of the oil well that exploded the previous April, killing 11 men. BP is accused of withholding interim claim payments to increase financial hardship on claimants; and persuading claimants to sign very low settlements that bar them from later legal action. The fate of 'whistle-blowers' was referred to. People who draw public attention to glaring cases of unethical behaviour by corporations and governments seem mostly to suffer from their good citizenship, even to death.

The chapter went on to describe another perception of corporate social responsibility: that of the Evangelical churches' mission to convert non-Christians to Christianity. In view of the fact that the vast majority of internal conflicts all over the world are sectarian and religious in origin, religious ethics is an important topic for discussion.

The same is true of international intellectual property rights, and the privatisation of essential services, two more controversial ethical issues. Granted the importance of including indigenous (local) knowledge with modern science for protection of the environment, including resources and public health, to what extent are multinationals entitled to exploit local knowledge for profit without compensating the people who traditionally owned it? The question leads to general discussion of intellectual property rights, and the risk to underprivileged and underdeveloped economies under the General Agreement on Trade in Services, for example. in the privatisation of water supplies.

Key points

1. The argument for competitive capitalism is that it achieves economic freedom as a necessary condition for political freedom.

2. However, businesses can no longer engage in unethical practices without the risk at least of attracting negative media publicity worldwide.

3. Also there is pressure from non-governmental organisations, demands from consumers, governments and society at large to persuade corporations to conduct sustainable business practices.

4. Moreover, to attract and retain employees and customers, companies are beginning to realise the importance of ethical corporate behaviour, now commonly known as corporate social responsibility, at least in highly regulated areas such as Europe, the UK and the US. They may behave differently elsewhere, for example, by exploiting cheap or child labour in less developed countries.

5. Corporate managers have to balance budgets, so they may be tempted to allocate insufficient resources to non-financial areas such as protecting human rights, pursuing business ethics and environmental policies, making corporate contributions to community causes, and so on. In many cases charitable projects, separate from the core business of the firm, take the place of an organisation-wide policy on corporate social responsibility.

6. Reports suggest excessive executive compensation imposes a high toll on society and creates instability in the economy.

7. Transnational organisations, including the Christian churches, now recognise that authority needs to be balanced by cultural sensitivity, and compromise has to take the place of ethnocentric ethical rigidity. There is an ethical dimension to the extent to which foreign investment of any kind, commercial, political, religious, can be imposed on native cultures.

8. Nevertheless global cultures are emerging, and in general they are favourable to pluralism (inclusion), to the market economy and to democracy. Hence some protest against them from members of traditional national cultures to whom their values are alien.

9. Traditional indigenous knowledge can benefit contemporary concerns for sustainable management of natural resources, but indigenous intellectual property rights are a major international ethical business concern, as are ways in which resources should be distributed between investors and local people.

10. Ethical dimensions exist to corporate practices under the provisions of the WTO agreements on trade, including trade in services.

Experiential exercises

Exercise 1

Ethical dilemma: The can of lemonade

Goal: To explore some ethical characteristics of 'universalistic' versus 'particularist' behaviour, as identified in *Riding the Waves of Culture* by Trompenaars and Hampden-Turner (1997).

Time required: About 45 minutes.

Number of players: Any number the instructor can handle, divided in small groups, say of 3 people each.

Materials: The presentation information below should be prepared in advance, either as PowerPoint or transparencies, or in some other form suitable for display to the group.

Activity

1. Explain that the purpose of the activity is to explore some culture-based aspects of ethical dilemmas. Talk the group through the prepared presentation and tell everybody the game that they are going to play is designed to illustrate differences between universalistic and particularist behaviour. On this dimension of human behaviour people from universalistic cultures focus more on rules and general standards applicable to all situations. Within more particularistic national cultures the focus is more on relationships; rules can be adapted to satisfy special requirements in given situations.

2. Form small groups, as mixed as possible. Distribute one copy of the dilemma to each person in each group.

3. Give everybody about 10 minutes to discuss it.

4. Call a plenary session for class discussion.

5. Ask the class: which is more important, dealing fairly and impersonally with everybody or 'bending the rules' if the situation seems to warrant it? What did group members suggest the manager should do?

6. Ask each group in turn to report on their findings.

7. Summarise in terms of the theory.

The can of lemonade

A teenager, in trouble with the police in the past but apparently eager to 'go straight', was recently employed in a small local branch of a much larger firm. Now he has been caught stealing a can of lemonade from the storeroom.

The company handbook clearly states that 'theft is theft' and that employees convicted of theft must be dismissed instantly, whether or not the theft is reported to the police.

Everybody in this local branch knows each other very well: often they are near neighbours and many know personally the teenager's parents and are aware of the family background. They all request the store manager to give the teenager another chance.

Should the manager rebuke the thief, issue a stern warning and leave it at that, or go by the rulebook?'

Background information to share with the class

Slide 1

Trompenaars and Hampden-Turner (1997) 'Riding the Waves of Culture: Understanding cultural diversity in business'

Their research focuses on the cultural dimensions of business executives. In *Riding the Waves of Culture* they identify seven value orientations.

Slide 2

Seven value orientations

1) Universalism<>particularism
2) Communitarianism<>individualism
3) Neutral<>emotional
4) Defuse<>specific
5) Achievement<>ascription
6) Human–Time relationship
7) Human–Nature relationship

Slide 3

Universalism/Particularism:
Universalism: Rules the same for everybody.
Particularism: Circumstances alter cases.

Lessons for international managers: Members of universalistic cultures (e.g., US) negotiating with potential partners from particularistic cultures (e.g., China) recognise relationships form the basis of trust and take time to develop. Rules (e.g., as specified in contracts) are only a rough guideline for decisions.

\---

Slide 4

Communitarianism/Individualism:

Examples:

Companies from individualistic cultures such as the USA will find it hard to introduce individual incentives to members of communitarian cultures such as Denmark or Japan.

Neutral/Emotional:

Examples:

Teams with members from cultures highly neutral (rational, e.g., German) and highly affective (emotional, e.g., Spanish) need inter-cultural understanding – or the Spanish will find the Germans cold and unfeeling; and the Germans will resist the more feelings-oriented views of the Spanish.

Slide 5

Specific/Diffuse:

Examples:

Managers from specific cultures, e.g., Danes or Germans, will 'tell it like it is', e.g., criticise subordinates directly, openly and impersonally.

Members of diffuse cultures, such as Indians or Thais, will regards this as causing loss of face for both the person giving and receiving the criticism. It must be expressed much more obliquely.

Slide 6

Human–Time relationship:

People in time-oriented cultures (e.g., the US) have sayings such as:
'Time and tide wait for no man'; 'Time is money'; 'Don't waste time'.

People in human-oriented cultures (such as Latin Americans) are more likely to say 'mañana' (tomorrow will do as well as today if there is something more important right now).

Human–Nature relationship:

'Nature is to be tamed and conquered for the benefit of humanity' (USA). 'People should live in harmony with nature' (Japan).

Exercise 2

Ethics quiz (answers at the end)

1. Which of the following best describes the concept of ethics?
a) the attempts of a business to balance its commitments to groups and individuals, including customers, other businesses, employees, investors and local communities
b) a form of social activism dedicated to protecting the rights of consumers in their dealings with businesses
c) beliefs about which is right or wrong or good or bad in actions that affect others
d) moral commitment to benefit individuals even at the expense of society

2. Ethics are based on individual beliefs and social concepts, and vary from ___
a) person to person
b) situation to situation
c) culture to culture
d) all of the above

3. Which of the following is likely to be considered unethical in all cultures?
a) a manager hires a friend rather than a more qualified applicant
b) a manager refuses a reasonable request by an employee for a pay rise, knowing the employee can't afford to quit
c) a retailer accepts a generous gift from a supplier in return for a large order
d) none of the above

4. Organisational stakeholders can best be defined as _____
a) individuals and businesses that own stock in a company
b) individuals and groups directly affected by the practices of an organisation
c) the officers and key employees of an organisation
d) government regulators who oversee an industry

5. Which of the following best describes a whistle-blower?
a) a union leader who calls a strike
b) an over-critical supervisor always finding fault with workers
c) an employee who reports the firm's unethical or illegal behaviour
d) an employee who creates a significant opportunity for social responsibility

6. Firms accused of paying excessive salaries to senior managers or providing frivolous 'perks' may be engaging in _____
a) human resources violations
b) protectionism
c) favouritism
d) improper financial management

7. A leading meat-processing firm has a long record of breaking environmental protection, labour and food processing laws; it tries to cover up its offences. This reflects what kind of stance on corporate social responsibility?
a) accommodative
b) obstructionist
c) proactive
d) defensive

8. Of the Asian companies surveyed by CSR in Asia, the business sector with the highest number of corporate social responsibility (CSR) members is:
a) energy
b) healthcare
c) hospitality
d) telecommunications

9. Researchers find that a number of global cultures are emerging, i.e., whose values are shared worldwide, and in general they are favourable to:
a) the use of English as an international language
b) the market economy and democracy
c) the emancipation of women and their achievement of management positions
d) freedom of speech

10. The world's biggest owners of intellectual property are:
a) media moguls
b) national governments
c) large corporations in the rich world
d) international non-government organisations

Answers
1: c; 2: a; 3: d; 4: b; 5: c; 6: d; 7: b; 8: a; 9: b; 10: c

Recommended reading

Books

Aras, G. and Crowther, D. (eds) 2010. *Global Perspectives on Corporate Governance and CSR.* Farnham, UK: Gower Publishing.

Berger, P.L. and Huntington, S.P. 2002. *Cultural Diversity in the Contemporary World.* New York: Oxford University Press.

Cavanagh, J. and Mander, J. (eds) 2002. *Alternatives to Economic Globalization: A Better World is Possible.* San Francisco: Berrett-Koehler..

Diamond, J. 2005. *Collapse: How Societies Choose to Fail or Succeed.* New York: Penguin.

Friedman, M. and Friedman, R.D. 2002. *Capitalism and Freedom.* Chicago: University of Chicago Press.

Kraidy, M.M. 2005. *Hybridity: Or the Cultural Logic of Globalization.* Philadelphia, PA: Temple University Press.

Loudon, D.L. and Della Bitta, A.J. 1993. *Consumer Behavior: Concepts and applications*, 4th edn. New York: McGraw-Hill.

Menzies, C.R. (ed.) 2006. *Traditional Ecological Knowledge and Natural Resource Management.* Lincoln, NB: University of Nebraska Press.

Journals

Bloomberg Business Week; http://www.businessweek.com
China Business Weekly
European Management Journal
Harvard Business Review
Journal of Advertising Research
Journal of Public Policy and Marketing
Journal of World Intellectual Property
National Interest
The Service Industries Journal
Sustainability Investment News

References

Barnhardt, R. and Kawagley, A.O. 2005. 'Indigenous knowledge systems and Alaska native ways of knowing'. *Anthropology and Education Quarterly*, 36 (1), pp. 8–23.

Berger, P.L. 1997. 'Four faces of global culture'. *National Interest*, 49, pp. 23–30.

Berger, P.L. and Huntington, S.P. 2002. *Cultural Diversity in the Contemporary World.* New York: Oxford University Press.

Berkes, F. 1999. *Sacred Ecology: Traditional Ecological Knowledge and Resource Management.* Philadelphia, PA: Taylor & Francis.

Berkes, F. and Turner, N.J. 2006. 'Knowledge, learning and the evolution of conservation practice for social–ecological system resilience'. *Human* Ecology, 34, pp. 479–94.

Berkes, F., Colding, H. and Folke, C. 2000. 'Rediscovery of traditional ecological knowledge as adaptive management'. *Ecological Applications*, 10 (5), pp. 1251–62.

Bombay, H. (ed.) 1996. *Aboriginal Forest-based Ecological Knowledge in Canada.* Ottawa: National Aboriginal Forestry Association.

Boyce, D.W. 1973. 'A glimpse of Iroquois culture history through the eyes of Joseph Brant and John Norton'. *Proceedings of the American Philosophical Society*, 117 (4) (Aug. 15, 1973), pp. 286–94

Briggs, J. 2005. 'The use of indigenous knowledge in development: Problems and challenges'. *Progress in Development Studies*, 5 (2), pp. 99–114.

Brockman, N.C. (ed.) 1994. *An African Biographical Dictionary.* Santa Barbara, CA: ABC-CLIO; http://www.dacb.org/stories/southafrica/livingstone1_david.html.

Brundtland Commission 1987. *Our Common Future: Report of the World Commission on Environment and Development.* Oxford: Oxford University Press.

Cobo, J.M. 1986/7. *Study of the Problem of Discrimination against Indigenous Populations,* UN Doc. E/CN.4/Sub.2/1986/7 and Add. 1–4; http://www.un.org./esa/socdev/unpfii/en/second.html [accessed 15 October 2010].

Davis, T. 2000. *Sustaining the Forest, the People, and the Spirit.* Albany, NY: State University of New York Press.

Dhall, A. and Sharma, R.T. 2010. 'What makes women successful in Indian banking industry?' *Times of India*, 19 September; http://timesofindia.indiatimes.com/business/india-business/What-makes-women-successful-in-Indian-banking-industry/articleshow/6584040.cms.

Diamond, J. 2005. *Collapse: How Societies Choose to Fail or Succeed.* New York: Penguin.

Ebert, R.J. and Griffin, R.W. 2007. *Business Essentials*, 6th edn. Upper Saddle River, NJ: Prentice Hall.

Friedman, M. and Friedman, R.D. 2002. *Capitalism and Freedom.* Chicago: University of Chicago Press.

Gema ORTEGA 2011. 'Writing hybridity: Identity, dialogics, and women's narratives in the Americas'. Dissertation submitted in partial fulfillment of the requirements for the degree of Doctor of Philosophy in Comparative Literature in the Graduate College of the University of Illinois at Urbana-Champaign, Urbana, Illinois.

H2O News 2010. 'Matteo Ricci: A Jesuit in the Kingdom of the Dragon', 5 November; http://www.h2onews.org/english/51-culture/224444382-matteo-ricci-a-jesuit-in-the-kingdom-of-the-dragon.html.

Haines, P. 2011. 'Famous cases of whistle-blowing', *The Brock Press*, 1 February; http://media.www.brockpress.com/media/storage/paper384/news/2004/03/30/Business/Famous.Cases.Of.WhistleBlowing-645453.shtml.

Hassol, S.J. 2004. *Impacts of a Warming Arctic: Arctic Climate Impact Assessment.* Cambridge: Cambridge University Press.

Hibbert, E. 2003. 'The new framework for global trade in services – All about GATS'. *Service Industries Journal*, 23 (2), pp. 67–78.

Hiebert, P. 1994. *Anthropological Reflections on Missiological Issues.* Grand Rapids, MI: Baker Books.

House, R. 1999. *Patterns and Portraits: Women in the History of the Reformed Church in America.* Grand Rapids, MI: Eerdmans.

Jena, P.R.J. and Grote, U. 2010. 'Changing institutions to protect regional heritage: A case for geographical indications in the Indian agrifood sector'. *Development Policy Review*, 28 (2), pp. 217–36.

Kihwelo, P.F. 2005. 'Indigenous knowledge: What is it? How and why do we protect it?', *Journal of World Intellectual Property*, 8, pp. 345–59.

Klooser, D.J. 2009. 'Toward adaptive community forest management: Integrating local forest knowledge with scientific forestry'. published online, 16 February; http://onlinelibrary. wiley.com/doi/10.1111/j.1944-8287.2002.tb00175.x/abstract.

Kraft, C. 1996. *Anthropology for Christian Witness*. Maryknoll, NY: Orbis.

Kraidy, M.M. 2005. *Hybridity: Or the Cultural Logic of Globalization*. Philadelphia, PA: Temple University Press.

Landlearnnsw.org.au n.d. http://www.landlearnnsw.org.au/sustainability/primary-industries-and-sustainability [accessed 8 February 2011].

Lauderdale, P. 2009. 'Collective indigenous rights and global social movements in the face of global development: From resistance to social change'. *Journal of Developing Societies*, 25 (3), pp. 371–91.

Long, T. 2010. 'The Jesuits in Canada', Suite101.com, 25 April; http://www.suite101.com/ content/the-jesuits-in-canada-a229847.

MacDonald, C. 2009. 'Drug companies make other companies do stupid, unethical things'; http://businessethicsblog.com/2009/05/10/drug-companies-make-other-companies-do-stupid-unethical-things/ [posted 10 May].

Mehta, L. and Madsen, Birgit la Cour 2005. 'Is the WTO after your water? The General Agreement on Trade in Services (GATS) and poor people's right to water'. *Natural Resources Forum*, 29 (2), pp. 154–64.

Mason, R. 2011. 'BP Gulf of Mexico oil spill fund "underpaying victims"', *Telegraph*, 3 February: http://www.telegraph.co.uk/finance/newsbysector/energy/oilandgas/8299361/ BP-Gulf-of-Mexico-oil-spill-fund-underpaying-victims.html.

Menzies, C.R. and Butler, C. 2006. 'Understanding ecological knowledge'. In C.R. Menzies (ed.), *Traditional Ecological Knowledge and Natural Resource Management*. Lincoln, NB: University of Nebraska Press.

Mercer, J. 2006. *Integrating Indigenous and Scientific Knowledge for Disaster Risk Reduction in Small Island Developing States*. Macquarie University, Sydney: Department of Human Geography; http://www.islandvulnerability.org/png.html.

Money.cnn.com 2005. 'Companies pitch in: Major companies – including Home Depot and Ford – pledge millions to hurricane relief efforts'. 15 September; http://money.cnn. com/2005/08/31/news/fortune500/firms_hurricane/index.htm.

Porter, A. 1997. '"Cultural imperialism" and Protestant missionary enterprise, 1780–1914'. *Journal of Imperial and Commonwealth History*, 25 (3), pp. 367–91.

Purcell, T.W. 1998. 'Indigenous knowledge and applied anthropology: Questions of definition and direction'. *Human Organization*, 57 (3), pp. 258–72.

Rheannon, F. 2007. 'Excessive CEO compensation hurting US companies and society', *Sustainability Investment News*, 14 September; http://www.socialfunds.com/news/article. cgi/2370.html.

Robert, D.L. 2009. *Christian Mission: How Christianity became a World Religion*. Chichester: Wiley-Blackwell.

Schwab, A. 2010. 'Hill's heresy a good role model for Australian banks'. 29 November; http:// www.crikey.com.au/2010/11/29/hills-heresy-a-good-role-model-for-australian-banks/.

Shaw, R. D. and Van Engen, C. 2003. *Communicating God's Word in a Complex World: God's Truth or Hocus Pocus?* Lanham, MD: Rowan & Littlefield.

Singh, R., Pretty, J. and Pilgrim, S. 2010. 'Traditional knowledge and biocultural diversity: Learning from tribal communities for sustainable development in northeast India'. *Journal of Environmental Planning and Management*, 53 (4), pp. 511–33.

Trompenaars, F. and Hampden-Turner, C. 1997. *Riding the Waves of Culture: Understanding Cultural Diversity in Business*. 2nd edn. London: Nicholas Brealey.

Trosper, R.L. 2007. 'Indigenous influence on forest management on the Menominee Indian reservation'. *Forest Ecology and Management*, 249 (1–2), pp. 134–9.

UK Department of Trade and Industry n.d. http://www.bis.gov.uk/site/foi/publication-scheme/categories/corporate-social-responsibility [accessed 30 January 2011].

UN Declaration on the Rights of Indigenous Peoples 2007. http://www.un.org/esa/socdev/unpfii/en/declaration.html [accessed 29 January 2011].

Weinstein, Bruce (2007) 'If it's legal, it's ethical … right?', *Bloomberg Business Week*, 15 October; http://www.businessweek.com/managing/content/oct2007/ca20071011_458606.htm.

Wilcox, D.R., Wiegand, P.C., Wood, J.S. and Howard, J.B. 2008. 'Ancient cultural interplay of the American Southwest in the Mexican Northwest'. *Journal of the Southwest*, 50 (2), pp. 103–206.

Index of Names and Subjects